ACCA
STUDY TEXT

Professional Paper 9

Information for Control and Decision Making

New in this June 2000 edition

- Thorough, reliable updating of material to 1 June 2000

- Many new exam focus points, giving you vital hints for the examination

- **FOR DECEMBER 2000 AND JUNE 2001 EXAMS**

BPP Publishing
June 2000

First edition 1993
Eighth edition June 2000

ISBN 0 7517 0192 0 (Previous edition 0 7517 0163 7)

British Library Cataloguing-in-Publication Data
A catalogue record for this book is available from the British Library

Published by

BPP Publishing Limited
Aldine House, Aldine Place
London W12 8AW

www.bpp.com

Printed by in Great Britain by Ashford Colour Press, Gosport, Hants

We are grateful to the Association of Chartered Certified Accountants for permission to reproduce in this text the syllabus and teaching guide of which the Association holds the copyright.

We are also grateful to the Association of Chartered Certified Accountants for permission to reproduce past examination questions in our Exam Question Bank. The Exam Answer Bank has been prepared by BPP Publishing Limited.

Contents

Page

BPP
PUBLISHING

Contents

HOW TO USE THIS STUDY TEXT

Aims of this Study Text

To provide you with the knowledge and understanding, skills and applied techniques required for passing the exam

The Study Text has been written around the ACCA's Official Syllabus and the ACCA's Official Teaching Guide (reproduced below, and cross-referenced to where in the text each topic is covered).

- It is **comprehensive**. We do not omit sections of the syllabus as the examiner is liable to examine any angle of any part of the syllabus - and you do not want to be left high and dry.

- It is **up-to-date as at 1 June 2000,** which means that it fulfils the requirement for the December 2000 exams that students should be up-to-date as at 1 June 2000.

- And it is **on-target**. We do not include any material which is not examinable. You can therefore rely on the BPP Study Text as the stand-alone source of all your information for the exam, without worrying that any of the material is irrelevant.

To allow you to study in the way that best suits your learning style and the time you have available, by following your personal Study Plan (see below)

You may be studying at home on your own until the date of the exam, or you may be attending a full-time course. You may like to (and have time to) read every word, or you may prefer to (or only have time to) skim-read and devote the remainder of your time to question practice. Wherever you fall in the spectrum, you will find the BPP Study Text meets your needs in designing and following your personal Study Plan.

To tie in with the other components of the BPP Effective Study Package to ensure you have the best possible chance of passing the exam

Recommended period of use	Elements of the BPP Effective Study Package
3-12 months before exam	**Study Text** Acquisition of knowledge, understanding, skills and applied techniques.

↓

| 1-6 months before exam | **Practice & Revision Kit**
Tutorial questions and helpful checklists of the key points lead you into each area. There are then numerous Examination questions to try, graded by topic area, along with realistic suggested solutions prepared by BPP's own authors in the light of the Examiner's Reports. June 2001 examinees will find the 2001 edition of the Kit invaluable for bringing them up-to-date as at 1 December 2000, the cut-off date for the June 2001 examinable material. |

↓

| last minute - 3 months before exam | **Passcards**
Short, memorable notes focused on what is most likely to come up in the exam you will be sitting. |

↓

| 1-6 months before exam | **Success Tapes**
Audio cassettes covering the vital elements of your syllabus in less than 90 minutes per subject. Each tape also contains exam hints to help you fine tune your strategy. |

↓

| 3-12 months before exam | **Breakthrough Videos**
These supplement your Study Text, by giving you clear tuition on key exam subjects. They allow you the luxury of being able to pause or repeat sections until you have fully grasped the topic. |

↓

| 3-12 months before exam | **Master CD**
Interactive CD-ROM containing questions on all aspects of the syllabus, cross referenced to help topics. |

Settling down to study

By this stage in your career you are probably a very experienced learner and taker of exams. But have you ever thought about *how* you learn? Let's have a quick look at the key elements required for effective learning. You can then identify your learning style and go on to design your own approach to how you are going to study this text - your personal Study Plan.

Key element of learning	Using the BPP Study Text
Motivation	You can rely on the comprehensiveness and technical quality of BPP. You've chosen the right Study Text - so you're in pole position to pass your exam!
Clear objectives and standards	Do you want to be a prizewinner or simply achieve a moderate pass? Decide.
Feedback	Follow through the examples in this text and do the Questions and the Quick quizzes. Evaluate your efforts critically - how are you doing?
Study Plan	You need to be honest about your progress to yourself - don't be over-confident, but don't be negative either. Make your Study Plan (see below) and try to stick to it. Focus on the short-term objectives - completing two chapters a night, say - but beware of losing sight of your study objectives
Practice	Use the Quick quizzes and Chapter roundups to refresh your memory regularly after you have completed your initial study of each chapter

These introductory pages let you see exactly what you are up against. However you study, you should:

- **read through the syllabus and teaching guide** - this will help you to identify areas you have already covered, perhaps at a lower level of detail, and areas that are totally new to you

- **study the examination paper section,** where we show you the format of the exam (how many and what kind of questions etc) and analyse all the papers set so far under the syllabus, **up to December 1999**

BPP
PUBLISHING

Key study steps

The following steps are, in our experience, the ideal way to study for professional exams. You can of course adapt it for your particular learning style (see below). Tackle the chapters in the order you find them in the Study Text. Taking into account your individual learning style, follow these key study steps for each chapter.

Key study steps	Activity
Step 1 *Chapter topic list*	Study the list. Each numbered topic denotes a numbered section in the chapter
Step 2 *Introduction*	Read it through. It is designed to show you *why* the topics in the chapter need to be studied - how they lead on from previous topics, and how they lead into subsequent ones
Step 3 *Knowledge brought forward boxes*	In these we highlight information and techniques that it is assumed you have 'brought forward' with you from your earlier studies. If there are matters which have changed recently due to legislation etc then these topics are explained in full. Do not panic if you do not feel instantly comfortable with the content - it should come back to you as we develop the subject for this paper. If you are really unsure, we advise you to go back to your previous notes
Step 4 *Explanations*	Proceed methodically through the chapter, reading each section thoroughly and making sure you understand. Where a topic has been examined, we state the month and year of examination against the appropriate heading. You should pay particular attention to these topics.
Step 5 *Key terms* and *Exam focus points*	• **Key terms** can often earn you *easy marks* if you state them clearly and correctly in an appropriate exam answer (and they are indexed at the back of the text so you can check easily that you are on top of all of them when you come to revise) • **Exam focus points** give you a good idea of how the examiner tends to examine certain topics - and also pinpoint *easy marks*
Step 6 *Note taking*	Take brief notes if you wish, avoiding the temptation to copy out too much
Step 7 *Examples*	Follow each through to its solution very carefully
Step 8 *Case examples*	Study each one, and try if you can to add flesh to them from your own experience - they are designed to show how the topics you are studying come alive (and often come unstuck) in the real world
Step 9 *Questions*	Make a very good attempt at each one
Step 10 *Answers*	Check yours against ours, and make sure you understand any discrepancies
Step 11 *Chapter roundup*	Check through it very carefully, to make sure you have grasped the major points it is highlighting

Key study steps	Activity
Step 12 *Quick quiz*	When you are happy that you have covered the chapter, use the **Quick quiz** to check your recall of the topics covered. The answers are in the paragraphs in the chapter that we refer you to
Step 13 *Examination question(s)*	Either at this point, or later when you are thinking about revising, make a full attempt at the **Examination question(s)** suggested at the very end of the chapter. You can find these at the end of the Study Text, along with the **Answers** so you can see how you did. We highlight for you which ones are introductory, and which are of the full standard you would expect to find in an exam

Developing your personal Study Plan

Preparing a Study Plan (and sticking closely to it) is one of the key elements in learning success.

First you need to be aware of your style of learning. There are four typical learning styles. Consider yourself in the light of the following descriptions. and work out which you fit most closely. You can then plan to follow the key study steps in the sequence suggested.

Learning styles	Characteristics	Sequence of key study steps in the BPP Study Text
Theorist	Seeks to understand principles before applying them in practice	1, 2, 3, 4, 7, 8, 5, 9/10, 11, 12, 13 (6 continuous)
Reflector	Seeks to observe phenomena, thinks about them and then chooses to act	
Activist	Prefers to deal with practical, active problems; does not have much patience with theory	1, 2, 9/10 (read through), 7, 8, 5, 11, 3, 4, 9/10 (full attempt), 12, 13 (6 continuous)
Pragmatist	Prefers to study only if a direct link to practical problems can be seen; not interested in theory for its own sake	9/10 (read through), 2, 5, 7, 8, 11, 1, 3, 4, 9/10 (full attempt), 12, 13 (6 continuous)

Next you should complete the following checklist.

Am I motivated?   (a) [ ]

Do I have an objective and a standard that I want to achieve?   (b) [ ]

Am I a theorist, a reflector, an activist or a pragmatist?   (c) [ ]

How much time do I have available per week, given: (d) [ ]

- the standard I have set myself

- the time I need to set aside later for work on the Practice and Revision Kit and Passcards

- the other exam(s) I am sitting, and (of course)

- practical matters such as work, travel, exercise, sleep and social life?

Now

- take the time you have available per week for this Study Text (d), and multiply it by the number of weeks available to give (e).

(e) [ ]

- divide (e) by the number of chapters to give (f)

(f) [ ]

- set about studying each chapter in the time represented by (f), following the key study steps in the order suggested by your particular learning style

This is your personal **Study Plan**.

Short of time?

Whatever your objectives, standards or style, you may find you simply do not have the time available to follow all the key study steps for each chapter, however you adapt them for your particular learning style. If this is the case, follow the Skim Study technique below (the icons in the Study Text will help you to do this).

Skim Study technique

Study the chapters in the order you find them in the Study Text. For each chapter, follow the key study steps 1-3, and then skim-read through step 4. Jump to step 11, and then go back to step 5. Follow through steps 7 and 8, and prepare outline Answers to Questions (steps 9/10). Try the Quick quiz (step 12), following up any items you can't answer, then do a plan for the Examination question (step 13), comparing it against our answers. You should probably still follow step 6 (note-taking), although you may decide simply to rely on the BPP Passcards for this.

Moving on...

However you study, when you are ready to embark on the practice and revision phase of the BPP Effective Study Package, you should still refer back to this Study Text:

- as a source of **reference** (you should find the list of key terms and the index particularly helpful for this)

- as a **refresher** (the Chapter roundups and Quick quizzes help you here)

And remember to keep careful hold of this Study Text - you will find it invaluable in your work

ACCA OFFICIAL SYLLABUS

1 Management framework

Management accounting operates in a changing environment in which management accounting techniques must be continuously appraised and reviewed. The management accounting framework must be reviewed in relation to the following areas.

(a) The evaluation of, and promotion of change in, management accounting techniques.
    (i) Budgetary planning and control
    (ii) Standard costing and variance analysis
    (iii) Decision making including quantitative aids

(b) Trends and developments in management accounting methods and techniques, business organisation and structure such as:
    (i) transfer pricing and divisionalised organisations;
    (ii) performance measurement and divisionalised organisations.

(c) Evaluating the impact of changes in business structure, functions and performance measures on the applicability and appropriateness of management accounting techniques and methods eg:
    (i) relevance of standard costing and variance analysis;
    (ii) use of traditional absorption costing methods.

(d) Identifying and evaluating existing and new methods and techniques and measures for management planning and control provision eg:
    (i) JIT (Just-in-Time) procedures;
    (ii) computer integrated manufacturing;
    (iii) world class manufacturing;
    (iv) total quality control;
    (v) activity based budgeting.

2 Design of management accounting systems

(a) Developing/implementing an appropriate system including:
    (i) identification of cost units, establishing cost/profit/responsibility centres;
    (ii) determining methods for recording relevant information;
    (iii) sources of information and recording/processing;
    (iv) computer based information storage and processing;
    (v) analysis of output information and its dissemination to relevant individuals/ departments.

	Covered in Chapter

(vi) Relationship between business performance and managerial performance	14-15, 17
(vii) Assessing management performance by reference to comparable internal and external information	
(viii) Performance measurement and developments in management accounting eg activity based budgeting, total quality management	

4 Information for decision making

(a) Pricing of goods and services	3, 4, 9, 16

    (i) Target and minimum pricing
    (ii) Price/demand relationships
    (iii) Pricing of special orders and short life products
    (iv) Transfer pricing between divisions in a group

(b) Identification and application of:	5, 7

    (i) Relevant costs (such as fixed/variable, direct/indirect, avoidable/unavoidable, opportunity/sunk);
    (ii) Appropriate techniques (CVP analysis, use of limiting factors, recognition of risk and uncertainty).

(c) Selection of relevant information for decision making	1, 5-8, 17

    (i) Application and interpretation of quantitative techniques in decision making:
       (1) decision criteria
       (2) expected value and expected profit, maximin
       (3) decision trees, rollback analysis
       (4) expected value of perfect and imperfect information
       (5) linear programming
- graphical and computer solution analysis
- assumptions and limitations
- shadow prices
- opportunity costs
- sensitivity analysis

    (ii) Use of indexing of costs and revenues
    (iii) Use of discounted cash flow techniques in longer term decision-making situations

(d) Use in a range of decision making situations: adoption of new products, product mix choice, discontinuance of products, make or buy, sell or further process, shutdown or temporary closure.	5 -7

ACCA OFFICIAL TEACHING GUIDE

This is the Official Teaching Guide, for the December 2000 and June 2001 exams.

Syllabus reference

Session 1 Accounting Information Systems - 1

2a,2c

- define information with particular reference to accounting systems
- explain ways in which accounting systems collect, process and disseminate information
- identify ways in which accounting information is used for internal and external reporting to different groups of interested parties
- contrast the roles of financial and non-financial information in management
- describe the information available from the financial accounting records
- name sources of monetary and non-monetary information available within and external to the organisation for use in the management accounting system
- describe the systems involved in collection and recording monetary and non-monetary information
- identify types of information which are relevant for different purposes
- identify how the collection and analysis of information is influenced by the management accounting principles and techniques in use
- describe how information requirements are influenced by trend, materiality and controllability considerations

Session 2 Accounting Information Systems - 2

2a,2c

- explain the use of information for planning, control and decision making
- describe the impact of responsibility accounting on information requirements
- describe and illustrate the use of cost, revenue, profit and investment centres
- identify and discuss controllable and non-controllable costs as part of cost analysis
- explain the nature and use of quantitative and qualitative information
- relate the required accuracy of information as related to its intended use
- explain and illustrate ways in which the measurement and processing of information may contribute to the degree of accuracy achieved
- explain how the impact of volume change and time may affect the accuracy of information
- explain and illustrate ways in which accuracy may be more controllable in some situations than in others
- outline ways in which uncertainty as to the accuracy of information may be allowed for in the operation of a management accounting system

Session 3 Information Technology and the Management Information System

2a

- identify the stages in the information processing cycle in the context of accounting information
- evaluate the transaction recording procedures in a computer based accounting system
- describe the use of software packages in the analysis of management accounting information
- identify the advantages and disadvantages of the use of spreadsheets databases in the provision and analysis of management accounting information
- list the procedures for the preparation and layout of a spreadsheet model
- evaluate the use of spreadsheet models in 'what-if' analysis of decision making information
- explain the use of spreadsheet data-tables in the provision of decision making information
- explain the use of spreadsheet modelling in the implementation of simulation techniques using random number generation

**Session 4 Impact of the Environment on the Accounting
Information Systems**

2c, 3a

- identify the accounting information requirements for strategic planning,
  management control and operational control for decisions
- distinguish between hierarchical and democratic management styles
- describe, with reference to management accounting, ways in which the
  information requirements of a management structure are affected by the
  features of that structure
- identify how hierarchical and democratic management structures affect
  information requirements
- evaluate the objectives of management accounting and management
  accounting information
- list the attributes and principles of management accounting information
- itemise and comment on factors which must be considered when setting up a
  management accounting system
- explain the integration of management accounting information within an
  overall management information system
- define and discuss the merits of open and closed systems
- define and discuss the use of programmed and non-programmed information,
  feedback and feedforward control
- suggest ways in which contingent factors (internal and external) influence
  management accounting information and its use
- illustrate the impact of human behaviour on the operation of a management
  accounting in an organisation

**Session 5 Modern Developments in Industry and Commerce
and The Accounting Response - 1**

1d, 2b, 3a

- list and comment on the goals of world class manufacturing
- name the main features of world class manufacturing and explain the principle
  benefits to be derived from them
- distinguish between value added and non-value added activities and carry out
  analysis which will identify and quantify each
- explain the principles of just-in-time procedures and discuss their implications
  for cost systems and cost control, including the use of backflush accounting
- identify benefits of production procedures (such as dedicated cell layout) for
  quality improvement, cost reduction and cost systems
- illustrate the use of activity based costing and discuss its impact on product
  costing and cost control

**Session 6 Modern Developments in Industry and Commerce
and The Accounting Response - 2**

1d, 2b, 3a

- discuss the meaning of quality in the context of total quality management
- describe the process of performance measurement in a total quality
  management environment
- explain how training for quality may be implemented and its associated costs
  and benefits
- explain the operation of design for quality and its associated costs and
  benefits
- describe the design and operation of a quality information system
- discuss ways in which the cost of quality may be measured, analysed and
  reported
- calculate and analyse the costs of quality from given data

Session 7   Decision Making and Short Run Decisions - 1

2c, 4c

- distinguish between relevant and irrelevant information using appropriate criteria
- identify cost classifications used in decision making
- explain the influence of size and type of entity on information requirements
- explain how quantitative and qualitative information is used in decision making
- evaluate and assess the frequency, timing, format and degree of accuracy in the provision of decision making information
- describe the basic decision making cycle for business decisions
- classify problems for the purpose of modelling, into simple problems, complex problems and dynamic problems
- define the relevance of endogenous and exogenous variables, policies and controls, performance measures and intermediate variables in model building
- tabulate typical management accounting decision situations and the quantitative techniques which may assist in each

Session 8   Decision Making and Short Run Decisions - 2

4b, 4d

- explain the nature of CVP analysis and name planning and decision making situations in which it may be used
- compare the accounting and economic models of CVP analysis
- explain the assumption of linearity and the principle of relevant range in the CVP model
- prepare breakeven charts and profit-volume graphs and interpret the information contained within each, including multi-product situations
- comment on the limitations of CVP analysis for planning and decision making including multiproduct situations
- explain the concept of avoidable or incremental cost
- describe the relationship between fixed costs and the time horizon used in a decision situation
- explain the meaning of opportunity cost and its use in decision making
- calculate relevant costs for specific decision situations from given data
- explain the meaning of throughput accounting and its use in decision making

Session 9   Decision Making and Short Run Decisions - 3

2b, 4b, 4d

- explain the nature of decision making and how it is affected by the time horizon which is used
- explain the use of incremental and opportunity costs in decision making
- specify qualitative factors which are relevant to sourcing and product line decisions
- describe the use of quantitative and qualitative factors in the decision making cycle
- explain and illustrate the impact of limiting factors on the decision making process
- calculate solutions to problems involving changes in product mix, discontinuance of products or departments
- implement make or buy sourcing decisions using relevant costs
- make decisions as to whether to further process a product before sale using relevant costs and revenues
- use relevant costs and revenues in decisions relating to the operation of internal service departments or the use of external services

BPP PUBLISHING

Session 15   Pricing - 1

- identify and discuss market situations which influence the pricing policy adopted by an organisation
- explain and discuss the variables (including price) which influence demand for a product or service
- explain the price elasticity of demand
- manipulate data in order to determine an optimum price/output level
- calculate prices using full cost and marginal cost as the pricing base
- compare the use of full cost pricing and marginal cost pricing as planning and decision making aids

Session 16   Pricing - 2

- calculate prices using activity based costing in the estimation of the cost element
- contrast and discuss the implications of prices using the activity based costing technique with those using volume related methods in assigning costs to products
- take informed pricing decisions in the context of special orders and new products
- discuss pricing policy in the context of skimming, penetration and differential pricing
- explain the problems of pricing in the context of short life products
- explain the operation of target pricing in achieving a desired market share

Session 17   Accounting Control Systems - 1

- describe the internal and external sources of planning information for an organisation
- list the information used in the preparation of the master budget and its functional components
- contrast the information used in the operation of zero based budgeting and incremental budgeting
- list the factors which distinguish long term from short term planning information requirements
- classify costs relevant to long term planning information
- discuss the significance of inflation and the time value of money in long term planning
- evaluate the significance of uncertainty in long term planning
- explain and illustrate the use of budgeting as a planning aid in the co-ordination of business activity
- explain and illustrate the relevance of budgeting in the co-ordination of business activities
- explain and quantify the application of positive and negative feedback in the operation of budgetary control
- explain and quantify the application of feedforward control in the operation of budgeting
- discuss the inter-relationship of planning, co-ordination and control in budgeting

Session 18   Accounting Control Systems - 2

- identify quantitative aids which may be used in budgetary planning and control
- discuss and evaluate methods for the analysis of costs into fixed and variable components
- give examples to demonstrate the use of forecasting techniques in the budgetary planning process
- explain the use of forecasting techniques in the budgetary planning process
- describe the use of learning curve theory in budgetary planning and control
- implement learning curve theory
- identify factors which may cause uncertainty in the setting of budgets and in the budgetary control process
- identify the effect of flexible budgeting in reducing uncertainty in budgeting
- illustrate the use of probabilities in budgetary planning and comment on the relevance of the information thus obtained
- explain the use of computer based models in accommodating uncertainty in budgeting and in promoting 'what-if' analysis

Session 19   Accounting Control Systems - 3

- identify the factors which affect human behaviour in budgetary planning and control
- contrast ways in which alternative management styles may affect the operation of budgetary planning and control systems
- explain budgeting as a bargaining process between people
- explain the conflict between personal and corporate aspiration and its impact on budgeting
- explain the application of contingency theory to the budgeting process
- discuss the impact of political, social, economic and technological change on budgeting
- discuss the impact of developments such as total quality management on budgeting
- critically review the use of budgetary planning and control
- enumerate and evaluate the strengths and weaknesses of alternative budget models such as fixed and flexible, rolling, activity based, zero based and incremental
- identify the effects on staff and management of the operation of budgetary planning and control

Session 20   Standard Costing

- discuss the uses of standard costing
- describe the installation of a standard cost system and the preparation and revision of standards
- calculate variances for sales, material, labour and overheads including sub-variances
- interpret the causes of variances, their inter-relationship one with another and their relevance to management
- calculate variances for mix and yield and their relevance to management
- calculate variances where budgeted labour or machine idle time exists and comment on the relevance of such variances to management
- prepare summary operating statements where standard absorption or standard marginal principles are applied
- differentiate between absorption and marginal cost approaches to variance calculation

Session 21   Advanced Variance Analysis

- explain planning and operational variances
- identify and discuss the advantages and limitations of planning and operational variance analysis
- calculate planning and operational variances for materials, labour and overhead cost variances including sub-variances
- calculate planning and operational variance for sales volume and price
- prepare summary operating statements which reconcile budgeted and actual profit using planning and operational variances
- explain the relevance to management of the variances detailed in a summary operating statement where planning and operational variances analysis is in use

Session 22   Interpretation and Investigation of Variances

- explain the meaning and significance of the terms trend, materiality and controllability in the context of variance analysis
- calculate the variance trend in absolute and percentage terms through time
- identify and discuss the 'management signals' which may be extracted from a set of variance figures for a number of successive time periods
- explain the planning, measurement, model, implementation and random deviations which contribute to uncertainty in variance analysis
- explain the implications of whether a variance is in control or out of control
- explain the use of statistical control charts in monitoring variance trend and controllability
- describe and illustrate the use of the statistical decision theory approach to variance investigation decisions
- critically appraise the use of standard costing and variance analysis in management accounting
- compare and evaluate alternative approaches to variance analysis
- discuss the impact of staff and management attitudes on the operation of variance analysis
- discuss the applicability of standard costing and variance analysis in changing environmental and cultural situations eg variances and quality costs

Session 23   Performance Measurement: The Principles

- describe the essential features of responsibility accounting
- identify the relevant factors in the design of a responsibility accounting system
- outline the essential features of an effective internal control system
- distinguish between quantitative and qualitative performance measures
- identify, explain and give examples of performance measures including monetary and non-monetary, percentages, ratios and indices
- analyse the application of financial performance measures including cost, profit, return on capital employed
- identify the areas in which performance measurement is required in a typical business
- assess and illustrate the measurement of profitability, activity and productivity
- discuss the measurement of quality and service
- discuss the conflict between profit and other objectives including reference to critical success factors
- describe management performance measures
- analyse the strengths and weaknesses of a range of management performance measures
- discuss the potential conflict in the use of a measure for both business and management performance

Session 24 Performance Measurement: Applications - 1

1b, 1c, 3c

- describe the qualitative and quantitative performance measures relevant for sales, material, labour and overhead in manufacturing industries
- analyse performance measures in job, batch, contract manufacturing environments
- analyse performance measures in process manufacturing environments
- describe quantitative and qualitative performance measures relevant in the service sector
- compute and discuss the implications of performance measures in the provision of a range of services such as accountancy and law, retail and distribution, transport
- discuss the behavioural implications of the performance measures used

Session 25 Performance Measurement: Applications - 2

1b, 1c, 3c

- describe quantitative and qualitative performance measures relevant in non-profit making organisations
- compute and discuss the implications of performance measures in the provision of non-profit making services such as education
- discuss the behavioural implications of the performance measures used
- describe the use of indices to allow for price and performance level changes through time
- implement calculations showing the use of indices in forecasting and trend analysis
- use suitable indices for inter-company performance comparison

Session 26 Transfer Pricing - 1

1b, 4a

- describe the organisation structure in which transfer pricing may be required
- explain divisional autonomy, divisional performance measurement and corporate profit maximisation and their link with transfer pricing policy
- formulate the 'general rule' for transfer pricing and explain its application
- describe, illustrate and evaluate the use of market price as the transfer price
- assess where an adjusted market price will be appropriate for transfer business
- assess the impact of market price methods on divisional autonomy, performance measurement and corporate profit maximisation

Session 27 Transfer Pricing - 2

1b, 4a

- describe the alternative cost based approaches to transfer pricing
- identify the circumstances in which marginal cost should be used as the transfer price and determine its impact on divisional autonomy, performance measurement and corporate profit maximisation
- illustrate methods by which a share of fixed costs may be included in the transfer price
- comment on these methods and their impact on divisional autonomy, performance measurement and corporate profit maximisation
- discuss the advantages which may be claimed for the use of standard cost rather than actual cost when setting transfer prices
- explain the relevance of opportunity cost in transfer pricing
- list the information which must be centrally available in order that the profit maximising transfer policy may be implemented between divisions where intermediate products are in short supply
- illustrate the formulation of the quantitative model for a range of limiting factors from which the corporate profit maximising transfer policy may be calculated

Session 28   Divisional Performance Evaluation

1b, 3c

- describe quantitative and qualitative performance measures relevant in a divisionalised organisation structure
- compute and evaluate performance measures used in a divisionalised organisation structure
- discuss the conflict between performance measures and decision making in a divisionalised organisation structure
- discuss the behavioural implications of the performance measures used
- discuss the impact of the divisional autonomy versus corporate goal congruence debate on divisional performance and transfer pricing
- recommend suitable measures and discuss the relevance of a range of monetary and non-monetary measures for divisional performance measurement
- interpret and discuss the behavioural implications of performance measures and transfer pricing methods in divisional structures
- recommend for a given situation the appropriate transfer pricing method and discuss its implications for performance measurement and corporate profit maximisation

Key areas of the Syllabus

The main areas of the syllabus for Paper 9 are as follows.

- New managerial philosophies
- Relevant information for decision making (uses to which information may be put and how these would be useful in a management accounting system)
- Pricing
- Budgeting and budgetary control
- Standard costing
- Performance evaluation
- Transfer pricing
- Strategic management accounting

Quantitative methods

Quantitative methods, such as the following, will be examined in the context of management accounting.

- Use of learning curve (will be built into a scenario type question)
- Calculus in pricing (students should be aware of how to implement basic calculus eg in price/demand formula derivation)
- Forecasting
- Probabilities
- Sensitivity analysis
- Use of indices
- Use of Discounted Cash Flow (DCF) (Use of NPVs - discussion of reasons for and against DCF - students should ignore taxation element)
- Use of linear programming - formulation and interpretation of model

THE EXAMINATION PAPER

Format of the paper

		Number of marks
Section A:	2 (out of 3) questions of 35 marks each	70
Section B:	2 (out of 3) questions of 15 marks each	30
		100

Time allowed: 3 hours

Present value and annuity tables will be provided in the exam.

Analysis of past papers

December 1999

Section A (2 out of 3 questions, 35 marks each)

1   Budget calculations (for situations including free replacements and process losses and for cost of quality); planning and operational variances (calculation and explanations); standard cost calculations (for situations including free replacements and process losses) and discussions of their benefit for product pricing and target costing.

2   Profit, RI, RO and NPV calculations for investment in a quality improvement programme; calculations of bonus paid on various rates and discussion of manager's preferred basis; discussion of factors influencing outcome of quality improvement programme.

3   Calculation of, explanation of, meaning and provision of examples of target costs and units of quality; discussion and quantitative analysis of proposal.

Section B (2 out of 3 questions, 15 marks each)

4   Discussion of behavioural problems associated with a focus on specific performance measures; commenting on actions to overcome problems associated with the operation of a performance measurement system.

5   Explanation of how certain actions can help to overcome uncertainty associated with budget preparation.

6   Transfer pricing.

June 1999

Section A (2 out of 3 questions, 35 marks each)

1   Relevant cost decision making; breakeven calculations; costs of quality

2   Learning curve theory; use of a forecasting model; overcoming production capacity constraints; suggesting ways to improve budget v actual comparisons

3   Absorption costing v activity based calculations; joint probability and EV calculations; attitude to risk

Section B (2 out of 3 questions, 15 marks each)

4   Applications of standard costing/variance analysis in the modern business environment

5   Traditional v modern purchasing/manufacturing/stockholding systems and the impact on the management accounting function

6   Balanced scorecard

December 1998

Section A (2 out of 3 questions, 35 marks each)

1   Decision making involving uncertainty; transfer pricing
2   Flexible budgeting; charge rates to user departments; performance measurement in service departments
3   Activity based budgeting; activity-based terminology; procedure for investigating activities

Section B (2 out of 3 questions, 15 marks each)

4   The relevance of standard costing and variance analysis in the application of particular areas of management accounting
5   The application of accountability and contingency theory to the structure and operation of management accounting systems
6   Benchmarking; performance measurement in not-for-profit organisations

June 1998

Section A (2 out of 3 questions, 35 marks each)

1   Decision making with uncertainty and risk; the impact of service organisation performance measures
2   Activity cost calculations; benchmarking exercise; strategic planning objectives
3   Decision making - early exit from the market for a product; make and/or subcontract decision

Section B (2 out of 3 questions, 15 marks each)

4   TQM, JIT and activity-based techniques: discussion of their principles and their impact on incremental budgeting system
5   Sources and content of total cost estimate in three situations
6   Performance measurement and aspiration levels

December 1997

Section A (2 out of 3 questions, 35 marks each)

1   NPV and IRR calculations; target costing; graphical representation of NPV and IRR; maximisation of price/ demand function
2   ROCE calculations using different transfer pricing bases (including ABC total cost); acceptability of various transfer pricing bases; shutdown decision (including the use of probabilities and expected values); factors affecting the shutdown decision
3   Variance calculations (material usage and price, process efficiency and expenditure); decision making using variances; determination of profit-maximising strategy (with respect to material sources and process methods); calculation of customer-specific contribution; limiting factor analysis; report on effect of decision-making focus on decision-making strategy

Section B (2 out of 3 questions, 15 marks each)

4   Continuous improvement and standard costing; the dysfunctional impact of focusing on certain variances
5   Costing in a processing industry
6   Alternative budgeting techniques

June 1997

Section A (2 out of 3 questions, 35 marks each)

1. Variance calculations and dysfunctional consequences of traditional measures; activity based costing calculations, activities and cost drivers
2. Interpretation of computerised linear programming output and limitations of linear programming
3. Performance measurement of service business: financial performance and other dimensions of performance

Section B (2 out of 3 questions, 15 marks each)

4. Pricing information and how it can be improved
5. Rolling budgets, flexible budgets, planning and operational variances and budgetary slack
6. Committed, discretionary and engineered costs and decision making in three scenarios

December 1996

Section A (2 out of 3 questions, 35 marks each)

1. Spreadsheet interpretation; calculation of standard costs (incorporating process losses); control standards v current standards; total quality management
2. Calculation of budgeted profit/loss involving inflation and various capacity levels; datatable interpretation; profit/loss calculations and probabilities; break-even calculation; use of spreadsheets
3. Preparation of operating statements (traditional expense-based analysis and activity-based analysis); advantages of activity based budgeting; performance measurement

Section B (2 out of 3 questions, 15 marks each)

4. Performance measurement in an education/training institution
5. Relevant costing and product valuation in various situations; the impact of timescale on decision making
6. Divisional performance measurement and transfer pricing

June 1996

Section A (2 out of 3 questions, 35 marks each)

1. Target costing/pricing involving the application of learning curve theory; factors which change the return on investment
2. Project appraisal using information provided on a range of performance measures, considering both the long and short term; annuity depreciation; zero base budgeting
3. Preparation of accounts using backflush accounting and a discussion of its merits; performance appraisal and NFIs; total quality management

Section B (2 out of 3 questions, 15 marks each)

4. Features of services; cellular organisation of a workforce
5. Total quality management and standard costing
6. Transfer pricing

Further guidance

The ACCA provides the following further guidance on the examination paper of Paper 9 *Information for Control and Decision Making*.

The objective of the Professional Stage

The main aim of the Professional Stage is to establish evidence of competence to practise as a professional accountant in public practice, public sector or in industry and commerce. This requires candidates to demonstrate not only that they have mastered the range of required knowledge, skills and techniques, but also that they are able to apply them in a managerial context.

By this stage, knowledge has to be fully integrated in the way it is used by professionals with a recognition of how the different subjects contribute to dealing with problems. This stage will present students with problems which test their skills and sensitivity in dealing with new contexts and unforeseen circumstances. In dealing with such situations, students will be expected to tailor solutions to previous problems appropriately and in a way which demonstrates their grasp of managerial skills.

Although emphasis will be given to practical issues, students will also be expected to criticise current practice and express views on developments in accounting. They will also be expected to show evidence of the necessary personal qualities and interpersonal skills required of the professional accountant.

Skills to be tested in the Professional Stage

Students should be able to demonstrate the ability to:

- draw on knowledge across all earlier papers studied;
- integrate that knowledge effectively and use it creatively in applying concepts and techniques;
- analyse and interpret data and information and present reasoned conclusions;
- diagnose and formulate appropriate solutions to problems which indicate commercial awareness;
- exercise judgement drawing on technical, political and commercial awareness in developing and evaluating alternatives and in proposing solutions;
- adapt to new systems and circumstances;
- communicate analyses and conclusions effectively and with sensitivity for differing purposes and to contrasting audiences with due emphasis on social expectations.

While the skills identified above will be tested directly by the questions set, in assessing the answers weight will be given to the students' ability to demonstrate a grasp of the following personal skills and attributes:

Interpersonal skills
Tact, sensitivity to political tensions and cultural differences, awareness of social, economic and political pressure, ability to influence

Management skills

Resource management: people, material, time and money, management of the client, management of change, in particular in technology, and contingency planning

Personal qualities

Persistence in pursuing inquiries and probing responses, integrity, objectivity, independence and public responsibility

Aim of paper 9

To ensure students are competent to prepare and analyse accounting data, apply it to a range of planning, control and decision-making situations and adapt it to accommodate change.

On completion of this paper students should be able to:

- review the objectives of management accounting and its role as part of a business information system;
- explain the meaning of and the accounting implications of trends in management accounting such as world class manufacturing and total quality management;
- explain the nature of information, its sources and analysis required for the operation of a management accounting system;
- describe, illustrate and comment on the planning and control uses of standard costing, budgeting and variance analysis;
- identify relevant costs and appropriate techniques for decision making and use them in various decision-making situations;
- identify, discuss and implement a range of product pricing methods applicable in particular market situations;
- discuss the characteristics of strategic management accounting decisions;
- discuss the performance measures appropriate to different business situations;
- demonstrate the skills expected at the Professional Stage.

Prerequisite knowledge

Paper 9 draws upon the coverage of management accounting in paper 8 Managerial Finance and costing in paper 3 Management Information.

Paper 9 develops the subject matter of papers 3 and 8 by:

- appraising and reviewing areas of change in the management accounting framework;
- incorporating risk and uncertainty in decision making;
- assessing the impact of uncertainty, materiality and controllability in budgeting and variance analysis;
- examining behavioural implications of planning and control;
- providing a more in depth view of performance measurement, including transfer pricing.

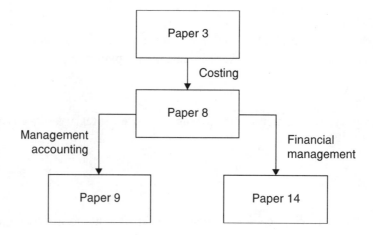

Extent of integration

Students must be prepared to apply quantitative techniques in management accounting decision making and will need to understand decision trees, probabilities, linear programming, indexing and discounted cash flows from paper 3 Management Information.

Paper 9 examines the scope for use of information technology in the provision and analysis of management accounting information and paper 5 Information Analysis will provide useful background knowledge for this area.

General notes

Students are advised to read the 'Exam notes' and 'Examiners' Reports' published in the *Students' Newsletter* as these contain details of examinable legislation, changes in the syllabuses and other useful information for each examination session.

Students are strongly advised to read articles published in the *Students' Newsletter* which are specified as relevant to this paper. Such articles are a useful source of learning materials for the examinations.

(*BPP note.* Recent articles by the Examiner which have appeared in the *ACCA Students' Newsletter* are provided in a bank at the end of this Study Text.)

Part A

Accounting information systems

Chapter 1

INFORMATION AND ACCOUNTING SYSTEMS

Chapter topic list	Syllabus reference
1 Information	2(a), 2(c)
2 Quantitative and qualitative information	2(a), 2(b), 2(c)
3 The accuracy of information	2(a), 2(b), 2(c)
4 Information technology and the MIS	2(a), 4(c)
5 Spreadsheets	2(a), 4(c)

Introduction

This chapter gives you some important facts about Paper 9 as a whole. It includes lots of examples of what **'information'** means in a management accounting context, as well as reminding you of ideas about information that you have studied already. Especially important is the section on **spreadsheets**, which are a favourite topic of the **Paper 9 examiner**. You have studied these before, too, but there are some very fundamental points about spreadsheets in the Paper 9 context that you **must** understand from the start.

Core areas of the syllabus identified by the examiner and covered in this chapter: **interpretation and use of data from IT output**.

1   INFORMATION

Information for control and decision making

1.1   ACCA Paper 9 has a grand title, but it is essentially a **management accounting** paper.

- **Control** in the context of Paper 9 is largely about budgeting, standard costs and performance measurement.

- **Decision making** involves the application of management accounting techniques such as probabilities and break-even analysis.

Exam focus point

In the exam you have to answer two from three 'written' questions that are usually fairly straightforward and can be answered from 'book knowledge'. These questions are worth 15 marks (they should take 15 × 1.8 minutes = 27 minutes). However, you also have to tackle two from three longer questions requiring quite difficult calculations and written commentary on the results of the calculations. They are worth 35 marks and should take 63 minutes each.

Accounting information

1.2   The principal distinction between management accounting and financial accounting is that management accounting serves **internal** users of accounting information while financial accounting reports to **external** users.

Financial and non-financial information

1.3   Traditionally for cost and management accounting, and still for the purposes of financial accounting and tax, the main type of information used by accountants is **monetary** information or **financial** information.

1.4   However, what we call 'financial information' is always capable of being broken down into a monetary price on the one hand, and a **non-monetary** component on the other. 'Wages' represents the price of the number of **hours** worked by a certain number of people. 'Materials costs' are the price of so many **kilograms** or **litres** or **units** of physical substances. The non-monetary component is likely to be more meaningful to many managers.

1.5   Non-financial information may also be expressed in terms of **percentages and ratios**. For example, details of the number of products returned, relative to the number sold (eg 2:100 or 2%), gives an indication of product quality.

1.6   Information need not be quantitative at all to be of interest to management. 'Closing down the factory will have a major adverse social impact in the area and will damage the organisation's reputation' is a highly significant **qualitative** factor to be taken into account when the decision is made about the future of the factory.

Knowledge brought forward from Papers 3, 5 and 8

Information must possess certain **qualities** if it is to be of any value. Information is good information if it is **ACCURATE** (**A**ccurate, **C**omplete, **C**ost-beneficial, **U**ser-targeted, **R**elevant, **A**daptable (in terms of communication), **T**imely, **E**asy to use).

Processing business data can be said to have the following features.

- **Collecting data in the first place**. The quality, accuracy and completeness of the data collected and input will affect the quality of information produced.

- **Processing the data into information,** by summarising it, say, or consolidating information from different sources, or classifying it and producing total figures.

- **Disseminating the information to users** via **scheduled** reports (routinely prepared on a regular basis (for example the payroll report)), **exception** reports (draw attention to deviations from plan), reports produced on **demand** (only when requested, not as a matter of course) and **planning** reports (for example forecasts).

Neutrality of information or freedom from bias

1.7   A point that has been examined a number of times in the past is the **'neutrality'** of information, a rather unpleasant way of saying that information should be **free from bias**. Bias may creep into management accounting information in ways such as the following.

(a)   A variance report may highlight a manager's failure to achieve a budget target **without recognising** that, say, the adverse variance against the budget is only half as large this month as it was last month. Comparative information should be presented as well if the information is to be interpreted fairly.

(b)   A manager in a large company will compare information about the price of supplies on the open market with the price that will be charged to her for the supplies if she buys them from another division of her company. If she finds that the goods produced by the competitor company are cheaper she will buy them from outside, but for a variety of reasons this **may not be in the best interests** of the company as a whole. The internal price needs to be 'neutral' so that it leads the manager to take the decision that is **in the best interests** of both her own division and of the company as a whole.

1.8   If you find point (b) a little hard to follow, don't worry. The topic of **transfer pricing** is explored in greater depth later in this Study Text.

Relevance

1.9   The **relevance** of management accounting information is clearly important in the very simple sense that there is no value in providing information about, say, **labour** rates if you are asked for information about **material** costs.

1.10 Likewise, though it may be on the right topic, **current** information may not be relevant to decisions about something that will happen in the **future**. For example it is not relevant to price a job due to be started in six months time using current labour rates if it is known that labour rates will have increased when the job commences.

1.11 Beyond this, however, **relevance** could be seen as the single most important quality of good information, embracing most of the other qualities (completeness, accuracy and so on) that useful information is supposed to possess.

(a)   A management accounting information system (MAIS) may not be designed or able to provide **complete** information, in other words *all* of the information that is relevant to a decision. For example, the system may not be capable of measuring, or reporting on **qualitative** matters such as the impact of a decision on staff morale.

(b)   The MAIS may be set up to provide **highly detailed** information, with analyses of costs down to the last penny, say. For many decisions this is **too high** a level of **accuracy**. Figures to the nearest thousand pounds may have been all that were required, so that most of the information provided was irrelevant.

(c)   The MAIS may use **inappropriate techniques** and therefore provide information which, although technically faultless, leads to bad decisions. An example would be the use of absorption costing on a **labour** hour basis in a highly **automated** production environment: the labour-hour based costs are not really **relevant** to the viability or otherwise of products, because very little labour is used.

Exam focus point

These two topics - bias and relevance - featured in a written question in **June 1994**. More generally, the qualities of good information should **always** be borne in mind when answering exam questions, which are themselves examples of data (the question) processed into information (the answer).

Question 1

(a)   How could an answer to an exam question display the qualities of good information?

(b)   Your finance director has just asked you to find out for him the current value of your organisation's stocks, as part of his preparation for a meeting. Describe the features of a report that you could prepare that would respond to this request in the *worst possible* way.

Answer

(a)   Work through each of items in the **ACCURATE** acronym with an exam solution in mind. For example an answer is not 'cost beneficial' or examiner-targeted, if it contains reams of writing in response to a section worth only 2 marks.

(b)   The **best** possible report would be a single top sheet showing the total figure: 'Total value of stocks as at [today's date]: £2.4m', say. This *might* be backed by a slightly more detailed analysis into raw materials, WIP and finished goods, or according to product types, but only rounded totals need be given.

The **worst** possible answer would be as far removed from this as possible. Work through each of the items in the *ACCURATE* acronym, thinking of ways that a report could fail to deliver the information required. For example, closing down production and calling in a team of management consultants to conduct a stock-take would be a highly cost-ineffective response.

As a further exercise you could consider in what circumstances the *bad* features that you identify for (b) would be regarded as *good* features. (The management consultants might be a good idea in a case of suspected fraud, for example.)

Sources of monetary and non-monetary information

The financial accounting records

1.12   You are by now very familiar with the idea of a system of sales ledgers and purchase ledgers, general ledgers, cash books and so on. These records provide a **history of an organisation's monetary transactions**.

1.13   Some of this information is of great value outside the accounts department - most obviously, for example, sales information for the marketing function. Other information, like cheque numbers, is of purely administrative value within the accounts department.

1.14   You will also be aware that to maintain the integrity of its financial accounting records, an organisation of any size will have systems for and **controls over transactions**. These also give rise to valuable information.

1.15   A stock control system is the classic example: besides actually recording the monetary value of purchases and stock in hand for external financial reporting purposes, the system will include purchase orders, goods received notes, goods returned notes and so on, and these can be analysed to provide management information about **speed** of delivery, say, or the **quality** of supplies.

Other internal sources

1.16   Much information that is not strictly part of the financial accounting records nevertheless is closely tied in to the accounting system.

(a)   Information about personnel will be linked to the **payroll** system. Additional information may be obtained from this source if, say, a project is being costed and it is necessary to ascertain the availability and rate of pay of different levels of staff.

(b)   Much information will be produced by a **production** department about machine capacity, movement of materials and work in progress, set up times, maintenance requirements and so on.

(c) Many service businesses - notably accountants and solicitors - need to keep detailed records of the **time** spent on various activities, both to justify fees to clients and to assess the efficiency of operations.

Question 2

Think of at least one piece of non-monetary information that a management accountant might obtain from the following sources in order to make a decision about a new product.

(a) Marketing manager   (d) Public relations officer
(b) Vehicle fleet supervisor (e) Head of research
(c) Premises manager

1.17 **Formal** information such as reports, memos and records of meetings may also be important. **Informal** information arises from employees' need to communicate with each other.

External sources

1.18 We hardly need say that an organisation's files are also full of invoices, letters, advertisements and so on received *from* customers and suppliers. But there are many occasions when an active search **outside the organisation** is necessary.

Knowledge brought forward from Papers 3 and 5

External sources of business information include:

- The government
- Newspapers, business magazines and specific reference works
- Television and radio
- Other businesses, for example through EDI and promotional material
- Professional bodies like the ACCA, and trade bodies
- Libraries, information services, and consultants or advisers
- The Internet

Larger organisations have information managers to assemble such information and pass it on to the people who need it.

Exam focus point

Paper 9 questions are usually concerned mainly with internal information gathered from the accounting system, although a question in the **December 1996** exam required you to work with a set of figures produced by a trade body, in addition to internally-generated figures, while a question in the **June 1998** exam provided recent industry average statistics for benchmarking purposes.

Management accounting principles and techniques

1.19 An organisation's needs for information are influenced profoundly by the **uses** to which it wants to put the information. For example, a great many organisations accumulate cost information for their products using **absorption costing**, whereas other businesses use **marginal costing**. Clearly if an organisation wants to change from marginal costing to absorption costing it may find that it cannot do so until it has **reanalysed** or **collected afresh** information about, say, machine hours, or about number of employees by function, or about whatever else is to be used as the absorption base.

1.20 This problem is more acute for organisations wishing to adopt modern techniques like **Just-in-Time** production or **activity based costing**, whose information needs are quite different from those of traditional methods.

1.21 The same applies to *ad hoc* decision-making situations: if an organisation wants to use, say, **learning curve theory**, it cannot do so without first understanding what information will be needed and then devising a means of collecting it.

Management accounting information in practice

1.22 It seems that much of what accountants learn in theory when they are gaining their qualification is **forgotten** in practice. An ACCA study of 300 companies found that management accounting methods are routinely ignored by many manufacturers. Many such companies make management decisions based on financial accounting information.

1.23 It is not clear whether this is because companies are **ignorant** of management accounting techniques or because they have **not invested** in measurement systems on top of those required to meet financial reporting requirements. Whatever the reason, it is not a desirable state of affairs, and the responsibility for instituting sounder practices in the future rests upon **your** shoulders.

Question 3

What information might be needed to determine an absorption rate for factory overheads?

Answer

Details of the amount and nature of the overheads; details of the physical characteristics of the factory and each of its departments (floor area, cubic capacity and so on), details of number of employees in each department; details of the value of machinery in each department; information about usage of service departments by production departments; details of an assortment of possible absorption bases like total labour or machine hours for the volume of production expected.

If you could not answer this, consider reviewing your earlier study material for cost and management accounting before proceeding with this text.

Exam focus point

One of the questions in the **June 1998** exam asked candidates to expand on the appropriate sources of the information used in, and the content of, total cost estimates for each of three situations. Most of the analysis should be knowledge brought forward from Papers 3 and 8, although an answer required mention of a number of Paper 9 topics, such as throughput (see Chapter 4).

2 QUANTITATIVE AND QUALITATIVE INFORMATION

KEY TERMS

Quantitative information is information that can be expressed in numbers. A sub-category of quantitative information is **financial information** (also known as **monetary information**), which is information that can be expressed in terms of money.

Qualitative information is information that cannot be expressed in numbers.

KEY TERMS

Non-financial information (or **non-monetary information**) is information that is not expressed in terms of money, although this does not mean that it cannot be expressed in terms of money.

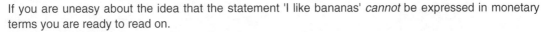

Question 4

Categorise the following statements as either financial, qualitative, quantitative or non-financial, whichever *one* of these you think is most appropriate.

(a)   I bought 4 bananas.

(b)   I bought £1's worth of bananas.

(c)   I like bananas.

(d)   I can afford 1lb of bananas.

Answer

We stressed that you should put each statement into one category only to make sure that you take in the essential points. For example, statement (a) is actually both quantitative and non-financial, but we would call it 'quantitative' only, because there is no suggestion of money being involved.

If you are uneasy about the idea that the statement 'I like bananas' *cannot* be expressed in monetary terms you are ready to read on.

Qualitative information

2.1   Colin Drury (*Management and Cost Accounting*, 1992) describes qualitative factors as those 'that can be expressed in monetary terms only with much difficulty or imprecision'. Thus the information 'German people are very fond of bananas' could be expressed as 'The value of the German banana market is £x million pa', but the value of x is very questionable.

2.2   EXAMPLE: QUALITATIVE INFORMATION

As a more elaborate example, consider the information that 'Joe is an excellent worker, much liked and respected by his workmates. He has a wife and two young children to support and unemployment in the area where he works is very high.' Now consider how difficult it would be to obtain the following information in order to appraise a decision whether or not to replace Joe with an untested machine.

(a)   The cost of **being sure** that the machine would do the job as well as Joe can.

(b)   The cost of **loss of morale** amongst other workers if Joe is made redundant.

(c)   The cost of **compensating** Joe for the psychological and financial impact of unemployment on himself and his family.

(d)   The cost of **relocating** Joe and his family to an area where he would have better job prospects.

(e)   The cost of **retraining** Joe to improve his job prospects.

(f)   The cost to Joe's community in **social and financial terms** of his unemployment or relocation.

2.3   These are not just political points. The company's treatment of Joe may have a profound impact upon its ability to **recruit** skilled employees in the future and on the way the company is **perceived** by potential customers. Whether the costs can be established or not, the questions need to be considered.

9

2.4   There will often be no conclusion that you as the management accountant can draw from qualitative information. Your job is to **be aware of its existence** and report it under the heading of **'other matters to be considered'**. In practice of course, many decisions are finally swayed by the strength of the qualitative arguments rather than the cold facts presented in the quantitative analysis, and rightly so.

Exam focus point

As a general guideline, if you are asked to comment on qualitative issues, you should consider matters such as the following.

(a)   The impact on or of **human behaviour**. What will be the reaction on the factory floor? How will managers feel? Will customers be attracted or deterred? Can suppliers be trusted?

(b)   The impact on or of the **environment** ('surroundings'). Is the country in a recession? Is government or legislation influential? Are there 'green' issues to be considered? What is the social impact? What action will competing companies take? Is changing technology a help or a hindrance?

(c)   The impact on or of **ethics**. Is the action in the public interest? Are we acting professionally? Are there conflicts of interest to be considered? Will fair dealing help to win business? Are we treating staff properly?

Easy marks

2.5   The topic of quantitative and qualitative information and the value of non-monetary information will be covered at several points later in this book. We have introduced it here because you should realise very early on that **Paper 9** is not just about number crunching. Numerical questions usually include written parts that offer relatively **easy marks** for common sense comments about qualitative management issues.

3   THE ACCURACY OF INFORMATION

3.1   One of the qualities of good information is that it is accurate within the user's needs. Various factors affect the degree of accuracy required and the degree that is achievable.

Exam focus point

An old syllabus exam question (set by the *current* Paper 9 examiner), asked how inaccuracy might exist in various management accounting information situations.

Measurement

3.2   The smaller the unit of measurement, the more accurately information may be expressed.

Case example

A firm of accountants that requires its staff to fill in timesheets measured by hourly divisions will get a less accurate analysis of time spent by staff than a firm whose staff are required to account for every five minutes of their time. The latter is probably highly appropriate for a firm whose staff carry out a wide variety of short tasks, but may be unnecessarily precise for a firm with few clients or one which only engages in highly specialised work.

Information processing

3.3 Accuracy in the sense of absolute correctness (rather than relative precision) is obviously affected by the care with which information is prepared. If the data that is collected is wrong then the final result will be inaccurate. The simplest example is an **error in data input** - putting in an extra nought, getting the decimal point in the wrong place and so on.

3.4 The way in which processed information is **stored** may also be important. An accounting system may preserve monthly totals from last year, for comparative purposes, but not store details of day-to-day transactions. Unless a back-up copy is kept, an analysis of, say, weekly sales trends to pinpoint likely peaks and troughs cannot be performed. So if you gave the production manager the information that 'last year sales hit a peak in **September**', and he then geared up production to have a full stock of goods ready for sale by the **second** week of September. If it subsequently transpired that maximum demand occurred in the **first** week of September, many potential sales may be lost because the information given to production was not accurate enough for its purpose and goods were not available on time.

Volume change

3.5 Volume change can affect the accuracy of information in a number of ways.

(a) From an administrative point of view an **increase in activities** may generate more data than information processors can cope with in the short term. This may mean that detailed analyses of information are not available until the system catches up. It may also increase the chance of error.

(b) Volume change may undermine assumptions about **cost behaviour**.

(i) The cost of hiring a machine may be **fixed** so long as only 1,000 units are produced per week but it may be doubled if 1,005 units are produced, because a second machine is needed. Materials may cost £1.80 per kg if only 1,000 kg are purchased, but £1.75 per kg for purchases over 1,000 kg, due to volume discount.

(ii) The accountant assumes variable costs increase in a **linear** fashion in relation to activity volume, but recognises that it is only within a certain activity range that this assumption holds good. The assumption is made because it is **sufficiently accurate** within the relevant range to serve the accountant's purpose.

3.6 As a general rule **the larger** the scale of operations, **the less accurate** the information obtainable is likely to become. Thus a manufacturer of specialised paints selling to a small number of regular buyers will be able to forecast its sales with a good deal more accuracy than can a company the size of ICI.

Time

3.7 The more **out-of-date** information is, the less likely it is to be accurate in the sense that it still holds true. Costs increase due to inflation, buyers' preferences change due to fashion, technology brings about improvements in efficiency, and so on.

3.8 On the other hand, time may **improve the accuracy** of information. For example a production manager may wish to assess the incidence of wastage of a certain material used in a certain process. He is far more likely to be given an accurate estimate if wastage is measured over a period of six months than if one day's wastage is taken at random.

BPP PUBLISHING

Accuracy and its controllability

3.9 Within an organisation it should be possible to control the accuracy of the information generated to a fine degree. For instance, the length of time it takes a machine to perform a job should be capable of measurement to the minute, second or millisecond, as required.

3.10 In some situations, however, accuracy is less controllable.

Control factor	Example
Some information relies for its accuracy upon individuals **telling the truth.**	A good example is an employee's timesheet. An employee may wish it to appear that he can perform a job more quickly than is really the case because he wants promotion; alternatively he may not wish to appear lazy and so ascribe time to the job that was really idle time. Inaccurate information about the time needed for the job will result in either case.
Information obtained from **outside the organisation** is more difficult, or even impossible, to verify.	Market research information is a good example: what people say they will do when asked face to face by a researcher in the street frequently differs from their real intentions. A manufacturer's product specification is another: a machine may be purchased because the manufacturer says it can produce 'over 1,000 widgets' per minute. This may mean that it averages 950 a minute under normal operating conditions, but is capable of operating at a higher speed for limited periods. Legislation may protect against blatant deception but it does not require accuracy to the degree that an organisation may need to plan effectively.

Accuracy and uncertainty

3.11 Management accounting information generally looks to the future and its accuracy is therefore subject to **uncertainty**. As we shall see in later chapters there are a number of ways in which this can be allowed for.

Question 5

In what sense is accuracy an issue in:

(a) the classification of costs as direct or indirect;
(b) the use of raw materials valuation methods like FIFO, LIFO or the weighted average method?

Answer

(a) Direct costs are costs that can be traced to the cost objective (a unit of product or whatever), but traceability is largely a question of the degree of accuracy that is necessary in practice.

(b) FIFO, LIFO and the weighted average method are all accounting conveniences to save the trouble of keeping precise records of the specific usage of every iota of raw material.

4 INFORMATION TECHNOLOGY AND THE MIS

Knowledge brought forward from Papers 3, 5 and 8

All but the tiniest of businesses now use **computerised** information systems because computers offer benefits of **speed** and **accuracy** and can handle large **volumes** of complex information processing.

It is useful to distinguish between various levels of information system.

Transaction processing systems record and arrange raw data, for example the details in what would be called day books and ledgers in a manual system.

Management information systems (MIS) take the raw data from transaction processing systems and present it in a form that makes it useful for managers who need to make decisions.

Executive information systems (EIS) are for more senior managers, and provide summary level data, user-friendly presentation and data manipulation.

Decision support systems (DSS) help to make decisions on poorly-defined problems, by providing access to information and information analysis tools.

Expert systems draw on a computerised knowledge base (such as the workings of tax legislation) and contain rules that indicate that if, say, x and y are the case, the appropriate course of action is z.

Accounting packages and management accounting information

4.1 Accounts systems for very large companies tend to be tailor-made and operate on a mainframe computers. Small and medium-sized companies tend to use off-the-shelf application software and PCs for their computerised accounting systems.

4.2 Accounting packages are amongst the most widely-used sort of 'off-the-shelf' package in business. A package may consist of a suite of program modules (such as for stock control, the purchase ledger, cash book and so on) and the computer user can use a **single module** for a specific application, or a **number of modules** in a more integrated system.

4.3 Each module may be **integrated** with the others, so that data entered in one module will be passed automatically or by simple operator request through into any other module where the data is of some relevance.

4.4 Each of these modules will have certain print-outs associated with it, giving standard **reports** like aged debtor analysis, stock valuation and so forth. Many packages also have a 'report generator' allowing the system to be tailored to supply special information needs. Sage, for example, claim that their Sterling package's report generator allows 'just about every piece of information in the system to be retrieved, re-sorted and printed out in the way you want it'. This is precisely what the management accountant needs to be able to do.

5   SPREADSHEETS

Knowledge brought forward from Papers 3 and 5

Spreadsheets

- A spreadsheet is a versatile type of software package for modelling.

- The model builder can decide how data should be manipulated and presented.

- Examples include Lotus 1-2-3 and Excel.

- The basic facilities featured in most spreadsheet programs are as follows.

    ° Print and file commands   ° Format
    ° Cell editing and spreadsheet rearrangement facilities   ° Macros
    ° Sorting   ° Protect
    ° Copying a formula   ° Search and replace

The advantages of spreadsheets

5.1   Here are some of the more common accounting applications of spreadsheets.

- Balance sheets
- Cash flow analysis/forecasting
- Inventory records
- Job cost estimates
- Market share analysis and planning

- Profit projections
- Profit statements
- Project budgeting and control
- Sales projections and records
- Tax estimation

5.2   The great value of spreadsheets derives from their **simple format** of rows, columns and worksheets of data, and the ability of the data **users** to have direct access themselves to their spreadsheet model via their own PCs. For example, an accountant can construct a cash flow model with a spreadsheet package on PC on his desk: he can **create** the model, **input** the data, **manipulate** the data and read or print the **output** direct. He will also have fairly **instant access** to the model, in just the time it takes to load the model onto his PC. Spreadsheets therefore bring computer modelling within the everyday reach of data users.

The disadvantages of spreadsheets

5.3   Spreadsheets have disadvantages if they are not properly used, including the following.

(a)   A **minor error in the design** of a model at any point can affect the validity of data throughout the spreadsheet. Such errors can be very difficult to trace. Good examples (though perhaps not to be used in exam answers!) are the errata that appeared in the ACCA's model answers to the December 1994 Paper 9 exam and in an article by the **examiner, George Brown,** in the April 1995 edition of the *ACCA Students' Newsletter*, both due to minor errors in spreadsheet design.

(b)   Even if it is properly designed in the first place, it is very easy to corrupt a model by **accidentally changing** a cell or inputting data in the wrong place.

Case example

KPMG Management Consulting discovered that up to 95% of models were found to contain major errors (ie those that could affect decisions based on the results of the model) and 59% were judged to have poor model design.

(c)   It is possible to become **over-dependent** on them, so that simple one-off tasks that can be done in seconds with a pen and paper are done on a spreadsheet instead. (Similarly most young accountants are dependent on their calculators, and incapable of performing anything but the most simple mental arithmetic.)

(d)   The possibility for experimentation with data is so great that it is possible to **lose sight** of the original intention of the spreadsheet.

Exam focus point

Spreadsheets are a **favourite topic** of the Paper 9 examiner, and you will see examples of their use **throughout this book**. Make absolutely sure that you understand the basics of spreadsheet construction explained on the following pages.

Constructing a spreadsheet model

5.4   The following steps are highly recommended.

Step	Explanation
Input	Pick out all the figures in the problem that are **subject to change** and enter them into the spreadsheet, with **clear labels**. For example if your problem involved five different figures you might enter the labels in cells A1 to A5 and the figures alongside in cells B1 to B5. This is the **input area** of the spreadsheet.
Calculations	In a different part of the spreadsheet enter the **formulae** that act upon the figures in the problem. If your problem involves multiplying one of your five figures by another and then adding the result to the sum of the other three, enter in the first cell (say B7) in your **calculation section** the formula B1*B2, in the second cell the formula SUM (B3:B7). Again **labels** should be included in column A.
Output	In a complex spreadsheet it is good practice to have a separate **output section** for the results of the calculations. The result of the calculation SUM (B3:B7) could be a figure that forms part of a budget. The budget would collect together, in a single area of the spreadsheet, the results of numerous calculations in the calculation area.

5.5   The value of this approach is that the only cells that need to be **changed** if the data changes (in next month's budget say) are the cells in the **input** area.

5.6 EXAMPLE: A SPREADSHEET FOR COST ABSORPTION

Tradco Ltd is a manufacturing business with four factories. It wants to develop a spreadsheet model for the **absorption of overheads**. Sample data for East Factory has been collected and **input** as rows 1 - 23 of a spreadsheet.

Input

The following **overhead costs** are allocated to East Factory.

	A	B	C	D	E
1	TRADCO LIMITED				
2	Input data				
3					
4	*Allocated overhead costs - East Factory*				
5		£			
6	Factory rent	5,000			
7	Machine depreciation	10,000			
8	Heat and light	6,450			
9					

The factory has three **departments**, further details of which are as follows.

	A	B	C	D	E
9					
10	*Departmental statistics*				
11		*Dept 1*	*Dept 2*	*Dept 3*	*Total*
12	Floor area (m²)	500	300	200	1,000
13	Cubic capacity (m³)	2,500	1,200	600	4,300
14	Value of machinery	100,000	20,000	80,000	200,000
15	Labour hours	3,000	2,150	11,800	16,950
16					

East Factory produces two products, x and y, and overheads are **absorbed** on a labour hour basis. The labour hours required in each department to produce one unit of each product are shown below.

	A	B	C	D	E
16					
17	*Labour hours per unit*				
18	Product x (hours)	3.0	1.0	2.0	
19	Product y (hours)	2.0	0.5	3.0	
20					

The direct costs of product x are £7 per unit and those of product y, £5 per unit.

	A	B	C	D	E
20					
21	*Direct costs*				
22	Product x (£)	7.00			
23	Product y (£)	5.00			
24					
25					

Required

The spreadsheet is to be designed so as to calculate the full cost of one unit of each product after the absorption of departmental overheads.

5.7 SOLUTION

Take your time with our solution to make sure you follow it. All the formulae used are shown on the final diagram following Paragraph 5.8. The curved lines should help you to follow the calculations. Note the **three areas**.

Calculations

The allocated overheads listed in rows 6 to 8 are first **apportioned** to the different departments using the bases shown in rows 12 to 15. For example Factory rent for Department 1 is £5,000 × (500m²/1,000m²) = £2,500.

	A	B	C	D	E
25					
26	**Apportionment**	*Dept 1*	*Dept 2*	*Dept 3*	*Total*
27	Factory rent	2,500	1,500	1,000	5,000
28	Heat and light	3,750	1,800	900	6,450
29	Machine depreciation	5,000	1,000	4,000	10,000
30	Total	11,250	4,300	5,900	21,450

The **absorption basis** is labour hours and so the absorption rate per labour hour is calculated by dividing the total department 1 overhead by the total labour hours. For example £11,250 divided by 3,000 hours is £3.75. The same procedure would be followed to calculate absorption rates for departments 2 and 3.

	A	B	C	D
31				
32	**Absorption rate**	*Dept 1*	*Dept 2*	*Dept 3*
33		3.75	2	0.5
34				

Output

Finally the absorption rates would be **applied to the hours spent by each product in each department**. For example £3.75 × 3 hours = £11.25.

	A	B	C	D	E
34					
35	**Total costs**				
36		*Product x*		*Product y*	
37		£		£	
38	Direct costs	7.00		5.00	
39	Dept 1 overheads	11.25		7.50	
40	Dept 2 overheads	2.00		1.00	
41	Dept 3 overheads	1.00		1.50	
42		21.25		15.00	
43					
44					

The total cost of product x is £21.25 and of product y £15.

5.8 Having built this basic model it could be **expanded and adapted** as appropriate for the other three factories, **used again** for subsequent periods, and used to perform **'what if' analyses**. In reality there may be many more different overheads, several more departments, and lots of different products, so you should appreciate the time saved in the long run by investing a little time at the outset to construct the model.

	A	B	C	D	E
1		TRADCO LIMITED			
2	**Input data**				
3					
4	*Allocated overhead costs*				
5		£			
6	Factory rent	5000			
7	Machine depreciation	10000			
8	Heat and light	6450			
9					
10	*Departmental statistics*				
11		*Dept 1*	*Dept 2*	*Dept 3*	*Total*
12	Floor area (m²)	500	300	200	=SUM(B12:D12)
13	Cubic capacity (m³)	2500	1200	600	=SUM(B13:D13)
14	Value of machinery	100000	20000	80000	=SUM(B14:D14)
15	Labour hours	3000	2150	11800	=SUM(B15:D15)
16					
17	*Labour hours per unit*				
18	Product x (hours)	3	1	2	
19	Product y (hours)	2	0.5	3	
20					
21	*Direct costs*				
22	Product x (£)	7			
23	Product y (£)	5			
24					
25					
26	**Apportionment**	*Dept 1*	*Dept 2*	*Dept 3*	*Total*
27	Factory rent	=B6*(B12/E12)	=B6*(C12/E12)	=B6*(D12/E12)	=SUM(B27:D27)
28	Heat and light	=B8*(B13/E13)	=B8*(C13/E13)	=B8*(D13/E13)	=SUM(B28:D28)
29	Machine depreciation	=B7*(B14/E14)	=B7*(C14/E14)	=B7*(D14/E14)	=SUM(B29:D29)
30	Total	=SUM(B27:B29)	=SUM(C27:C29)	=SUM(D27:D29)	=SUM(B30:D30)
31					
32	**Absorption rate**	*Dept 1*	*Dept 2*	*Dept 3*	
33		=B30/B15	=C30/C15	=D30/D15	
34					
35	**Total costs**				
36		*Product x*		*Product y*	
37		£		£	
38	Direct costs	=B22		=B23	
39	Dept 1 overheads	=B18*B33		=B19*B33	
40	Dept 2 overheads	=C18*C33		=C19*C33	
41	Dept 3 overheads	=D33*D18		=D19*D33	
42		=SUM(B38:B41)		=SUM(D38:D41)	
43					

Spreadsheets and databases

5.9 A **database** is a computer file of common data that can be accessed so as to serve a wide variety of users and user needs. A spreadsheet can be linked to, and extract information from, an existing database, or a database can be created using a spreadsheet so as to allow easy **access** to, and **manipulation** of, complex data or large volumes of data.

- The database can be searched to find specific data.

- Data can be sorted alphabetically and numerically by rows or columns in ascending or descending order.

- Sub-sets of the data can be extracted according to defined criteria.

- Statistical calculations can be performed on the data.

5.10 Beyond a certain level of complexity it is easier to use a proper database package such as **Microsoft Access** in preference to Microsoft Excel.

5.11 EXAMPLE: USING A DATABASE FOR DECISION MAKING

A company wishes to rationalise its materials handling procedures and has a number of options for **automating** this part of its operations. A vital factor in choosing the new machinery is what **load-bearing capacity** will be necessary.

5.12 The company has a database on a spreadsheet which is mainly used for stock control: it is in part number order, and shows the **weight and cost** of each part, **numbers delivered** and issued and the **balance** in stock. It also shows how many of each part are required for each of its 30 products. An extract is shown below to illustrate this.

5.13 By manipulating this database in the various ways suggested above it would be possible to extract an analysis **sorting** the data, product by product, showing parts used by each product, and **multiplying** the number of parts needed by the weight of each part, thus calculating the total weight of parts needing to be moved for each product.

5.14 This information could be linked to a production schedule for the different products, to find the total weight of parts to be moved for each production run. The machinery purchased to move the parts would need to be adequate to move that weight of parts within a certain amount of time.

	A	B	C	D	E	F	G	H	I	J	K	L
1	Stock no.	Description	Weight (kg)	Cost/kg	In	Out	Ordered	Balance	Product 1	Product 2	Product 3	Product 4
2	001	Nut	0.001	5.00		2,000		10,000	10		5	
3	002	Bolt	0.005	10.00				10,000	10		5	
4	003	Screw	0.002	7.50		2,000		20,000		50		20
5	004	Hinge	0.100	10.00				4,000		6		
6	005	Bracket	0.090	4.80	1000			7,500			12	
7	006	Corner	0.046	3.20		2,000		8,000	4			
8	007	Panel	1.000	14.00			1000	780	6	8		
9	008	Socket	0.053	2.53				5,250				4
10	009	Plug	0.067	3.97				5,250				4
11												

5.15 There may in practice be **further complications** (like the **size** of the different parts) but this too could be recorded on the database and brought to bear upon the decision.

More advanced spreadsheets

5.16 There are examples of spreadsheets throughout this book: you will see how they can be used to help with specific management accounting tasks and techniques wherever it is appropriate to show you this.

5.17 In particular we shall be looking at the various ways the **examiner** has incorporated spreadsheets into exam questions, using features such as **datatables** and others.

Chapter roundup

- **Good information** (such as an exam answer) has certain qualities that can be remembered by the **ACCURATE** acronym. **Relevance** is particularly important. Information should also be free from **bias**.

- **Sources** of monetary and non-monetary information include the accounting records, other internal sources, and external sources.

- **Qualitative** information is as relevant to control and decision making as **quantitative** information.

- The degree of **accuracy** required in information and the degree that is actually achievable are affected by the following factors.

○ Measurement	○ Routine changes	○ Controllability
○ Processing	○ Time	○ Uncertainty

- You should be aware of the advantages and disadvantages of **spreadsheets** and know how to prepare and lay out a **spreadsheet model**. Good spreadsheets are built up from three sections (**input, calculations and outputs**).

Quick quiz

1   What sort of information is used in management accounting? (see paras 1.3 -1.6)

2   Explain the acronym ACCURATE. (1.6)

3   Where does management accounting information come from, besides the financial accounting records? (1.12 - 1.18)

4   What are the implications for information systems of adopting JIT and ABC? (1.20)

5   How might you be able to earn **easy marks** in a Paper 9 exam? (2.5)

6   Give an example of how the system of measurement used affects the accuracy of information (3.2)

7   How does volume change affect the accuracy of information? (3.5)

8   What is an accounting module? (4.2 - 4.4)

9   What are the possible disadvantages of spreadsheets? (5.3)

10 Explain why a good spreadsheet model should be divided into three areas. (5.4 - 5.5)

11 How can a database be used to manipulate data? (5.9)

Question to try	Level	Marks	Time
1	Exam standard	15	27 mins

Chapter 2

THE ENVIRONMENT AND THE ACCOUNTING INFORMATION SYSTEM

Chapter topic list	Syllabus reference
1 Planning, control and decision making	2(a), 2(b), 2(c)
2 Strategic management accounting	1(a), 1(b)
3 Management accounting information systems	2(a), 2(c)

Introduction

An accounting information system is part of a larger information **environment** called the management information **system**, which itself is just one system within a larger environment called an organisation. In this chapter we look at some more advanced ideas about information and its use. As you will see, the **Paper 9 examiner** has written **articles** on some of the topics covered in this chapter.

Core areas of the syllabus identified by the examiner and covered in this chapter: **definition and main features of strategic management accounting; link between strategic management accounting and operational planning**.

1   PLANNING, CONTROL AND DECISION MAKING

1.1   Within an organisation, and at all levels of the organisation, information is continually flowing back and forth, being used by people to formulate **plans** and take **decisions,** and to draw attention to the need for **control** action, if the plans and decisions are not working as intended.

> **KEY TERMS**
>
> **Planning** means formulating ways of proceeding. **Decision making** means choosing between various alternatives. These two terms are virtually inseparable: you decide to plan in the first place and the plan you make is a collection of decisions.
>
> **Control** is used in the sense of monitoring something so as to keep it on course, like the 'controls' of a car, not (or not merely) in the sense of imposing restraints, or exercising tyrannical power over something. We have more to say about control later in this Study Text.

Question 1

This simple scenario may help you to understand how these terms are interrelated.

Mr and Mrs Average need to go to Sainsbury's to buy food and other household items. They make a list beforehand which sets out all the things they need. As they go round the supermarket they tick off the items on the list. If any particular item is not available they choose an alternative from the range on the shelves. They also buy a bottle of wine and two bars of chocolate. These were not on their original list.

(a)   What part or parts of this activity would you describe as planning?
(b)   There are several examples of decision making in this story. Identify three of them.
(c)   What part or parts of this activity would you describe as control?

Answer

We would describe making the list as planning, but making the list is also an example of decision making, since Mr and Mrs Average have to decide what items will go on the list. Ticking off the items is control and choosing alternatives is 'control action' involving further decision making.

You should be able to answer the various parts of this question without further help.

The decision-making hierarchy

1.2   Robert Anthony, a leading writer on organisational control, suggested what has become a widely-used hierarchy, classifying the information used at different management levels into three tiers: strategic planning, management control and operational control.

> ### KEY TERMS
>
> **Strategic planning.** The process of deciding on objectives of the organisation, on changes in these objectives, on the resources used to attain these objectives, and on the policies that are to govern the acquisition, use and disposition of these resources.
>
> **Management control.** The process by which managers assure that resources are obtained and used effectively and efficiently in the accomplishment of the organisation's objectives. It is sometimes called tactics or tactical planning.
>
> **Operational control** (or operational *planning*). The process of assuring that specific tasks are carried out effectively and efficiently.

1.3   You should have studied the Anthony hierarchy as part of your earlier studies, so we shall concentrate on how it features in **Paper 9** exams.

Strategic planning

1.4   The **strategic planning** process would include such matters as the selection of products to make and markets to sell them to, the required levels of company profitability, the purchase and disposal of subsidiary companies or major fixed assets, and so on.

1.5   Notable **characteristics** of strategic planning are as follows.

(a)   Generally formulated in **writing,** after much after discussion by committee (the **Board**)

(b)   **Circulated** to all interested parties within the organisation, and perhaps to the press

(c)   Does not trigger direct action but rather a series of **lesser plans** for sales, production and so on.

(d)   **Information** often obtained from outside the organisation and may be qualitative or quantitative.

Operational control

1.6 **Operational control** works out what **specific tasks** need to be carried out in order to achieve the strategic plan. For example a strategy may be to increase sales by 5% per annum for at least five years, and an operational plan to achieve this would be sales reps' weekly sales targets.

1.7 Notable characteristics of operational planning are the **speed of response** to changing conditions, and the use and understanding of **non-financial information** such as data about customer orders or raw material input.

Management control: co-ordinating the strategic and operational levels

1.8 **Management control** sits between strategy and operations and tries to ensure that operations achieve the intended strategic results. For example, a statement showing variances from flexed budget for materials costs might result in management control action such as asking purchasing staff to identify cheaper suppliers.

1.9 Notable characteristics of management control are that it is concerned with **efficient** and **effective** use of **resources**. Management control **information** is often quantitative and is commonly expressed in **financial** terms. The role of management control in co-ordinating operations and strategy is further discussed in the next section.

Question 2

Explain the terms, 'resources', efficiency', and 'effectiveness'.

Answer

You should remember this from earlier studies of subjects such as economics, as well as from earlier management accounting studies.

(a) **Resources**, sometimes referred to as the '4 Ms', are men, materials, machines and money. Time and space might also be included. Information itself is also a hugely valuable resource - some argue that it is becoming the most important of all.

(b) **Efficiency** in the use of resources means that optimum **output** is achieved from the **input** resources used.

(c) **Effectiveness** in the use of resources means that the *outputs* obtained are in line with the intended **objectives** or targets.

Exam focus point
The **June 1995** exam included a question that asked about the key features of strategic planning and operational planning. Candidates had to detail strategic planning objectives relevant to a particular situation in the **June 1998** exam.

2 STRATEGIC MANAGEMENT ACCOUNTING

Strategic management accounting and traditional management accounting

2.1 Traditional management accounting grew out of cost accounting. The 'management' that it was primarily intended to serve was **production** management, and hence the traditional emphasis on accounting for labour costs, materials costs and production overheads.

2.2 In the 1980s many commentators began to argue that traditional management accounting was too **backward-looking** and **inward-looking**, whereas decision making should be a **forward-looking** process which must be substantially **outward looking**.

2.3 **Strategic management accounting** is a logical development of this argument. Where strategic questions are being addressed, the management accounting system should provide information that is strategically significant.

> **KEY TERMS**
>
> A **strategy** is the sum of an organisation's long-term objectives, affecting its position in its environment.
>
> Following on from this, **strategic management accounting** means accounting procedures which stress extra-organisational variables such as competitors' actions and political, economic, social and technological (PEST) factors, as well as internal activities and non-financial data evaluation.

Management accounting information and strategic management

2.4 The **information** that is needed for strategic management could be grouped into eight categories.

Category	Strategic management information needs
Competitors' costs	What are they? How do ours compare? Can we beat them?
Product profitability	What profits or losses are being made by each of our products? Why is product A making good profits whereas equally good product B is making a loss?
Pricing decisions for new products	They can have crucial implications for the success or failure of the product when it is launched on the market. Accounting information can help to analyse how profits and cash flows will vary according to price and prospective demand.
The value of market share	A firm ought to be aware of what it is worth to increase the market share of one of its products.
Price reductions	Price reductions will probably be necessary at some stage in a product's life cycle, to increase or sustain market demand. When should they be made, by how much should prices be reduced?
Future prices	What will prices be next year, and in two to five years' time? What implications will these changes have for our products and markets?
Capacity expansion	Should the firm expand its capacity, and if so by how much? Should it diversify into a new area of operations or new market?
Falling prices	Management needs to know whether a sharp fall will be long term, and how much further prices might fall.

The Paper 9 examiner's view: linking strategy and operations

2.5 The Paper 9 examiner has written an **article** on this topic. The article includes a case study of a fictional company that adopts new management ideas like TQM, JIT and ABC (see Chapter 3) as its strategy for dealing with a high level of customer complaints. The company is trying to improve **quality** and **speed of delivery** while **controlling costs**, but it faces a number of problems.

> 'The achievement of long-term goals will require strategic planning which is linked to short-term operational planning ... . If there is no link between strategic planning and operational planning the result is likely to be *unrealistic plans, inconsistent goals, poor communication and inadequate performance measurement.*'
>
> (George Brown, 'Management Accounting and Strategic Management', *ACCA Students' Newsletter*, March 1994)

2.6 Providing the **links** referred to in this quotation is, effectively, what you are required to do in most of numerical questions that feature in the **Paper 9 examination,** and also in some of the written ones. In other words the figures or commentary that you provide in your answers are precisely the sort of information that will help to avoid problems of not achieving strategic aims.

2.7 We shall now consider the results of a lack of proper links (as *italicised* in the quotation).

Unrealistic plans

2.8 Unrealistic operational plans will force staff to **try too hard** with **too few resources**. Mistakes and failure are almost inevitable. This means poor quality products: costs include lost sales, arranging for returns, and time wasted dealing with complaints.

2.9 **Over-ambitious** plans may also mean that more stocks are produced than an organisation could realistically expect to sell (so costs of write-offs, opportunity costs of wasted resources, and unnecessary stock holding costs are incurred).

Inconsistent goals

2.10 Inconsistent strategic planning and operational planning goals may mean **additional costs** are incurred. An operational plan may require additional inspection points in a production process to ensure quality products are delivered to customers. The resulting extra costs will be at odds with the strategic planning goal of **minimum cost**.

Poor communication

2.11 Poor communication between senior management who set strategic goals and lower-level operational management could mean that operational managers are **unaware** of the strategic planning goal, say to sustain competitive advantage at minimum cost through speedy delivery of quality products to customers.

2.12 Some operational managers may therefore choose to focus on quality of product while others attempt to produce as many products as possible as quickly as they can; still others will simply keep their heads down and do as little as possible. This will lead to **lack of co-ordination**: there will be bottlenecks in some operational areas, needing expensive extra resources in the short term, and wasteful idle time in other areas.

BPP PUBLISHING

Inadequate performance measurement

2.13 Inadequate performance measurement will mean that an organisation has little idea of which areas are performing well and which **need to improve**. If quality of product and speed of delivery are the main sources of competitive advantage a business needs to know how good it is at these things.

2.14 For example, if an organisation measures only **conventional accounting results** it will know how much stock it has and how much it has spent, say, on 'carriage out', but it will not know the **opportunity cost** of cancelled sales through not having stock available when needed, or not being able to deliver it on time. Equally the **quality** of products needs to be measured in terms not only of sales achieved, but also in terms of **customer complaints** and feedback: again the cost is the opportunity cost of lost sales.

Exam focus point

The consequences and cost implications of lack of co-ordination between strategic planning and operational planning featured in an exam question in June 1995.

Note that the **examiner's articles** are very important, and points and techniques featured in them frequently appear in exam questions. There is more on this later, but if you are impatient look up **'Brown, George'** in the **index** for a full list of places where we cover his writings.

Question 3

(a) What does the Paper 9 examiner say about links?
(b) Why are articles by the Paper 9 examiner important?
(c) Define strategic management accounting.

Answer

If you can't answer these questions you have obviously not read Section 2 of this Chapter properly, which is **daft** considering how important it is. Is this a good time for you to be studying?

3 MANAGEMENT ACCOUNTING INFORMATION SYSTEMS

The attributes and principles of management accounting information

3.1 A classic study in the 1950s by Simon *et al* identified three attributes of accounting information as follows.

(a) Useful for **scorekeeping** - seeing how well the organisation is doing overall

(b) **Attention-directing** - indicating problem areas that need to be investigated.

(c) Useful for **problem-solving** - providing a means of evaluating alternative responses to the situations in which the organisation finds itself.

Setting up a management accounting system

3.2 Taking a very broad view the following factors should be considered when setting up a management accounting system. This modifies the basic **input-process-output** model to focus on **user** requirements.

(a) The **output** required. This is just another way of saying that the management accountant must identify the information needs of managers. If a particular manager finds pie-charts most useful the system should be able to produce them. If another manager needs to know what time of day machinery failures occur, this information should be available. Levels of detail and accuracy of output and methods of **processing** to produce it must be determined in each case.

(b) **When** the output is required. If information is needed within the hour the system should be capable of producing it at this speed. If it is only ever needed once a year, at the year end, the system should be designed to produce it **on time**, no matter how long it takes to produce.

(c) The **sources** of input information. It is too easy to state that the outputs required should dictate the inputs made. The production manager may require a report detailing the precise operations of his machines, second by second. However, the management **accounting** system could only acquire this information if suitable **production** technology had been installed.

3.3 Another way of looking at the design question is to consider the **circumstances** in which the management accounting system will be used and take account of **contingent factors.**

KEY TERM

A **contingent factor** is a factor that may or may not apply, depending upon the specific circumstances. The three main contingent factors are technology, organisation structure and the environment.

Factor	Explanation
Technology	Obviously a **computerised accounting system** is differently designed to a manual one. Also, the nature of the **production process** determines the level of detail and accuracy that can be achieved. In Part B we shall see the profound impact that **advanced manufacturing technology** is having on management accounting.
Organisation structure	Essentially this is the 'social' factor, the different **relationships** that can exist between the various **parts** of an organisation and the **people** within them, the relative size of those parts and the degree of interdependence. **Responsibility accounting** systems are a good example.
The environment	Factors include the **competitive** environment in which the organisation operates and the degree of **uncertainty** that subsists. For example, where there is intense competition on **price**, the accounting system needs to control **costs** very closely; where competition is based on **product differentiation**, information about product **quality** is vital. An organisation that is continually launching **new products** needs more sophisticated **forecasting** capability from its system than one that is well-established in a **stable, predictable** market.

Exam focus point
You might find either or both of the modified input-process-output framework or the contingent factors framework useful if asked to suggest how a management accounting system should be designed, given a specific scenario.

BPP PUBLISHING

Cost classifications in the management information system

3.4   You should remember from earlier studies that the main ways in which costs are **classified** are as follows.

(a)   According to **behaviour**: fixed, variable, mixed, step and so on
(b)   According to **function**: production, administration, distribution and so on
(c)   According to **type of expense**: electricity, salaries and so on
(d)   According to **relevance**: future cash flows against sunk costs, for example
(e)   According to **controllability**: advertising expenditure against corporation tax, say

3.5   Each of these classifications can be examined in terms of how **useful** they are as information for planning, control and decision-making information. The analysis below will also serve to **jog your memory** of a wide number of issues in management accounting studied at earlier levels.

Exam focus point

The relevance of different cost classifications to planning, control and decision making when designing a management accounting system was the subject of a written question in the **December 1995** exam.

Planning

3.6   Planning for costs is another way of describing **budgeting**.

Classification	Usefulness/Example
Behaviour	The distinction between fixed and variable costs is crucial to the use of **flexible budgeting**, where different activity levels (and so different variable costs) can be planned for in advance.
Function	There will be separate plans or budgets for each function, all of which have to be **co-ordinated** into a master budget to make a **coherent** plan. The plans of a function such as sales and marketing will affect the plans of others, such as production and distribution.
Expense type	Different types of expense are subject to **different influences**. Just because raw material costs, say, have risen by 5%, this does not mean that, say, electricity costs have risen by 5% too.
Relevance	Irrelevant costs such as past costs may not be a reliable guide to future costs.
Controllability	If certain costs are not within the control of the business there is little point in devoting resources to planning for them in detail.

Control

3.7   **Budgetary control** and **variance analysis** is usually the most prominent method of control within an organisation.

Classification	Usefulness/Example
Behaviour	This is an important consideration for the **other** use of flexible budgets, as a means of making meaningful comparisons with actual figures once known. The distinction between fixed and variable costs allows the original budget to be flexed to actual levels of activities.

Classification	Usefulness/Example
Function	Analysis by **function** is part of the system of **responsibility** accounting. For example, if distribution costs are lumped together with administration costs rather than being analysed out separately, then there is no way of knowing how cost effectively or otherwise the distribution manager is doing his job. If he is doing it ineffectively the lack of analysis might mean that blame for excessive costs is unfairly attributed to the administration manager.
Expense type	They must be known so that like is compared with like. For example **actual** production costs may be **as budgeted** at, say, £10,000. However, if the budget was for £8,000 of materials and £2,000 of labour and the actual figure was for £5,000 each of both materials and labour, things have clearly not gone according to plan.
Relevance	This is an issue in control. Past costs again provide an example: the most sophisticated form of variance analysis compares actual results with what would have been budgeted if the future had been known when drawing up the plans, not with the original budget, which was based on what had happened in the past.
Controllability	It is self-evident that controllability is an issue in control. Significant adverse variances in costs that are regarded as **within** managers' control need to be explained and eliminated in subsequent periods. Costs **beyond** the control of the business (for example a sudden rise in employers' National Insurance) should certainly be *measured* by the budgetary control system so that they can be incorporated into subsequent plans, but there is no point in wasting resources 'investigating' the variance that arises through this cause.

Decision making

3.8 Relevance is a major factor in decision making, but as the following analysis shows, the other classifications are necessary too, to determine what is and is not relevant.

Classification	Usefulness/Example
Behaviour	Very many management accounting techniques (breakeven analysis, limiting factor analysis, and so on) require the identification of **contribution** (selling price minus variable cost).
Function	Analysis by *function* may be important in certain decisions, most notably where the function is a **discretionary** one such as R & D.
Expense type	This is an issue because for a decision involving, say, raw materials, the cost to be used must be determined from amongst the **replacement cost** (if any), the **value in other use** and the **disposal value**. For a decision involving the use of labour, replacement, alternative value and disposal costs would entail quite different considerations such as recruitment costs, or company policy on redundancy payments.
Relevance	Relevant costs are the **only** sort of costs that should be used for decision making. Examples of irrelevant costs have already been given: past costs or sunk costs, committed costs, notional costs. Relevant costs are **future incremental cash flows**.

Classification	Usefulness/Example
Controllability	Committed costs are a good example of costs that are **irrelevant** for decision making: whatever decision is taken the cost will still be incurred. For the purposes of the decision, therefore, committed costs are effectively **incapable** of being controlled.

Chapter roundup

- Key words to distinguish **strategic planning**, **management control** and **operational control** are **objectives**, **resources**, and **tasks** respectively. You should be able to explain how information requirements reflect these different focal points.

- Strategic management accounting looks to the **long term** and looks **outwards**, whereas traditionally management accounting has been internally focused.

- Strategic aims must be **linked** with operational actions through management control. If not, an organisation is liable to make unrealistic plans, form inconsistent goals, and suffer from poor communication and inadequate performance measurement.

- The classic division of management accounting into the tasks of **scorekeeping**, **attention directing**, and **problem solving** remains highly valid.

- A **user**-focused model for the design of management accounting systems looks first at the **output** required and **when** it is required and only then at the **inputs** and **processing** and **access** needed to provide the output.

- Another useful approach to a discussion of the design of management accounting systems concentrates on three **contingent variables**: technology, organisation structure and the environment.

- Traditional and familiar ideas about **cost classification** are also highly relevant to the design of management accounting systems.

Quick quiz

1   Define three tiers of management information and decision making. (see para 1.2)

2   What are the characteristics of strategic planning? (1.5)

3   What is a resource and which level of management controls resources? (1.9)

4   What is a strategy? (2.3)

5   What information is needed for strategic management? (2.4)

6   What costs arise from unrealistic plans? (2.8)

7   What opportunity costs arise if performance measurement is inadequate? (2.13, 2.14)

8   How does organisation structure affect management accounting system design? (3.3)

9   Why is classification according to expense type important for planning purposes? (3.6)

10 Why should a management accounting system classify costs according to behaviour? (3.6 - 3.8)

Question to try	Level	Marks	Time
2	Exam standard	15	27 mins

Part B
Modern developments and the accounting response

Chapter 3

MODERN DEVELOPMENTS

Chapter topic list	Syllabus reference
1 World class manufacturing	1(a) - 1(d), 2(b), 3(a)
2 Dedicated cell layout	1(a) - 1(d), 2(b), 3(a)
3 Just-in-time	1(a) - 1(d), 2(b), 3(a)
4 Total quality management	1(a), 2(b), 3(a), 3(c)
5 Target costing	1(d), 4(a)
6 Activity based approaches	1(a) - 1(d), 2(b), 3(a)

Introduction

In this chapter we look at business organisations in the context of modern management thought and new technology. Developments such as JIT, TQM and ABC invariably form the **background** for Paper 9 questions and you will usually be required to write some sort of **commentary** about the pros and cons of JIT, the difficulty of implementing TQM and so on.

There are no numbers in this chapter, but in the next chapter we shall work through some full Paper 9 style **numerical questions** as we look at some of the accounting techniques that have been developed in response to the trends identified in this chapter.

Core areas of the syllabus identified by the examiner and covered in this chapter: **just-in-time; ABC/ABB/ABM; total quality programmes**.

1 WORLD CLASS MANUFACTURING

1.1 World Class Manufacturing (WCM) was a term coined in the mid 1980s to describe fundamental changes that have taken place in manufacturing companies.

1.2 Above all a WCM policy is to develop close relationships with **customers** in order to achieve the following.

(a) Know what their requirements are.

(b) Supply customers on time, with short delivery lead times.

(c) Supply goods of the appropriate quality.

(d) Change the product mix quickly and develop new products or modify existing products as customer needs change.

1.3 WCM is a very broad term but in the context of **Paper 9 questions** it has the following elements, all in some way connected with **reducing costs** and improving **customer satisfaction** and **sales**.

- Dedicated cell production
- Just-in-time (JIT) manufacturing (less stock, faster delivery to customers)

- Total quality management (TQM) programmes
- Target costing
- Activity based approaches

Question 1

You have encountered things like JIT and ABC in your previous studies. See if you can write a paragraph or two on each explaining what they are.

---

2 DEDICATED CELL LAYOUT

Traditional production procedures

2.1 Traditionally, manufacturing industries have fallen into a few broad groups according to the **nature of the production process** and **materials flow**.

Type of production	Description
Jobbing industries	**Items are produced individually**, often for a specific customer order, as a 'job'. Versatile equipment and highly skilled workers are needed to give businesses the flexibility to do a variety of jobs. The jobbing factory is typically laid out on a **functional** basis with, say, a milling department, a cutting department and so on.
Batch processing	The manufacture of **standard goods in batches**. 'Batch production is often carried out using **functional** layouts but with a greater number of more **specialised machines**. With a functional layout batches move by different and complex routes through various specialised departments travelling over much of the factory floor before they are completed.' (Drury, *Management and Cost Accounting*)
Mass production	Involves the **continuous production of standard items** from a sequence of continuous or repetitive operations. Often uses a **product-based** layout whereby product A moves from its milling machine to its cutting machine to its paint-spraying machine, product B moves from its sawing machine to its milling machine and so on. There is **no separate 'milling department'** or 'assembly department' to which all products must be sent to await their turn on the machines: **each product has its own dedicated machine**.

Dedicated cell layout

2.2 The modern development in this sphere is to merge the flexibility of the functional layout with the speed and productivity of the product layout. **Cellular** manufacturing involves a **U-shaped flow** along which are arranged a number of different machines that are used to make products with similar machining requirements.

2.3 The machines are operated by workers who are **multi-skilled** rather than limited to one operation such as 'grinder', or whatever. The aim is to facilitate **Just-in-time** production and obtain the associated improvements in **quality** and reductions in **costs**.

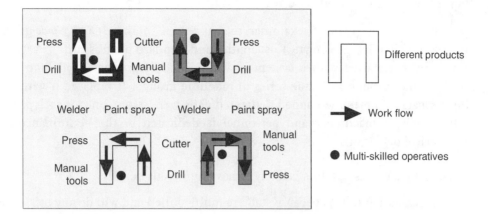

Case example: Dedicated cells

In January 1994 the *Financial Times* carried a good example of this approach in an article about the Paddy Hopkirk car accessory factory in Bedfordshire.

> One morning the factory was just an untidy sprawl of production lines surrounded by piles of crates holding semi-finished components. Two days later, when the workforce came to work [after Christmas], the machines had been brought together in tightly grouped "cells". The piles of components had disappeared, and the newly cleared floor space was neatly marked with colour-coded lines mapping out the flow of materials.

> Overnight there were dramatic differences. In the first full day, productivity on some lines increased by up to 30%, the space needed for some processes had been halved, and work in progress had been cut considerably. The improved layout had allowed some jobs to be combined, freeing up operators for deployment elsewhere in the factory.

The new layout encourages 'one-piece production, with as many processes as possible being carried out on a single part consecutively rather than one process being done in a big batch. Parts are only delivered to the next stage of the production or assembly process when they are needed' rather than piling up in huge storage bins, as before. Unnecessary walking and movements are eliminated by setting up production in a horseshoe shape rather than a straight line: 'in this way an operator doing a number of tasks will end up at the starting point for the next cycle'.

Case example: Operations

New approaches are not necessarily restricted to manufacturing. In January 1994 the *Financial Times* described the application of a 'production-line' approach to operations in a Swedish hospital. This is not as gruesome as it sounds: it simply means that more efficient use is made of operating theatre time so that more operations can be carried out. The hospital is now organised according to 'patient flow' - how the patient moves through the system. Previously separate functions like medical and surgical departments have been brought together to facilitate flow.

Exam focus point

Dedicated cell production has featured as **background** for many Paper 9 questions. Typically a scenario is given describing a company that has just moved over to dedicated cell production from another method. You are given a set of **before and after** figures and asked to assess whether the change has been a success.

Questions have also asked you to comment on the implications and benefits of dedicated cell production in other terms, such as employee motivation and customer satisfaction. The **examiner** has written about this, as explained in the following paragraphs.

BPP PUBLISHING

The Paper 9 examiner and the benefits of dedicated cell production

2.4 An **article** by the Paper 9 examiner that appeared in the *ACCA Students' Newsletter* in February 1996 (George Brown, 'Cost control and standard process costs - Part 3') described a company that started with a system in which each of products X, Y and Z passed in a straight line through the same series of **machine groups.** It replaced it with one in which three separate **horseshoe-shaped dedicated cells** were set up, one for each product. In each cell a bank of machinery and personnel is dedicated to the performance of a specific sequence of operations.

2.5 As the article points out, this is likely to have numerous benefits.

(a) Increased **flexibility,** because staff are multi-skilled and will do any task necessary.

(b) Reductions in **idle time,** because temporary lulls in activity will be filled by routine maintenance work rather than sitting waiting for production to pick up.

(c) Reduction in **work in progress,** because products do not have to wait in a queue for a machine to be available. This frees up working capital for other uses.

(c) Reduction in unnecessary **movement** of operatives and **handling** of materials (and associated **costs**), because of the horseshoe layout.

(d) Reduction in process **losses** and **returns** of faulty goods, because ongoing **training** means that staff are more highly skilled and more careful, have more responsibility for the whole product, and are committed to producing high quality output.

(e) **Rapid response** to sudden changes in demand or requirements, because of increased skills and the reduced likelihood of bottlenecks. **Late delivery** will be much reduced or eliminated, increasing **customer satisfaction**.

(f) Better **motivation** amongst workers, partly because they will probably receive better rates of **pay** to allow for increased responsibilities, but also because the cultivation of a **team spirit** should increase levels of performance as employees take more pride in their work, and more account of each others' needs.

(g) The improvement in the working environment and the support offered by team members should **reduce the level of staff turnover** and its associated costs.

Question 2

A question in the **June 1996** exam asked how a dedicated cell approach might bring about improvements in a section of a *service* business whose members dealt by phone or in writing with a wide variety of customer enquiries about the organisation's offerings. Work was organised on the basis of geographical area. The section suffered from high levels of overtime, backlogs, complaints and staff turnover.

How would you have answered this question?

---

3 JUST-IN-TIME

3.1 Dedicated cell layout is normally associated with a **just-in-time** approach to production.

KEY TERMS

Just-in-time (JIT) is a system whose objective is to produce or to procure products or components as they are required by a customer or for use, rather than for stock. A just-in-time system is a 'pull' system, which responds to demand, in contrast to a 'push' system, in which stocks act as buffers between the different elements of the system, such as purchasing, production and sales.

Just-in-time production is a production system which is driven by demand for finished products whereby each component on a production line is produced only when needed for the next stage.

Just-in-time purchasing is a purchasing system in which material purchases are contracted so that the receipt and usage of material, to the maximum extent possible, coincide.

CIMA *Official Terminology* 1996

Exam focus point

JIT would have been just one of the techniques or philosophies to include in an answer to a **June 1999** exam question on alternative systems to the traditional approach to purchasing, production, stockholding and satisfying customer demand. You will encounter others as you work through this chapter.

3.2 EXAMPLE: JUST-IN-TIME

Here is a highly simplified scenario illustrating the JIT concept. This company only ever receives one order at a time. Suppose that it takes 1 hour to convert raw materials into a *nearly* finished product. It takes a further hour to turn WIP into the *finished* product (for example to paint it the required colour and add extras).

		Stock levels		
		Finished goods	WIP	Raw materials
9 am	Stock levels at this point are as shown.	0	1	0
10am	An order is received for a finished item. The WIP is completed and the supplier is asked to deliver new raw materials sufficient to make the next item.	1	0	0
11am	The finished item is despatched. Raw materials are received.	0	0	1
12am	The raw materials are worked on.	0	1	0
1pm		0	1	0
2pm		0	1	0
3pm	Another order is received. The process begins again.	1	0	0
4pm	The order is despatched and raw materials are received.	0	0	1

PUBLISHING

JIT philosophy

3.3 Although described as a system in the CIMA *Official Terminology*, JIT is more of a **philosophy** or approach to management since it encompasses a commitment to continuous improvement and the search for excellence in the design and operation of the production management system.

3.4 The aim, according to the **examiner's article** in the February 1996 *ACCA Students' Newsletter*, is to 'streamline the flow of products through the production process and into the hands of customers'.

3.5 E J Hay (*The Just-in-Time Breakthrough*) identified seven aspects of JIT, which helps to tie it in with what we have studied so far.

Aspect	Explanation
JIT purchasing	Small, frequent deliveries against bulk contracts, requiring close integration of suppliers with the company's manufacturing process.
Machine cells	The grouping of machines or workers by product or component instead of by type of work performed.
Set-up time reduction	The recognition of machinery set-ups as non 'value-adding' activities (see below) which should be reduced or even eliminated.
Uniform loading	The operating of all parts of the productive process at a speed which matches the rate at which the customer demands the final product.
Pull system (Kanban)	The use of a Kanban, or signal, to ensure that products/components are only produced when needed by the next process. Nothing is produced in anticipation of need, to then remain in stock, consuming resources.
Total quality	The design of products, processes and vendor quality assurance programmes to ensure that the correct product is made to the appropriate quality level on the first pass through production.
Employee involvement	JIT involves major cultural change throughout an organisation. This can only be achieved if all employees are involved in the process of change and continuous improvement inherent in the JIT philosophy.

Value added

3.6 JIT aims to eliminate all **non-value-added costs**. Value is only added while a product is actually being processed. Whilst it is being inspected for quality, moving from one part of the factory to another, waiting for further processing and held in store, value is not being added. Non value-added activities should therefore be eliminated.

KEY TERM

'A **value-added** cost is incurred for an activity that cannot be eliminated without the customer's perceiving a deterioration in the performance, function, or other quality of a product. The cost of a picture tube in a television set is value-added.

The costs of those activities that can be eliminated without the customer's perceiving deterioration in the performance, function, or other quality of a product are non-value-added. The costs of handling the materials of a television set through successive stages of an assembly line may be non-value-added. Improvements in plant layout that reduce handling costs may be achieved without affecting the performance, function, or other quality of the television set.'

(Horngren)

Problems associated with JIT

3.7   JIT might not be appropriate in all circumstances.

(a) It is not always easy to predict **patterns of demand**.

(b) JIT makes the organisation far more vulnerable to **disruptions in the supply chain**.

(c) JIT was originated by Toyota when all of Toyota's manufacturing was done within a 50 km radius of its headquarters. **Wide geographical spread** makes JIT difficult.

(d) Suppliers are likely to charge a **premium price** for contractually guaranteed frequent small deliveries.

Case example

In October 1991 the workforce at Renault's gear-box production plant at Cléon went on strike. The *day afterwards* a British plant had to cease production. Within two weeks Renault was losing 60% of its usual daily output a day. The weaknesses were due to the following.

• Sourcing components from one plant only

• Heavy dependence on in-house components

• Low inventory

• The fact that Japanese-style management techniques depend on stability in labour relations, something in short supply in many European countries.

Modern versus traditional stock control systems

3.8   There is no reason for the newer approaches to supersede the old entirely. A **restaurant** might find it preferable to use the traditional economic order quantity approach for staple non-perishable food stocks, but adopt JIT for perishable and 'exotic' items. In a **hospital** a stock-out could, quite literally, be fatal, and JIT would be quite unsuitable.

Question 3

Placing an order for an item of stock costs £170. The stock costs £30 a unit, and annual storage costs are 15% of purchase price. Annual demand is 600,000 units. What is the economic order quantity?

Answer

C = £170, D = 600,000, H = £30 × 15% = £4.50 and so EOQ $= \sqrt{2 \times 170 \times 600{,}000 / 4.5} = 6{,}733$ units

If this mystifies you, you had better revise stock control from your earlier studies.

Exam focus point

JIT and TQM (see below) feature in exam questions in the same way as dedicated cells, as something that a company has just introduced, and with before and after costs to compare and comment on.

4   TOTAL QUALITY MANAGEMENT

4.1   **Quality** means 'the degree of excellence of a thing' - how well made it is, or how well performed if it is a service, how well it serves its purpose, and how it measures up against its rivals. These criteria imply two things.

(a)   That quality is something that requires **care** on the part of the **provider**.

(b)   That quality is largely **subjective** - it is in the eye of the beholder, the **customer**.

4.2   The **management** of quality is the process of:

(a)   establishing **standards of quality** for a product or service;

(b)   establishing **procedures or production methods** which ought to ensure that these required standards of quality are met in a suitably high proportion of cases;

(c)   **monitoring** actual quality;

(d)   taking **control action** when actual quality falls below standard.

4.3   Quality management becomes **total** when it is applied to everything a business does.

KEY TERM

Total quality management (TQM) is the process of applying a zero defect philosophy to the management of all resources and relationships within the firm as a means of developing and sustaining a culture of continuous improvement which focuses on meeting customers' expectations

Get it right, first time

4.4   One of the basic principles of TQM is that the cost of **preventing** mistakes is less than the cost of **correcting** them once they occur. The aim should therefore be **to get things right first time**.

> 'Every mistake, every delay and misunderstanding, directly costs a company money through **wasted time and effort**, including time taken in pacifying customers. Whilst this cost is important, the impact of poor customer service in terms of **lost potential for future sales** has also to be taken into account'.
>
> (Robin Bellis-Jones and Max Hand, *Management Accounting,* May 1989)

Continuous improvement

4.5 A second basic principle of TQM is dissatisfaction with the *status quo*: the belief that it is **always possible to improve** and so the aim should be to 'get it **more** right next time'.

Case example

In an average factory only one second is spent adding value - like drilling holes or packing - for every 1,000 seconds spent not adding value. Experts say that they have never seen a factory cut this ratio to less than 1:200. This nevertheless indicates the extent to which continuous improvement is possible and how workers should continuously be seeking ways to reduce time-wasting effort.

The requirements of quality

4.6 Mark Lee Inman usefully lists 'eight requirements of quality' in the May 1995 *ACCA Students' Newsletter*. Each of these points will be developed in the remainder of this chapter.

(a) Accept that the only thing that matters is the **customer**.

(b) Recognise the all-pervasive nature of the **customer-supplier relationship**, including internal customers: passing sub-standard material to another division is not satisfactory.

(c) Move from relying on inspecting to a predefined level of quality to **preventing the cause** of the defect in the first place.

(d) Each operative or group of operatives must be **personally responsible** for defect-free production or service in their domain.

(e) Move away from 'acceptable' quality levels. Any level of defects is **unacceptable.**

(f) **All departments** should try obsessively to get things right first time: this applies to misdirected telephone calls and typing errors as much as to production.

(g) **Quality certification** programmes should be introduced.

(h) The **cost of poor quality** should be emphasised: good quality generates savings.

4.7 When quality improvements are achieved by introducing **new technology** that makes it easier for people to do their jobs, or **new practices** that are designed to make workers take more care, then **training** to show people how to use the new technology or implement the new practices will be required.

4.8 However, workers themselves are frequently the best source of information about how (or how not) to improve quality. 'Training' means training workers to **want** to improve things: it is matter of **changing attitudes**.

(a) Workers can be **motivated** by a positive approach to quality: producing quality work is a tangible and worthwhile objective. Where responsibility for quality checking has been given to the worker himself (encouraging self-supervision), job satisfaction may be increased: it is a kind of job enrichment, and also a sign of trust and respect, because imposed controls have been removed.

(b) **Cultural** orientation (the deep 'belief' in quality, filtered down to all operatives) and work group norms and influence can be used. Competition to meet and beat quality standards, for example, might be encouraged. Quality circles may be set up, perhaps with responsibility for implementing improvements which they identify.

Empowerment

4.9 **Empowerment** has a vital place in the quality control process: 'the people lower down the organisation possess the knowledge of what is going wrong within a process but lack the authority to make changes. Those further up the structure have the authority to make changes but lack the profound knowledge required to identify the right solutions. The only solution is to **change the culture** of the organisation so that everyone can become involved in the process of improvement and work together to make the changes'. (Max Hand)

4.10 Empowerment has two key aspects.

(a) Allowing workers to **decide how to do** the necessary work, using the skills they possess and acquiring new skills as necessary to be an effective team member.

(b) Making those workers personally **responsible** for achieving production targets and for quality control. (The French word for empowerment is 'responsibilisation'.)

Quality circles

4.11 A quality circle consists of a group of employees who meet regularly to discuss **problems of quality** and **quality control** in their area of work, and perhaps to suggest ways of improving quality. The quality circle has a leader who directs discussions and possibly also helps to train other members of the circle. It is also a way to encourage **innovation**.

The costs and benefits of training for quality

4.12 **Benefits of training for quality**

(a) Improved quality of output
(b) Improved productivity
(c) Greater job satisfaction and commitment on the part of employees

4.13 **Costs**

(a) The cost of the non-productive time taken to learn new attitudes and skills
(b) The cost of qualified instructors or training courses and materials, as necessary
(c) The cost of mistakes when learning on the job, including wasted materials and lost time

Quality-related costs are considered in more depth in a moment.

Design for quality

4.14 Quality control happens at various stages in the process of **designing** a product or service.

(a) At the **product design stage**, quality control means trying to design a product or service so that its specifications provide a suitable balance between price and quality (of sales and delivery, as well as manufacture) which will make the product or service competitive.

Modern manufacturing businesses use Computer Aided Design (CAD) to identify or rectify design features such as the following.

(i) Opportunities to reduce the **number of parts** in a product overall. The fewer the number of parts, the less parts there are to go wrong.

(ii) Opportunities to use parts or materials that are **already used** (or could be used) by other products. The more common parts overall the less chance there is of a product failing to meet quality standards due to a rogue supplier of just one of many components. For example if a car with electric windows can be designed to use the same *glass* as a cheaper model with manually-wound windows, there will only be one glass supplier to keep a check on.

   (iii)   Opportunities to improve **physical characteristics** such as shape, size or positioning of controls and so on to make the product more user-friendly.

(b) **Production engineering** is the process of designing the **methods** for making a product (or service) to the design specification. It sets out to make production methods as efficient as possible, and to avoid the manufacture of sub-standard items.

(c) **Administration: information systems** should be designed to get the required information to the right person at the right time; **distribution systems** should be designed to get the right item to the right person at the right time; and so on.

Quality control and inspection

4.15   A distinction should be made between **quality control** and **inspection**.

(a) **Quality control** involves setting controls for the **process** of manufacture or service delivery. It is a aimed at **preventing** the manufacture of defective items or the provision of defective services.

(b) **Inspection** is concerned with looking at products made, supplies delivered and services provided, to establish whether they are up to specification. It is a technique of **identifying** when defective items are being produced at an unacceptable level. Inspection is usually carried out at three main points.

   (i)   Receiving inspection - for raw materials and purchased components

   (ii)   Floor or process inspection for WIP

   (iii)   Final inspection or testing for finished goods.

The costs and benefits of design for quality

4.16   Design for quality incurs **costs** such as the costs of **employing** design staff and of obtaining and using monitoring **equipment** for process control, obtaining and using inspection equipment, and employing quality control staff. The **benefits** of quality control come from **savings** in quality-related costs, and from improvements in **customer relations** and hopefully (because of the quality of the final product) in sales **demand**.

Quality-related costs

4.17   It is quite misleading to use the term 'quality costs' without further qualifications. A concern for **good** quality source money; it is **poor quality that costs money.**

> **KEY TERMS**
>
> **Prevention costs** represent 'the cost of any action taken to investigate, prevent or reduce defects and failures.
>
> **Appraisal costs** are the costs of assessing quality achieved.
>
> **Internal failure costs** are costs arising within the organisation of failure to achieve the quality specified.

KEY TERMS CONT'D

External failure costs are costs arising outside the manufacturing organisation of failure to achieve specified quality (after transfer of ownership to the customer).

The **costs of conformance** are those incurred in ensuring that the level of quality required is achieved. Appraisal costs and prevention costs are costs of conformance.

Costs of non-conformance are incurred when the level of quality which should apply is not achieved. Internal and external failure costs are costs of non-conformance.

Quality-related costs	Example
Prevention costs	Quality engineering
	Design/development of quality control/inspection equipment
	Maintenance of quality control/inspection equipment
	Administration of quality control
	Training in quality control
Appraisal costs	Acceptance testing and performance testing
	Inspection of goods inwards
	Inspection costs of in-house processing
Internal failure costs	Failure analysis and re-inspection costs
	Losses from failure of purchased items
	Losses due to lower selling prices for sub-quality goods
	Costs of reviewing product specifications after failures
External failure costs	Administration and costs of customer complaints section
	Product liability costs
	Cost of repairing products returned from customers
	Cost of replacements due to sub-standard products/marketing errors

Exam focus point

Candidates in the **June 1999** exam had to provide examples relevant to the question scenario of costs of conformance and non-conformance. Quality related costs were also examined heavily in the **December 1999** exam, in both numerical and written questions.

The relationship between the costs of conformance and non-conformance

4.18 The relationship can be shown graphically.

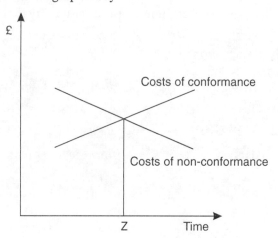

In theory, an organisation should continue to incur costs of conformance until they are greater than the costs of non-conformance. If the trend in costs continues after point Z there will be a net cost to the organisation (although it is debatable whether such improvement levels could be attained).

Question 4

A manufacturer's inspection procedures indicate that one faulty item out of every 1,000 good items produced is sent to a customer. The management regards this as acceptable, as a replacement will be supplied free of charge. Unit sales are 10,000,000 per year, and each unit costs £20 to manufacture and makes a profit of £5. It is probable that every customer who buys a faulty product will return it, and will thenceforth buy a similar product from another company. The average customer buys two units a year. Marketing costs per new customer are £10 per year.

(a)   What is your best estimate of the net cost of this policy for a year?
(b)   What name(s) would you give to quality-related costs of this type?
(c)   Could the situation be improved by incurring other types of quality-related cost?

Answer

(a)   Presumed number of bad units delivered a year = 10,000,000/1,000 = 10,000

	£
Cost of defects 10,000 × £20	200,000
Cost of free replacement 10,000 × £20	200,000
Manufacturing cost	400,000
Marketing costs for replacement customers £10 × 10,000	100,000
Gross cost of poor quality	500,000
Less income from original sale	250,000
Net cost of poor quality	250,000

Although the cost of the original defective item is recovered, this does not alter the fact that the company does not get it right first time. The company has still suffered the cost of the replacement and the cost of replacing the customer by marketing to new customers.

(b)   The cost of replacements is an external failure cost; the cost of defects and the new marketing costs are internal failure costs.

(c)   It appears that the manufacturer already incurs *appraisal* costs, since there are inspection procedures for goods about to be despatched. The reason(s) for the fault should be established (a further *internal failure* cost) and the extent of the problem should be more precisely ascertained (further *appraisal* costs), since it is not certain that all dissatisfied customers return their goods, though it is highly likely that their business is lost. Once this has been done it will be possible to decide whether, by spending more on *prevention,* the overall cost of poor quality can be reduced.

The Paper 9 examiner and quality

4.19   The following features of TQM were highlighted by the examiner in an article in the March 1994 edition of the *ACCA Students' Newsletter*, and repeated (*verbatim*) in an article in the February 1996 edition.

(a)   It aims towards an environment of **zero defects** at minimum cost.

(b)   It requires an awareness by **all personnel** of the quality requirements compatible with supplying the **customer** with products of the agreed design specification.

(c)   It aims towards the **elimination of waste,** where waste is defined as anything other than the minimum essential amount of equipment, materials, space and workers' time.

(d)   It must embrace **all aspects of operation** from pre-production to post-production stages in the business cycle.

(e) It recognises the need to **maximise** the ratio of **added value** time to total cycle time. Non-value added activities incur costs which should be eliminated. For example, stockholding costs, inspection costs, costs incurred in unnecessary movement of goods.'

5   TARGET COSTING

5.1   To compete effectively in today's competitive market, organisations must continually redesign their products with the result that **product life cycles** have become much shorter. The **planning, development and design stage** of a product is therefore critical to an organisation's cost management process. Considering possible cost reductions at this stage of a product's life cycle is now one of the most important issues facing management accountants in industry.

> ### KEY TERM
>
> **Target cost** means a product cost estimate derived by subtracting a desired profit margin from a competitive market price. This may be less than the planned initial product cost, but will be expected to be achieved by the time the product reaches the mature production stage.   (CIMA, *Official Terminology*)
>
> Target cost = Market price – Desired profit margin

5.2   The technique requires managers to change the way they think about the relationship between cost, price and profit.

(a) Traditionally the approach is to develop a product, determine the production **cost** of that product, set a selling price, with a resulting profit or loss.

(b) The target costing approach is to develop a product, determine the market selling **price** and desired profit margin, with a resulting cost which must be achieved.

5.3   In 'Product costing / pricing strategy' (**ACCA Students Newsletter,** August 1999), which we have reproduced at the end of the text, the examiner provided a useful summary of the **steps in the implementation of the target costing prices.**

Step 1.   Determine a product specification of which an adequate sales volume is estimated.

Step 2.   Set a selling price at which the organisation will be able to achieve a desired market share.

Step 3.   Estimate the required profit based on return on sales or return on investment.

Step 4.   Calculate the target cost = target selling price – target profit.

Step 5.   Compile an estimated cost for the product based on the anticipated design specification and current cost levels.

Step 6.   Calculate cost gap = estimated cost – target cost.

Step 7.   Make efforts to close the gap. This is more likely to be successful if efforts are made to 'design out' costs prior to production, rather than to 'control out' costs during the production phase. (See para 5.5 below.)

Step 8.   Negotiate with the customer before making the decision about whether to go ahead with the project.

5.4 When a product is first manufactured, its target cost may well be much lower than its currently-attainable cost, which is determined by current technology and processes. Management can then set **benchmarks for improvement** towards the target costs, by improving technologies and processes.

5.5 Various techniques can be employed.

- Reducing the **number of components**
- Using **standard components** wherever possible
- **Training** staff in more efficient techniques
- Acquiring new, more efficient **technology**
- Cutting out **non-value-added activities** (identified using **activity analysis** etc)
- Using **different materials**
- Using **cheaper staff**

Exam focus point

Target costing was examined in **December 1994, December 1995, June 1996 and December 1997.** Questions typically ask you to explain what target costing is, how a target cost might be achieved in the context of the scenario in the question, and/or how target costing can be used to achieve some specified aim.

Question 5

How does target costing fit in with TQM?

Answer

TQM emphasises continuous improvement, which is essential if a business is eventually to get its costs down to the target level. On the other hand, there is a danger with target costing that once the target is achieved no further improvement will be attempted.

Exam focus point

The cost gap between a target cost and current expected cost can be analysed into internal and external failure costs, while appraisal and prevention costs may be incurred in an effort to reduce the incidence of internal and external failure costs in order that the total cost may be brought closer to the target cost. Such an inter-relationship was examined in **December 1999.**

6 ACTIVITY BASED APPROACHES

6.1 A focus on the **activities** that a business carries out, as opposed to how its activities have traditionally been organised into separate **functions,** lies behind much modern thinking. For instance it has been found to be more fruitful to think of what may have once been called the **warehousing** department (function) in terms what that department *does*, such as **inspection of goods, stock control** and **materials movement** (activities).

6.2 Depending what subject you are studying or who wrote the article you are reading you might find that this modern development has different names.

(a) **Business Process Re-engineering** might be the term used, for instance, if you are looking at how **information technology** can help to eliminate non-value added activities or co-ordinate two previously separate activities, or replace one way of doing things with a completely new, quicker and cheaper way.

(b) **Activity based** analysis might be the term used if you are looking, say, at how **costs** can be calculated in a more meaningful way.

6.3 The **Paper 9 examiner** has always used some variant of 'activity based': activity based costing, activity based budgeting, activity based management or whatever.

Exam focus point

Activity based analysis has been very frequently examined. It has featured in **all except two** of the exams set so far under the current syllabus. Questions typically ask you to calculate costs using absorption costing and then activity based costing and to provide comments. (This was the case in **June 1999**, for example.) We shall be looking at just such a question in the next chapter.

6.4 The key point, whatever terminology is used, is that this modern development entails finding new and better ways of doing existing things so as to give greater satisfaction to customers at less cost to the business. This in turn means that **new and better information** is needed.

6.5 For instance, **activity based costing (ABC)** was developed because it was realised that older methods such as absorption costing using labour hours as the basis for absorbing overheads, did not provide useful information about what was causing the overheads to be incurred in the first place: the **cost drivers**.

Knowledge brought forward from Papers 3 and 8

You have studied basic ABC and the rationale behind it at earlier levels.

New **technology** means that **overheads** are now likely to represent a far larger proportion of overall costs than in the past.

The proponents of ABC argue that **traditional cost accounting** techniques result in a **misleading** and inequitable division of cost between low value and high value products, and that ABC provides a more meaningful allocation of costs which make unit costs more accurate. This in turn is part of a **shift** in emphasis **away** from costing merely for **stock valuation** towards costing of products made to meet actual **customer demand**.

Most overhead costs can be analysed between **short-term** variable costs, that vary with the **volume** of production, and **long-term** variable costs, that do *not* vary with the volume of production, but do vary with a different measure of **activity**.

The ABC approach is to relate overhead costs to the activities that cause or 'drive' them to be incurred in the first place and to change subsequently.

The **mathematics** involved are covered in full in the next chapter, because this is still very important for Paper 9.

New terms

6.6 In late 1996 the leading **management accounting body** in the UK, the Chartered Institute of Management Accountants (CIMA), published a new edition of its *Official Terminology*, which included some new and more rigorous definitions.

KEY TERMS

Activity based budgeting. A method of budgeting based on an activity framework and utilising cost driver data in the budget-setting and variance feedback processes.

Activity based costing (ABC). An approach to the costing and monitoring of activities which involves tracing resource consumption and costing final outputs. Resources are assigned to activities and activities to cost objects based on consumption estimates. The latter utilise cost drivers to attach activity costs to outputs.

Activity-based management (ABM). System of management which uses activity-based cost information for a variety of purposes including cost reduction, cost modelling and customer profitability analysis.

Activity cost pool. A grouping of all cost elements associated with an activity

Activity driver. A measure of the frequency and intensity of the demands placed on activities by cost objects. For example, the number of customer orders measures the consumption of order entry activities by each customer

Activity driver analysis. The identification and evaluation of the activity drivers used to trace the cost of activities to cost objects. It may also involve selecting activity drivers with potential to contribute to the cost management function with particular reference to cost reduction.

Cost driver. Any factor which causes a change in the cost of an activity, eg the quality of parts received by an activity is a determining factor in the work required by that activity and therefore affects the resources required. An activity may have multiple cost drivers associated with it

The merits of activity based approaches

6.7   Merits of activity based approaches include the following.

(a)   The **complexity** of many businesses has increased, with wider product ranges, shorter product life cycles, the greater importance of quality and more complex production processes. Activity based analysis recognises this complexity with its **multiple cost drivers,** many of them **transaction-based** rather than volume-based.

(b)   In a more **competitive** environment, companies must be able to assess **product profitability** realistically. To do this, they must have a good understanding of what drives overhead costs. Activity based analysis gives a meaningful analysis of costs which should provide a better basis for pricing decisions, product mix decisions, design decisions and production decisions.

(c)   In modern manufacturing systems, **overhead** functions include a lot of **non-factory-floor activities** such as product design, quality control, production planning, sales order planning and customer service. Activity based analysis is concerned with all overhead costs, including the costs of these functions, and so it takes cost accounting beyond its 'traditional' factory floor boundaries.

(d)   **Service** businesses have characteristics very similar to those required for the successful application of activity based analysis in modern manufacturing industry.

    (i)   A highly **competitive** market

    (ii)   **Diversity** of products, processes and customers

    (iii)   **Significant overhead costs** not easily assigned to individual products

    (iv)   Demands on overhead resources related to products/customers, **not volume**

(e) Cost **control** may be improved because the **causes of increases** in costs can be more readily identified (poor use of storage space, for example) and means of reducing costs can be investigated (extra shelving, perhaps, or automated packing procedures).

(f) ABC techniques can be used in **customer profitability analysis.**

Case example

As a result of an ABC study, a FMCG manufacturer discovered that three of its top five customers in terms of gross profit using traditional techniques were in the bottom five and loss making when ABC was used.

Criticisms of activity based approaches

6.8 It has been suggested by critics that activity based approaches have some serious flaws.

(a) The **costs** of obtaining and interpreting the **new information** may be considerable. Activity based analysis should not be introduced unless it can provide additional information for management to use in planning or control decisions.

(b) Many overheads relate neither to volume nor to complexity and diversity. The ability of a **single cost driver** to fully explain the cost behaviour of all items in its associated pool is **questionable**.

(c) Some measure of **arbitrary** cost apportionment may still be required at the cost pooling stage for items like building depreciation. If an activity based system has many cost pools the amount of apportionment needed may be greater than ever.

(d) Some people have questioned the fundamental assumption that activity **causes** cost, suggesting that it could be argued that **decisions** cause cost or the passage of **time** causes cost or that there may be **no one clear cause** of cost.

Question 6

One of the directors of the company that employs you as a management accountant observes wryly that the thing that drives sales administration costs is customers ringing up and ordering things, and that if only they did this less often sales administration costs could be dramatically reduced!

How would you respond to this implied criticism of ABC?

Answer

The director is correct after a fashion, but what this really means is that the company needs to find more cost-effective ways of taking orders, not that it needs to take fewer orders. Activity analysis, if properly directed, is likely to identify the customers who take up the most time and encourage investigation of alternatives such as EDI links.

Activity-based information and decision making

6.9 The traditional cost behaviour patterns of fixed cost and variable cost are felt by advocates of ABC to be unsuitable for **longer-term decisions**, when resources are not fixed and changes in the volume or mix of business can be expected to have an impact on the cost of all resources used, not just short-term variable costs. A **five-level hierarchy of costs** has therefore been suggested to **facilitate the analysis of costs**.

Level	Basis	Costs are dependant on....	Example
1	Unit	Volume of production	Machine power
2	Batch	Number of batches	Set-up costs
3	Process	Existence of a process	Quality control
4	Product	Existence of a product group/line	Product management
5	Facility	Existence of a production facility or plant	Rent and rates

6.10 As Innes and Mitchell say, 'This analysis of cost highlights the decision level at which each element of cost can be influenced. For example, the reduction of production cost levels will not simply depend on a general reduction in output volumes, but also on reorganising production to perhaps increase *batch* size and reduce batch volume, on eliminating or modifying a *process*, on cutting out or merging product lines or on altering or removing *facility* capacity'.

Exam focus point

Six easy marks were available in the **December 1998** exam for discussing, and providing relevant examples of, cost pool, cost drivers and hierarchy of activities.

The Paper 9 examiner and activity analysis

6.11 Exam questions in **December 1996** and **June 1997** have used certain terminology that you should know about.

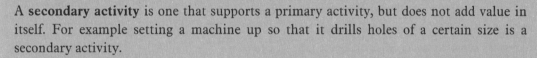

KEY TERMS

A **primary activity** is one that adds value to a product, for example cutting and drilling materials and assembling them. These are sometimes called *core* activities.

A **secondary activity** is one that supports a primary activity, but does not add value in itself. For example setting a machine up so that it drills holes of a certain size is a secondary activity.

Discretionary activities (or 'diversionary' activities) do *not add value* and are symptoms of *failure* within the organisation. For instance repairing faulty production work is such an activity because it should not have been faulty in the first place.

BPP PUBLISHING

Chapter roundup

- Paper 9 questions are generally written against a **'world cl*ss manufacturing'** background in which every aspect of production is designed with the aim of **satisfying customers.**
- **Dedicated cell layout** merges the flexibility of functional layouts (eg separate cutting departments) with the speed and productivity of the product layout.
  - ° Workers are **multi-skilled,** highly **trained** and highly **motivated**
  - ° Products move through their dedicated cells in a **U-shaped flow**, cutting down on **materials movements** and **bottlenecks**
  - ° JIT and TQM principles are applied
- **Just-in-time** (JIT), whereby items are produced or purchased only when they are needed, aims to eliminate **non-value-added** activities and costs such as moving and storing materials. It may be **difficult to apply** where **demand** is unpredictable or **suppliers** are unreliable or inaccessible or charge a high premium and more traditional **EOQ-type** approaches may sometimes be preferable.
- **Total quality management** (TQM) means getting it right first time, and improving continuously.
- **Quality-related costs** can conveniently be categorised as prevention costs and appraisal costs (**costs of conformance**) and internal failure costs and external failure costs (**costs of non-conformance**).
- **Target costing** is an approach that takes as its starting point the **price** that **customers** will pay for a product and tries to design a product and production method that will produce it for **less than that price** and give a satisfactory return.
- **Activity based approaches** look at businesses in terms of what **activities** they do rather than where they are done or who does them.

Quick quiz

1. What does a WCM policy aim to achieve? (see para 1.2)
2. What are the benefits of dedicated cell layout? (2.5)
3. What is just-in-time production? (3.1)
4. What do you understand by the terms value-added and non-value-added? (3.6)
5. Give an example of a situation in which JIT is appropriate. (3.7, 3.8)
6. What are the two basic principles of TQM? (4.4, 4.5)
7. Give four categories of quality cost and two examples of each category. (4.17)
8. Give a simple formula for target cost. (5.1)
9. How can a target cost be achieved? (5.5)
10. What is a cost driver? (6.6)
11. What are the merits of activity analysis? (6.7)
12. What is a secondary activity? (6.11)

Question to try	Level	Marks	Time
3	Exam standard	35	63 mins

Chapter 4

THE ACCOUNTING RESPONSE

Chapter topic list	Syllabus reference
1 The accounting response	1(a) - 1(d), 2(b), 3(a)
2 ABC v absorption costing	1(a) - 1(d), 2(b), 3(a)
3 ABC in Paper 9	1(a) - 1(d), 2(b), 3(a)
4 Total quality management programmes	1(a), 2(b), 3(a), 4(c)
5 JIT and backflush accounting	1(a) - 1(d), 2(b), 3(a)
6 JIT and throughput accounting	4(b), 4(d)

Introduction

At long last we introduce you to some **real** Paper 9-type questions in this chapter. This chapter looks at some of the management accounting techniques that have developed in response to the modern business environment described in the previous chapter. It is one of the **most important chapters** in the whole of this book.

In Section 1 we are going over old ground, but **please** work through it fully because we are also trying to help you develop habits that will **really help** you in the exam. Sections 2, 3, 4 and 5 explain several tricks that you may well encounter in **your exam**. Section 5 also tries, amongst other things, to explain the whole rationale behind Paper 9 questions.

Core areas of the syllabus identified by the examiner and covered in this chapter: **ABC**; **total quality programmes**; **backflush accounting**; **throughput accounting**.

1 THE ACCOUNTING RESPONSE

1.1 Traditional management accounting makes various **assumptions,** such as the idea that the amount spent on overheads is in some way related to labour hours, or that a certain level of 'loss' in a production process is 'normal', or that 'buffer' stocks should be held (and carefully valued) to avoid stock-outs, or that the price of a product is decided by slapping a mark-up on its 'fully absorbed cost'.

1.2 Such assumptions are clearly **invalid** in a modern environment that may use robots to build products, accept no losses at all, have virtually nil stock, and be unable to charge more for products than customers are willing to pay and than competitors are charging.

1.3 If the assumptions are invalid, then the **techniques** developed in the past to support them must also be **questioned**, and **replaced** with new ones if they are found lacking.

Absorption costing: an old technique

1.4 Absorption costing is a technique you have studied before, and there was a reminder in the context of spreadsheets in Chapter 1.

BPP
PUBLISHING

1.5   However, it has featured regularly in Paper 9 scenarios as the **before** technique to be compared with the **after** of ABC, so here is a step by step approach and a thorough example. (In Section 2 you will realise that the example is intended to draw attention to some of the **pitfalls** of this old-fashioned approach.)

Step 1.   Take the **total** of the cost(s) to be absorbed
Step 2.   Take the **total quantity** of whatever is the **absorption base**
Step 3.   **Divide** Step 1 by Step 2 to give the **absorption rate** for that overhead
Step 4.   Take the amount of the **absorption base** used by **one unit** of a product
Step 5.   Multiply this amount (Step 4) by the **absorption rate** (Step 3)
Step 6.   Call the result of Step 5 the **cost absorbed per unit** of this product
Step 7.   Multiply the **cost absorbed per unit** (Step 6) by the **number of units** produced

1.6   EXAMPLE: ABSORPTION COSTING

Got The T-Shirt Ltd manufactures four products, A, B, C and D. Relevant information for a certain period is as follows.

	Output	Material cost per unit	Direct labour hours per unit	Machine hours per unit
	Units	£	Hours	Hours
A	25	5	2	3
B	25	20	6	7
C	250	5	2	3
D	250	20	6	7

Direct labour cost per hour	£8.00

Other production costs	£
Short run variable costs	6,160
Set-up costs	22,000
Expediting and scheduling costs	18,000
Materials handling costs	15,440

Required

Using a conventional absorption costing approach and an absorption rate for all 'other production costs' based on direct labour hours, calculate the total product cost per unit.

1.7   SOLUTION

Work through our solution carefully using a **calculator** to check all the numbers. Make sure you **refer back to the information** given in the question to see where all the figures are coming from. (In this solution we may get this wrong deliberately, too.)

> **Exam focus point**
>
> Get into the habit of working though all of the numerical examples in this book in this way. Paper 9 questions deliberately try to reflect life in the sense that they don't give you neatly arranged figures on a plate. They make you work to find the information you need in the first place and decide which bits are and are not relevant.
>
> A key skill in Paper 9 exams is the ability to **find and extract** the information you need.

Step 1.   *Take the **total** of the cost(s) to be absorbed*. In this case **all** 'other production costs' are to be absorbed on the same basis so we can just add them all up.

	£
Short run variable costs	6,160
Set-up costs	22,000
Expediting and scheduling costs	18,000
Materials handling costs	15,440
	61,600

Step 2. *Take the **total quantity** of whatever is the absorption base. The absorption base is* **labour hours** *so we need to find the total quantity. (But first **check**! Is it labour hours, or is this a deliberate mistake on our part?)*

	Output Units	Direct labour hours per unit Hours	Total hours per product Hours
A	25	2	50
B	25	6	150
C	250	2	500
D	250	6	1,500
			2,200

Step 3. ***Divide** Step 1 by Step 2 and call the result the **absorption rate** for that cost.* **Absorption rate = £61,600/2,200 = £28 per labour hour**

Step 4. *Take the amount of the absorption base used by **one unit** of a product. This is given in the question. Find it and check that the table below is the same.*

Product	A	B	C	D
Direct labour hours per unit (hours)	2	6	2	6

Step 5. *Multiply this amount (Step 4) by the absorption rate (Step 3).*

Step 6. *Call the result of Step 5 the **cost absorbed per unit** of this product. In practice you would **combine steps 4 and 5 and 6**. (Step 4 is separate to emphasise that you concentrate on **one unit** at this stage. Step 6 is separate to emphasise what you get as a result.)*

	Direct labour hours per unit Hours	Absorption rate £	Cost absorbed per unit £
A	2	28	56
B	6	28	168
C	2	28	56
D	6	28	168

Step 7. *Multiply the cost absorbed per unit (Step 6) by the number of units produced. In practice you could **just add another two columns** to the table you have already produced, as follows.*

	Direct labour hrs per unit Hours	Absorption rate £	Cost absorbed per unit £	Number of units produced	Total amount absorbed
A	2	28	56	25	1,400
B	6	28	168	25	4,200
C	2	28	56	250	14,000
D	6	28	168	250	42,000
					61,600

Question 1

(a) Are there any **errors** in the material above?

(b) Work out the cost of **direct materials** and **direct labour** for each of products A to D. For instance if 25 units of A are produced, each unit takes 2 hours and labour costs £8 per hour, how much is the labour cost for product A in this period?

Answer

(a) Yes, but only one on this occasion. Did you spot it?

(b) Fill in your answer here and check it with ours, below.

	A	B	C	D
Direct material				
Direct labour				

1.8 Combining our step by step approach to overheads with the materials and labour calculations that **you** did for Question 1 we get the following results.

	A	B	C	D
	£	£	£	£
Direct material	125	500	1,250	5,000
Direct labour	400	1,200	4,000	12,000
Overheads	1,400	4,200	14,000	42,000
Total cost	1,925	5,900	19,250	59,000
Units produced	25	25	250	250
Cost per unit (Total cost divided by units produced)	**£77**	**£236**	**£77**	**£236**

Question 2

(a) Analyse the cost of a **unit** of product A into its separate components.

(b) Look at the final results. Can you detect any sort of pattern? If so, look closely at the information in the question. Can you explain why these patterns have emerged?

Answer

(a)

	£
Direct material (£125/25)	5
Direct labour (£400/25)	16
Overheads (see Step 6 above)	56
	77

Note that you can do the final steps either on a total basis or on a per unit basis. In the exam **read the question** and do what you are asked to do.

(b) Answers are suggested in the next section.

2 ABC v ABSORPTION COSTING

2.1 The sales director of Got The T-Shirt Ltd looks at the above figures and says that efforts must be made to **increase sales of product A**: it is one of the cheapest to produce and yet only 25 units are made per period.

2.2 However, a newly appointed management accountant has been doing some investigation and believes that none of the other production costs incurred are actually related to labour at all. Her findings suggest that the **drivers** of these costs are as follows.

Cost	Cost driver
Short run variable costs	Machine hours
Set-up costs	Number of production runs per product
Expediting and scheduling costs	Number of production runs per product
Materials handling costs	Number of production runs per product

2.3 The number of production runs is as follows.

Product	A	B	C	D
No of production runs in the period	3	3	7	7

2.4 Having obtained all the information the management accountant takes the sales director step by step through an approach to **activity based costing** calculations.

Step 1. List the **total cost** of each activity

Step 2. List the **total** of each **cost driver** unit (hours, runs, etc) and the **overall total**

Step 3. Divide Step 1 by Step 2 and call the result the **cost per cost driver unit**

Step 4. Multiply the **cost per cost driver unit** (Step 3) by the **total cost driver units per product** (Step 2)

Step 5. Call the amount calculated in Step 4 the **total (overhead) cost per product per activity**

Step 6. Incorporate with other costs (such as materials) if necessary, and divide the overall totals by the number of units of each product produced. Call this the **total cost per unit.**

Steps 4 and 5 will be combined in one table in practice: we separate them here for emphasis.

2.5 EXAMPLE: ACTIVITY BASED COSTING

Again, work through this example carefully.

Step 1. *List the total overhead cost of each activity.* This is given in the question as follows.

Overhead costs	£
Short run variable costs	6,160
Set-up costs	22,000
Expediting and scheduling costs	18,000
Materials handling costs	15,440

Step 2. *List the **total** of each **cost driver** unit (hours, runs, etc) and the **overall total**.* This has to be calculated as follows. Don't forget to check where the information is coming from.

	Output	Machine hours per unit	Total machine hours	No of prodn runs in the period
	Units	Hours	Hours	
A	25	3	75	3
B	25	7	175	3
C	250	3	750	7
D	250	7	1,750	7
			2,750	20

Step 3. *Divide Step 1 by Step 2 for each activity and call the result the cost per cost driver* **unit.**

Activity	Cost	Total cost driver units	Cost per cost driver unit
	£	Units	£
Short run variable costs	6,160	2,750	2.24
Set-up costs	22,000	20	1,100.00
Expediting and scheduling costs	18,000	20	900.00
Materials handling costs	15,440	20	772.00

Step 4. *Multiply the cost per cost driver unit (Step 3) by the total cost driver units per product (Step 2).*

Step 5. *Call the amount calculated in Step 4 the total (overhead) cost per product per activity*

	Cost per cost driver unit	Total driver units per product				Total 'other' costs per product per activity			
		A	B	C	D	A	B	C	D
	£								
Short run variable	2.24	75	175	750	1,750	168	392	1,680	3,920
Set-up costs	1,100	3	3	7	7	3,300	3,300	7,700	7,700
Expediting etc	900	3	3	7	7	2,700	2,700	6,300	6,300
Materials handling	772	3	3	7	7	2,316	2,316	5,404	5,404

Step 6. *Combine our activity-based step by step approach to other production costs with the materials and labour calculations that you did earlier.*

	A	B	C	D
	£	£	£	£
Direct material	125	500	1,250	5,000
Direct labour	400	1,200	4,000	12,000
Short-run variable overheads	168	392	1,680	3,920
Set-up costs	3,300	3,300	7,700	7,700
Expediting and scheduling cost	2,700	2,700	6,300	6,300
Materials handling	2,316	2,316	5,404	5,404
Total cost	9,009	10,408	26,334	40,324
Units produced	25	25	250	250
Cost per unit (total cost ÷ units produced)	**£360.36**	**£416.32**	**£105.336**	**£161.296**

Question 3

Analyse the cost of a **unit** of product A above into its separate components.

Answer

	£
Direct material	5.00
Direct labour	16.00
Short-run variable overheads	6.72
Set-up costs	132.00
Expediting and scheduling cost	108.00
Materials handling	92.64
Total cost	360.36

Again, the way you present the answer depends on what you are asked to do in the question.

Comparison of ABC v absorption costing

2.6 Here is a summary of our calculations in Sections 1 and 2. Note that the under/over allocations in total add up to nil (check for yourself), because the overall costs are the same: we are just allocating them to products in different ways.

Product	Units	Absorption costing unit cost £	ABC unit cost £	Under/over allocation per unit £	Under/over allocation in total £
A	25	77.00	360.36	- 283.36	- 7,084
B	25	236.00	416.32	- 180.32	- 4,508
C	250	77.00	105.336	- 28.336	- 7,084
D	250	236.00	161.296	+ 74.704	+ 18,676

2.7 The figures suggest that the traditional **volume**-based absorption costing system based on labour or machine hours is **flawed**.

(a) It under-allocates costs to low-volume products (here, A and B with 25 units of output) and over-allocates overheads to higher-volume products (here C and D in particular, with 250 units).

(b) It under-allocates costs to quickly-produced products (here A and C with just 5 hours of work needed per unit) and over-allocates overheads to products that take longer (here B and particularly D take 13 hours).

Why is this? Because most of the other production costs are **not caused** by the number of units produced or the amount of time spent on them. They are mostly caused by the resources that need to be devoted to setting up machines, organising the work and getting materials in place ready to start.

Question 4

Was the sales director correct? Should Got The T-Shirt Ltd try to increase sales of product A?

Answer

Clearly not if you look at the figures. Product A may well be priced at less than activity based cost. The company should try to increase the sales of products C and D, and possibly discontinue A and B, or else look for ways to reduce the (activity-based) costs of A and B dramatically.

Section summary

2.8 As we say in the introduction to this chapter it is worth working through the (rather laboured) example in Sections 1 and 2 thoroughly because this topic comes up frequently in exams. Make sure you fully understand all the calculations before moving on. We are now going to look at a **Paper 9** standard question.

3 ABC IN PAPER 9

> **Exam focus point**
> Here is an **ABC question** closely based on one set in the **December 1994** Paper 9 exam. For good measure it also includes **target costing,** which you met in the previous chapter.

3.1   EXAMPLE: LETHAL AND DEADLY

Lethal and Deadly are two types of poison made by Killitt plc. Each sales unit is produced by means of a two-stage process – manufacturing and bottling. At present, conversion costs are absorbed by the two products using estimated time based rates. However, Killitt's management accountant thinks that there is a good case for implementing activity based costing and she has gathered some new information about the production process.

Absorption costing information

The following figures are available for Period 1. All figures are estimates.

		Manufacturing	Bottling
		£	£
Conversion costs:	Variable	47,500	31,500
	Fixed	25,000	18,000

30% of fixed costs are product specific, the remainder are company fixed costs. Fixed costs will not change within the activity levels currently being considered.

	Lethal	Deadly
Production/sales (bottles)	75,000	50,000
Selling price per bottle (£)	3.50	3.70
Direct material cost per bottle (£)	2.50	2.60
Production time per bottle:		
Manufacturing (minutes)	10	10
Bottling (minutes)	8	6

(Direct materials consist of liquids and chemicals, all of which are input at the start of the manufacturing process.)

Activity based costing information

Manufacturing is a process of mixing and then reducing the chemicals. *Bottling* involves filling two different types of bottle. Product specific production costs (variable and fixed) have thus been analysed to give the following percentages.

	Manufacturing	Bottling
Mixing	55%	
Reducing	45%	
Filling		75%
Bottling materials		25%

Manufacturing

(a) The *mixing* product specific costs are incurred in proportion to the level to which vats can be filled without boiling over during production. The proportions are: Lethal: Deadly = 3:2

(b) The product specific *reducing* costs are incurred in proportion to the viscosity of the liquid when it emerges from the vats. The proportions are: Lethal: Deadly = 4:7.

Bottling

(a) The product specific *filling* cost required for each product is attributable in the following proportions: Lethal:Deadly = 5:4.

(b) Bottling *materials* are also a part of the product specific bottling cost, and costs are incurred in the proportion Lethal: Deadly = 2:4.

Under the activity based system company fixed costs are to be apportioned to products at an overall average rate per bottle.

Required

(a) (i) Calculate costs per bottle (analysed by type of cost) for each product using the absorption costing information. (10 marks)

(ii) In the light of your answer to (a)(i), evaluate a proposal by the management accountant that one of the products should no longer be produced. (4 marks)

(b) (i) Calculate costs per bottle for each product using the activity based costing information. (12 marks)

(ii) In the light of your answer to (b)(i), reconsider the management accountant's proposal to alter the production pattern. (4 marks)

(c) To achieve its parent company's *targets* for return on capital Killitt plc needs to make an overall net profit margin of 5% on sales. The management accountant suggests that *target costing* could be helpful in this respect.

Required

How do you interpret the management accountant's suggestion? What specific areas should be examined? (5 marks)

(35 marks)

Part (a)(i): absorption costing

3.2 Part (a) (i) requires you to calculate **costs per bottle** for each of the two products, Lethal and Deadly, using absorption costing. You have to **analyse** cost per bottle into the separate types of costs.

3.3 This sounds pretty similar to what we did in Section 1 of this chapter: the first step is to find out what the total costs to be absorbed are. This was **easy** enough in the previous example. There was a nice little list of them and you just had to add it up and find the total. Paper 9 questions will **not be so straightforward**. Note the following points about the Lethal and Deadly question.

(a) There is no mention at all of labour hours and machine hours.

(b) The figures are given partly in absolute terms (eg £47,500) and partly in percentage terms (30% ... the remainder).

3.4 This is because the Paper 9 examiner is doing two things.

(a) He is describing the **modern** manufacturing environment, where most people are paid salaries, not by the hour, and they are paid whether they work or not, and where most costs associated with technology are related to supporting the technology rather than actually running it.

(b) He is trying to imitate real life in making it **hard to extract** the information you need in the first place rather than giving it to you on a plate.

> **KEY TERMS**
>
> **Conversion costs** are the costs of turning raw materials into finished goods. The term may include both the cost of paying employees and the cost of operating machinery. Some conversion costs will be variable according to some activity (not necessarily how many units are produced) and others will be fixed.

BPP PUBLISHING

KEY TERMS

Product specific fixed costs are, as you might expect, specific to a particular product. For example it may be necessary to pay a fixed annual fee for the right to use the formula for a product, or a fixed annual salary to the resident scientific expert on that product.

Company fixed costs are things like rent and rates for a factory.

3.5   *Step 1: total costs to be absorbed*

The **conversion costs** to be absorbed in this question, then, are as follows.

		Workings
Variable manufacturing cost	£7,500	
Variable bottling cost	31,500	
Product specific fixed costs		
Manufacturing	7,500	(£25,000 □ 30%)
Bottling	5,400	(£18,000 □ 30%)
Company fixed costs		
Manufacturing	17,500	(£25,000 □ 70%)
Bottling	12,600	(£18,000 □ 70%)

(a)   It is worth **re-arranging the layout** given in the question, if only to help you to sort out what is what.

(b)   It is a very good habit to **show any workings** that you do.

Exam focus point

You may realise when you are half-way through a question that the approach you have chosen was not necessarily the best or quickest way to approach it.

This **does not matter in the slightest**. If you are making sense of the figures, getting your calculations right and **laying out your workings clearly** so that the marker can see that you have read the questions carefully and understand the relationships between the numbers in the question, you are likely to score marks.

In any case, there is no 'best way' of answering a Paper 9 question.

3.6   *Step 2: the absorption basis*

The absorption bases are **estimated time based rates, as** we are told in the second paragraph of the question. Fortunately this does not mean that you have to estimate the times yourself, it simply means that they are a sort of standard time based on past experience. The times are given to you in the question, as follows.

Production time per bottle	*Lethal*	*Deadly*
Manufacturing (minutes)	10	10
Bottling (minutes)	8	6

You want a separate figure which you will then divide into each of the costs to be absorbed.

	Bottles	*Minutes per bottle*	*Total*
Basis for variable manufacturing cost			
Lethal	75,000	10	750,000
Deadly	50,000	10	500,000
			1,250,000

	Bottles	Minutes per bottle	Total
Basis for variable bottling costs			
Lethal	75,000	8	600,000
Deadly	50,000	6	300,000
			900,000

The same figures are used for the fixed manufacturing and bottling costs.

3.7 *Step 3: absorption rates*

Divide Step 1 by Step 2.

			Rate
	£	Minutes	£
Variable manufacturing cost	47,500	1,250,000	0.038
Variable bottling cost	31,500	900,000	0.035
Product specific fixed costs			
Manufacturing	7,500	1,250,000	0.006
Bottling	5,400	900,000	0.006
Company fixed costs			
Manufacturing	17,500	1,250,000	0.014
Bottling	12,600	900,000	0.014

3.8 *Steps 4, 5 and 6: apply the rates to the resources consumed by one unit*

	Rate	Lethal		Deadly	
	£	Mins	£	Mins	£
Variable manufacturing cost	0.038	10	0.380	10	0.380
Variable bottling cost	0.035	8	0.280	6	0.210
Product specific fixed costs					
Manufacturing	0.006	10	0.060	10	0.060
Bottling	0.006	8	0.048	6	0.036
Company fixed costs					
Manufacturing	0.014	10	0.140	10	0.140
Bottling	0.014	8	0.112	6	0.084
Total conversion cost			1.020		0.910
Direct material cost			2.500		2.600
Total cost per bottle			3.520		3.510

3.9 *Step 7* is not necessary here, because the information given in the question for direct costs is on a per bottle basis already.

3.10 Note that we have added in **direct material** costs, as given in the question, at the end. You could easily forget to do this in an exam. It is good practice to stop for a moment when you have finished a part of a question and think about whether you have **missed anything out**.

Question 5

Look back at the requirements and see if you can suggest an answer to part (a)(ii). We shall come back to this later.

---

63 **BPP**
PUBLISHING

Part (b)(i): activity based costing

3.11 The first step is to list out the costs to be dealt with, re-analysed as appropriate. Again, because this is Paper 9, the information has to be **teased out** of the question.

(a) The question tells us that 55% of the **product specific costs** (variable and fixed) are spent on the mixing activity. This means, say, that 55% of **variable** manufacturing cost of £47,500 (all product specific) is spent on mixing (0.55 × £47,500 = £26,125) and 55% of **product specific fixed** manufacturing costs (30% of £25,000) is spent on mixing (0.55 × 0.30 × £25,000 = £4,125).

(b) The question tells us costs such as this £4,125 are split between products in certain **ratios** or **proportions**. So, for example, the mixing cost is split in the ratio Lethal: Deadly = 3:2.

£4,125 divided by (3+2) = £825

∴ Lethal (3 × £825) = £2,475 and Deadly (2 × £825) = £1,650

(c) The question tells us that **company fixed costs** are to be apportioned at an overall average rate per **bottle.**

KEY TERM

An **overall average rate per (something)** means you take the total cost to be turned into a rate and the total of whatever the rate is per, and divide the first by the second.

Total company fixed costs (£25,000 + £18,000) × 70%	£30,100
Total bottles (75,000 + 50,000)	125,000
Overall average rate per bottle	£0.2408

Exam focus point
This calculation was required in the **December 1998** exam.

Activity based results

3.12 Here are the final results if you work through the information in the manner suggested above. The full workings are then shown separately. Make sure you follow the calculations through from the workings to the final result.

	Lethal	Deadly
Unit costs using ABC	£	£
Direct material (given)	2.50	2.60
Variable conversion (W1)	0.52	0.80
	3.02	3.40
Product specific (W2)	0.09	0.13
	3.11	3.53
Apportioned (W3)	0.24	0.24
Total	3.35	3.77

Workings

1   *Variable costs using ABC*

These are calculated in total then apportioned to the products in the ratios given.

	Total	Lethal	Deadly
	£	£	£
Mixing ((£47,500 × 0.55) in ratio 3:2)	26,125	15,675.00	10,450.00
Reducing ((£47,500 × 0.45) in ratio 4:7)	21,375	7,772.73	13,602.27
Filling ((£31,500 × 0.75) in ratio 5:4)	23,625	13,125.00	10,500.00
Bottling material((£31,500 × 0.25) in ratio 2:4)	7,875	2,625.00	5,250.00
Total		39,197.73	39,802.27
Per unit (totals divided by 75,000 or 50,000)		0.52	0.80

2 *Product specific fixed costs using ABC*

	£	£	£
Mixing ((£25,000 × 30% × 55%) in ratio 3:2)	4,125	2,475.00	1,650.00
Reducing ((£25,000 × 30% × 45%) in ratio 4:7)	3,375	1,227.27	2,147.73
Filling ((£18,000 × 30% × 75%) in ratio 5:4)	4,050	2,250.00	1,800.00
Bottling material ((£18,000 × 30% × 25%) in ratio 2:4)	1,350	450.00	900.00
Total		6,402.27	6,497.73
Per unit (totals divided by 75,000 or 50,000)		0.09	0.13

3 *Apportioned fixed costs using ABC*

Total costs (£25,000 + £18,000) × 70%	£30,100
Total units (75,000 + 50,000)	125,000
Average cost per unit	£0.2408

Cost drivers and ratios

3.13 Be *very* careful with **ratios**.

(a) If you are told, say, that 'the cost is incurred **per kg** of material in the ratio 2:1 ' you need to **weight** the total kg of each material used **by the ratio** and then split the cost according to the weighted kg.

(b) If you are told that 'the cost is attributable to the materials in the ratio 2:1' you can simply split the cost in this ratio.

3.14 EXAMPLE: RATIOS

Suppose total storage costs are £22,000 and there are typically 3,000 kg of material A in stock and 5,000 kg of material B.

(a) Given the first wording the cost is split (3,000 ×2):(5000 × 1) = 6,000:5,000 (A: £12,000; B: £10,000).

(b) Given the second wording the cost is split 2:1 (A: £14,667; B: £7,333).

> **Exam focus point**
> ABC questions with added complications like ratios and weighting have been a feature of Paper 9 exams. This point was relevant, for example, in the **December 1995** and **December 1998** exams.

BPP PUBLISHING

Written parts of the question

3.15 In this case, if you can grab, say, 10 marks out of the 13 available for written comments, you only need another 8 marks from all of your calculations, and you should be able to get these for sensible well-labelled **workings** (see Chapter 6) whether or not your final calculations are correct.

3.16 On the other hand, your written answers do need to be a **sensible interpretation** of the figures you have calculated. A 'sensible' interpretation is one that draws on your **knowledge of the issues** surrounding the technique in question (in this case you know that ABC is supposed to give more accurate product costs and often draws attention to the fact that some products are unprofitable to produce) and **makes commercial sense**.

3.17 Parts a(ii) and b(ii) simply ask you to look at your results and see what implications they have. In part (a)(i) we get a cost for Lethal that is £0.02 higher than the selling price of £3.50. This might suggest that **Lethal** should be discontinued. Similarly the figures in (b)(i) suggest that **Deadly** should be discontinued because it costs £0.07 more to produce than it can be sold for.

3.18 Does this make **commercial sense**?

- In the first place, both products make a **contribution to fixed costs** so stopping production will mean that the company is less profitable overall unless it can find this contribution from elsewhere.

- There may be **other implications** such as letting down faithful customers which will be more damaging to the company than a small loss on Lethal will be.

- The amount of the loss is so small in this case that it would be highly susceptible to **errors in cost estimates**. If just one of the figures given turns out to be slightly wrong the whole picture may change.

- It may be possible to **raise prices**.

3.19 Part (c) of the question needs a brief explanation of **target costing**, and some suggestions of how it might be implemented. Look back at Chapter 3 for suggestions and then attempt your own answer, applying what you read to the information in the question. You can also do a few additional figures, even though these are not asked for directly.

Question 6

Do the two products currently make an overall net profit of 5% on sales?

Answer

Total sales are (75,000 × £3.50) + (50,000 × £3.70) = £447,500. Total costs (using either absorption costing or ABC, since the overall costs are the same) work out to £439,500. Check this for yourself. This gives a net profit of £8,000 or 1.8%, so the products are not achieving the target at present.

Developing an activity model – the examiner's approach

3.20 You might be asked, as part of another question on ABC, to describe how and activity model might be developed. In his article, reproduced at the end of this text, 'Product costing/pricing strategy' (**ACCA Students' Newsletter**, August 1999), the examiner suggests the following approach.

Step 1. **Determine the activities** that are being carried out and whether or not they need to be carried out. (Classifying activities as primary or support or value added or non value added will help.)

Step 2. Ascertain **how effectively** activities are being carried out and to what quality and standard.

Step 3. Discover the **principal cost** driver which determines the level of resource required for an activity.

Step 4. Work out the **relationship** between an activity's cost driver and its root cause.

3.21 The examiner's example focuses on the cutting of a steel sheet, a primary, value-added activity. The effectiveness of the steel sheet cutting activity could be determined by studying the type of machinery used, the skills level of the machine operators and the effectiveness of the machinery. The cost driver for the activity might be the number of cuts required, which may be linked to the steel sheet purchasing policy. it may be possible to reduce the number of cuts (and hence the cost of the activity) by purchasing smaller sheets.

4   TOTAL QUALITY MANAGEMENT PROGRAMMES

> **Exam focus point**
> Here is a **quality management question,** again closely based on one set in the **December 1994** Paper 9 exam.

4.1   EXAMPLE: QUALITY WITH KNOBS ON

Turner-Down Bros, a supplier to the music industry, moulds nylon granules to produce plastic knobs for electronic instruments and equipment. There are two types of knob – Large and Small. Current performance is regarded as less than satisfactory and Turner-Down Bros is deciding whether to undertake a quality management programme. Implementation of the programme will cost £100,000.

(a) The firm currently buys nylon granules for £25 per thousand. Goods inwards checks cost £8,250 pa. An average of 3% of nylon granules received are rejected because they are too large to feed into the moulding machines. The granule manufacturer accepts returns, giving a credit of £0.50 per thousand granules.

An agreement with a new granule manufacturer will mean that inspection and rejection costs will no longer be incurred in respect of raw materials. The new manufacturer guarantees the size of the granules and is willing to make Just-in-time deliveries. The cost of granules and delivery will be £30 per thousand units.

(b) The moulding process incurs variable conversion costs of £16 per thousand granules input. Misshapen units from the process have to be scrapped but they can be sold for £2.50 per thousand units. Misshapes amount to 12% of input to the process.

Misshapes cannot be eliminated entirely, but improved procedures under the TQM programme are expected to reduce losses by 9%.

(c) The threading and grooving process entails a series of processes to which the freshly moulded knobs are subjected in order to produce the finished product. The variable conversion costs in the threading and grooving process for Large and Small knobs are £12 and £20 per thousand units respectively. Production problems in the threading and grooving process result in 17.5% of units becoming flawed. Flawed units are sold for scrap at £7.50 per thousand units.

Cellular manufacturing will be introduced into the threading and grooving process, with one cell for each of types Large and Small. The revised variable costs per thousand knobs processed will be £10 and £18 respectively. This will largely solve the current production problems and only 4% of the input to each cell is expected to be flawed. Flawed units will be sold as scrap as at present.

(d) Demand for finished goods is unpredictable and so a stock of Large and Small plastic knobs of 100,000 and 150,000 units respectively is held all year round. Variable stock holding costs are £17.50 per ten thousand units. Stocks also allow immediate replacement of knobs found to be flawed by customers. Returns amount to 3% of plastic knobs delivered to customers.

Faster response times will be possible with cellular production in the threading and grooving process and this will mean that it is no longer necessary to hold finished goods stocks to meet fluctuating demand. Some knobs will still be held to allow for the immediate replacement of those found to be flawed in customer hands. Initially one month's worth of replacements (estimated at 10,000 and 15,000 units for the Large and Small types respectively) will be carried in stock. Variable stockholding costs will not change.

An accurate summary of the effect of these changes on production requirements has already been prepared by the production manager. This is reproduced below.

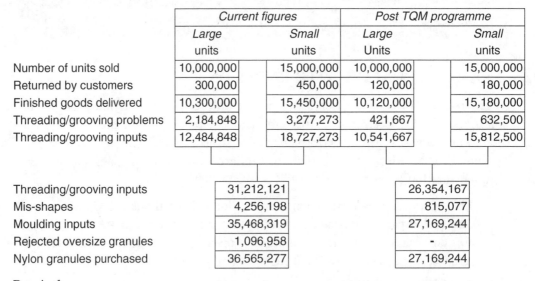

	Current figures		Post TQM programme	
	Large units	Small units	Large Units	Small units
Number of units sold	10,000,000	15,000,000	10,000,000	15,000,000
Returned by customers	300,000	450,000	120,000	180,000
Finished goods delivered	10,300,000	15,450,000	10,120,000	15,180,000
Threading/grooving problems	2,184,848	3,277,273	421,667	632,500
Threading/grooving inputs	12,484,848	18,727,273	10,541,667	15,812,500

Threading/grooving inputs	31,212,121	26,354,167
Mis-shapes	4,256,198	815,077
Moulding inputs	35,468,319	27,169,244
Rejected oversize granules	1,096,958	-
Nylon granules purchased	36,565,277	27,169,244

Required

(a) The above scenario contains examples of each of the standard categories of quality costs – internal failure costs, external failure costs, appraisal costs, and prevention costs. Explain what these terms mean illustrating your answer as appropriate. (8 marks)

(b) Prepare a statement which sets out the net benefit or loss of implementing the quality management programme. All figures should be rounded to the nearest pound. Show all workings. (27 marks)

(35 marks)

Solution to part (a)

4.2 **Part (a)** asks for some straightforward explanations of terms you should have learned from the previous chapter. It also asks for **examples** however. Here are some suggestions.

Quality cost	Example from the question
Internal failure costs	Mis-shapes in the moulding process and the flawed units lost in the threading and grooving process.
External failure costs	Knobs discovered to be flawed by customers
Appraisal costs	Goods inwards checks, detection of mis-shapes and detection of flawed units following the threading/grooving process
Prevention costs	The agreement with the JIT supplier, the improved procedures aimed at reducing the number of mis-shapes, and the introduction of cellular manufacturing

Question 7

Explain why we have chosen these examples. In other words explain what each category of cost means. Look back to the previous chapter and **learn** these terms if you can't do this.

Solution to part (b)

4.3 Part (b) asks for a **statement** setting out the net benefit or loss of implementing the programme, but it does not tell you how to lay out your statement and we have not suggested an ideal answer deliberately. The key thing is that it is clear to the marker **how you have derived your figures** and what your **overall answer** is.

4.4 We suggest you work **calmly and methodically** through the question making a rough note of all the costs and benefits that arise from the quality management programme.

- Cost of implementation
- Savings on inspection and rejection costs for nylon granules
- Extra cost of higher quality materials
- Reduced losses through mis-shapes
- Fewer flawed units through cellular manufacturing
- Savings in stockholding costs for finished goods

4.5 Before leaping into the question, however, look at the table at the end of the question and make sure you understand it. Work through it with a calculator. For instance to achieve **sales** of 10m large units it is necessary to **produce** 10.3m large units because 0.3m are returned.

4.6 Even with no other problems this would mean that you had to **buy** enough raw materials to make 10.3m units, and you would incur **conversion costs** for 10.3m units. If you could change things so that only 0.2m were returned you would save money **at each stage of production,** because your inputs would be lower and your conversion efforts would be less. We can add therefore add to our checklist above as follows.

- Savings in purchase volumes for raw materials
- Savings in conversion costs at each stage

4.7　On the next page is an analysis of the thought processes that you would need to go through to answer this question successfully. See if **you** can rearrange this into a proper **statement** with **workings** attached.

Exam focus point

This question illustrates a number of very common **'tricks'** in Paper 9 exams.

- The idea that to make **one whole unit** you need to input the equivalent of more than one unit's worth of materials and effort is very common. (For instance to make one cup of tea, you need to put more than one cup of tea's worth of water into the kettle, because some will be lost into the kitchen as steam.) Question 1 of the **December 1999** exam provides another example.

- Figures are often given per something. In this case most of the costs are **per thousand** granules. It is very easy to forget this in the heat of the exam. Watch out!

- Figures are often given in an **unfamiliar way**. The table at the end of the question is an example. It is well worth spending a few minutes working out the logic of tables such as this before launching headlong into the question.

- This is really a **relevant costs** question wrapped up in 'modern environment' clothing.

Question 8

You are told that the table given at the end of the question is an **accurate** analysis. Verify this using the percentages given in the question.

Answer

Do this for yourself. You will find that all of the figures work out as described. For instance mis-shapes come to 12% of inputs before the TQM programme and (12-9) = 3% afterwards.

35,468,319 × 12% = 4,256,198
27,169,244 × 3% = 815,077.

Note, therefore, that just like real life a question may sometimes give you more information than you require.

Thought process	(Cost)/Saving
	£
There does not seem to be anything to do with the **implementation** cost other than note it down	(100,000)
Inspection is not necessary because quality is now guaranteed. This **saves** £8,250.	8,250
The **rejects** amount to **3%** of the granules received, but this is a red herring because the penultimate line of the table at the end of the question tells us exactly how many are rejected at present: 1,096,958.	
These can be returned for a credit of £0.50 per thousand, reducing costs by (1,096,958/1,000 × £0.50) = £548.48. Since there will no longer be any rejects this reduction will no longer apply, so this is a **cost**.	(548)
The extra **purchase cost** of higher quality materials is £30 – £25 = £5 per thousand units, but the cumulative effect of all the changes on the **volume** purchased is that the amount purchased is significantly lower.	
(36,565,277 × £25/1,000) = £914,132 is replaced by (27,169,244 × £30/1,000) = £815,077, so the net effect is in fact a **saving** of £99,055	99,055
Mis-shapes are reduced by (4,256,198 – 815,077) = 3,441,121 units and these could formerly be sold for £2.50 per thousand. This income will no longer be received, so it is a **cost** of the TQM programme	(8,603)
Conversion costs in the moulding process are unchanged at £16 per 1,000, but they apply to fewer units so there is a **saving** here. (35,468,319 – 27,169,244) × £16/1,000 = £132,785	132,785

Follow the same logic with the **threading/grooving** improvements from cellular manufacturing.

	£
Existing cost (Large) (12,484,848 × £12/1,000) =	149,818
Existing cost (Small) (18,727,273 × £20/1,000) =	374,545
	524,363
Amended cost (Large) (10,541,667 × £10/1,000) =	105,417
Amended cost (Small) (15,812,500 × £18/1,000) =	284,625
	390,042

Thought process	(Cost)/Saving
The net **saving** here is £134, 321	134,321
Scrap sales forgone in this instance are ((2,184,848 + 3,277,273) – (421,667 + 632,500)) × £7.50/1,000 = £33,060	(33,060)
Finally we have reductions in **finished goods stock** to deal with.	
A total of 250,000 units are held at present at a cost of £17.50 per 10,000 units. This will be reduced to 25,000 units at the same cost. 225,000 × £17.50/10,000 = £394 saving	394
TOTAL SAVING	**232,594**

5 JIT AND BACKFLUSH ACCOUNTING

5.1 The substantial reduction in stocks that is a feature of **JIT** means that stock valuation is less relevant and can therefore be simplified to a certain extent.

> ### KEY TERM
>
> **Backflush accounting** (or backflush costing) is a method of costing associated with a JIT production system which applies cost to the output of a process. Costs do not mirror the flow of products through the production process, but are attached to the output produced (finished goods and cost of sales), on the assumption that such backflushed costs are a realistic measure of the actual costs incurred.   (CIMA, *Official Terminology*)

5.2 In other words, backflush accounting challenges the principle enshrined in SSAP 9, and the staple of cost accounting for decades, that stock and WIP should be accounted for by calculating cost and net realisable value of '**each item of stock separately**', so that overall costs need to be carefully traced back to individual 'equivalent units' of production to get a true and fair idea of the value of WIP.

5.3 Backflush accounting is more appropriate in a modern world where organisations are doing their utmost **not to hold stocks** at all (hence WIP valuation is not needed), and where the **recording** of every little increase in stock value, as each nut and bolt is added, is simply an expensive and **non-value-added activity** that should be eliminated.

5.4 EXAMPLE: WORKING BACKWARDS FROM OUTPUT

To take a **much simplified example,** if backflush accounting is used, the management accountant might extract the following information from the monthly accounting transaction records and production records.

Orders completed and despatched in July	196 units
Orders prepared in advance 1 July	3 units
Orders prepared in advance 31 July	2 units
Scrapped items	5 units
Conversion costs in the month	£250,000
Material costs in the month	£475,000

This is enough to place a value on stocks and production as follows.

	Units		£
B/f	(3)	Conversion costs	250,000
Dispatched	196	Material costs	475,000
Scrapped	5	Total costs	725,000
C/f	2		
Units produced	200		

Cost per unit is 725,000 units divided by 200 = £3,625

In this case a single process account could be drawn up as follows.

	Dr (£)	Cr (£)
Stock b/fwd (3 × £3,625)	10,875	
Materials	475,000	
Conversion costs	250,000	
To finished goods (196 × £3,625)		710,500
Losses etc written off to P& L (5 × £3,625)		18,125
Stock c/fwd (2 × £3,625)		7,250
	735,875	735,875

5.5 **Traditional** management accountants might propose two arguments.

(a) That the figure for **losses** here is **inaccurate**. They would say that in reality the faulty goods would have been scrapped when only partially complete and it is wrong to value them at the same cost as a fully finished good unit.

(b) Using this approach, the figure for stocks b/fwd and c/fwd will not tie up with the accounts for last month and next month, because the material and conversion costs may be different.

5.6 **Modern** management accountants might reply as follows.

(a) **Losses** represent only about 2% of total cost and are **not material**. In any case putting a value to them is less important than improving the quality of **production** procedures (on the basis of TQM practices and **non-financial** production information) to ensure that they do not occur again;

(b) Finished good stocks represent between 1% and 2% of total cost and are **immaterial**. Slight discrepancies in valuation methods of b/fwds and c/fwds will be amount to a *fraction* of a percentage, and can be written off in the month as a small **variance**.

5.7 Above all the modern management accountant would argue that (even with computers) the **cost** of tracing units every step of the way through production - with 'normal' and 'abnormal losses', equivalent units and numerous process accounts - is simply not worth it, in terms of the **benefit** derived from the information it provides.

Exam focus point

Note the way we justify our argument, by analysing the figures we have produced and expressing them in terms of what **percentage** one represents of another. This is frequently a useful technique for the written parts of Paper 9 questions.

Now we go on to look at how backflush costing has featured in the Paper 9 exam.

The Paper 9 examiner and backflush accounting: before and after

5.8 In the second of the three parts of the examiner's lengthy article 'Control information and standard process costs' (*ACCA Students' Newsletter*, January 1996) there is an explanation of how **conventional standard process accounts** can be condensed into a set of bookkeeping records which adopt a **backflush accounting** approach.

5.9 Our example which follows is similar to one in the examiner's article, but it is **more accessible** and still illustrates all of the principles involved in backflush accounting. It is **based on an exam question** that appeared in **June 1996**.

5.10 EXAMPLE: BACKFLUSH ACCOUNTING

Product X is produced by Z Ltd by passing raw material Y through three processes (A, B and C). Z Ltd currently uses a system of standard process costing. This has the following implications for the bookkeeping system.

(a) All transfers into and between processes, transfers to finished goods and losses are valued at the standard cost for their degree of completion.

(b) Labour and overheads are recorded at cost.

(c) Normal loss is the expected loss *in units*. Abnormal loss is the difference between units input to a process and output (such as normal loss, WIP losses and finished goods).

(d) Residual variances are recorded for each process. They are the difference between standard *cost* and actual *cost* of operating the process *after* the value of abnormal loss has been deducted.

Z Ltd maintains constant stock levels.

Raw material Y (standard cost per litre £300)	150 litres
Work in progress in process B	70 units
Work in progress in process C	70 units
Finished goods	70 units

Because work in progress is held at the **beginning** of a process there is none in Process A. (Any raw material stocks would be recorded separately and transferred in as part of input.) The perishable nature of product X means that once finished goods have been transferred to the finished goods store, losses are bound to occur.

The standard process costing accounts for 19X8 are shown below.

PROCESS A

	Units	£'000		Units	£'000
Raw material input	2,200*	257,400	Normal loss	12	-
Labour and o/hds	-	159,000	Transfers to Process B	2,175	413,250
			Abnormal loss	13	2,470
			Residual variance	-	680
	2,200	416,400		2,200	416,400

* raw material input in terms of units, not litres

PROCESS B

	Units	£'000		Units	£'000
WIP b/f	70	13,300	Normal loss	10	-
Transfers from Process A	2,175	413,250	Transfers to Process C	2,145	589,875
Labour and o/heads	-	183,150	Units damaged in WIP	5	1,250
			Abnormal loss	15	4,125
			Residual variance		1,150
			WIP c/f	70	13,300
	2,245	609,700		2,245	609,700

PROCESS C

	Units	£'000		Units	£'000
WIP b/f	70	19,250	Normal loss	20	-
Transfers from Process B	2,145	589,875	Transfers to finished		
Labour and o/hds	-	540,820	Goods	2,112	1,123,584
			Units damaged in WIP	7	2,800
			Abnormal loss	6	3,000
			Residual variance		1,311
			WIP c/f	70	19,250
	2,215	1,149,945		2,215	1,149,945

A **profit and loss account** for the same period is as follows.

	£'000	£'000
Sales		1,849,700
Less: standard cost of sales		1,121,090
Standard contribution		728,610
Less: units damaged in WIP	4,050	
abnormal losses	9,595	
residual variances	3,141	
stock losses	2,494	
		(19,280)
Profit		709,330

The recently appointed assistant management accountant, having just passed the ACCA Paper 9 exam, believes that it would be more appropriate for Z Ltd to use backflush accounting than conventional standard process cost bookkeeping.

(a) **Inventory levels are low** and the vast majority of manufacturing costs form part of the cost of sales, rather being deferred in closing stock values. The amount of work involved in tracking costs through work in progress, cost of sales and finished goods is therefore unlikely to be justifiable.

(b) Z Ltd has predictable levels of efficiency and fixed price and quality of materials, so that **cost variances** are **insignificant**. This is vital for the operation of backflush accounting.

Required

Prepare a 'materials and in-process account' and a 'finished goods' account using the principles of backflush accounting.

5.11 SOLUTION

A possible simplified bookkeeping system using backflush accounting is shown below. As usual, check that you understand where the figures come from and how they are calculated in case we have made any **deliberate errors**.

The materials and in process account is a simplified version of the process accounts for all three processes but it also records the value of the **raw material stock** held. Note that the transfers between process A and B, and between processes B and C are eliminated.

The finished goods account simply records stocks of, transfers in and out of, and any losses of finished goods.

Note in particular the method of calculating **finished goods stock**.

Exam focus point
Remember that the problem described above was examined in **June 1996**. The solution below shows how it might have been tackled.

MATERIALS AND IN-PROCESS A/C

	£		£
Material and stock in process b/f (W1)	77,550	Transfers to finished goods (W4)	1,123,584
Material cost (W2)	257,400	Residual variances (W5)	16,786
Labour and o/hds (W3)	882,970	Material and stock in process c/f	77,550
	1,217,920		1,217,920

FINISHED GOODS

	£		£
Finished goods stock b/f (W6)	37,240	To cost of sales (P&L a/c) (W7)	1,121,090
From materials and in-process a/c	1,123,584	Stock losses (P&L a/c) (W7)	2,494
		Finished good stock c/f	37,240
	1,160,824		1,160,824

Workings

1   (150 litres × £300) (from the second main paragraph n the question) + £13,300 (**Process B**) + £19,250 (**Process C**)

2   From **Process A**

3   Total from **all three**

4   From **Process C**

	£
5 Residual variance (for **all processes**)	3,141
Abnormal loss (for **all processes**)	9,595
Units damaged in WIP (for **all processes**)	4,050
	16,786

6   70 units (finished goods stock) × £1,123,584/2,112 (from **Process C**) = 70 × £532 = £37,240 (where £532 is the unit valuation)

7   From **profit and loss account**

KEY TERM

Residual variances is a term used by the Paper 9 examiner to refer to the sum of conventional process costing variances, all of which will be replaced in the modern environment by more useful non-financial data.

Possible problems with backflush accounting

5.12   (a)   It is most appropriate for JIT systems with minimum raw materials and WIP inventories. If used in conjunction with a computerised materials requirements or manufacturing resources planning (**MRP**) system, for instance, **production times must be short,** otherwise the MRP system will 'think' that materials and components are available when they have actually been transferred to WIP. (On the other hand a company that has invested in and still uses MRP is unlikely to try backflush costing in the first place.)

(b)   Some have claimed that it should **not** be used **for external reporting** purposes. If, however, **stocks are low** or are practically **unchanged** from one accounting period to the next, operating income and stock valuations derived from backflush accounting will **not be materially different** from the results using conventional systems and hence, in such circumstances, backflush accounting is acceptable for external financial reporting.

(c)   It is **vital** that adequate production controls exist so that **cost control during the production process is maintained**.

Advantages of backflush accounting

5.13 (a) It is **simple,** there being no separate accounting for WIP

(b) There are **fewer accounting entries,** supporting vouchers, documents and so on.

(c) The system may **discourage** managers from **producing for stock** since working on material does not add value if it moves into stock.

(d) Even the **finished goods** account is **unnecessary,** as we showed in the first example in this section, and as the examiner concedes at the end of his January 1996 article.

(e) By focusing on the **total output of a process,** there is no subjective dividing of apportioned overheads.

> **Exam focus point**
>
> Knowledge from Papers 3 and 8 had to be merged with knowledge from Paper 9 for one of the **December 1997** questions. Candidates had to discuss the factors which should be considered when preparing and agreeing the manufacturing cost per product unit in a **processing industry.** Simply Papers 3 and 8 knowledge you might think! But they should also have considered the impact on such valuations of **JIT, TQM and backflush accounting.**

The point of all these new methods

5.14 In the case of **backflush accounting** this approach may well leave you wondering **what is the point?** For instance, in the example above, the information seems to be collected and analysed in the old way anyway, and the new method turns out to be **just a summary** of totals derived from the old method.

5.15 The **point** is this:

(a) The Paper 9 examiner is going out of his way to **encourage the adoption** of more sensible and useful management accounting techniques (refer back to paragraphs 5.6 and 5.7, for instance).

(b) **Transitions** between different methods of doing things **will occur** for all companies at some time, and **you** may well find yourself in the position of being **the accountant** who has to **implement** the change. You may as well get some practice!

5.16 Once again this demonstrates the **typical trend of Paper 9** questions, which we can summarise as follows.

Before: Company X used to do so and so and here are some **figures**

After: Company X has now decided to do such and such, and here are some **more figures**

Required

Process both sets of figures in the way suggested and then **write comments** comparing the two sets of results.

> **Exam focus point**
>
> In the **June 1998** exam, a question followed the above structure, the company having decided to implement an IT initiative.

6 JIT AND THROUGHPUT ACCOUNTING

6.1 The concept of throughput accounting has been developed as an **alternative system of cost and management accounting in a JIT environment.**

KEY TERM

'**Throughput accounting** (TA) is an approach to accounting which is largely in sympathy with the JIT philosophy. In essence, TA assumes that a manager has a given set of resources available. These comprise existing buildings, capital equipment and labour force. Using these resources, purchased materials and parts must be processed to generate sales revenue. Given this scenario the most appropriate financial objective to set for doing this is the maximisation of throughput (Goldratt and Cox, 1984) which is defined as: sales revenue *less* direct material cost.

(Tanaka, Yoshikawa, Innes and Mitchell, *Contemporary Cost Management*)

6.2   TA for JIT is said to be based on three concepts.

(a) *Concept 1*. In the short run, **most costs in the factory (with the exception of materials costs)** are fixed (the opposite of ABC, which assumes that all costs are variable). These fixed costs include direct labour. It is useful to group all these costs together and call them **Total Factory Costs (TFC)**.

(b) *Concept 2*. In a JIT environment, all stock is a 'bad thing' and the **ideal inventory level is zero**. Products should not be made unless there is a customer waiting for them. This means **unavoidable idle capacity in some operations must be accepted**, except for the operation that is the bottleneck of the moment.

Work in progress should be **valued at material cost only** until the output is eventually sold, so that no value will be added and no profit earned until the sale takes place. Working on output just to add to work in progress or finished goods stock creates no profit, and so should not be encouraged.

(c) *Concept 3*. Profitability is determined by the rate at which 'money comes in at the door' (that is, sales are made) and, in a JIT environment, this depends on how quickly goods can be produced to satisfy customer orders. Since the goal of a profit-orientated organisation is to make money, stock must be sold for that goal to be achieved.

Question 9

How are these concepts a direct contrast to the fundamental principles of conventional cost accounting?

Answer

Conventional cost accounting	Throughput accounting
Stock is an asset.	Stock is *not* an asset. It is a result of unsynchronised manufacturing and is a barrier to making profit.
Costs can be classified either as direct or indirect.	Such classifications are no longer useful.
Product profitability can be determined by deducting a product cost from selling price.	Profitability is determined by the rate at which money is earned.
Profit can be increased by reducing cost elements.	Profit is a function of material cost, total factory cost and throughput.

Bottleneck resources

6.3 The aim of modern manufacturing approaches is to match production resources with the demand for them. This implies that there are **no constraints, termed bottleneck resources** in TA, within an organisation. The throughput philosophy entails the identification and elimination of these bottleneck resources. Where it cannot be eliminated, and to avoid the build-up of work in progress, **production must be limited to the capacity of the bottleneck resource**. If a rearrangement of existing resources or buying-in resources does not alleviate the bottleneck, investment in new equipment may be necessary. The elimination of one bottleneck is likely to lead to the creation of another at a previously satisfactory location, however. The management of bottlenecks therefore becomes a primary concern of the manager seeking to increase throughput.

6.4 There are other factors which might limit throughput other than a lack of production resources (bottlenecks).

    (a) The existence of an uncompetitive selling price
    (b) The need to deliver on time to particular customers
    (c) The lack of product quality and reliability
    (d) The lack of reliable material suppliers

Throughput measures

6.5 In a throughput environment, **production priority** must be given to the products best able to generate throughput, that is those **products that maximise throughput per unit of bottleneck resource** (which is similar in concept to maximising contribution per unit of limiting factor). Such product rankings are for **short-term production scheduling only**. In throughput accounting, bottlenecks should be eliminated and so rankings should change very quickly. Customer demand can, of course, cause the bottleneck to change at short notice too.

6.6 Products can be ranked according to the **TA ratio**.

    TA ratio = return per factory hour/cost per factory hour

    where   return per factory hour = throughput/time on bottleneck resource

                cost per factory hour (for all products) = TFC/total time available on bottleneck resource

6.7 The **TA ratio** is **similar in concept to contribution per unit of limiting factor**. (In fact, if materials were the only variable cost, contribution and throughput would be identical and there would be no difference between traditional contribution analysis and throughput analysis.) The TA ratio can be **used to assess the relative earning capabilities of different products** and hence can help with decision making.

Calculating product costs

6.8 TFC can be attributed to products according to the product's usage of bottleneck resources.

    TFC cost per unit = usage of bottleneck resource × TFC per unit of bottleneck resource
    Total TA product cost = material cost per unit + share of TFC

    A product which makes little or no use of the bottleneck resource will have little or no TFC attributed to it.

Is it good or bad?

6.9 TA is seen by some as **too short term**, as all costs other than direct material are regarded as fixed. Moreover, it **concentrates on direct material costs** and does nothing for the control of other costs such as overheads. These characteristics make throughput accounting a **good complement for ABC**, however, since ABC focuses on labour and overhead costs.

6.10 TA attempts to maximise throughput whereas traditional systems attempt to maximise profit. By attempting to maximise throughput an organisation could be producing in excess of the profit-maximising output. **Production scheduling** problems inevitably mean that the profit-maximising output is never attained, however, and so a **throughput maximising approach** could well **lead to the profit-maximising output** being achieved.

6.11 TA helps to direct attention to bottlenecks and focus management on the key elements in making profits, inventory reduction and reducing the response time to customer demand.

Case example

An article in *Management Accounting* in April 1992 gives a case study of a company which has adopted TA, with a particular emphasis on managing and alleviating bottlenecks in the production process. Although the company identified three areas of difficulty (the correct identification of constraints and bottlenecks, a one-off profit reduction because fewer overheads are carried forward in closing stocks, the appearance of previously hidden problems such as the inability of suppliers to meet delivery schedules), financial benefits have ensued and other benefits reported include a much enhanced realisation throughout the company of the critical need to adhere to production schedules and of the importance of 'first-time capability' (getting it right first time). The monthly management report has been reduced from forty pages to five and it is made available if requested to all employees. Above all, TA has forced management accounting staff at this company to get back to understanding what is actually happening on the shop floor and to be inventive about performance measures.

6.12 The following example illustrates the value of throughput accounting for decision making.

6.13 EXAMPLE: THROUGHPUT ACCOUNTING

Corrie Ltd produces three products, X, Y and Z. The capacity of Corrie's plant is restricted by process alpha. Process alpha is expected to be operational for eight hours per day and can produce 1,200 units of X per hour, 1,500 units of Y per hour, and 600 units of Z per hour.

Selling prices and material costs for each product are as follows.

Product	Selling price	Unit material cost	Throughput
	£	£	£
X	150	70	80
Y	120	40	80
X	300	100	200

Total factory cost (TFC) is £720,000 per day.

Required

(a) Calculate the profit per day if daily output achieved is 6,000 units of X, 4,500 units of Y and 1,200 units of Z.

(b) Determine the efficiency of bottleneck use.

(c) Calculate the TA ratio for each product.

(d) In the absence of demand restrictions for the three products, advise Corrie Ltd's management on the optimal production plan.

6.14 SOLUTION

(a) Profit = Throughput (sales revenue less direct material cost) – TFC = [(£80 × 6,000) + (£80 × 4,500) + (£200 × 1,200)] – £720,000 = £360,000

(b) Efficiency of bottleneck use = attributed TFC as % of actual TFC

TFC cost per unit = usage of bottleneck resource × TFC per unit of bottleneck resource

TFC per unit (minute) of bottleneck = £720,000/(8 hrs × 60 mins) = £1,500

TFC cost per unit is therefore as follows.

Product	Time in process alpha	× TFC per minute	= TFC cost per unit
	Minutes	£	£
X	60/1,200 = 0.05	1,500	75
Y	60/1,500 = 0.04	1,500	60
Z	60/600 = 0.10	1,500	150

TFC cost for the day is as follows.

Product	Output in day	TTFC cost per unit	TFC
		£	£'000
X	6,000	75	450
Y	4,500	60	270
Z	1,200	150	180
			900

Efficiency of bottleneck use = £900,000 ÷ £720,000 = 1.25 = 125%

Check. Equivalent hours produced

X	6,000/1,200 =	5	
Y	4,500/1,500 =	3	
Z	1,200/600 =	2	
		10	

Hours available 8, hours produced 10, ∴ 125% efficiency.

(c) TA ratio = return per factory hour/cost per factory hour

Return per factory hour = throughput/time on bottleneck resource
Cost per factory hour = TFC/availability of bottleneck resource = £720,000/8 = £90,000

Product	Return per factory hour	Cost per factory hour	TA ratio
X	(£80 ÷ 0.05 min) × 60	£90,000	1.07
Y	(£80 ÷ 0.04 min) × 60	£90,000	1.33
Z	(£200 ÷ 0.10 min) × 60	£90,000	1.33

(d) An attempt should be made to remove the restriction on output caused by the limited process alpha capacity. This will, of course, result in another bottleneck emerging elsewhere.

Extra capacity could possibly be obtained by overtime working, process improvements or product specification changes but until the volume of throughput can be increased, output should be concentrated upon products Y and Z (greatest TA ratios), unless there are good marketing reasons for continuing the current production mix.

Case example

In 'Accounting for Throughput' (*Management Accounting,* May 1996), Dugdale and Jones discuss the consequences of introducing throughput ideas into the accounting, production and marketing functions of a particular company.

(a)   'Measures of efficiency and overhead recovery were no longer considered useful ... The danger of traditional measures causing sub-optimal behaviour was now recognised and the key measure became "schedule adherence" ... The use of schedule adherence was later accompanied by the introduction of a throughput profit and loss account ... [which was] extremely simple.

	£
Sales revenue	X
Materials	(X)
Materials price and exchange variances	X
Throughput	X
Expense	(X)
Net profit	X

Gradually other measures were added to cell managers' monthly accounting packages - days' inventory on-hand, manufacturing cycle time, cost of quality, customer due-date performance.'

(b)   '... most [cell managers] thought that schedule adherence was a good measure but its credibility depended on the creation of realistic schedules ... Without such [financially-based] measures [of departmental performance], many managers considered that they were operating in a measurement vacuum in which they had insufficient information ... It may be that this [creating new local performance measures] is an intractable problem in accounting for throughput.'

(c)   'Whilst there was some disagreement about the use of throughput measures in production there were no such reservations in marketing... the move towards marginal cost pricing [throughput accounting being a form of marginal costing, only material costs being treated as variable] and away from absorbed costs and gross margin targets was an unmitigated success.'

Exam focus point

A question in the **June 1999** exam looked at the differences between the traditional approach to purchasing/production/stockholding/satisfying customer demand, and one most appropriate to the modern business environment. Candidates were asked to name ways in which the management accounting function would be affected by the more modern approach. Any of the topics covered in this chapter would have been suitable for inclusion in an answer.

CVP analysis and throughput accounting

6.15   The examiner in his article 'Quantitative Applications in paper 9 - part 2' (in the *ACCA Students' Newsletter, May 2000*) suggested that contribution analysis can be applied to throughput accounting.

(a)   'Where there is a limitation in the availability of input resource, contribution per unit of that limiting factor may be used to rank the products in order to get the best financial results'.

(b)   In throughput accounting, a 'bottleneck' *could* be a maximum capacity in hours in a particular production operation. As this is the bottleneck, then the firm should align the product mix by maximising **contribution per bottleneck hour.**

6.16   Moreover, if there is a bottleneck in one area of the business, it could imply that excess stocks are being built up elsewhere. Goldratt suggests three measures.

(a) Throughput: rate at which system generates money (sales less material cost)

(b) 'Inventory': **all** money investing in achieving goods for sale. He suggests that:

(c) Operational expenses: money spent converting inventory to throughput

$$\text{ROI} = \frac{\text{'Throughput'} - \text{'Operational expense'}}{\text{'Inventory'}}$$

Chapter roundup

- This chapter is intended to give you a massive **insight** into what to expect from the **Paper 9 exam**, and how to deal with the questions you will face. If you have not studied it very thoroughly indeed you will need to come back to it (**and** re-read chapters 1 to 3, which are essential background) again at a later date.

- Many of the **assumptions** behind traditional management accounting techniques are **invalid** in a modern environment.

- You should nevertheless be thoroughly familiar with techniques like absorption costing since exam questions typically ask you to **compare** figures calculated **using both older and newer methods.**

- Learn **step by step** approaches to absorption costing and ABC so that you are completely comfortable with the **basics.** However, be prepared to **adapt your approach** to the requirements of specific questions which may give you the information in an unexpected way.

- Take care with **cost drivers and ratios**.

- **Easy marks** are often available for written comments, provided they are a **sensible interpretation** of the figures drawing on **knowledge of the issues** and making **commercial sense.**

- Questions on **TQM** typically ask you to identify **how costs will change** after a TQM programme has been implemented.

- **Backflush accounting** may be appropriate where **stocks are low.** Costs are not traced through the production process but are simply attached to final output. Questions on backflush costing are likely to look at how the old style accounts can be consolidated into a **single account**.

- **Throughput accounting** should focus attention on bottlenecks and on the key elements in making profits (inventory reduction and reducing response time to customer demand).

BPP PUBLISHING

Quick quiz

1   Why is the validity of traditional management accounting techniques open to question? (see paras 1.1 - 1.3)

2   What are the seven steps for absorption costing? (1.5)

3   What are the six steps for ABC? (2.4)

4   Why might absorption costing produce flawed results? (2.7)

5   What is a conversion cost? (3.4)

6   What is meant by 'commercial sense'? (3.16, 3.18)

7   Define backflush accounting (5.1)

8   How might modern accountants reply to objections to backflush accounting? (5.6, 5.7)

9   What are the advantages and disadvantages of backflush accounting? (5.12, 5.13)

10   Why might it be important for practical reasons for you to learn new techniques? (5.15)

11   What are the three concepts upon which throughput accounting is based? (6.2)

Question to try	Level	Marks	Time
4	Exam standard	20	36 mins

Part C
Decision making

Chapter 5

DECISION MAKING

Chapter topic list	Syllabus reference
1 Decision making	2(c), 4(c)
2 Decision modelling	2(c), 4(c)
3 Relevant costs	4(b), 4(d)
4 Identifying relevant costs	4(b), 4(d)
5 Contribution	4(b), 4(d)

Introduction

This chapter introduces the topic of decision making, firstly with some general considerations about the **process** of decision making and the **context** in which it is done. In Section 2 we move on to set out some important **terminology** which you *must* be comfortable with because it may well be used in exam questions. Identifying **relevant costs** is a vital skill in Paper 9 questions and there are some notes on how to do this and a chance to get some practice. Finally there is a reminder of **CVP analysis** - you have covered this before but **contribution** is central to many Paper 9 questions, so you must make sure that you know what it is and how to manipulate it.

Core areas of the syllabus identified by the examiner and covered in this chapter: **relevant cost analysis**.

1 DECISION MAKING

The decision-making cycle

1.1 Decision making involves several steps.

> *Step 1.* Identify **objectives.**
> *Step 2.* Identify **alternative opportunities (strategies)** for achieving them.
> *Step 3.* Collect and **analyse relevant data** about each alternative.
> *Step 4.* **Make the decision**. State the **expected** outcome.
> *Step 5.* **Implement** the decision.
> *Step 6.* Obtain data about **actual results**.
> *Step 7.* **Compare actual** results with the **expected** outcome.
> *Step 8.* Evaluate achievements and **make further decisions** in this light.

1.2 Steps 3 to 8 will be dealt with as appropriate in the following chapters, but there are some points to be noted about Steps 1 and 2.

Identifying objectives

1.3 Objectives can be either long term or short term. In the **short term,** profit maximisation or cost minimisation (for example improved productivity) is often used as an objective towards which decision making should be aimed. However, alternative short-term objectives might be avoiding a loss, avoiding unnecessary risks or achieving a given growth in sales or profits compared with a previous year.

1.4 At the same time, some recognition might be given to **non-financial objectives** in the short term, such as maintaining or improving the **quality** of products or services, **employee welfare** (for example deciding to spend more money on health and safety at work) and **environmental considerations**.

1.5 The primary **long-term** objective of a profit-making organisation may be to maximise the return to shareholders, but without taking risks that shareholders might consider excessive.

Identifying alternative opportunities

Exam focus point

By preparing a schedule of costs, candidates in the **December 1997** exam had to determine which of **four alternative strategies** would lead to profit maximisation.

1.6 The search for things to do which might help an organisation achieve its objectives is one of the major tests of good management. Decisions might not be taken, and opportunities might be missed, simply because managers failed to recognise that opportunities existed.

Exam focus point

The Paper 9 examiner occasionally uses the term **alternative choice decision making**, which seems to mean choosing between different options, as opposed to choosing whether or not to do a particular thing.

Question 1

Distinguish between information gathered for alternative choice decision making and information gathered to decide whether or not to do something once the best option has been identified.

Answer

(a) Alternative choice decision making needs **factual** information: what are the **costs and benefits** (quantitative and qualitative) of each of the various options and how do they compare? This is a **management control**-type decision.

(b) Deciding whether or not to go ahead with an option is more dependent upon information about the **environment:** customers' and competitors' likely reactions, forecasts of future trading conditions and so on. (The decision to go ahead may also be dependent on **historical** information to an extent, in the sense that managers will judge on the basis of their past experience.)

Exam focus point

Candidates in the **December 1997** exam had to write a report explaining how **decision-making strategy** is affected by the degree of information available and the extent to which a decision maker has access to such information.

The organisational context of decisions

1.7 The **size** of an organisation has an impact on the information required to make decisions. The larger the organisation, the wider the consequences of a decision, and so the more complex the information required to make it. For example, a **small** business need only take account of **local conditions**, whereas a larger, **national** business needs to take account of different labour rates in **different parts of the country** and different costs of transporting materials from source to where they are needed. The problems are compounded for **international** businesses, and these also need to consider different **legal and political** constraints, the impact of **exchange rate** variations and so on.

1.8 The **type** of entity may also affect information requirements. Here are some examples.

(a) A manufacturer of a **well-established staple food** product like Heinz Beans, say, has less need to take account of market conditions than the manufacturer of a product which is highly sensitive to economic conditions and faces a good deal of competition, like a small hatchback car.

(b) **Service businesses** tend to have a very high proportion of fixed costs (buildings, substantial fixed assets like computer systems, and people). Decisions, and the information required to make them, tend to take a longer perspective than they might in a manufacturing business where the resources used are more short-lived.

(c) An **accountancy** firm offers a service uniquely tailored to each client and to decide on staffing requirements it needs records of time spent specifically on that client. A bank, in contrast, offers standard services like current accounts and can decide staffing requirements by, say, periodically undertaking a work study in selected branches.

(d) A **railway company** knows how long it takes to deliver a service and what manpower is required without collecting any information. However, it needs attendance records to be available very quickly to permit decisions about the *level* of service it is able to offer.

The qualitative factors in decision making

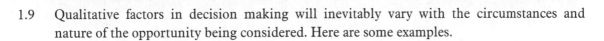

Exam focus point
Providing additional factors which could influence a particular decision strategy was worth 6 marks in both the **December 1997** and **June 1998** exams.

1.9 Qualitative factors in decision making will inevitably vary with the circumstances and nature of the opportunity being considered. Here are some examples.

Factor	Comment
Availability of cash	An opportunity may be profitable, but there must be sufficient cash to finance any purchases of **equipment** and build-up of **working capital**. If cash is not available, new sources of funds must be sought.
Employees	Any decision involving the shutdown of plant, changes in work procedures and so on will require acceptance by employees, and ought to have regard to **employee welfare**.
Customers	Decisions about new products or product closures, the quality of output or after-sales service will inevitably affect customer **loyalty** and customer **demand**. A decision involving one product may have repercussions on customer **attitudes** towards a range of company products. The **reliability** of a customer and the risk of incurring a bad debt may be a factor in some decisions.

BPP
PUBLISHING

Factor	Comment
Competitors	Some decisions may stimulate a response from rival companies. The decision to reduce selling prices in order to raise demand may not be successful if all competitors take similar **counter-action**.
Suppliers	Suppliers' long-term **goodwill** may be damaged by a decision. Decisions to change the specifications for bought-out components, or to change stockholding policies so as to create patchy, uneven demand, might put a strain on suppliers. If a company is the supplier's main customer, a decision might drive the supplier **out of business**.
Feasibility	A proposal may look good on paper, but managers may have some reservations about their ability to carry it out in practice.
Unquantified opportunity costs	It may be useful to qualify a recommended decision by stating, for example, that 'Project X would appear to be viable on the assumption that there are no other more profitable opportunities available'.
Political pressures	Large companies must recognise that there might be political pressures applied by the government or society to influence their investment or disinvestment decisions. The Labour government's imposition of a windfall tax on privatised utilities like British Telecom is an example.
Legal constraints	A decision might occasionally be deferred or rejected because of doubts about the legality of the proposed action.

Exam focus point

Learn this list: it is invaluable as a source of ideas for written comments in exam questions

Time and decision making

1.10 Decision making is affected by the **time horizon** which is used because, in the longer term, more costs become **variable**, the **time value of money** starts to have an impact and all information becomes subject to **uncertainty**.

1.11 If you need to think in terms of time periods, it is common to think of the short-run in terms of months, and the long-run in terms of years, but this is not a strict definition.

1.12 There are various other aspects to the time element in decisions.

(a) What would be the consequences of estimating incorrectly time to carry out a decision?

(b) Should a decision aim at a **time-minimising** option?

(c) Can a decision be **delayed**, and implemented later?

(d) Can a decision be **reversed** later?

2 DECISION MODELLING

2.1 One aid to decision making is to build a mathematical **model** in which variables in the 'real' system are represented by mathematical symbols and equations.

2.2 A question in the **December 1994** exam asked for explanations and examples of each of the following elements of models.

(a) **Exogenous variables** (literally, variables 'growing or originating from outside', from the Greek) are those determined **externally**, for example the cost of a raw material imposed by the supplier. These might be called **input variables.**

(b) **Endogenous variables** (literally, variables 'growing or originating from within') are variables that are produced **within** the model by means of the interaction between other variables. To an extent they are controlled by the decision maker, who can influence the relationships between variables. They might alternatively be called **output variables.** For example, the **re-order level** for an item stock may be an endogenous variable, perhaps determined by means of the EOQ model, or simply an arbitrary percentage of the annual requirement of that item. (The formula or percentage is usually known as an **intervening** variable.)

The term is sometimes used more simply to describe a variable whose value can be **decided by management,** for example the level of a bonus for employees. It is hard to think of universally applicable examples in modern business, where variables depend on customer needs.

(c) **Policies** are **general guidelines** for decision making. For example a company may have a positive discrimination policy that requires it to do business with third world organisations in preference to others, to encourage economic development. In a manufacturing decision this would place constraints on the sourcing of components. Policies may also be imposed from outside. For example a product may have to adhere to certain safety standards imposed as a policy of the government.

(d) **Performance measures** are standards that the outputs arising from the decision must meet. They would generally derive from the overall objectives of a company's strategy.

(e) **Controls** in a model are devices used to regulate the operation of the model. For example the model might incorporate a control designed to reject an option in which labour costs exceed a certain figure. The control is the **function** of accepting or rejecting, not the figure itself: for instance the formula $=IF(A5>B5, B5,A5)$ is a control in a spreadsheet which returns the value in cell B5 (the limit) if the value in A5 is over the limit.

(f) The term **intermediate variable** (as mentioned in the Paper 9 Teaching Guide) may be taken literally to mean something that (actively) **comes between other things,** such as the EOQ formula mentioned above (an 'intervening variable'). They are used to link **endogenous** and **exogenous** variables to the performance measure. For instance the ranking technique in limiting factor analysis calculates **contribution per unit of limiting factor,** an intermediate variable which is then used to find the profit maximising production plan.

3 RELEVANT COSTS

3.1 You studied relevant costs for Paper 8. Make sure you still understand the following terms, which are just as important for Paper 9.

KEY TERMS

A **relevant cost** is a future cash flow arising as a direct consequence of a decision. Thus, only costs which differ under some or all of the available opportunities should be considered; relevant costs are therefore sometimes referred to as **incremental costs** or **differential costs**.

- **Avoidable costs** are usually associated with shutdown or disinvestment decisions and are defined as: 'those costs which can be identified with an activity or sector of a business and which would be avoided if that activity or sector did not exist'.

- An **opportunity cost** is the benefit forgone by choosing one opportunity instead of the next best alternative.

Non-relevant costs are irrelevant for decision-making because they are either not future cash flows or they are costs which will be incurred anyway, regardless of the decision that is taken.

- A **sunk cost** is used to describe the cost of an asset which has already been acquired and which can continue to serve its present purpose, but which has no significant realisable value and no income value from any other alternative purpose.

- A **committed cost** is a future cash outflow that will be incurred anyway, whatever decision is taken now about alternative opportunities. They may exist because of contracts already entered into by the organisation, which it cannot get out of.

- A **notional cost** or **imputed cost** is a hypothetical accounting cost to reflect the benefit from the use of something for which no actual cash expense is incurred. Examples include notional rent and notional interest.

- **Historical costs** are irrelevant for decision making.

Question 2

A research project undertaken on behalf of a client has already incurred costs of £200,000. It is estimated that further costs of £280,000 (materials £100,000, staff costs £60,000 and overheads £120,000) will be charged to the project before its completion in one year's time. The overheads comprise depreciation of plant and equipment (£40,000), and an allocation of general overheads incurred by the business based on 80% of material costs. You have been asked to review the project because the project's total estimated costs of £480,000 exceed the contracted value of £350,000 for the completed research.

If the project is abandoned the client will receive £150,000 as compensation. You obtain the following information about the estimated cost to completion of the project.

Materials: contracts have already been exchanged for the purchase of £100,000 of materials. The material is highly specialised and has no alternative use on other projects. If not used on this project the material would have to be disposed of, incurring costs of £15,000.

Staffing: two highly skilled researchers each receive a salary of £25,000 pa. The other £10,000 is an allocation of part of the salary of a supervisor who is in overall charge of several projects. If the project is abandoned, the research workers would be declared redundant, each receiving £10,000 in compensation.

Overheads: plant and equipment costing £80,000 was bought at the commencement of the project, and a second year's depreciation charge (£40,000) is included in the estimated costs. The plant and equipment is highly specialised and has no other use. Estimated scrap value now is £10,000, but it is £4,000 in one year's time.

Required

(a) Give your recommendation whether on financial grounds the project should be continued or abandoned. Your calculations must be supported by clear statements of the reasons why a particular figure is included or excluded, and of any assumptions you make.

(b) Briefly explain any non-financial factors which need to be considered before finally deciding to abandon such a research project.

Answer

(a)

	Note	£	
Costs already incurred	(i)	0	
Materials	(ii)	(15,000)	saving
Staff costs	(iii)	30,000	
Overheads: plant and equipment	(iv)	6,000	
general overhead	(v)	0	
		21,000	
Contracted value		350,000	
Relevant future contribution from project		329,000	
Saving in compensation		150,000	
Total gain from continuing with project		479,000	

Therefore, on financial grounds the project should be continued.

Notes

(i) Costs already incurred are sunk and are not relevant to any future decision.

(ii) Contracts have already been exchanged and so the material must be paid for and the £100,000 cost is sunk. Using the material on this project would save the disposal costs.

(iii) The £10,000 allocated salary of the supervisor would not be affected by this project and so is not relevant. To continue to employ the skilled researchers would cost £15,000 more each than declaring them redundant.

(iv) The original cost of the equipment is a sunk cost. Depreciation is not a cash flow and is irrelevant. The relevant cost of using the equipment for this project is the £6,000 reduction in scrap value which would occur.

(v) General overheads are allocations of overheads which are unaffected by this decision.

(b) Non-financial factors which would need to be considered are as follows.

(i) The effect on the company's reputation for completing projects once commenced
(ii) The likelihood of further projects being received from the same customer
(iii) The effect on the morale of the research staff
(iv) Other opportunities which could use the facilities currently being employed
(v) The ease with which the skilled researchers could be replaced for future projects

4 IDENTIFYING RELEVANT COSTS

Exam focus point

The identification of relevant and non-relevant costs was an important technique in answering a **June 1999** question.

4.1 In this section we provide a fairly gentle introduction to the sort of thought processes that you will have to go through when you encounter a decision-making question. First some general points about machinery, labour, and particularly materials, that often catch people out.

(a) **Machinery user costs**

Once a machine has been bought its cost is a **sunk** cost. **Depreciation** is not a relevant cost, because it is not a cash flow. However, **using** machinery may involve some incremental costs. These costs might be referred to as **user costs** and they include hire charges and any fall in resale value of owned assets, through use.

(b) **Labour**

Often the labour force will be paid irrespective of the decision made and the costs are therefore **not incremental**. Take care, however, if the labour force could be put to an **alternative use**, in which case the relevant costs are the **variable costs** of the labour and associated variable overheads **plus** the **contribution forgone** from not being able to put it to its alternative use.

(c) **Materials**

(i) The relevant cost of raw materials is generally their current **replacement** cost, unless the materials have already been purchased and would not be replaced once used.

(ii) If materials have already been purchased but will not be replaced, then the relevant cost of using them is **either** (a) their current **resale** value **or** (b) the value they would obtain if they were put to an **alternative use**, if this is greater than their current resale value.

The **higher** of (a) or (b) is then the opportunity cost of the materials. If the materials have no resale value and no other possible use, then the relevant cost of using them for the opportunity under consideration would be nil.

The flowchart below shows how the relevant costs of materials can be identified, **provided that** the materials are **not in short supply**, and so have **no internal opportunity cost**.

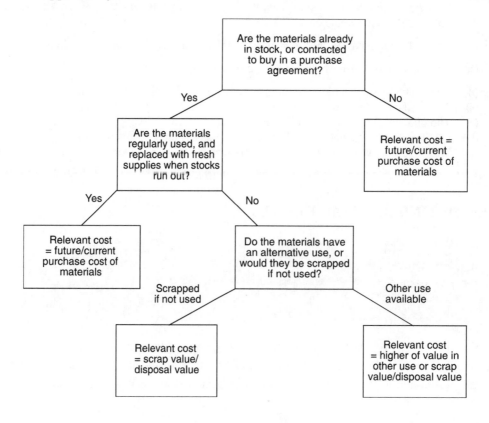

Question 3

O'Reilly Ltd has been approached by a customer who would like a special job to be done for him, and who is willing to pay £22,000 for it. The job would require the following materials:

Material	Total units required	Units already in stock	Book value of units in stock £/unit	Realisable value £/unit	Replacement cost £/unit
A	1,000	0	-	-	6
B	1,000	600	2	2.5	5
C	1,000	700	3	2.5	4
D	200	200	4	6.0	9

(a) Material B is used regularly by O'Reilly Ltd, and if units of B are required for this job, they would need to be replaced to meet other production demand.

(b) Materials C and D are in stock as the result of previous over-buying, and they have a restricted use. No other use could be found for material C, but the units of material D could be used in another job as substitute for 300 units of material E, which currently costs £5 per unit (of which the company has no units in stock at the moment).

What are the relevant costs of material, in deciding whether or not to accept the contract?

Answer

(a) Material A is not owned and would have to be bought in full at the replacement cost of £6 per unit.

(b) Material B is used regularly by the company. There are existing stocks (600 units) but if these are used on the contract under review a further 600 units would be bought to replace them. Relevant costs are therefore 1,000 units at the replacement cost of £5 per unit.

(c) Material C: 1,000 units are needed and 700 are already in stock. If used for the contract, a further 300 units must be bought at £4 each. The existing stocks of 700 will not be replaced. If they are used for the contract, they could not be sold at £2.50 each. The realisable value of these 700 units is an opportunity cost of sales revenue forgone.

(d) Material D: these are already in stock and will not be replaced. There is an opportunity cost of using D in the contract because there are alternative opportunities either to sell the existing stocks for £6 per unit (£1,200 in total) or avoid other purchases (of material E), which would cost 300 × £5 = £1,500. Since substitution for E is more beneficial, £1,500 is the opportunity cost.

(e) Summary of relevant costs:

	£
Material A (1,000 × £6)	6,000
Material B (1,000 × £5)	5,000
Material C (300 × £4) plus (700 × £2.50)	2,950
Material D	1,500
Total	15,450

4.2 EXAMPLE: RELEVANT COSTS

The following problem is a **minimum pricing** problem, calling for a pricing decision for a one-off product.

A company has just completed production of an item of special equipment for a customer only to be notified that this customer has now gone into liquidation. After much effort, the sales manager has been able to interest a potential buyer, White Knight Ltd, which has indicated a willingness to buy the machine if certain conversion work could first be carried out.

(a) The sales price of the **machine** to the original buyer had been fixed at £138,600 and had included an estimated normal profit mark-up of 10% on total costs. The costs incurred in the manufacture of the machine were:

	£
Direct materials	49,000
Direct labour	36,000
Variable overhead	9,000
Fixed production overhead	24,000
Fixed sales and distribution overhead	8,000
	126,000

(b) If the machine is **converted**, the production manager estimates that the cost of the extra work required would be:

Direct materials (at cost)   £9,600

Direct labour: Dept X - 6 men for 4 weeks @ £210 per man/week
                                              Dept Y - 2 men for 4 weeks @ £160 per man/week

(c) Variable overhead would be 20% of direct labour cost, and fixed production overhead would be absorbed at 83.33% of direct labour cost in Dept X and at 25% of direct labour cost in Dept Y.

(d) (i)   In the original machine, there are three types of material. Type A could be sold for scrap for £8,000. Type B could be sold for scrap for £2,400 but it would take 120 hours of casual labour paid at £3.50 per hour to put it into a condition in which it would be suitable for sale. Type C would need to be scrapped, at a cost to the company of £1,100.

(ii)   The direct materials required for the conversion are already in stock. If not needed for the conversion they would be used in the production of another machine in place of materials that would otherwise need to be purchased, and that would currently cost £8,800.

(iii) The conversion work would be carried out in two departments, X and Y. Department X is currently extremely busy and working at full capacity; it is estimated that its contribution to fixed overhead and profits is £2.50 per £1 of labour. Department Y, on the other hand, is short of work but for organisational reasons its labour force, which at the moment has a workload of only 40% of its standard capacity, cannot be reduced below its current level of 8 employees, all of whom are paid a wage of £160 per week.

(iv)   The designs and specifications of the original machine could be sold to an overseas customer for £4,500 if the machine is scrapped.

(v)   If conversion work is undertaken, a temporary supervisor would need to be employed for 4 weeks at a cost of £1,500. It is normal company practice to charge supervision costs to fixed overhead.

(vi)   The original customer has already paid a non-returnable deposit to the company of 12.5% of the selling price.

Required

Calculate the minimum price that the company should accept from White Knight Ltd for the converted machine. Explain clearly how you have reached this figure.

4.3   SOLUTION

Note that the money received from the original customer should be ignored. Just as costs incurred in the past are not relevant to a current decision about what to do in the future, **past revenues** are also irrelevant.

ESTIMATE OF MINIMUM PRICE FOR THE CONVERTED MACHINE

	£	£
Opportunity cost of using the direct materials types A, B and C (W1)		8,880
Opportunity cost of additional materials for conversion (W2)		8,800
Opportunity cost of work in department X		
Labour (W3)	5,040	
Variable overhead (W3)	1,008	
Contribution forgone (W3)	12,600	
		18,648
Opportunity cost: sale of design and specifications (W4)		4,500
Incremental costs:		
Variable production overheads in department Y (W5)		256
Fixed production overheads (W6)		1,500
Minimum price		42,584

Workings

1   The **cost of the original machine** is a past cost and so is not relevant, and the £126,000 of cost incurred should be excluded from the minimum price calculation. It is necessary, however, to consider the alternative use of the direct **materials** (opportunity costs) which would be forgone if the conversion work is carried out.

	£
Type A: Revenue from sales as scrap (note (a))	8,000
Type B: Revenue from sales as scrap, minus the additional cash	
costs necessary to prepare it for sale (£2,400 − (120 × £3.50))	1,980
Type C: Cost of disposal if the machine is not converted	
(a negative opportunity cost)	(1,100)
Total opportunity cost of materials Types A, B and C	8,880

By agreeing to the conversion of the machine, the company would therefore lose a net revenue of £8,880 from the alternative use of these materials.

2   The cost of additional direct **materials** for conversion is £9,600, but this is an historical cost. The relevant cost of these materials is the £8,800 which would be spent on new purchases if the conversion is carried out. If the work goes ahead, the materials in stock would be unavailable for production of the other machine mentioned in item (d)(ii) of the question and so the extra purchases of £8,800 would then be needed.

3   **Direct labour** in Departments X and Y is a fixed cost and the labour force will be paid regardless of the work they do or do not do. The cost of labour for conversion in Department Y is not a relevant cost because the work could be done without any extra cost to the company. In Department X, however, acceptance of the conversion work would oblige the company to divert production from other profitable jobs. The minimum contribution required from using Department X labour must be sufficient to cover the cost of the labour and variable overheads and then make an additional £2.50 in contribution per £1 of labour.

Department X - costs for direct labour hours spent on conversion:

6 men × 4 weeks × £210 =	£5,040
Variable overhead cost: £5,040 × 20% =	£1,008
Contribution forgone by diverting labour from other work:	
£2.50 per £1 of labour cost = £5,040 × 250% =	£12,600

4   If the machine is converted, the company cannot sell the designs and specifications. £4,500 is a relevant (**opportunity**) cost of accepting the conversion order.

5   **Variable overheads** in Department Y are relevant costs because they will only be incurred if production work is carried out. (It is **assumed** that if the workforce is idle, no variable overheads would be incurred.)

6   **Fixed overheads**, being mainly unchanged regardless of what the company decides to do, should be ignored because they are not relevant (incremental) costs. The additional cost of supervision should, however, be included as a relevant cost of the order because the £1,500 will not be spent unless the conversion work is done.

The assumptions in relevant costing

4.4   Many of the assumptions that are typically made in relevant costing may be **dropped** in **Paper 9 questions**.

Assumption	Comment
Cost behaviour patterns are known	If a department closes, say, the attributable fixed cost savings would be known.
The amount of fixed costs, unit variable costs, sales price and sales demand are known with certainty	It is possible to apply risk and uncertainty analysis to decisions and so recognise that what will happen in the future is not certain.
The objective of decision making in the short run is to maximise 'satisfaction'	Satisfaction is often regarded as 'short-term profit'. However, there are many other qualitative factors or financial considerations which may influence a final decision.
The information on which a decision is based is complete and reliable	Decisions usually have to be based on **imperfect information.**

4.5   We shall be exploring the implications of dropping these assumptions in the next few chapters.

5   CONTRIBUTION

5.1   Here is a brief reminder of some very basic material on **contribution**. As you will see in the next chapter this is often a key consideration in **Paper 9 questions**, so make sure you have a good grasp of the basics before continuing, by doing Questions 4 and 5.

Knowledge brought forward from Paper 3

CVP (breakeven) analysis: arithmetic

- Contribution = selling price − variable costs

- Total contribution required to achieve a target profit = fixed costs + target profit

- Breakeven point = activity level at which there is neither profit nor loss = activity level where total contribution equals fixed costs = total fixed cost ÷ contribution per unit = contribution required to break even ÷ contribution per unit

- Contribution/sales (C/S) ratio = profit/volume (P/V) ratio = (contribution ÷ sales) × 100%

- Sales revenue at breakeven point = fixed costs ÷ C/S ratio

- Margin of safety = budgeted sales units − breakeven sales units

---

Question 4

Tripod Ltd makes and sells three products, X, Y and Z. The selling price per unit and costs are as follows.

	X	Y	Z
Selling price per unit	£80	£50	£70
Variable cost per unit	£50	£10	£20

Fixed costs per month are £160,000. The maximum sales demand per month is 2,000 units of each product and the minimum sales demand is 1,000 of each.

Required

(a) Comment on the potential profitability of the company.

(b) Suppose that there is a fixed demand for X and Y of 1,500 units per month, which will not be exceeded, but for which firm orders have been received. How many units of Z would have to be sold to achieve a profit of at least £25,000 per month?

Answer

(a) When there is no indication about whether marginal or absorption costing is in use, it is simpler (and more informative too) to assess profitability with contribution analysis and marginal costing. This is the requirement in part (a) of the problem. The obvious analysis to make is a calculation of the worst possible and best possible results.

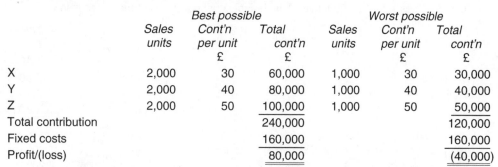

	Best possible			Worst possible		
	Sales units	Cont'n per unit £	Total cont'n £	Sales units	Cont'n per unit £	Total cont'n £
X	2,000	30	60,000	1,000	30	30,000
Y	2,000	40	80,000	1,000	40	40,000
Z	2,000	50	100,000	1,000	50	50,000
Total contribution			240,000			120,000
Fixed costs			160,000			160,000
Profit/(loss)			80,000			(40,000)

The company's potential profitability ranges from a profit of £80,000 to a loss of £40,000.

(b) The second part of the problem is a variation of a 'target profit' calculation.

		£	£
Required (minimum) profit per month			25,000
Fixed costs per month			160,000
Required contribution per month			185,000
Contribution to be earned from:	product X 1,500 × £30	45,000	
	product Y 1,500 × £40	60,000	
			105,000
Contribution required from product Z			80,000
Contribution per unit of Z			£50
Minimum required sales of Z per month			1,600 units

Question 5

Lisbon Ltd achieved the following results in 19X1.

	£'000	£'000
Sales (200,000 units)		2,000
Cost of sales		
Direct materials	800	
Direct labour	400	
Overheads	600	
		1,800
Profit		200

Throughout 19X1, sales were £10 per unit, and variable overheads, which vary with the number of units produced, amount to £1 per unit.

Required

Using CVP analysis, calculate the sales volume necessary to achieve a profit of £330,000 in 19X2 if, at the beginning of the year, the sales price is increased by £0.50 per unit, but the increases in costs above 19X1 levels are expected to be direct material 10%, direct labour 15%, variable overhead 10% and fixed overhead 20%. Comment on the result obtained.

Answer

In 19X1 sales were 200,000 units. The variable cost per unit is therefore as follows.

	19X1	19X2 prediction
	£	£
Direct materials	4	4.40
Direct labour	2	2.30
Variable overhead	1	1.10
	7 per unit	7.80 per unit

Fixed costs	£
19X1 total overhead (fixed plus variable)	600,000
Variable overhead in 19X1 (200,000 × £1)5	200,000
Fixed overhead in 19X1	400,000
Add 20%	80,000
Estimated fixed overhead in 19X2	480,000

In 19X2, a profit of £330,000 is required.

	£
Required profit	330,000
Fixed costs	480,000
Required contribution	810,000

Contribution per unit in 19X2 (£10.50 - £7.80) = £2.70
Required sales £810,000/£2.70 = 300,000 units

This is an increase of 50% on 19X1 volumes. It is first of all questionable whether such a large increase could be achieved in one year. Secondly, given such an increase, it is likely that output will be outside the *relevant range* of output (see below). Thirdly, estimates of fixed costs and variable costs are unlikely to be reliable.

Exam focus point

The calculation of estimated **customer specific contribution** was worth 9 marks in the **December 1997** exam. A breakeven calculation was required in the **June 1999** exam.

Chapter roundup

- Decisions should take the organisation's **objectives** as their point of reference.

- **Relevant costs**, the organisational **context** and **qualitative** matters are the chief factors to be considered.

- **Decision modelling** is a means of trying out a range of decisions before implementing the one that seems most appropriate. Successful modelling requires all the relevant variables to be identified and proper definition of the relationships between them.

- Relevant costs are **future incremental cash flows.**

- Key terms include **avoidable** cost, **opportunity** cost, **sunk** cost, **committed** cost and **notional** (or **imputed** cost).

- The total relevant cost a scarce resource consists of the **contribution**/incremental profit forgone from the next-best opportunity for using the scarce resource *plus* the **variable cost** of the scarce resource, that is, the cash expenditure to purchase the resource.

- Be sure that you read examination questions very carefully to determine the treatment of **labour**, **material** costs and **machinery** user costs.

- Despite its limitations it is very important to be fully conversant with the concept of CVP analysis and particularly **contribution** because it is central to many Paper 9 questions.

Quick quiz

1   What objectives might an organisation have? (see paras 1.3 - 1.5)

2   How might the organisational context affect the nature of a decision? (1.7, 1.8)

3   List nine qualitative matters that may affect decisions. (1.9)

4   What is the importance of the time horizon in decision making? (1.10)

5   What is an endogenous variable? (2.2)

6   Explain the terms incremental cost, sunk cost and committed cost. (3.1)

7   Draw a flowchart to identify how materials should be valued in decision making. (4.1)

8   How do you find the total contribution required to achieve a target profit? (5.1)

9   How do you find the maximum amount that should be paid in fixed costs, given a specific profit target? (5.1)

Question to try	Level	Marks	Time
5	Exam standard	30	54 mins

Chapter 6

PAPER 9 AND DECISION-MAKING TECHNIQUES

Chapter topic list	Syllabus reference
1 Old hat!	2(b), 4(b), 4(d)
2 Missing numbers	2(b), 4(b), 4(d)
3 Inputs and outputs from processes	2(b), 4(b), 4(d)
4 Choosing between options	2(b), 4(b), 4(d)
5 Do now or do later?	2(b), 4(b), 4(d)
6 Discounted cash flow techniques	4(c)
7 Spreadsheets and discounted cash flow	4(c)

Introduction

We start this chapter by briefly reviewing decisions using the **conventional** categories of 'make or buy' and so on. However, these pigeon holes are not especially useful for Paper 9. **Paper 9** decision making techniques are largely a matter of multiplying, dividing, adding, subtracting and applying percentages. The problem is working out which numbers to do what to!

The main part of this chapter therefore presents a series of examples illustrating some of the typical hurdles that the examiner expects you to be able to cope with. It also contains some useful advice on **presentation** and how to score **easy marks**.

At the end of the chapter we give a fairly full reminder of **discounted cash flow** techniques, since students are often unnecessarily frightened of the time value of money.

Core areas of the syllabus identified by the examiner and covered in this chapter: **use of DCF** in decision making.

1 OLD HAT!

1.1 In this section we work very briefly through some material that should be very familiar to you from **Paper 8** studies, just to reassure you that you are on fairly familiar territory.

> **Exam focus point**
> **Paper 9** questions do not fit comfortably into the conventional 'make or buy', 'discontinuance', 'process further' etc categories, even though these terms are used in the Teaching Guide.

Make or buy decisions

1.2 These involve a decision by an organisation about whether it should either make a product using its own resources or pay another organisation to make the product.

1.3 Relevant costs are the **differential costs** between the two options (differences in unit variable costs plus differences in directly attributable fixed costs).

1.4 **Other considerations**

(a) The **make** option gives management direct control of the work.

(b) The **buy** option has the benefit of sub-contractor's skill and expertise, but their reliability has to be considered.

(c) The **buy** option means that it may be possible to put the internal spare capacity freed up to other uses.

1.5 In a situation where a company must sub-contract work to make up a **shortfall in its own in-house capabilities,** its total costs will be minimised if those units bought out from a sub-contractor have the **lowest extra variable cost per unit of scarce resource**.

1.6 For example if machine hours are scarce a company should minimise the extra variable costs of sub-contracting per machine hour saved. The calculation might look like this.

	A	B	C
	£	£	£
Variable cost of making	20	36	24
Variable cost of buying	29	40	34
Extra variable cost of buying	9	4	10
Machine hours saved by buying (say)	3 hrs	2 hrs	4 hrs
Extra variable cost of buying per hour saved	£3	£2	£2.50

1.7 The priority for **making** the items in-house will be in the order: **A then C then B**. It is better to pay £2 extra to an outsider than to pay £3 extra.

(We shall look at the technique of **limiting factor analysis** in full in the next Chapter.)

> **Exam focus point**
> What might be termed a 'make or buy' decision featured in a **June 1998** exam question but, typically, vast reams of information had to be trawled through and the relevant information picked out.

Shutdown or discontinuance decisions

1.8 In Paper 9 these tend to be questions about product-line profitability using different methods of costing, such as ABC versus absorption costing. We have covered this in some detail already.

Joint product decisions

1.9 When a manufacturing company carries out **process** operations in which two or more joint products are made from a common process, a number of decision problems can arise.

(a) If the joint products can be sold either in their existing condition at the 'split-off' point at the end of common processing or after further separate processing, a decision should be taken about whether to sell each joint product at the split-off point or after **further processing.**

(b) If there is extra sales demand for one joint product but not another, it will be necessary to decide whether it is worth making more output of *both* joint products in order to sell the extra output of one (and dispose of the unwanted quantities of the other).

1.10 In either case the decision is made on the basis of a comparison of the **incremental costs and revenues**.

Exam focus point

In spite of the above, it is safer **not to think in formulaic terms** about the 'sort' of question you are doing, because in Paper 9 you are likely to have to draw techniques from a number of different areas of study, or else **follow the instructions you are given**, perhaps using a technique invented by the management accountant described in the question (ie by the **examiner**).

2   MISSING NUMBERS

2.1 In the next few sections we look at some typical examples of problems that have come up in Paper 9 questions, draw your attention to a number of useful 'tricks' or **ways of phrasing things** that might catch you out or confuse you in the exam and give you a few tips on scoring **easy marks**.

2.2 To start with an easy example, quite often you will read a question and **think** you know what to do with the figures but then find that certain information that you would **expect** to have does not seem to be there.

2.3 The information is not there because the examiner expects you to be totally familiar with standard techniques and to be able to derive the missing numbers from the information you have by **working backwards**.

2.4   EXAMPLE: MISSING NUMBERS

Sales of product X are 50,000 units per annum. Fixed costs are £100,000. Net profit per unit is £5. The producers are considering a change in design which will reduce production costs by £0.75 per unit but it is estimated that this will also reduce annual sales by 7% per annum.

Required

(a) Prepare an analysis which shows the estimated effect on annual profit if this change is implemented and enables management to check whether the proposal will achieve an annual target profit increase of £10,000.

(b) Calculate the percentage reduction in sales at which the implementation of the change would result in the same total profit as that earned before the change.

Exam focus point

This example is based on a question set under the old syllabus, but by the current Paper 9 examiner.

2.5   SOLUTION: PART (a)

If you are not sure how the numbers fit together or what information you do and do not have, begin by doing a **proforma**. (There is no need to fill in the question marks. These are to remind how the figures link up.)

	£
Sales price per unit	?
Production costs per unit	(?)
Contribution	?
Fixed costs	(?)
Net profit	?

Now fill in the gaps working from the bottom up.

	£
Sales price per unit	?
Production costs per unit	?
Contribution (balance)	7
Fixed costs (£100,000/50,000)	2
Net profit per unit	5

There are still some missing numbers, but do we actually need to know the selling price or the variable costs per unit?

(a) The effect on sales is a 7% drop: $50,000 \times 7\% = 3,500$ units.

(b) This means a loss of contribution of $3,500 \times £7 = £24,500$

(c) Remaining units however, will each make £0.75 extra contribution because of the reduction in production costs. $(50,000 – 3,500) \times £0.75 = £34,875$.

(d) The net benefit is therefore $£(34,875 – 24,500) = \underline{\textbf{£10,375}}$. The proposal **will** achieve the required increase in profit.

2.6 SOLUTION: PART (b)

The missing number here seems to be the total profit earned before the change. This is easy $(50,000 \times £5 = £250,000)$.

However, the number you really want is the **contribution** that needs to be achieved. Again this is now easy (target contribution = total profit + fixed costs = £250,000 + £100,000 = £350,000).

The change means that contribution increases by £0.75 to £7.75 per unit. To earn £350,000 we therefore need to sell £350,000/£7.75 = **45,162 units**. (Note that we **round up**, because we cannot sell a fraction of a unit.)

The reduction in absolute terms is 4,838 units.

However, read the question. The **percentage** reduction is 4,838/50,000 = **9.7%**.

Commentary (easy marks)

2.7 If you were asked to comment on your results, the main point to note is that the original **estimate** of the reduction in demand must be **highly uncertain**. The reduction only needs to be 2.7% higher for the company to gain no benefit from the change at all.

2.8 You might also note that if the reduction in cost is achieved by reducing **quality** this may have a knock-on effect on customers' **perceptions** of the company's **other products**.

Question 1

In part (b) of the above example, why not simply divide the target profit by the new profit per unit of £5.75?

Answer

Think about the way that fixed costs are spread over the number of units sold. Is the new profit per unit £5.75?

2.9 EXAMPLE: MORE MISSING NUMBERS

A company produced 15,000 units last year which represented 80% capacity utilisation. The selling price per unit was £15. Variable costs were £8.25 per unit and fixed costs were £5 per unit. Next year prices will be increased by 2%. All costs will be subject to 3% inflation.

Required

Calculate the **percentage capacity utilisation** at which the company will break even next year.

2.10 SOLUTION

This can be solved using algebra.

The company will break even where sales revenue – variable costs = fixed costs.

Let x = the break even number of units sold

Sales revenue = £15 × 1.02 × x = £15.3x
Variable costs = £8.25 × 1.03 × x = £8.5x
Fixed costs = 15,000 × £5 × 1.03 = £77,250

∴ 15.3x – 8.5x = 77,250 and so x = 11,360

However, now we need to know what proportion 11,360 units is of **full** capacity. If 15,000 units represents 80% capacity then full capacity must be 15,000/80% = 18,750.

The company will therefore break even at 11,360/18,750 = **60%** capacity.

3 INPUTS AND OUTPUTS FROM PROCESSES

3.1 As mentioned in Chapter 4 another favourite feature in a Paper 9 question is forcing students to deal with the idea that **what goes into** a manufacturing process generally needs to be **more than what comes out**. Some people find this quite hard to get to grips with, so we shall elaborate on the idea.

3.2 Here are some figures.

Loss in Process 1   7%   Loss in Process 2   2%   Loss in Process 3   17%

Another way of putting this would be to say that, for example, 93% (ie 100% - 3%) of the inputs to Process 1 are carried forward to Process 2.

Another way would be to say that **what goes in** to Process 1 is 107.53% (1/0.93) **more than what comes out** and goes into Process 2.

3.3 Suppose 100 units are input to Process 1. Here are two different ways of looking at what will happen.

	Input	Proportion c/fwd	Output		Input	Proportion b/fwd	Output
Process 1	100.00	0.93	93.00	**Process 3**	75.65	1/0.83	91.14
Process 2	93.00	0.98	91.14	**Process 2**	91.14	1/0.98	93.00
Process 3	91.14	0.83	75.65	**Process 1**	93.00	1/0.93	100.00

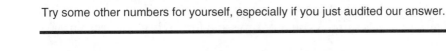

Question 2

(a) How many units must be input in the above example to produce 20 units of finished goods?
(b) If 20 units are input to Process 1 how many units of finished goods will be produced?

Answer

(a) $20 \times 1/0.83 \times 1/0.98 \times 1/0.93 = 26.44$.
(b) $20 \times 0.93 \times 0.98 \times 0.83 = 15.13$

Try some other numbers for yourself, especially if you just audited our answer.

3.4 EXAMPLE: INPUTS TO PROCESSES

A bicycle manufacturer is considering trying a new supplier for pedals. At present pedals cost £124 for 50, but the new supplier has offered them for £110 for 50. If the cheaper pedals are used they are more likely to be damaged in production: estimates suggest that 4% will have to be scrapped as compared with 2% at present.

Required

If the company makes 10,000 bicycles per year what will be the effect on profit of changing to the new supplier?

3.5 SOLUTION

Don't forget that a bicycle has **two** pedals!

	£
Present inputs $(2 \times 10,000) \times 1/0.98 \times £124/50$	50,612.25
Revised inputs $(2 \times 10,000) \times 1/0.96 \times £110/50$	45,833.33
Extra profit	4,778.92

4 CHOOSING BETWEEN OPTIONS

4.1 In this section we look at an alternative choice type question, which is basically a matter of comparing relevant costs and revenues, although this example has a typical Paper 9 twist in the wording.

4.2 The example we have chosen is one where there is a strong temptation to just tap away on a calculator and write down the final answer. This will not earn you any marks if you happen to tap the wrong figure, because nobody will know what you did wrong. In other words the main issue in this section is the value of **good presentation**.

Exam focus point
The original question, set in **June 1994**, was worth 8 marks and was linked up to a larger question.

BPP
PUBLISHING

4.3 EXAMPLE: OPTIONS AVAILABLE

A Ltd has three options for Machine A.

Option 1 Dispose of Machine A in one years time for £8,750

Option 2 Modify Machine A now at a cost of £6,250. This choice is being considered in conjunction with another decision, Decision A.

Decision A would mean that production output would increase by 25,000 units per annum except in the first year when 25% of the production enhancement would be lost due to running in. Production units sell for £20 per unit and have variable costs of £7.50 per unit.

The modification will mean that Machine A can only be sold for £5,000 in one year's time. However, it will reduce the production enhancement loss from 25% to 15%.

Option 3 Modify Machine A now at a cost of £2,500, which will mean that the company does not have to hire an alternative machine at a cost of £7,500. This modification would mean that Machine A could only be sold for £625 in one year's time.

Required

What should the company do with Machine A? *Ignore the time value of money.*

4.4 SOLUTION: EASY MARKS IF YOU'RE A PRIZE WINNER

Here is how to lay out a **summary** of your answer that would instantly put you in the running for **Best Overall Answer**.

Summary final answer

	(Saving)/Cost	*Reference*
Option 1	£(8,750)	W1
Option 2	£(30,000)	W2
Option 3	£(4,375)	W3

Conclusion: <u>Option 2 is clearly the best because it gives the highest revenue.</u>

4.5 SOLUTION: EASY MARKS IF YOU'RE KEEN TO GET ON

Here, on the other hand, is how good **pass-standard** students should **lay out** the **Workings** that markers would scrutinise if the overall answer happened **not** be right.

Workings for Question X (a)

1   **Option 1**

The revenue from this **Option 1** is given in the question: £8,750.

2   **Option 2**

	£
Reduction in impact of production losses(25,000 × (25-15)% × £(20 –7.50)	(31,250)
Modification (given)	6,250
Sales value after one year (given)	(5,000)
Saving	(30,000)

3   **Option 3**

	£
Modification (given)	2,500
Hire costs avoided (given)	(7,500)
Disposal cost (given)	625
Saving	(4,375)

Wording

4.6   The 'double negative' **wording of Option 2** may have confused you. The enhancement is 25,000 units × £12.50 contribution = £312,500. Decision A reduces this enhancement **by 25%** to £234,375. Use of machine A only reduces it **by 15%** to £265,625 and therefore *saves* £31,250

The importance of showing workings

4.7   If the marker can **see** from your workings that you have **read the question**, extracted the **right information**, and had a good go at **using the techniques** that you should know about, having studied for this paper, there is a good chance that you will get through the exam quite comfortably.

Show 'em what you've got!

4.8   The **key point** is that you **let the marker see** what you are doing. This is simply a matter of layout and labelling. **Every examiner**, in every subject, for every professional body, **always complains** about the **layout and labelling** of students' answers. **Get wise to this!**

   (a)   **Number your workings** consecutively. You may end up with Workings 1 to 50 if you are not quite sure how to proceed at the outset, and experiment with the numbers a bit, or just Workings 1 –3 if you sorted out exactly how to do the question from the start. It does not matter **how many** workings you do. Only **layout, labelling** and **cross-referencing** matter in the exam.

   (b)   Always **label your workings** and tables with headings and side-headings, and show units used (£, kg, units, etc). (Note the extent of the labelling in the workings shown above, in spite of the fact that most of the figures are given.)

   (c)   As you go along, **do a summary** on a separate clean page of whatever you expect to be your **final figures** and **state your conclusion** if it is not immediately clear.

   (d)   Without fail your summary **must be CROSS-REFERENCED** to your **Workings**, because you will get marks for sensible workings, even if the answer is wrong. (See any **Solution** in this book.)

Developing good practice

4.9   Our advice is simple: you will not go far wrong if you learn to **copy** the style of the **SOLUTIONS** to the examples or questions that you see in **this book** (except, of course, where we say 'work out such and such for yourself' to make you join in: you should **not** ask the marker to do this!).

5 DO NOW OR DO LATER?

5.1 The next example shows you how to lay out an answer to a more complicated relevant costs question.

5.2 EXAMPLE: DO NOW OR DO LATER?

A Ltd currently carries out process B the output from which can be sold for £20 per unit and has variable unit costs of £7.50 per unit. Process B has directly attributable fixed operating costs of £40,000 per annum.

A Ltd also carries out process C by using equipment that has running costs of £25,000 per annum. The equipment could be sold *now* for £50,000 (but this would incur dismantling costs of £7,500) or in one year's time for £45,000 with dismantling costs of £8,750.

Process B could be adapted so that it incorporated Process C.

(a) The existing process B machinery would have to be removed, either now at a dismantling cost of £12,500 and with the sale of the machinery for £100,000, or in one year's time for £75,000 with dismantling costs of £13,750.

(b) Alternative Process B machinery would have to be leased. This would cost £10,000 per annum and have annual fixed running costs of £30,000.

The existing Process B machinery originally cost £250,000 when bought five years ago. It is being depreciated at 10% per annum.

Required

Prepare an analysis on an incremental opportunity cost basis to decide on financial grounds whether to adopt Process B immediately or to delay it for one year. *Ignore the time value of money.*

5.3 SOLUTION

The best approach to a complex either/or problem like this is to draw up a **three-column table** with columns for the first option (adapt now) and the second (adapt later), and a third column for the **differences** between the options (Column 1 minus Column 2).

	Adapt now	*Adapt in One year*	*Net (savings)/ costs*
Savings	£	£	£
Sale of Process C equipment	(50,000)	(45,000)	(5,000)
Sale of Process B machinery	(100,000)	(75,000)	(25,000)
Costs			
Fixed operating costs	0	40,000	(40,000)
Removal of Process B machinery	12,500	13,750	(1,250)
Process C – running costs	0	25,000	(25,000)
Process C – dismantling costs	7,500	8,750	(1,250)
Leased Process B equipment running costs	30,000	0	30,000
Leasing costs	10,000	0	10,000
Net (savings) less costs			(57,500)

Conclusion: <u>The analysis shows that adapting now will bring savings of £57,500 more than adapting in one year.</u>

A methodical answer

5.4 There are lessons to be learned here about extracting information from complex Paper 9 questions. Note the following points.

(a) You should do **savings and costs separately** and put **one type in brackets** (it doesn't matter which way round you do this as long as you are consistent: we have put savings in brackets in keeping with the accounting convention that they are credits). This is important because it is easy to get the signs wrong when you come to work out the differences.

(b) Subtract column 2 from column 1 taking **care with the minus signs**. For instance:

$$-50{,}000 - (-45{,}000) = -5{,}000$$

(c) Adapting now means that the fixed operating costs of £40,000 will not be incurred so a **nought** goes in the Now column. Adapting in one year means that fixed operating costs of £40,000 will have to be paid for another year. The net benefit of adapting now is therefore a saving of £40,000.

(d) There are some **red herrings** in the information given. Unit selling prices and costs are not relevant, since they do not change, whenever Process B is adapted. Original cost and depreciation are not relevant because they are not future cash flows.

6 DISCOUNTED CASH FLOW TECHNIQUES

6.1 The magic words **ignore the time value of money** appeared in the last two examples, but we **cannot** ignore it any more.

Exam focus point

The knowledge brought forward boxes below show you what you should know already. **Paper 9** does not require any more advanced knowledge than this (**very** simple calculations were required in **December 1999** for example), but it may well **combine** DCF with other techniques that you have already seen, such as adjusting cash flows for inflation before discounting. A question set in **December 1995** asked for this approach.

Knowledge brought forward from Paper 8

Discounted cash flow techniques

- **Discounting** involves determining the equivalent worth today (**present value (PV)**) of a future cash flow (FV). Only **relevant costs** are used.

  PV = FV × 1/(1+r)n, where 1/(1+r)n = discount factor

  Example: the PV of £100,000 received in five years if r is 6%pa = £100,000 × 1/(1.06)5 = £74,726.

- DCF techniques look at the **cash flows** of a project, not accounting profits. The timing of cash flows is taken into account by discounting them.

- The **net present value (NPV) method** of using DCF to evaluate an investment is as follows.

  - Work out the PVs of all cash flows (income and expenditure) related to the investment using an organisation's cost of capital/target rate of return.

  - Work out a net total (a net present value (NPV)).

  - If the NPV is positive the investment is acceptable, if it is negative it is unacceptable.

- The **internal rate of return (IRR) method** calculates the exact rate of return at which the investment's NPV = 0.

  - If IRR > target rate of return, the investment is acceptable.
  - If IRR < target rate of return, the investment is unacceptable.

- To determine the IRR of a one-or-two-year investment, equate the PV of costs with the PV of benefits.

- To determine the IRR of a more lengthy investment, use **interpolation**.

  - Calculate a rough estimate of the IRR using 2/3 × (profit ÷ initial investment).

  - Calculate the NPV using the rough estimate of the IRR as r. If the NPV is negative, recalculate the NPV using a lower rate but if the NPV is positive, recalculate the NPV using a higher rate.

  - Calculate the IRR using a% + [(A/(A − B)) × (b − a)]% where

    a = one interest rate   b = the other interest rate
    A = NPV at rate a   B = NPV at rate b

- The following **timing of cash flow conventions** are used in DCF.

  - A cash flow at the beginning of an investment project (ie 'now') occurs in year 0, for which the discount factor is always 1.

  - Cash flows during the course of a time period are assumed to occur at the period end.

  - Cash flows at the beginning of a time period are assumed to occur at the end of the previous time period.

- An **annuity** is a constant sum of money each year for a given number of years. The PV of an annuity is calculated using cumulative PV factor tables. The cumulative PV factor for years 3 to 6 = cumulative PV factor for years 1 to 6 minus cumulative PV factor for years 1 to 2.

- **Other methods of investment appraisal** include the **accounting rate of return (ARR) method** and the **payback method**.

Question 3

LCH Limited manufactures product X which it sells for £5 per unit. Variable costs of production are currently £3 per unit, and fixed costs 50p per unit. A new machine is available which would cost £90,000 but which could be used to make product X for a variable cost of only £2.50 per unit. Fixed costs, however, would increase by £7,500 per annum as a direct result of purchasing the machine. The machine would have an expected life of 4 years and a resale value after that time of £10,000. Sales of product X are estimated to be 75,000 units per annum. If LCH Limited expects to earn at least 12% per annum from its investments, should the machine be purchased?

Answer

Savings are 75,000 × (£3 - £2.50) = £37,500 per annum. Additional costs are £7,500 per annum. Net cash savings are therefore £30,000 per annum. (Remember, depreciation is not a cash flow and must be ignored as a 'cost'.)

The first step in calculating an NPV is to establish the relevant costs year by year. All future cash flows arising as a direct consequence of the decision should be taken into account.

It is assumed that the machine will be sold for £10,000 at the end of year 4.

Note. It is a convention of DCF that receipts and payments made during the course of a year are assumed to be made at the year end. Thus the net savings of £30,000 are assumed to occur at the end of year 1, year 2 etc.

Year	Cash flow £	PV factor (12%)	PV of cash flow £
0	(90,000)	1.000	(90,000)
1	30,000	0.893	26,790
2	30,000	0.797	23,910
3	30,000	0.712	21,360
4	40,000	0.636	25,440
		NPV	+7,500

The NPV is positive and so the project is acceptable: it will earn more than 12% pa.

Question 4

LC Ltd is considering the manufacture of a new product which would involve the use of both a new machine (costing £150,000) and an existing machine, which cost £80,000 two years ago and has a current net book value of £60,000. There is sufficient capacity on this machine, which has so far been under-utilised. Annual sales of the product would be 5,000 units, selling at £32 per unit. Unit costs would be as follows.

	£
Direct labour (4 hours @ £2)	8
Direct materials	7
Fixed costs including depreciation	9
	24

The project would have a 5 year life, after which the new machine would have a net residual value of £10,000. Because direct labour is continually in short supply, labour resources would have to be diverted from other work which currently earns a contribution of £1.50 per direct labour hour. The fixed overhead absorption rate would be £2.25 per hour (£9 per unit) but actual expenditure on fixed overhead would not alter. Working capital requirements would be £10,000 in the first year, rising to £15,000 in the second year and remaining at this level until the end of the project, when it will all be recovered. The company's cost of capital is 20%.

Required

Assess whether the project worthwhile.

Answer

The relevant cash flows are as follows.

			£
(a)	Year 0	Purchase of new machine	150,000

			£
(b)	Years 1-5	Contribution from new product (5,000 units × £(32 – 15))	85,000
		Less contribution forgone ((5,000 × 4) × £1.50)	30,000
			55,000

(c) The project requires £10,000 of working capital at the beginning of year 1 and a further £5,000 at the start of year 2. Increases in working capital reduce the net cash flow for the period to which they relate. When the working capital tied up in the project is 'recovered' at the end of the project, it will provide an extra cash inflow (for example debtors will eventually pay up).

(d) All other costs, which are past costs, notional accounting costs, or costs which would be incurred anyway without the project, are not relevant to the investment decision.

(e) The NPV is calculated as follows

Year	Equipment £	Working capital £	Contribution £	Net cash flow £	Discount factor 20%	PV of net cash flow £
0	(150,000)	(10,000)		(160,000)	1.000	(160,000)
1		(5,000)		(5,000)	0.833	(4,165)
1-5			55,000	55,000	2.991	164,505
5	10,000	15,000		25,000	0.402	10,050
					NPV =	10,390

The NPV is positive and the project is worthwhile, although there is not much margin for error. Some risk analysis of the project is recommended.

Question 5

Find the IRR of the project given below and state whether the project should be accepted if the company requires a minimum return of 17%.

Time		£
0	Investment	(4,000)
1	Receipts	1,200
2	"	1,410
3	"	1,875
4	"	1,150

Answer

The total receipts are £5,635 giving a total profit of £1,635 and average profits of £409. The average investment is £2,000. The ARR is £409 ÷ £2,000 = 20%. Two thirds of the ARR is approximately 14%. The initial estimate of the IRR that we shall try is therefore 14%.

		Try 14%		Try 16%	
Time	Cash flow £	Discount factor 14%	PV £	Discount factor 16%	PV £
0	(4,000)	1.000	(4,000)	1.000	(4,000)
1	1,200	0.877	1,052	0.862	1,034
2	1,410	0.769	1,084	0.743	1,048
3	1,875	0.675	1,266	0.641	1,202
4	1,150	0.592	681	0.552	635
		NPV	+ 83	NPV	(81)

The IRR must be less than 16%, but higher than 14%. The NPVs at these two costs of capital will be used to estimate the IRR. Using the interpolation formula:

$$IRR = 14\% + [(83/(83 + 81)) \times (16\% - 14\%)] = 15.01\%$$

The IRR is, in fact, exactly 15%.

The project should be rejected as the IRR is less than the minimum return demanded.

---

7 SPREADSHEETS AND DISCOUNTED CASH FLOW

7.1 Modern spreadsheet packages take all of the hard work out of discounted cash flow calculations. All you have to do to create a presentable document is set up the initial table. Some examples follow, using Microsoft Excel. Other packages, like Lotus 1-2-3, work in a very similar way.

> ## Exam focus point
>
> The examiner will **not** expect you to know about the **specific function names** used by a particular spreadsheet package (this would be unfair because different people use different packages), but you might be asked to **comment generally** on how the use of a spreadsheet package could help with a DCF problem.
>
> What follows should help to undermine the popular misconception that DCF is laborious and difficult to do in practice. You might even like to try it yourself.

7.2 EXAMPLE: THE NPV METHOD

To find the NPV of a project all you need do is enter the project's estimated cash flow details into a spreadsheet. Here is an example for an organisation which has a cost of capital of 15%.

	A	B	C	D	E	F
1	Year	Cash flow				
2		£				
3	0	(100,000)				
4	1	60,000				
5	2	80,000				
6	3	40,000				
7	4	30,000				
8						
9	NPV	£56,119				
10						
11						
12						
13						
14						

This cell contains the formula:

=NPV (15%, B4:B7) + B3

7.3 Cell B9 contains a '**function reference**' which tells the computer to do a NPV calculation. The reference in Excel is, believe it or not, **NPV**. In brackets are the interest rate and the range of cells containing the values to be discounted. (The = sign tells Excel that this entry is a formula, like @ in Lotus 123.)

7.4 In Excel the package assumes that the **first** cash flow given occurs at the end of time 1 and so time 0 cash flows have to be added (or subtracted as appropriate) outside the brackets. The time 0 flow is not discounted because it occurs *now*.

7.5 EXAMPLE: CUMULATIVE DISCOUNTING

The spreadsheet package for a project with a cash outflow of £30,000 every year for 6 years, assuming a cost of capital of 14%, could be set out as follows.

	A	B	C	D
1	Year	Cash flow		
2		£		
3	1 to 6	(30,000)	£116,660.03	
4				
5				
6				
7				
8				
9				
10				
11				
12				
13				
14				

This cell contains the formula:

=PV (14%, 6, B3)

7.6 The function reference is **PV**, the period is 6 years, the cell referred to (B3) contains the absolute value, £30,000. Note that the answer given by Excel is **more accurate** than the one calculated using cumulative present value tables because of **rounding**.

7.7 EXAMPLE: INTERNAL RATE OF RETURN

Perhaps best of all, spreadsheet packages can calculate IRRs at lightning speed. Here is an example.

	A	B	C	D	E
1	Year	Cash flow			
2		£			
3	0	(60,000)			
4	1	20,000			
5	2	40,000			
6	3	30,000			
7	4	10,000			
8					
9	IRR	26.03%			
10					
11					
12					
13					
14					

This cell contains the formula:

=IRR (B3:B7)

Why learn to do DCF 'by hand'?

7.8 You may be wondering why accountancy bodies put you through the agony of learning the 'manual' method of DCF calculations when they are so easy on a computer. The pragmatic reason, of course, is that you will not have a computer to hand when you are doing your Paper 9 exam. Far more importantly, however, you **must learn the theory** behind the method for two reasons.

(a) So that when, in practice, you are using a computer you can see whether it is giving you **reasonable results**. It is still very easy to key in the wrong figure, the wrong formulae, the wrong cell references and so on.

(b) So that you can **explain** what your computer's calculations mean to managers not familiar with these techniques.

Exam focus point

A graphical representation of the relationship between NPV and IRR was required in the **June 1997** exam. Could you have remembered how to do this from your Paper 8 Studies?

Chapter roundup

- Decision making in management accounting is **conventionally** divided into categories such as 'make or buy', 'shutdown' and so on, but in Paper 9 it is **not helpful to pigeon-hole your knowledge** in this way.

- A common problem in Paper 9 questions is what appears to be **missing information**. The information is not missing really: it has to be extracted by working around the problem. This requires a firm grasp of basic concepts such as contribution.

- Another favourite feature of Paper 9 question is the concept that **what goes in** to a manufacturing process must often be **more than what comes out,** because of losses in process.

- Well presented **workings** are the key to **easy marks** in most exams that involve calculations. **Number** your workings, **label** them clearly and make sure you have a **final answer** (clearly labelled as such) which is **cross referenced** to the relevant workings.

- Relevant cost questions involving choices are often best laid out in **columns** (Do this/Do that/Difference). Care is needed with minus signs.

- Examination questions sometimes tell you to **ignore** the time value of money, but not always. You need to be confident at using the **discounted cash flow** techniques that you learned for Paper 8.

Quick quiz

1 How should a company decide on a production strategy if it has limited in-house production facilities, but can buy components from outside? (see para 1.5).

2 Can sales price be found given a figure for variable costs and fixed costs? (2.5)

3 Draw up a table showing how to deal with inputs and outputs to processes that experience losses. (3.3)

4 What four features should final answers and workings have? (4.8)

5 What is the formula for calculating a present value? (6.1)

Question to try	Level	Marks	Time
6	Exam standard	35	63 mins

Chapter 7

SCARCE RESOURCES AND LINEAR PROGRAMMING

Chapter topic list	Syllabus reference
1 Scarce resources	2(b), 4(b), 4(d)
2 Linear programming: the graphical technique	4(c)
3 Linear programming: computer models	4(c)
4 Assumptions and limitations of linear programming	4(c)

Introduction

This chapter begins with a reminder of what a scarce resource is and how to do the technique of **ranking** products in order of **contribution-earning ability.** You should have studied this before, but it has featured in several Paper 9 questions, and serves as a good introduction to linear programming.

Linear programming is a more complicated technique of allocating resources in order to achieve the best results. You will have covered the basics of the **graphical approach** to linear programming in your studies for Paper 3 and so we just give a summary of what you should already know. We then move on to consider **sensitivity analysis**, **shadow prices** and **allowable increases.** In the second half of the chapter we look at how **computer models** can be used to solve all types of limiting factor problem, both simple and complex.

Core areas of the syllabus identified by the examiner and covered in this chapter: **use of limiting factors** in decision making, **formulation and interpretation of linear programming models**.

1   SCARCE RESOURCES

1.1   When an organisation provides a range of products or services to its markets, but has a restricted amount of resources available to it, then it will have to make a decision about what **product mix** (or mix of services) it will provide. Its volume of output and sales will be constrained by the limited resources rather than by sales demand, and so management faces a decision about **how scarce capacity should best be used**. The scarce resource might be material, machine time, cash or labour, for example.

KEY TERM

An organisation has a **scarce resource** if it does not have enough of the resource to undertake every available opportunity for making more contribution towards profit. Thus machine time would be scarce if every machine was being operated at full capacity, without being able to produce enough output to meet sales demand in full.

1.2   From a management accounting point of view, the assumption would be that a firm faced with a problem of one or more scarce resources would select a product or service mix that would maximise overall profitability, and so **maximise** total **contribution**.

1.3   The technique for establishing the contribution-maximising product or service mix differs according to whether there is **just one** or **two or more** scarce resources.

Question 1

The word 'scarce' in this context is potentially misleading, because it does not necessarily mean that there is a worldwide shortage, it simply means that the firm cannot in the short-term obtain all the resources it needs to carry out a particular task. Consider the following cases.

(a)   What resources would be scarce for a two-partner firm of certified accountants that wished to tender for the audit of Barclays Bank?

(b)   What resources would be scarce for a small building firm that wished to build a football stadium?

As you probably realise yourself in practice, the commonest scarce resources are **time** and **money**.

Decisions involving one scarce resource

1.4   When there is just one scarce resource, the technique for establishing the contribution-maximising product mix or service mix is to **rank** the products or services in order of **contribution-earning ability per unit of the scarce resource**. You should have learned this technique of **limiting factor analysis** for Paper 8, but it is still important for Paper 9. Here are a series of examples to illustrate this technique and the further considerations involved.

1.5   EXAMPLE: ONE SCARCE RESOURCE

Spice Ltd makes two products, Posh and Ugly, for which there is unlimited sales demand at the budgeted sales price of each. A Posh takes 8 hours to make, and has a variable cost of £36 and a sales price of £72. An Ugly takes 5 hours to make, and has a variable cost of £24 and a sales price of £48. Both products use the same type of labour, which is in restricted supply. Which product should be made in order to maximise profits?

1.6   SOLUTION AND DISCUSSION

(a)   There is no limitation on sales demand, but **labour** is in restricted supply, and so to determine the profit-maximising production mix, we must rank the products in order of **contribution-earning capability per labour hour**.

	Posh	Ugly
	£	£
Sales price	72	48
Variable costs	36	24
Contribution	36	24
Hours per unit	8 hrs	5 hrs
Contribution per labour hour	£4.50	£4.80
Ranking	**2nd**	**1st**

Although Posh units have the higher unit contribution, Ugly units are more profitable because they make a **greater contribution per unit** in each scarce hour of labour time worked. For instance, eight Ugly units (worth 8 × £24 = £192) can be made in the same time as five Posh (worth only 5 × £36 = £180).

(b) *Other considerations*

A profit-maximising budget would therefore be to produce Ugly units only, within the assumptions made. It is important to remember, however, that other considerations, so far excluded from the problem, might alter the decision entirely.

(i) Can the **sales price** of either product be **raised**, thereby increasing unit contribution, and the contribution per labour hour, without reducing sales demand? Since sales demand is apparently unlimited, it would be reasonable to suspect that both products are underpriced.

(ii) To what extent are sales of each product **interdependent**? For example, a manufacturer of knives and forks could not expect to cease production of knives without affecting sales demand for the forks.

(iii) Would a decision to cease production of Posh units really have no effect on fixed costs? The assumption that **fixed costs** are unaffected by limiting factor decisions is not always valid, and closure of either the Posh or Ugly production line might result in **fixed cost savings** (for example a reduction in production planning costs, product design costs, or equipment depreciation).

(c) *Qualitative factors*

There are also qualitative factors to consider.

(i) Would a decision to make and sell just Ugly units have a harmful effect on **customer loyalty** and sales demand?

(ii) Is the decision going to affect the long-term plans of the company as well as the short-term? If Posh units are not produced next year, it is likely that **competitors** will take over the markets vacated by Spice Ltd. **Labour** skilled in the manufacture of Posh units will be lost, and a decision in one year's time to reopen manufacture of Posh units might not be possible.

(iii) **Why is there a shortage of labour?** Are the skills required difficult to obtain, perhaps because the company is using very old-fashioned production methods, or is the company a high-tech newcomer located in a low-tech area? Or perhaps the conditions of work are so unappealing that people simply do not want to work for the company.

Question (c) (iii) should be asked whatever the scarce resource. If machine hours are in short supply is this because more machines are needed, or newer, more reliable and efficient machines? If materials are in short supply, what are competitors doing? Have they found an equivalent or better substitute? Is it time to redesign the product?

1.7 When there is a maximum **limit on sales demand** for an organisation's products or services, they should still be ranked in order of contribution-earning ability per unit of the scarce resource. However, the profit-maximising decision will be to produce the **top-ranked products** (or to provide the top-ranked services) **up to the sales demand limit**.

1.8 EXAMPLE: ONE SCARCE RESOURCE AND LIMITED SALES DEMAND

Ferguson Ltd manufactures and sells three products, Beckham, Scholes and Neville, for which budgeted sales demand, unit selling prices and unit variable costs are as follows.

Budgeted sales demand	Beckham 550 units		Scholes 500 units		Neville 400 units	
	£	£	£	£	£	£
Unit sales price		16		18		14
Variable costs: materials	8		6		2	
labour	4		6		9	
		12		12		11
Unit contribution		4		6		3

The company has existing stocks of 250 units of Beckham and 200 units of Neville, which it is quite willing to use up to meet sales demand. All three products use the same direct materials and the same type of direct labour. In the next year, the available supply of materials will be restricted to £4,800 (at cost) and the available supply of labour to £6,600 (at cost). What product mix and sales mix would maximise the company's profits in the next year?

1.9 SOLUTION AND DISCUSSION

There appear to be **two** scarce resources, direct materials and direct labour. However, this is not certain, and because there is a limited sales demand as well, it might be that there is:

(a) no limiting factor at all, except sales demand - ie none of the resources is scarce;

(b) only one scarce resource preventing the full potential sales demand being achieved.

Step 1. Begin by establishing **how many scarce resources** there are, and if there are any, which one or which ones they are. In this example we have:

	Beckham Units	Scholes Units	Neville Units
Budgeted sales	550	500	400
Stock in hand	250	0	200
Minimum production to meet demand	300	500	200

	Minimum production to meet sales demand Units	Required materials at cost £	Required labour at cost £
Beckham	300	2,400	1,200
Scholes	500	3,000	3,000
Neville	200	400	1,800
Total required		5,800	6,000
Total available		4,800	6,600
(Shortfall)/Surplus		(1,000)	600

Materials are a limiting factor, but labour is not.

Step 2. The next step is to rank Beckham, Scholes and Neville in order of contribution earned per £1 of direct materials consumed.

	Beckham £	Scholes £	Neville £
Unit contribution	4	6	3
Cost of materials	8	6	2
Contribution per £1 materials	£0.50	£1.00	£1.50
Ranking	**3rd**	**2nd**	**1st**

Step 3. Neville should be manufactured up to the limit where units produced plus units in stock will meet sales demand, then Scholes second and Beckham third, until all the available materials are used up.

Ranking	Product	Sales demand less units in stock Units	Production quantity Units		Materials cost £
1st	Neville	200	200	(× £2)	400
2nd	Scholes	500	500	(× £6)	3,000
3rd	Beckham	300	175	(× £8)	* 1,400
			Total available		4,800

* Balancing amount using up total available.

Step 4. The profit-maximising budget is as follows.

	Beckham Units	Scholes Units	Neville Units
Opening stock	250	0	200
Add production	175	500	200
Sales	425	500	400

	Beckham £	Scholes £	Neville £	Total £
Revenue	6,800	9,000	5,600	21,400
Variable costs	5,100	6,000	4,400	15,500
Contribution	1,700	3,000	1,200	5,900

Question 2

What other considerations should be taken into account by Ferguson Ltd?

Answer

Refer back to the previous example for suggestions if you cannot think of any for yourself.

Exam focus point

Overall production capacity was the **limiting factor** in a question in the **December 1997** exam. Customer contribution per unit of sale had to be used to determine the optimum sales strategy. The available production capacity had to take into account products replaced free of charge. Of course, candidates weren't given a figure for free replacements. It had to be calculated using a wealth of data provided in the question.

In the **June 1999** exam candidates had to suggest ways in which a production capacity constraint could be overcome, whereas in the **December 1999** exam, they had to explain how recognition and overcoming of production constraints may help in the formulation of budgets which provide the desired annual profit.

Assumptions in limiting factor analysis: one scarce resource

1.10 In the previous examples, the following assumptions were made. If any of the assumptions are not valid, then the profit-maximising decision might be different.

(a) **Fixed costs will be the same** regardless of the decision that is taken, and so the profit maximising and contribution-maximising output level will be the same. This will not necessarily be true, since some fixed costs might be **directly attributable** to a product or service. A decision to reduce or cease altogether activity on a product or service might therefore result in some fixed cost savings, which would have to be taken into account.

(b) The **unit variable cost is constant**, regardless of the output quantity of a product or service. This implies that:

    (i)   the price of resources will be unchanged regardless of quantity; for example, there will be no bulk purchase discount of raw materials;

    (ii)   efficiency and productivity levels will be unchanged; regardless of output quantity, the direct labour productivity, the machine time per unit, and the materials consumption per unit will remain the same.

(c) The **estimates** of sales demand for each product, and the resources required to make each product, are **known with certainty.** In the previous example, there were estimates of the maximum sales demand for each of three products, and these estimates were used to establish the profit-maximising product mix. **Suppose the estimates were wrong?** The product mix finally chosen would then either mean that some sales demand of the most profitable item would be unsatisfied, or that production would exceed sales demand, leaving some stock unsold. Clearly, once a profit-maximising output decision is reached, management will have to **keep their decision under continual review,** and adjust their decision as appropriate in the light of actual results.

(d) **Units of output are divisible,** and a profit-maximising solution might include fractions of units as the optimum output level. Where fractional answers are not realistic, some rounding of the figures will be necessary.

Exam focus point

A suitable adjustment will have to be made for any problem involving a scarce resource where one (or more) of the assumptions is invalid. A Paper 9 question would almost certainly ask you to perform calculations that dropped one or more of the assumptions.

Scarce resources and opportunity costs: shadow prices

1.11   If there are scarce resources, there will be **opportunity costs** (the benefits forgone by using a scarce resource in one way instead of in the next most profitable way).

1.12 EXAMPLE: SHADOW PRICE

For example, suppose that a company manufactures two items X and Y, which earn a contribution of £24 and £18 per unit respectively. Product X requires 4 machine hours per unit, and product Y 2 hours. Only 5,000 machine hours are available, and potential sales demand is for 1,000 units each of X and Y. What should the product mix be?

1.13 SOLUTION (NO EXTRA RESOURCES)

Machine hours would be a limiting factor, and with X earning £6 per hour and Y earning £9 per hour, the profit-maximising decision would be:

	Units	Hours	Contribution £
Y	1,000	2,000	18,000
X (balance)	750	3,000	18,000
		5,000	36,000

Priority is given to Y because the opportunity cost of making Y instead of more units of X is £6 per hour (X's contribution per machine hour), and since Y earns £9 per hour, the incremental benefit of making Y instead of X would be £3 per hour.

1.14 SOLUTION WITH EXTRA RESOURCES

If extra machine hours could be made available, more units of X (up to 1,000) would be made, and an extra contribution of £6 per hour could be earned. Similarly, if fewer machine hours were available, the decision would be to make fewer units of X and to keep production of Y at 1,000 units, and so the loss of machine hours would cost the company £6 per hour in lost contribution.

1.15 This £6 per hour, the marginal contribution-earning potential of the scarce resource at the profit-maximising output level, is referred to as the **shadow price** (or **dual price**) of the scarce resource.

KEY TERM

The **shadow price** of a resource is the marginal contribution that can be earned for each unit of the scarce resource that is available.

2 LINEAR PROGRAMMING: THE GRAPHICAL TECHNIQUE

2.1 The linear programming technique can be applied to problems with the following features.

(a) There is a **single objective**, which is to *maximise* or *minimise* the value of a certain function. The objective in commercial decision making is usually to maximise contribution and thus maximise profit.

(b) There are **several constraints**, typically scarce resources, that limit the value of the objective function.

2.2 The graphical approach to linear programming is not examinable but you would be well advised to read through the following 'Knowledge brought forward box' to remind yourself of the terminology.

Knowledge brought forward from Paper 3

Linear programming: the graphical approach

- The graphical approach can be used for linear programming problems with only two decisions variables (typically, two products) which can be represented on a graph, with one axis for each variable.

- Suppose that a company makes two products, the standard and the deluxe.

	Standard	Deluxe	Availability per month
Contribution per unit	£15	£20	
Labour hours per unit	5	10	4,000
Kgs of material per unit	10	5	4,250

Find the production plan which will maximise contribution.

Knowledge brought forward from Paper 3 (cont'd)

- *Step 1.* Define the variables.

    ○ Let x = number of standard produced each month
    ○ Let y = number of deluxe produced each month

- *Step 2.* Establish the **constraints** (by converting them into equations).

    ○ Labour : $5x + 10y \leq 4{,}000$
    ○ Material: $10x + 5y \leq 4{,}250$
    ○ Non negativity: $x \geq 0, y \geq 0$

- *Step 3.* Establish the **objective function**: Contribution (C) = $15x + 20y$

- The **graphical method** of finding the optimal solution is as follows.

    ○ **Graph the constraints**

    ○ Establish the **feasible area/region**, which is the area where all inequalities are satisfied (area above the x axis and y axis ($x \geq 0$, $y \geq 0$), below the material constraint ($\leq$) and below the labour constraint ($\leq$)).

    ○ Determine the vertices of the feasible area using **simultaneous equations** and then calculate the contribution at each vertex to determine which is the **optimal solution**.

---

3 LINEAR PROGRAMMING: COMPUTER MODELS

3.1 The graphical approach to linear programming cannot be used if there are more than two decision variables. There are then two alternatives: a technique called the **Simplex** method (which you are **not required to know** for Paper 9) or **computer** models.

3.2 The following example will illustrate how a typical modern **spreadsheet** package can be used to solve linear programming problems.

Exam focus point

Paper 9 questions use a different package, as we shall see, but first we will teach you something that may be useful in practice.

3.3 EXAMPLE: A COMPUTER MODEL

Let us suppose that Austen Ltd makes 2 products, X and Y, which make a unit contribution of £20 and £16 respectively. Sales demand is unlimited at current selling prices, but there is a potential shortage of labour, materials and machine time.

The constraints, ignoring the expected sales demands, are:

Materials	$5x + 2y \leq 3{,}000$	Machine time	$3x + 2y \leq 2{,}100$
Labour hours	$x + 3y \leq 1{,}750$	Non-negativity	$x \geq 0, y \geq 0$

where x and y are the quantities of product X and product Y respectively.

Using Microsoft Excel, set up the problem on a spreadsheet as follows.

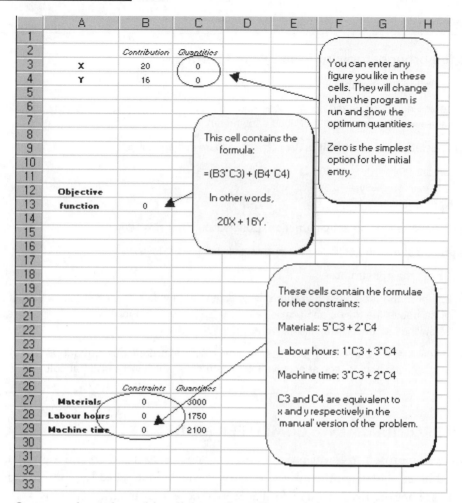

Once you have done this, click on the cell containing the objective function (B13 in our example) so that it is highlighted. Then run Excel's analysis tool called 'Solver', which throws up the following menu. (Lotus 1-2-3's tool is also called **Solver**.)

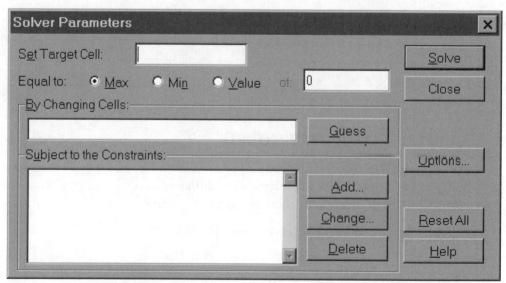

(a)   Your **target cell** is the objective function - cell B13 in our example.

(b)   You want to maximise the objective function so you click with your mouse on the **Max** button.

(c)   The values you can change (**changing cells**) are the quantities of X and Y you produce. These values will appear in cells C3 and C4.

(d) Now you set up the **constraints**, putting them into 'spreadsheet style'. For example 5x + 2y ≤ 3,000 is, in terms of the spreadsheet, B27 ≤ C27. Each constraint, plus the negativity constraints, are added in turn by clicking on the **Add** button and entering the cell references as appropriate.

(e) Finally, click on **Options** which gives you another menu allowing you (amongst other things) to instruct the computer that it should assume the model is linear.

Your completed menu should look like the one below.

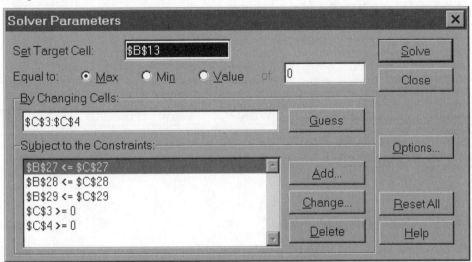

If you now click the **Solve** button the optimum solution is found in about 5 seconds.

3.4 SOLUTION

The solution is provided on your initial spreadsheet.

This shows that the optimal solution is to produce 400 X and 450 Y, with a resulting contribution of £15,200, leaving 100 units of unused materials. All labour hours and machine time will be used.

	A	B	C	D
1				
2		*Contribution*	*Quantities*	
3	X	20	400	
4	Y	16	450	
5				
6				
7				
8				
9				
10				
11				
12	**Objective**			
13	**function**	15200		
14				
15				
16				
17				
18				
19				
20				
21				
22				
23				
24				
25				
26		*Constraints*	*Quantities*	
27	**Materials**	2900	3000	
28	**Labour hours**	1750	1750	
29	**Machine time**	2100	2100	
30				

Computer output

3.5   Solver also gives you the option of obtaining three reports.

3.6   The **limits report** basically shows the same information as provided in the solution spreadsheet.

Cell	Target Name	Value
$B$13	function Contribution	15200

Cell	Adjustable Name	Value	Lower Limit	Target Result	Upper Limit	Target Result
$C$3	X Quantities	400	0	7200	400	15200
$C$4	Y Quantities	450	0	8000	450	15200

> **KEY TERMS**
>
> The **shadow price of a limiting factor** shows by how much contribution would change if an additional unit of the resource were made available at its normal variable cost (but with the availability of other resources and demand constraints being held constant).
>
> The shadow price only applies in a range between **allowable minimum** and **allowable maximum** supplies of the resource (that is, between an **allowable decrease** below the original quantity available and an **allowable increase** above the original quantity available). If supply of the resource is outside this range the optimal solution will change.

3.7   The **sensitivity report** tells you the final values of X, Y and the resources used as before but it also provides the following information.

(a)   The amounts by which **contribution** from X and Y could increase or decrease before the optimum production quantities would change (the **allowable increase**). For example, if the contribution from X were £23 it would still be best to produce 400 units of X and 450 of Y. If it were £25, the optimal solution would change. If Y's contribution were £60 (16 + 44), the optimal solution would again change.

(b)   The amounts by which the various **constraints** could increase or decrease before the optimum solution would change (**allowable increase** column).

(c)   The **shadow prices** of the labour and machine hour constraints (the materials constraint is not binding - there are spare materials left).

(*Note*. **R H Side** simply means the right hand side of the equation. The allowable increase for materials ($1E + 30 = 10^{30}$) is effectively infinity, because we already have more than enough materials.)

Changing Cells

Cell	Name	Final Value	Reduced Cost	Objective Coefficient	Allowable Increase	Allowable Decrease
$C$3	X Quantities	400	0	20	4	14.66666667
$C$4	Y Quantities	450	0	16	44	2.666666667

Constraints

Cell	Name	Final Value	Shadow Price	Constraint R.H. Side	Allowable Increase	Allowable Decrease
$B$27	Materials Constraints	2900	0	3000	1E+30	100
$B$28	Labour hours Constraints	1750	1.142857143	1750	1400	175
$B$29	Machine time Constraints	2100	6.285714286	2100	53.84615385	933.3333333

3.8 The third report is called an **answer report**, which summarises the problem and the solution.

Target Cell (Max)

Cell	Name	Original Value	Final Value
$B$13	function Contribution	0	15200

Adjustable Cells

Cell	Name	Original Value	Final Value
$C$3	X Quantities	0	400
$C$4	Y Quantities	0	450

Constraints

Cell	Name	Cell Value	Formula	Status	Slack
$B$27	Materials Constraints	2900	$B$27<=$C$27	Not Binding	100
$B$28	Labour hours Constraints	1750	$B$28<=$C$28	Binding	0
$B$29	Machine time Constraints	2100	$B$29<=$C$29	Binding	0
$C$3	X Quantities	400	$C$3>=0	Not Binding	400
$C$4	Y Quantities	450	$C$4>=0	Not Binding	450

Do-it-yourself!

3.9 If you have access to a modern spreadsheet package you may wish to set up the problem we have described and experiment with different values for the variables.

3.10 Computer tools such as Microsoft Excel's Solver can also be used to find the answers to highly complex 'What if?' problems with **hundreds of constraints** and variables.

STORM and Paper 9

3.11 Unfortunately (in terms of being able to practise yourself) the Paper 9 examiner prefers to use a computer package called STORM to derive his output for Paper 9 questions.

(Lecturers may wish to know that STORM is an American quantitative modelling package made by Storm Software Inc. It has eighteen modules offering facilities such as queueing analysis, production scheduling, statistical process control and decision trees, as well as linear programming. Its commercial price is over £500, though it can be obtained more cheaply for academic use. It appears not to have been updated since 1993 and it is DOS based.)

3.12 STORM output looks like this.

Optimal solution – detailed report

	Variable	Value
1	Variable A	11,253.33
2	Variable B	5,760.00
3	Variable C	3,456.00
4	Variable D	7,200.00
5	Variable E	1,728.00

		Constraint	Type	RHS	Slack	Shadow price
1	Max	Hours	<=	35,000.00	5,602.67	0.0000
2		Variable A	>=	2,880.00	8,373.33	0.0000
3		Variable B	>=	5,760.00	0.00	–2.2000
4		Variable C	>=	3,456.00	0.00	–6.9333
5		Variable D	>=	7,200.00	0.00	–20.8000
6		Variable E	>=	1,728.00	0.00	–33.0667
7	Max	Funds	<=	7,200,000.00	0.00	0.1389

Objective function value = 756,467.2

Sensitivity Analysis of Objective Function Coefficients

	Variable	Current coefficient	Allowable minimum	Allowable maximum
1	Variable A	30.00	27.36	– Infinity
2	Variable B	22.80	– Infinity	25.0000
3	Variable C	26.40	– Infinity	33.3333
4	Variable D	19.20	– Infinity	40.0000
5	Variable E	33.60	– Infinity	66.6667

Sensitivity Analysis of Right-hand Side Values

		Constraint	Type	Current value	Allowable minimum	Allowable maximum
1	Max	Hours	<=	35,000.00	29,397.33	– Infinity
2		Variable A	>=	2,880.00	– Infinity	11,253.33
3		Variable B	>=	5,260.00	0.00	15,808.00
4		Variable C	>=	3,456.00	0.00	10,992.00
5		Variable D	>=	7,200.00	0.00	13,480.00
6		Variable E	>=	1,728.00	0.00	5,496.00
7	Max	Funds	<=	7,200,000.00	5,391,360.00	8,410,176.00

3.13 The only significant difference between this output and the output from Solver is that it shows **allowable minimum** and **maximum** instead of allowable increase and decrease. So, for example, the allowable minimum of variable A, 27.36, would be shown as an allowable decrease (30 – 27.36 = 2.64) in Solver.

Exam focus point

Output from STORM featured in a question set in **June 1997**.

Question 3

Study the STORM output and answer the following questions.

(a) In the optimum solution how many resources are devoted to variable D?

(b) What does the 'Type' column indicate?

(c)   What does RHS mean?

(d)   Explain the two numbers in the 'Slack' column.

(e)   The shadow price of variable B is –2.20. What does this mean?

(f)   If 11,253.33 units of resources are devoted to Variable A at a cost of its current coefficient, 30.00, and likewise variables B to E, what is the overall value?

Answer

(a)   7,200

(b)   It shows what type of constraint applies. For instance Variable A must be greater than or equal to (> =) 2,880.

(c)   It means the Right Hand Side of the constraint equation, for instance '2,880' in the inequality A >= 2,880.

(d)   The figure 5602.67 is the difference between the maximum amount (type is <=) of resources (Hours) available and the amount used in the optimal solution.

Maximum available		35,000.00
Variable A	11,253.33	
Variable B	5,760.00	
Variable C	3,456.00	
Variable D	7,200.00	
Variable E	1,728.00	
		29,397.33
		5,602.67

The figure 8373.33 shows the difference between the optimal amount for variable A, 11,253.33 and the minimum (type >=) of 2880.

(e)   This is the amount by which the coefficient of variable B (22.80) could change before the overall solution changed.

(f)

11,253.33 × 30	337,600.00
5,760.00 × 22.80	131,328.00
3,456.00 × 26.40	91,238.40
7,200.00 × 19.20	138,240.00
1,728.00 × 33.60	58,060.80
	745,467.20

This, of course, is the value of the objective function. You may have got a small rounding difference.

---

4   ASSUMPTIONS AND LIMITATIONS OF LINEAR PROGRAMMING

4.1   The assumptions that are made in linear programming are similar to the assumptions in **limiting factor analysis** with one scarce resource, and these limit its usefulness for planning and decision making.

(a)   **Fixed costs will be the same** regardless of the product mix that is selected, and there are no step costs, so the profit-maximising product mix and the contribution-maximising product mix are the same.

(b)   The **unit variable cost is constant,** regardless of the output quantity of a product or service. (*Note.* Paying a premium for *extra* units of a scarce resource is a separate matter. Within the constraints of the initial linear programming problem, unit variable costs are constant.)

(c) The **estimates** of sales demand and the resources required to make each product are **known with certainty**.

(d) **Units of output are divisible** and fractions of units may appear in the optimal solution.

4.2 In addition, there are the following further assumptions.

(a) The total **amount available** of each scarce resource is **known with accuracy**. (The optimal product mix or service mix is based on these known quantities, hence the need for some accuracy in estimating the quantities available.)

(b) There is **no interdependence** between the **sales demand** for the different products or services, so that there is a completely free choice in the product or service mix without having to consider the consequences for maximum sales demand or selling prices.

4.3 Difficulties with applying the linear programming technique **in practice** include the following.

(a) It may be difficult to determine **which resources** are likely to be in short supply, **how much** will be available, and whether **all possible uses** have been identified.

(b) It is by no means certain that management make product mix decisions which are profit-maximising. They may be more concerned to develop a **production/sales plan** which:

   (i)   is **realistic**;
   (ii) is **acceptable** to the individual **managers** throughout the organisation;
   (iii) is **acceptable** to the rest of the **workforce**; and
   (iv) promises a **satisfactory profit** and accounting return.

Linear programming in practice

4.4 In spite of these limitations, linear programming appears to be a **useful** technique in practice. Some statistical studies have been carried out suggesting that linear cost functions do apply within fairly wide relevant ranges of output, and so the assumptions underlying linear programming are reasonably valid.

4.5 In practice a computer is essential, since there may be hundreds of constraints and variables. But *because* computers can cope with this volume of data, linear programming **is used in practice**, it is not just a theoretical technique.

Application	Comment
Budgetary planning	LP will help to decide on the optimum product mix and on anticipated usage (and therefore cost) of resources. It can also show the amount of premium it is worth paying to obtain extra units of scarce resources, in the event that other factors in the budget dictate that the level of activity should be different to that suggested by the solution to the linear programming problem.
Production scheduling	LP models have helped demand requirements to be met at minimum cost, subject to constraints concerning production capacity, subcontracting, and inventory holdings.
Blending of materials	Successful applications have been reported in such diverse settings as the mixing of paint, the mixing of meats to make sausages and the blending of chocolate products.

Application	Comment
Transportation/ distribution	The typical aim of this application is to meet demand for a product from different geographical markets using several geographically dispersed plants, while minimising transportation and distribution costs.
Personnel planning	An example is the assignment of nurses to hospital departments that undergo peaks and troughs in demand. Key inputs in these applications include the cost of each type of nurse for normal hours and the cost of overtime and supplemental staff.

Exam focus point

The **uses** of linear programming in budgeting featured in a question in **June 1995**. The **limitations** of the technique featured in a question in **June 1997**.

Chapter roundup

- When operations have to be planned with just **one scarce resource**, products can be ranked in order of contribution earning ability per unit of the scarce resource.

- Other matters also need to be taken into account such as **interdependence** between products, **fixed cost** savings, and the impact on **customers, suppliers** and **employees.**

- The **shadow price** of a resource is the marginal contribution that can be earned for each unit of the scarce resource that is available.

- **Linear programming** is a means of dealing with problems involving more than one scarce resource.

- If there are only two variables the **graphical technique** can be used.

- If there are more than two decision variables a **software package** is likely to be used.

- Linear programming is limited by some of its **assumptions**, such as constant fixed costs and unit variable costs, accurate knowledge of sales demand and resource availability, and the objective of profit-maximisation.

Quick quiz

1 Why might an organisation not be able to provide whatever mix of products it likes? (see para 1.1)

2 What are three qualitative matters to be considered when making decisions involving scarce resources? (1.6)

3 What assumptions about limiting factor analysis might be dropped in a Paper 9 question? (1.10)

4 What is the shadow price of a resource? (1.15)

5 How is a linear programming model formulated? (2.2)

6 What is an allowable maximum? (3.6)

7 List three limitations of linear programming. (4.1 - 4.3)

8 Describe two applications of linear programming. (4.5)

Question to try	Level	Marks	Time
7	Exam standard	20	36 mins

Chapter 8

RISK AND UNCERTAINTY

Chapter topic list	Syllabus reference
1 Risk and uncertainty	4(c)
2 Allowing for uncertainty	4(c)
3 Spreadsheets and data tables	2(a), 4(c)
4 Probabilities and expected values	4(c)
5 Decision trees	4(c)
6 Perfect and imperfect information	4(c)

Introduction

Decision making involves making decisions now about what will happen in the **future**. Obviously, decisions can turn out badly, or actual results can prove to be very different from the estimates on which the original decision was made. Ideally the decision maker would know with **certainty** what the future consequences would be for each choice facing him. But the real world is not normally so helpful, and decisions must be made in the knowledge that their consequences, although probable perhaps, are rarely 100% certain.

Various methods of bringing **uncertainty and risk analysis** into the evaluation of decisions will be described in this chapter. You may well think that some methods are more sensible or practical than others but you should judge each method on its merits, and be able to apply it if necessary in an examination.

Core areas of the syllabus identified by the examiner and covered in this chapter: **allowing for uncertainty** in decision making; **use of probabilities involving such areas as maximax, maximin and minimax regret**; **value of perfect information**; **use of quantitative techniques** in decision making; **interpretation and use of data from IT output such as spreadsheet data tables**.

1   RISK AND UNCERTAINTY

Uncertainty and risk

> ### KEY TERMS
>
> **Risk** involves situations or events which may or may not occur, but whose probability of occurrence can be calculated statistically and the frequency of their occurrence predicted from past records. Thus insurance deals with risk.
>
> **Uncertain events** are those whose outcome cannot be predicted with statistical confidence.

1.1 In everyday usage the terms risk and uncertainty are not clearly distinguished. If you are asked for a definition, do not make the mistake of believing that the latter is a more extreme version of the former. It is not a question of degree, it is a question of whether or not **sufficient information** is available to allow the lack of certainty to be quantified. As a rule, however, the terms are used interchangeably.

Risk preference

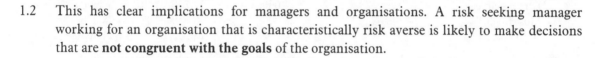

> **KEY TERMS**
>
> A **risk seeker** is a decision maker who is interested in the best outcomes no matter how small the chance that they may occur.
>
> A decision maker is **risk neutral** if he is concerned with what will be the most likely outcome.
>
> A **risk averse** decision maker acts on the assumption that the worst outcome might occur.

1.2 This has clear implications for managers and organisations. A risk seeking manager working for an organisation that is characteristically risk averse is likely to make decisions that are **not congruent with the goals** of the organisation.

1.3 There may be a role for the management accountant here, who could be instructed to **present** decision-making information in such a way as to ensure that the manager considers **all** the possibilities, including the worst.

> **Exam focus point**
> Risk preference featured in questions in the **June 1994, June 1998, December 1998** and **June 1999** exams.

2 ALLOWING FOR UNCERTAINTY

Conservatism

2.1 This approach simply involves estimating outcomes in a conservative manner in order to provide a built-in safety factor.

2.2 However, the method fails to consider explicitly a **range** of outcomes and, by concentrating only on conservative figures, may also fail to consider the **expected** or most likely outcomes.

2.3 Conservatism is associated with **risk aversion** and prudence (in the general sense of the word). In spite of its shortcomings it is probably the **most widely used** method in practice.

Worst/most likely/best outcome estimates

2.4 A more scientific version of conservatism is to measure the most likely outcome from a decision, and the worst and best possible outcomes. This will show the **full range of**

possible outcomes from a decision, and might help managers to reject certain alternatives because the worst possible outcome might involve an unacceptable amount of loss.

2.5 EXAMPLE: WORST/BEST POSSIBLE OUTCOMES

Omelette Ltd is trying to set the sales price for one of its products. Three prices are under consideration, and expected sales volumes and costs are as follows.

Price per unit	£4	£4.30	£4.40
Expected sales volume (units)			
Best possible	16,000	14,000	12,500
Most likely	14,000	12,500	12,000
Worst possible	10,000	8,000	6,000

Fixed costs are £20,000 and variable costs of sales are £2 per unit.

Which price should be chosen?

2.6 SOLUTION

	£4	£4.30	£4.40
Contribution per unit	£2	£2.30	£2.40
Total contribution towards fixed costs	£	£	£
Best possible	32,000	32,200	30,000
Most likely	28,000	28,750	28,800
Worst possible	20,000	18,400	14,400

(a) The highest contribution based on **most likely** sales volume would be at a price of £4.40 but arguably a price of £4.30 would be much better than £4.40, since the most likely profit is almost as good, the worst possible profit is not as bad, and the best possible profit is better.

(b) However, only a price of £4 guarantees that the company would **not make a loss,** even if the worst possible outcome occurs. (Fixed costs of £20,000 would just be covered.) A risk averse management might therefore prefer a price of £4 to either of the other two prices.

The maximin decision rule

KEY TERM

The **maximin** decision rule suggests that a decision maker should select the alternative that offers the least unattractive worst outcome. This would mean choosing the alternative that *maxi*mises the *mini*mum profits.

2.7 EXAMPLE: MAXIMIN DECISION RULE

A businessman is trying to decide which of three mutually exclusive projects to undertake. Each of the projects could lead to varying net costs which the businessman classifies as outcomes I, II, and III. He has constructed the following payoff table or matrix.

		Net profit in £'000s if outcome turns out to be		
		I (Worst)	*II (Most likely)*	*III (Best)*
	A	50	85	130
Project	B	70	75	140
	C	90	100	110

Which project should he undertake? Use the maximin decision rule.

2.8 SOLUTION

The maximin decision rule suggests that he should select the 'smallest worst result' that could happen. This is the decision criterion that managers should 'play safe' and either minimise their losses or costs, or else go for the decision which gives the higher minimum profits. If he selects project A the worst result is a net profit of 50. Similarly, the worst results for B and C are 70 and 90 respectively. The best worst outcome is 90 and project C would therefore be selected (because this is a better 'worst possible' than either A or B).

2.9 The maximin decision rule is also known as the **minimax cost** rule - minimise the maximum costs or losses.

Criticisms of the maximin decision rule

2.10 The maximin decision rule is subject to two major criticisms.

(a) It is **defensive** and **conservative**, being a safety first principle of avoiding the worst outcomes without taking into account opportunities for maximising profits.

(b) It ignores the **probability** of each different outcome taking place. In the previous example, we ignored the fact that outcome II was the most likely outcome.

Maximax

> ### KEY TERM
>
> The **maximax** criterion looks at the best possible results. Maximax means 'maximise the maximum profit'. An alternative name that amounts to the same thing is **minimin** (minimise the minimum costs or losses).

2.11 EXAMPLE: MAXIMAX

Here is a payoff table showing the profits that will be achieved depending upon the action taken (A, B or C) and the circumstances prevailing (I, II or III).

		Profits *Actions*		
		A	*B*	*C*
	I	100	80	60
Circumstances	II	90	120	85
	III	(20)	10	85
Maximum profit		100	120	85

Action B would be chosen if the maximax rule is followed.

2.12 **Criticisms** of this approach would again say that it ignores probabilities and that it is over-optimistic.

Question 1

A company is considering which one of three alternative courses of action, A, B and C to take. The profit or loss from each choice depends on which one of four economic circumstances, I, II, III or IV will apply. The possible profits and losses, in thousands of pounds, are given in the following payoff table. Losses are shown as negative figures.

		Action		
		A	*B*	*C*
	I	70	60	70
Circumstance	II	-10	20	-5
	III	80	0	50
	IV	60	100	115

Required

State which action would be selected using each of the maximax and maximin criteria.

Answer

(a) The best possible outcomes are as follows.

A (circumstance III):	80
B (circumstance IV):	100
C (circumstance IV):	115

As 115 is the highest of these three figures, action C would be chosen using the maximax criterion.

(b) The worst possible outcomes are as follows.

A (circumstance II):	-10
B (circumstance III):	0
C (circumstance II):	-5

The best of these figures is 0 (neither a profit nor a loss), so action B would be chosen using the maximin criterion.

Minimax regret rule

> **KEY TERM**
>
> The **minimax regret** rule aims to minimise the regret from making the wrong decision. **Regret** is the opportunity lost through making the wrong decision.

This is cited in an article by the examiner 'Quantitative Applications in Paper 9 – part 1' (*ACCA Students' Newsletter, April 2000*).

2.13 We first consider the extreme to which we might come to regret an action we had chosen.

Regret for any combination of action and circumstances	=	Profit for best action in those circumstances	–	Profit for the action actually chosen in those circumstances

The minimax regret decision rule is that the decision option selected should be the one which **minimises the maximum potential regret** for any of the possible outcomes.

2.14 EXAMPLE: MINIMAX REGRET

A manager is trying to decide which of three mutually exclusive projects to undertake. Each of the projects could lead to varying net costs which the manager calls outcomes I, II and III. The following payoff table or matrix has been constructed.

		Outcomes (Net profit)		
		I	*II*	*III*
		(Worst)	*(Most likely)*	*(Best)*
	A	50	85	130
Project	B	70	75	140
	C	90	100	110

Which project should be undertaken?

2.15 SOLUTION

A table of regrets can be compiled, as follows, showing the amount of profit that might be forgone for each project, depending on whether the outcome is I, II or III.

	Outcome			Maximum
	I	*II*	*III*	
Project A	40 ★	15 ★★★	10	40
Project B	20 ★★	25	0	25
Project C	0	0	30	30

★ 90 – 50   ★★ 90 – 70   ★★★ 100 – 85   etc

The **maximum regret** is 40 with project A, 25 with B and 30 with C. The lowest of these three maximum regrets is 25 with B, and so project B would be selected if the minimax regret rule is used.

Sensitivity analysis

> **KEY TERM**
>
> **Sensitivity analysis** is a term used to describe any technique whereby decision options are tested for their vulnerability to changes in any 'variable' such as expected sales volume, sales price per unit, material costs, or labour costs.

2.16 Here are three useful approaches to sensitivity analysis, all of which have featured in **Paper 9 questions.**

(a) To estimate by **how much costs and revenues would need to differ** from their estimated values before the decision would change.

(b) To estimate whether a decision would change **if estimated costs were x% higher** than estimated, or estimated revenues y% lower than estimated.

(c) To estimate by how much costs and/or revenues would need to differ from their estimated values before the decision maker **would be indifferent** between two options.

2.17 The essence of the approach, therefore, is to carry out the calculations with one set of values for the variables and then substitute other possible values for the variables to see how this affects the overall outcome.

(a) From your studies of information technology you may recognise this as **what if analysis** that can be carried out using a **spreadsheet.**

(b) From your studies of **linear programming** you may remember that sensitivity analysis can be carried out to determine over which ranges the various constraints have an impact on the optimum solution.

(c) **Flexible budgeting** can also be a form of sensitivity analysis.

(d) Sensitivity analysis is one method of analysing the risk surrounding a **capital expenditure project** and enables an assessment to be made of how responsive the project's NPV is to changes in the variables that are used to calculate that NPV.

> **Exam focus point**
>
> A capital expenditure project featured in the **December 1995** exam. The following example covers all the key points.

2.18 EXAMPLE: SENSITIVITY ANALYSIS

Kenney Ltd is considering a project. The 'most likely' cash flows associated with the project are as follows.

Year	0	1	2
	£'000	£'000	£'000
Initial investment	(7,000)		
Variable costs		(2,000)	(2,000)
Cash inflows (650,000 units at £10 per unit)		6,500	6,500
Net cash flows	(7,000)	4,500	4,500

The cost of capital is 8%.

Required

Calculate the increase/decrease in each of the variables affecting the project's NPV at which Kenney Ltd would be indifferent between accepting or rejecting the project. (*Note.* Consider each of the variables in turn, the other variables remaining unchanged.).

2.19 SOLUTION

Work carefully through this solution making sure you understand all the calculations, and noting how the figures are analysed (percentages, unit costs etc).

The PVs of the cash flow are as follows.

Year	Discount factor 8%	PV of initial investment £'000	PV of variable costs £'000	PV of cash inflows £'000	PV of net cash flow £'000
0	1.000	(7,000)			(7,000)
1	0.926		(1,852)	6,019	4,167
2	0.857		(1,714)	5,571	3,857
		(7,000)	(3,566)	11,590	1,024

The project has a positive NPV and would appear to be worthwhile. The changes in cash flows which would need to occur for the project to only just breakeven (and hence be on the point of being unacceptable) are as follows.

Variable		Increase/decrease to make Kenney indifferent
Initial investment	(W1)	+14.6%
Sales volume	(W2)	−12.7%
Selling price	(W3)	−8.8%
Variable costs	(W4)	+28.7%
Cost of capital	(W5)	+133.0%

Workings

1 Initial investment

The initial investment can rise by £1,024,000 before the investment breaks even. The initial investment may therefore increase by 1,024/7,000 = **14.6%.**

2 Sales volume

The present value of the cash inflows minus the present value of the variable costs is £8,024,000. This will have to fall to £7,000,000 for the NPV to be zero.

We need to find the net cash flows in actual values. The cumulative discount factor for 8% and year 2 is 1.783. If the discount factor is divided into the required present value of £7,000,000 we get an annual cash flow of £3,925,968. Given that the most likely net cash flow is £4,500,000, the net cash flow may decline by approximately £574,032 each year before the NPV becomes zero.

Net cash flow is 4,500/6,500 of sales, so sales = £574,032 × 6,500/4,500 = £829,157. At a selling price of £10 per unit this represents 82,916 units. Alternatively we may state that sales volume may decline by **12.7%** (82,916/650,000) before the NPV becomes negative.

3   **Selling price**

When sales volume is 650,000 units per annum, total sales revenue can fall to £5,925,968 (£(6,500,000 – £574,032 (W2)) per annum before the NPV becomes negative. This assumes that total variable costs and sales volume remain unchanged. This represents a selling price of £9.12 per unit (£5,925,968/650,000), an **8.8%** (£0.88/£10) reduction in the selling price.

4   **Variable costs**

The variable cost per year can increase by £574,032 (W3), or £0.88 per unit. This represents an increase of £574,032/2,000,000 = **28.7%**.

5   **Cost of capital**

We need to calculate the IRR. Let us try discount rates of 15% and 20%.

Year	Net cash flow	Discount factor	PV	Discount factor	PV
	£'000	15%	£'000	20%	£'000
0	(7,000)	0.870	(6,090)	0.833	(5,831)
1	4,500	0.756	3,402	0.694	3,123
2	4,500	0.658	2,961	0.579	2,606
			NPV = 273		NPV = (102)

IRR = 0.15 + [(273/(273 + 102)) × (0.20 – 0.15)] = 18.64%

The cost of capital can therefore increase by ((18.64 – 8)/8) = **133%** before the NPV becomes negative.

Question 2

Nevers Ure Ltd is considering a project with the following 'most-likely' cash flows.

Year	Purchase of plant £	Running costs £	Savings £
0	(7,000)		
1		2,000	6,000
2		2,500	7,000

The cost of capital is 8%.

Required

Measure the sensitivity (in percentages) of the project to changes in the levels of expected costs and savings.

Answer

The PVs of the cash flows are as follows.

Year	Discount factor 8%	PV of plant cost £	PV of running costs £	PV of savings £	PV of net cash flow £
0	1.000	(7,000)			(7,000)
1	0.926		(1,852)	5,556	3,704
2	0.857		(2,143)	5,999	3,856
		(7,000)	(3,995)	11,555	560

BPP
PUBLISHING

The project has a positive NPV and would appear to be worthwhile. The changes in cash flows which would need to occur for the project to break even (NPV = 0) are as follows.

(a) Plant costs would need to increase by a PV of £560, that is by (560/7,000) × 100% = 8%
(b) Running costs would need to increase by a PV of £560, that is by (560/3,995) × 100% = 14%
(c) Savings would need to fall by a PV of £560, that is by (560/11,555) × 100% = 4.8%

Problems with this approach

2.20 This approach to sensitivity analysis has a number of weaknesses.

(a) The method requires that **changes** in each key variable are **isolated** but management is more interested in the **combination** of the effects of changes in two or more key variables. Looking at factors in isolation is unrealistic since they are often interdependent.

(b) Sensitivity analysis does not examine the **probability** that any particular variation in costs or revenues might occur.

3 SPREADSHEETS AND DATA TABLES

> **KEY TERM**
>
> The term **data table** is used by some spreadsheet packages (for example Lotus 1-2-3 and Excel), and by the Paper 9 examiner, to refer to a group of cells that show the results of changing the value of variables.

3.1 Data tables **come up in exams,** so it is worth spending some time on them. They can be most clearly explained using a simple example.

3.2 EXAMPLE: A ONE-INPUT DATA TABLE

Don't be put off by the terminology here. All this means is that **one** of the bits of the calculation changes and the other bits don't.

Suppose a company has production costs which it would expect to be in the region of £5m were it not for the effects of inflation. Economic forecasts for the inflation rate in the coming year range from 2% to 10%.

If this were part of a scenario that the company was trying to model on a spreadsheet a 'data table' could be produced showing the range of effects of these various possible levels of inflation simply by:

(a) Entering the basic data

(b) Entering just one formula per item affected (production costs and profits in the example illustrated)

(c) Using the computer's data table tool

3.3 Here is the problem set up on Microsoft Excel.

	A	B	C	D	E	F	G	H	I	J	K
1											
2	Input variable (eg inflation rate)						5%				
3	Constant (eg production costs)						£ 5,000,000				
4	Constant (eg profit before inflation is taken into consideration)						£ 475,000				
5											
6											
7				Production							
8				costs	Profit						
9				5,250,000	225,000						
10			2%								
11			3%								
12			4%								
13			5%								
14			6%								
15			7%								
16			8%								
17			9%								
18			10%								
19											
20											

This cell contains the formula G4 - (G3*G2) ie the profit (G4) less the increase in production costs due to inflation. It is positioned at the top of the answer column in a one-input table.

This cell contains the formula G3 + (G3*G2) ie the production costs plus the increase due to inflation. It must be at the head of the 'answer' column for a one-input table.

The cells shown here with a heavy border are selected and then the Data 'Table' menu is called up. This asks you to enter the 'column input cell' (we are varying a *column* of percentages), which is the cell with our original value of 5%, cell G2.

3.4 This is what happens after a single cell reference (G2) is entered, as prompted by the data table menu.

	A	B	C	D	E	F	G	H	I
1									
2	Input variable (eg inflation rate)						5%		
3	Constant (eg production costs)						£5,000,000		
4	Constant (eg profit before inflation is taken into consideration)						£ 475,000		
5									
6									
7				Production					
8				costs	Profit				
9				5,250,000	225,000				
10			2%	5,100,000	375,000				
11			3%	5,150,000	325,000				
12			4%	5,200,000	275,000				
13			5%	5,250,000	225,000				
14			6%	5,300,000	175,000				
15			7%	5,350,000	125,000				
16			8%	5,400,000	75,000				
17			9%	5,450,000	25,000				
18			10%	5,500,000	(25,000)				
19									

The shaded cells are automatically filled by the spreadsheet package to show the impact of inflation on production costs and profits.

Two-input data tables

3.5 This facility can also be used if **two** of the numbers in the calculation are to be changed.

3.6 EXAMPLE: A TWO-INPUT DATA TABLE

Suppose the company is not sure that its production costs will be £5m - they could alternatively be only £4.5m or else they could be up to £5.5m. The problem is set up in a similar way on Excel. Study the diagram carefully.

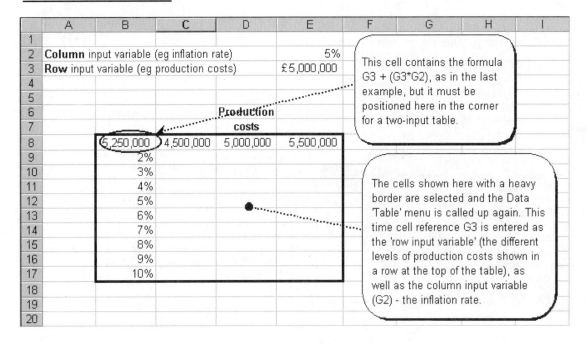

3.7 SOLUTION

Here is the solution, obtained with three or four clicks of the mouse!

	A	B	C	D	E	F	G	H
1								
2	**Column** input variable (eg inflation rate)				5%			
3	**Row** input variable (eg production costs)				£5,000,000			
4								
5								
6				**Production**				
7				**costs**				
8		5,250,000	4,500,000	5,000,000	5,500,000			
9		2%	4,590,000	5,100,000	5,610,000			
10		3%	4,635,000	5,150,000	5,665,000			
11		4%	4,680,000	5,200,000	5,720,000			
12		5%	4,725,000	5,250,000	5,775,000			
13		6%	4,770,000	5,300,000	5,830,000			
14		7%	4,815,000	5,350,000	5,885,000			
15		8%	4,860,000	5,400,000	5,940,000			
16		9%	4,905,000	5,450,000	5,995,000			
17		10%	4,950,000	5,500,000	6,050,000			
18								

Once more the cells shown here with shading are filled in automatically by the spreadsheet package

The Paper 9 examiner's article

3.8 A very comprehensive illustration was given in the form of a case study in: George Brown, 'Is this a spreadsheet I see before me?', *ACCA Students' Newsletter*, December 1994. It is rather long and complicated but the following exercise is based on the article.

Exam focus point

Topics covered in Question 3 were examined in **June 1995** and again in **December 1996**. We strongly recommend that you try out these questions for yourself using Excel or Lotus 1-2-3.

Question 3

Moist, Damp and Brown is a firm of solicitors mainly engaged in conveyancing business, domestic disputes and small claims. The partners are trying to assess their likely income from conveyancing in the next year. They charge a standard fee of £300 for conveyancing work. On average they reckon that a conveyancing job takes about 5 hours but this varies considerably from case to case due to the large number of unknown factors involved.

Years of experience enable them to assess the likely difficulty of a job (based on their knowledge of the other solicitor involved, the lending organisation, the local authority, the price of the property and so on). They have assigned weighting factors to as many of the variables as possible such that an average job has a total weighting factor of 1. They have a policy of refusing any jobs with a total weighting factor greater than 2. The most likely scenario for the coming year has been set up on a spreadsheet as follows.

	A	B	C	D	E	F	G	H
1								
2	Standard fee (£)	300						
3	Number of clients (£)	100						
4	Average time (hours)	5						
5	Variable costs per hour (£)	20						
6	Fixed costs per annum (£)	5,000						
7								
8	Variability index	1.00						
9								
10		£						
11	Fee income	30,000.00						
12	Variable costs	(10,000.00)						
13	Fixed costs	(5,000.00)						
14	Net profit	15,000.00						
15								

A data table is needed to assess the consequences of different scenarios. However the partners cannot remember how to set this up.

Required

Tell them what should be put in the top left hand corner and what should be the row variable and the column variable. Either manually or with a spreadsheet calculate the figures that will appear in the data table. What will be the net profit if 125 jobs are taken on with an overall average weighting factor of 1.25?

	A	B	C	D	E	F	G	H
18	=B14	0.50	0.75	1.00	1.25	1.50	1.75	2.00
19	0							
20	25							
21	50							
22	75							
23	100							
24	125							
25	150							
26	200							
27	225							
28	250							

Answer

Cell A18 should contain the formula =B14. The row variable is B8 and the column variable is B3. The figures are as follows. Reading from the table the net profit in the circumstances described will be £16,875.

	A	B	C	D	E	F	G	H
18	15,000.00	0.50	0.75	1.00	1.25	1.50	1.75	2.00
19	0	(5,000)	(5,000)	(5,000)	(5,000)	(5,000)	(5,000)	(5,000)
20	25	1,250	625	0	(625)	(1,250)	(1,875)	(2,500)
21	50	7,500	6,250	5,000	3,750	2,500	1,250	0
22	75	13,750	11,875	10,000	8,125	6,250	4,375	2,500
23	100	20,000	17,500	15,000	12,500	10,000	7,500	5,000
24	125	26,250	23,125	20,000	16,875	13,750	10,625	7,500
25	150	32,500	28,750	25,000	21,250	17,500	13,750	10,000
26	200	45,000	40,000	35,000	30,000	25,000	20,000	15,000
27	225	51,250	45,625	40,000	34,375	28,750	23,125	17,500
28	250	57,500	51,250	45,000	38,750	32,500	26,250	20,000

4 PROBABILITIES AND EXPECTED VALUES

4.1 Although the outcome of a decision may not be certain, there is some likelihood that *probabilities* could be assigned to the various possible outcomes from an analysis of previous experience.

Knowledge brought forward from Paper 3

- If X, Y and Z are the mutually exclusive outcomes of an event (which means that no two outcomes can happen at the same time), P(X or Y or Z) = P(X) + P(Y) + P(Z) = 1.

- Suppose X and Y are independent events (which means that the occurrence of X in no way effects the occurrence of Y).

  - Probability that both events occur (joint probability), P(X and Y) = P(X).P(Y)
  - Probability that either or both events occur, P(X or Y) = P(X) + P(Y) − P(X and Y).

- If event Y is dependent upon/conditional upon event X taking place, the probability that both events will occur, P(X and Y) = P(X) × P(Y/X) = P(Y) × P(X/Y).

Exam focus point

It is most unlikely that you would have to calculate probabilities from first principles in a Paper 9 exam.

Expected values

4.2 Where probabilities are assigned to different outcomes we can evaluate the worth of a decision as the **expected value**, or weighted average, of these outcomes. The principle is that when there are a number of alternative decisions, each with a range of possible outcomes, the optimum decision will be the one which gives the highest expected value.

4.3 EXAMPLE: EXPECTED VALUES

Suppose a manager has to choose between mutually exclusive options A and B, and the probable outcomes of each option are as follows.

	Option A			Option B	
Probability	Profit £		Probability	Profit £	
0.8	5,000		0.1	(2,000)	
0.2	6,000		0.2	5,000	
			0.6	7,000	
			0.1	8,000	

The expected value (EV) of profit of each option would be measured as follows.

	Option A				Option B		
Prob	Profit £		EV of profit £	Prob	Profit £		EV of profit £
0.8 ×	5,000	=	4,000	0.1 ×	(2,000)	=	(200)
0.2 ×	6,000	=	1,200	0.2 ×	5,000	=	1,000
	EV	=	5,200	0.6 ×	7,000	=	4,200
				0.1 ×	8,000	=	800
					EV	=	5,800

In this example, since it offers a higher EV of expected profit, option B would be selected in preference to A, unless further risk analysis is carried out.

> **FORMULA TO LEARN**
>
> The **expected value** of an opportunity is equal to the sum of the probabilities of an outcome occurring multiplied by the return expected if it does occur:
>
> $$EV = \sum px$$
>
> where p is the probability of an outcome occurring and x is the value (profit or cost) of that outcome.

Question 4

A manager has to choose between mutually exclusive options C and D and the probable outcomes of each option are as follows.

	Option C		Option D	
Probability	Cost £	Probability	Cost £	
0.29	15,000	0.03	14,000	
0.54	20,000	0.30	17,000	
0.17	30,000	0.35	21,000	
		0.32	24,000	

Both options will produce an income of £30,000. Which should be chosen?

Answer

Option C. Do the workings yourself in the way illustrated above. Note that the probabilities are for *costs* not profits.

Limitations of expected values

4.4 The preference for B over A on the basis of expected value is marred by the fact that A's **worst possible** outcome is a profit of £5,000, whereas B might incur a loss of £2,000 (although there is a 70% chance that profits would be £7,000 or more, which would be more than the best profits from option A).

4.5 Since the decision must be made **once only** between A and B, the expected value of profit (which is **merely a weighted average** of all possible outcomes) has severe limitations as a decision rule by which to judge preference.

4.6 Expected values are more valuable as a guide to decision making where they refer to outcomes which will occur **many times over**. Examples would include the probability that so many customers per day will buy a can of baked beans, the probability that a customer services assistant will receive so many phone calls per hour, and so on.

Cumulative probability tables

4.7 As we have seen, EVs can be used to compare two or more mutually exclusive alternatives. The alternative with the most favourable EV of profit or cost would normally be preferred. However, alternatives can also be compared by looking at the **spread of possible outcomes**, and the probabilities that they will occur. The technique of drawing up **cumulative probability tables** might be helpful, as the following example shows.

4.8 EXAMPLE: CUMULATIVE PROBABILITY

QRS Ltd is reviewing the price that it charges for a major product line. Over the past three years the product has had sales averaging 48,000 units per year at a standard selling price of £5.25. Costs have been rising steadily over the past year and the company is considering raising this price to £5.75 or £6.25. The sales manager has produced the following schedule to assist with the decision.

Price	£5.75	£6.25
Estimates of demand		
Pessimistic estimate (probability 0.25)	35,000	10,000
Most likely estimate (probability 0.60)	40,000	20,000
Optimistic estimate (probability 0.15)	50,000	40,000

Currently the unit cost is estimated at £5.00, analysed as follows.

	£
Direct material	2.50
Direct labour	1.00
Variable overhead	1.00
Fixed overhead	0.50
	5.00

The cost accountant considers that the most likely value for unit variable cost over the next year is £4.90 (probability 0.75) but that it could be as high as £5.20 (probability 0.15) and it might even be as low as £4.75 (probability 0.10). Total fixed costs are currently £24,000 pa but it is estimated that the total for the ensuing year will be £25,000 with a probability of 0.2, £27,000 with a probability of 0.6 or £30,000 with a probability of 0.2.

(Demand quantities, unit costs and fixed costs can be assumed to be statistically independent.)

Required

Analyse the foregoing information in a way which you consider will assist management with the problem, give your views on the situation and advise on the new selling price. Calculate the expected level of profit that would follow from the selling price that you recommend.

4.9 DISCUSSION AND SOLUTION

In this example, there are two mutually exclusive options, a price of £5.75 and a price of £6.25. Sales demand is uncertain, but would vary with price. Unit contribution and total contribution depend on sales price and sales volume, but total fixed costs are common to both options. Clearly, it makes sense to begin looking at EVs of contribution and then to think about fixed costs and profits later.

(a) A table of probabilities can be set out for each alternative, and an EV calculated, as follows.

(i) **Price £5.75**

Sales demand Units	Prob	Variable cost per unit £	Prob	Unit cont'n £	Total cont'n £'000	Joint prob	EV of cont'n £'000
35,000	0.25	5.20	0.15	0.55	19.25	0.037	0.722
		4.90	0.75	0.85	29.75	0.187	5.578
		4.75	0.10	1.00	35.00	0.025	0.875
40,000	0.60	5.20	0.15	0.55	22.00	0.090	1.980
		4.90	0.75	0.85	34.00	0.450	15.300
		4.75	0.10	1.00	40.00	0.060	2.400
50,000	0.15	5.20	0.15	0.55	27.50	0.022	0.619
		4.90	0.75	0.85	42.50	0.112	4.781
		4.75	0.10	1.00	50.00	0.015	0.750
				EV of contribution			33.005

The EV of contribution at a price of £5.75 is £33,005. This EV could have been calculated more quickly and simply by calculating the EV of sales demand and the EV of variable cost, but an extended table of probabilities will help the risk analysis when the two alternative selling prices are compared.

(ii) **Price £6.25**

Sales demand Units	Prob	Variable cost per unit £	Prob	Unit cont'n £	Total cont'n £'000	Joint prob	EV of cont'n £000
10,000	0.25	5.20	0.15	1.05	10.50	0.0375	0.394
		4.90	0.75	1.35	13.50	0.1875	2.531
		4.75	0.10	1.50	15.00	0.0250	0.375
20,000	0.60	5.20	0.15	1.05	21.00	0.0900	1.890
		4.90	0.75	1.35	27.00	0.4500	12.150
		4.75	0.10	1.50	30.00	0.0600	1.800
40,000	0.15	5.20	0.15	1.05	42.00	0.0225	0.945
		4.90	0.75	1.35	54.00	0.1125	6.075
		4.75	0.10	1.50	60.00	0.0150	0.900
				EV of contribution			27.060

The EV of contribution at a price of £6.25 is £27,060.

(b) **Fixed costs**

The EV of fixed costs is £27,200.

Fixed costs £	Probability	EV £
25,000	0.2	5,000
27,000	0.6	16,200
30,000	0.2	6,000
		27,200

(c) **Conclusion**

On the basis of EVs alone, a price of £5.75 is preferable to a price of £6.25, since it offers an EV of contribution of £33,005 and so an EV of profit of £5,805; whereas a price of £6.25 offers an EV of profit of only £27,060 and so an EV of loss of £140.

The disadvantages of point estimate probabilities

4.10 A point estimate probability means an estimate of the probability of **particular outcomes** occurring. In the previous example, there were point estimate probabilities for variable costs (£5.20 or £4.90 or £4.75) but in reality, the actual variable cost per unit might be any amount, from below £4.75 to above £5.20. Similarly, point estimate probabilities were given for period fixed costs (£25,000 or £27,000 or £30,000) but in reality, actual fixed costs might be **any amount between** about £25,000 and £30,000.

4.11 This is a disadvantage of using point estimate probabilities: they can be **unrealistic**, and can only be an **approximation** of the risk and uncertainty in estimates.

The advantages of point estimate probabilities

4.12 In spite of their possible disadvantages, point estimate probabilities can be very helpful for a decision maker.

(a) They provide some estimate of risk, which is probably **better than nothing**.

(b) If there are **enough** point estimates they are likely to be a **reasonably good** approximation of a continuous probability distribution.

(c) Alternatively, it can be **assumed** that point estimate probabilities **represent a range** of values, so that if we had the probabilities for variable cost per unit, say, of £5.20, £4.90, and £4.75 we could assume that those actually represent probabilities for the ranges, say, £5.05 to £5.30, and £4.82 to £5.04 and £4.70 to £4.81.

(d) The estimates are relatively easy to make, and so are **more practical** than attempting continuous probability distribution estimates.

Question 5

In examination questions you are usually **told** the probability of various outcomes. Where would this information come from in practice and how reliable would you expect it to be?

Answer

Probabilities can be calculated from historical records. For example if your train was late four mornings out of five last week there is an 80% chance of your train being late. Obviously the larger the sample the more reliable the information is likely to be - you may live on a particularly bad line, or there may have been engineering works last week.

As a further exercise, use your bank statements for the last year or so to calculate the probability that you will have over, say, £500 in the bank on the 20th day of a month. (Choose another amount if £500 is unrealistically high or low.)

Exam focus point

Straightforward EV calculations were required in the **June 1998** and **December 1998** exams. Joint probability calculations were needed in the **June 1999** exam. Candidates needed to use a two-way data table provided in the question to calculate the resulting EV.

5 DECISION TREES

Knowledge brought forward from Paper 3

Decision trees

- Decision trees are diagrams which illustrate the choices and possible outcomes of a decision.

- The preparation of a decision tree is as follows.

  o Start with a (labelled) *decision point.*

  o Add branches for each option/alternative.

  o If the outcome of an option is 100% certain, the branch for that alternative is complete.

  o If the outcome of an option is uncertain (ie there are a number of possible outcomes), add a (labelled) *outcome point.*

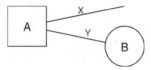

  o For each possible outcome, a branch (with the relevant probability) should be added to the outcome point.

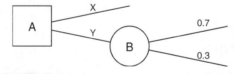

  o Always work *chronologically* from left to right.

Exam focus point

A question in **December 1994** asked for a decision tree illustration of a problem that involved deciding whether or not to investigate a variance given various probabilities.

Knowledge brought forward from Paper 3

Rollback analysis

Rollback analysis is the technique used to evaluate a decision with a decision tree. Working from **right to left**, the EV of revenue/cost/contribution/profit is calculated at each *outcome point.*

Example: As a result of an increase in demand for a town's car parking facilities, the owners of a car park are reviewing their business operations. A decision has to be made now to select one of the following three options for the next year.

Option 1: Make no change. Annual profit is £100,000. There is little likelihood that this will provoke new competition this year.

Option 2: Raise prices by 50%. If this occurs there is a 75% chance that an entrepreneur will set up in competition this year. The Board's estimate of its annual profit in this situation would be as follows.

Knowledge brought forward from Paper 3 (cont)

	2A WITH a new competitor		2B WITHOUT a new competitor	
Probability	Profit		Probability	Profit
	£			£
0.3	150,000		0.7	200,000
0.7	120,000		0.3	150,000

Option 3: Expand the car park quickly, at a cost of £50,000, keeping prices the same. The profits are estimated to be like 2B above, except the probabilities would be 0.6 and 0.4 respectively

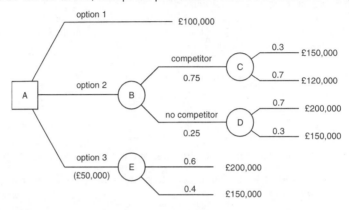

At C, expected profit = (150 × 0.3) + (120 × 0.7) = £129,000
At D, expected profit = (200 × 0.7) + (150 x 0.3) = £185,000
At B, expected profit = (129 × 0.75) + (185 × 0.25) = £143,000
At E, expected profit = (200 × 0.6) + (150 × 0.4) = £180,000

Option	Expected profit
	£'000
1	100
2	143
3 (180 – 50)	130

Question 6

A software company has just won a contract worth £80,000 if it delivers a successful product on time, but only £40,000 if it is late. It faces the problem now of whether to produce the work in-house or to sub-contract it. To sub-contract the work would cost £50,000, but the local sub-contractor is so fast and reliable as to make it certain that successful software is produced on time.

If the work is produced in-house the cost would be only £20,000 but, based on past experience, would have only a 90% chance of being successful. In the event of the software *not* being successful, there would be insufficient time to rewrite the whole package internally, but there would still be the options of either a 'late rejection' of the contract (at a further cost of £10,000) or of 'late sub-contracting' the work on the same terms as before. With this late start the local sub-contractor is estimated to have only a 50/50 chance of producing the work on time or of producing it late. In this case the sub-contractor still has to be paid £50,000, regardless of whether he meets the deadline or not.

Required

(a) Draw a decision tree for the software company, using squares for decision points and circles for outcome (chance) points, including all relevant data on the diagram.

(b) Calculate expected values as appropriate and recommend a course of action to the software company with reasons.

Answer

(a)   All values in £'000

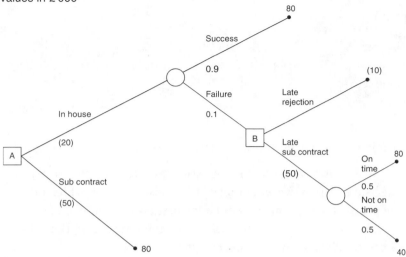

(b)   *At decision point B*
EV of late rejection = -10
EV of late sub-contract = (80 × 0.5) + (40 × 0.5) - 50 = 10
The optimum strategy at B is therefore to subcontract with EV = 10.

At decision point A
EV of sub-contract = 80 - 50 = 30
EV of in-house = (80 × 0.9) + (10* × 0.1) - 20 = 53
The optimum strategy at A is therefore to produce in-house with EV = 53.

*This is the optimum EV at decision point B.

Conclusions

The decisions which will maximise expected profits are to attempt initially to produce in-house and if this fails to sub-contract. The expected profit is £53,000.

Assuming that the probabilities have been correctly estimated, the company has a 90% chance of making a profit of £60,000, a 5% chance of making £10,000 and a 5% chance of making a £30,000 loss. If the company is not willing to risk making a loss, the initial option of subcontracting should be taken since this offers a guaranteed profit of £30,000.

---

6   PERFECT AND IMPERFECT INFORMATION

6.1   Whenever a decision is made whose outcome is uncertain, there will always be some **doubt that the correct decision has been taken**. If a decision is based on selecting the option with the highest EV of profit, it can be assumed that in the long run (that is, with a sufficient repetition of the outcomes), the decision option so selected will give the highest average profit. But if the decision involves a once-only outcome, there will be a big risk that the outcome will be worse than the EV, and that in retrospect it will eventually be seen that the wrong decision was taken.

6.2   The uncertainty about the future outcome from taking a decision can sometimes be reduced by **obtaining more information** first about what is likely to happen. Information can be obtained from various sources, such as market research surveys, other surveys or questionnaires, conducting a pilot test or building a prototype model.

6.3   We can categorise information depending upon how reliable it is likely to be for predicting the future and hence for helping managers to make better decisions.

The value of perfect information

> ## KEY TERM
>
> **Perfect information** removes *all* doubt and uncertainty from a decision, and it would enable managers to make decisions with complete confidence that they have selected the most profitable course of action.

6.4 We can estimate a value of perfect information, based on expected values (EVs) as follows.

Step 1. If we **do not have perfect information** and we must choose between two or more decision options, we would select the decision option which offers the **highest EV of profit**. This option will not be the best decision under all circumstances. There will be some probability that what was really the best option will not have been selected, given the way actual events turn out.

Step 2. **With perfect information**, the **best decision option** will always be selected. Just what the profits from the decision will be must depend on the future circumstances which are predicted by the information; nevertheless, the EV of profit with perfect information should be higher than the EV of profit without the information.

Step 3. The **value** of perfect information is the **difference** between these two EVs.

6.5 EXAMPLE: THE VALUE OF PERFECT INFORMATION

The management of Ivor Ore Ltd must choose whether to go ahead with either of two mutually exclusive projects, A and B. The expected profits are as follows.

	Profit if there is strong demand	*Profit/(loss) if there is weak demand*
Option A	£4,000	£(1,000)
Option B	£1,500	£500
Probability of demand	0.3	0.7

(a) What would be the decision, based on expected values, if no information about demand were available?

(b) What is the value of perfect information about demand?

6.6 SOLUTION

Step 1. If there were **no information** to help with the decision, the project with the higher EV of profit would be selected.

Probability	*Project A*		*Project B*	
	Profit	*EV*	*Profit*	*EV*
	£	£	£	£
0.3	4,000	1,200	1,500	450
0.7	(1,000)	(700)	500	350
		500		800

Project B would be selected, and this is clearly the better option if demand turns out to be weak. However, if demand were to turn out to be strong, project A would be more profitable. There is a 30% chance that this could happen.

Step 2. **Perfect information** will indicate for certain whether demand will be weak or strong. If demand is forecast 'weak' project B would be selected. If demand is forecast 'strong', project A would be selected, and perfect information would improve the profit from £1,500, which would have been earned by selecting B, to £4,000.

Forecast demand	Probability	Project chosen	Profit £	EV of profit £
Weak	0.7	B	500	350
Strong	0.3	A	4,000	1,200
EV of profit with perfect information				1,550

Step 3.

	£
EV of profit without perfect information (that is, if project B is always	800
EV of profit with perfect information	1,550
Value of perfect information	750

Provided the information does not cost more than £750 to collect, it would be worth having.

Question 7

Watt Lovell Ltd must decide at what level to market a new product, the urk. The urk can be sold nationally, within a single sales region (where demand is likely to be relatively strong) or within a single area. The decision is complicated by uncertainty about the general strength of consumer demand for the product, and the following conditional profit table has been constructed.

		Demand		
		Weak £	Moderate £	Strong £
Market	nationally (A)	(4,000)	2,000	10,000
	in one region (B)	0	3,500	4,000
	in one area (C)	1,000	1,500	2,000
Probability		0.3	0.5	0.2

(a) What should the decision be, based on EVs of profit?
(b) What would be the value of perfect information about the state of demand?

Answer

(a) Without perfect information, the option with the highest EV of profit will be chosen.

	Option A (National)		Option B (Regional)		Option C (Area)	
Probability	Profit £	EV £	Profit £	EV £	Profit £	EV £
0.3	(4,000)	(1,200)	0	0	1,000	300
0.5	2,000	1,000	3,500	1,750	1,500	750
0.2	10,000	2,000	4,000	800	2,000	400
		1,800		2,550		1,450

Marketing regionally (option B) has the highest EV of profit, and would be selected.

(b) If perfect information about the state of consumer demand were available, option A would be preferred if the forecast demand is strong and option C if the forecast demand is weak.

Demand	Probability	Choice	Profit £	EV of profit £
Weak	0.3	C	1,000	300
Moderate	0.5	B	3,500	1,750
Strong	0.2	A	10,000	2,000
EV of profit with perfect information				4,050
EV of profit, selecting option B				2,550
Value of perfect information				1,500

The value of imperfect information

6.7   There is one serious drawback to the technique we have just looked at: in practice **useful information is never perfect** unless the person providing it is the sole source of the uncertainty. Market research findings or information from pilot tests and so on are likely to be reasonably accurate, but they can still be wrong: they provide imperfect information. It is possible, however, to arrive at an assessment of how much it would be worth paying for such imperfect information, **given that we have a rough indication of how right or wrong it is likely to be**.

6.8   The assessment of the value hinges on the calculation of **posterior probabilities** (the probability of something happening once the information has been obtained) and **prior probabilities** (the probability of something happening based on past experience only).

Exam focus point

The examiner has confirmed that, although the topic of imperfect information may feature within an exam question, you will not be required to perform any quantitative work on this topic. So you don't need to worry about the way in which prior and posterior probabilities are calculated.

6.9   A decision tree can be drawn based on the probabilities calculated and rollback analysis carried out. The value of imperfect information is then calculated in a similar way to that of perfect information as the difference between the EV if information is obtained and the EV if information is not obtained.

Chapter roundup

- Management accounting directs its attention towards the **future** and the future is **uncertain**. For this reason a number of methods of taking uncertainty and risk into consideration have evolved.

- **Sensitivity analysis** can be used in any situation so long as the relationships between the key variables can be established. Typically this involves changing the value of a variable and seeing how the results are affected.

- Approaches like **conservatism** or **maximax** are often used intuitively in practice. It may be that psychological factors (feelings of safety on the one hand or exhilaration at the risk on the other) need to be taken into account.

- **Expected values** indicate what an outcome is likely to be in the long term with repetition. Fortunately, many business transactions do occur over and over again

- A **data table** is a group of cells in a spreadsheet that show the results of changing the value of variables.

- **Decision trees** should be drawn from left to right using different symbols to distinguish decision points and outcome points. They are evaluated by 'rolling back' from right to left, calculating the EVs of each outcome point to enable the decision(s) to be made.

- Information is unlikely to be **perfect** in practice unless it is so general as to be of limited value. However, it may be worth paying for **imperfect** information especially if it is also possible to ascertain how likely it is to be correct.

Quick quiz

1 What do you understand by the term 'risk preference'? (see para 1.2)

2 What is the maximin decision rule? (2.7 - 2.8)

3 What might sensitivity analysis attempt to establish? (2.16)

4 What is a data table? (3.1)

5 How is expected value calculated? (4.3)

6 What are the limitations of expected values? (4.4 - 4.6)

7 What are the advantages of point estimate probabilities? (4.12)

8 What are the three steps for determining the value of perfect information? (6.4)

9 What is the drawback of perfect information? (6.7)

Question to try	Level	Marks	Time
8	Exam standard	15	27 mins

BPP PUBLISHING

Chapter 9

PRICING

Chapter topic list	Syllabus reference
1 Costs and pricing policy	1(d), 4(a)
2 Pricing policy and the market	4(a)
3 The optimum price/output level	4(a)
4 Special cases in pricing	4(a)

Introduction

This is the last chapter in the decision making part of this book. We look briefly at some traditional cost-based approaches to the pricing of costs and services, and in more detail at **activity based** approaches. Then we consider some of the practical issues, since pricing has a great deal to do with **customers**, **competitors** and **markets**. The third section is derived from **economic theory**, but don't neglect it because it has been examined - and that in the context of **spreadsheets**. Finally we mention one or two special cases that may crop up in pricing.

Core areas of the syllabus identified by the examiner and covered in this chapter: **price/demand relationships**, **use of elementary calculus**; **life cycle aspects**, **short life products**, **impact of features such as ABC**, **costs and pricing**; **costing and pricing of internal services**.

1 COSTS AND PRICING POLICY

1.1 Price can go by many names: fares, tuitions, rent, assessments and so on. All profit organisations and many non-profit organisations face the task of setting a price for their products or services.

1.2 In modern marketing philosophy, price, whilst important, is not necessarily the predominant factor. Modern businesses seek to interpret and **satisfy consumer wants and needs** by modifying existing products or introducing new products to the range. This contrasts with earlier production-oriented times when the typical reaction was to cut prices in order to sell more of an organisation's product.

1.3 Nevertheless proper pricing of an organisation's products or services is essential to its **profitability** and hence its **survival**, and price has an important role to play as a **competitive tool** which can be used to differentiate a product and an organisation and thus exploit market opportunities.

Traditional approaches

1.4 You studied traditional ideas about pricing at **Paper 8**. Read the notes below and then try the questions, which will give you some practice on **basic techniques**, and also reinforce your understanding of how to deal with **uncertainty**.

Knowledge brought forward from Paper 8

- With **full cost-plus pricing** the sales price is determined by calculating the full cost of the product and then adding a percentage mark-up for profit.

  - This ensures that **all costs are covered**.
  - It is useful if prices have to be **justified** to customers.
  - However it takes **no account of market or demand** conditions.
  - It requires **arbitrary** decisions about **absorption** of costs.
  - There may be problems in determining the **profit mark up.**

- With **marginal cost plus pricing**, a profit margin is added on to either the marginal cost of production or the marginal cost of sales. This is sometimes called 'mark-up' pricing.

  - This draws attention to **contribution**.
  - It is convenient if there is a **readily identifiable variable cost** (eg in retail).
  - However, again it takes **no account of market or demand** conditions.
  - Pricing decisions **cannot ignore fixed costs** in the long term.

- **Minimum pricing** is an approach based on relevant costs. It may be useful when tendering for work. The minimum price consists of the **incremental** cost of producing and selling an item and the **opportunity** costs of the resources used to do so.

  - It shows an **absolute minimum** below which price should not be set.
  - Actual price – minimum price = the **incremental profit** that would be obtained per item.

Question 1

A product's full cost is £4.75 and it is sold at full cost plus 70%. A competitor has just launched a similar product selling for £7.99. How will this affect the first product's mark up?

Answer

The cost-plus percentage will need to be reduced by 2%.

Question 2

Markup Ltd has begun to produce a new product, Product X, for which the following cost estimates have been made.

	£
Direct materials	27
Direct labour: 4 hrs at £5 per hour	20
Variable production overheads: machining, ½ hr at £6 per hour	3
	50

Production fixed overheads are budgeted at £300,000 per month and because of the shortage of available machining capacity, the company will be restricted to 10,000 hours of machine time per month. The absorption rate will be a direct labour rate, however, and budgeted direct labour hours are 25,000 per month. It is estimated that the company could obtain a minimum contribution of £10 per machine hour on producing items other than product X.

The direct cost estimates are not certain as to material usage rates and direct labour productivity, and it is recognised that the estimates of direct materials and direct labour costs may be subject to an error of ± 15%. Machine time estimates are similarly subject to an error of ± 10%.

The company wishes to make a profit of 20% on full production cost from product X. What should the full-cost-plus based price be?

Answer

Even for a relatively 'simple' cost plus pricing estimate, some problems can arise, and certain assumptions must be made and stated. In this example, we can identify two problems.

(a)   Should the opportunity cost of machine time be included in cost or not?

(b)   What allowance, if any, should be made for the possible errors in cost estimates?

Using different assumptions, we could arrive at any of four different unit prices in the range £117.60 to £141.66.

(a)   *Exclude machine time opportunity costs: ignore possible costing errors*

	£
Direct materials	27.00
Direct labour (4 hours)	20.00
Variable production o/hds	3.00
Fixed production o/hds (at £300,000/25,000 = £12 per direct labour hour)	48.00
Full production cost	98.00
Profit mark-up (20%)	19.60
Selling price per unit of product X	117.60

(b)   *Include machine time opportunity costs: ignore possible costing errors*

	£
Full production cost as in (a)	98.00
Opportunity cost of machine time (contribution forgone (½ hr × £10))	5.00
Adjusted full cost	103.00
Profit mark-up (20%)	20.60
Selling price per unit of product X	123.60

(c)   *Exclude machine time opportunity costs but make full allowance for possible under-estimates of cost*

	£	£
Direct materials	27.00	
Direct labour	20.00	
	47.00	
Possible error (15%)	7.05	
		54.05
Variable production overheads	3.00	
Possible error (10%)	0.30	
		3.30
Fixed production overheads (4 hrs × £12)	48.00	
Possible error (labour time) (15%)	7.20	
		55.20
Potential full production cost		112.55
Profit mark-up (20%)		22.51
Selling price per unit of product X		135.06

(d)   *Include machine time opportunity costs and make a full allowance for possible under-estimates of cost*

	£
Potential full production cost as in (c)	112.55
Opp cost of machine time (potential contrib'n forgone (½ hr × £10 × 110%))	5.50
Adjusted potential full cost	118.05
Profit mark-up (20%)	23.61
Selling price per unit of product X	141.66

Exam focus point

Information for the functional/process analysis required for the traditional cost plus profit mark-up approach to pricing will differ considerably depending on the type of product (use of direct and indirect costs, basis for the absorption of overhead costs), as examined in question 5 of the **June 1998** paper.

1.5   In his article 'Product costing/pricing strategy' (*ACCA Students' Newsletter*, August 1999), the examiner suggests four alternatives to a selling price based on an organisation's standard cost plus approach.

(a) **Lower the profit mark-up** if **considerable competition** exists.

(b) **Set the price equal to its total cost** if **competition** is **very tough.** (Fixed units will at least be covered.)

(c) If an organisation has **spare capacity,** the **total variable (marginal) cost** can be used as a starting point in deciding on the acceptability of a price below total cost.

(d) If an organisation has **spare capacity** and there are some **product (order) specific fixed costs** which would be avoidable if the order did not go ahead, the **marginal cost of the order must include these costs.**

1.6 This article, which we have reproduced at the end of the text, covers a wide range of topics. We have summarised the main points at relevant places throughout the text but we strongly advise you to study it in general.

Pricing and ABC

1.7 As you know, under the ABC approach overheads are allocated to products on the basis of the activities that cause them to be incurred, rather than according to some arbitrary base like labour hours. The implication for pricing is that the **full cost** on which prices are based may be **radically different** if ABC is used.

1.8 EXAMPLE: ACTIVITY BASED COSTING AND PRICING

This example uses information from 'Markup Ltd' in Question 2, plus additional details. (Do Question 2 before proceeding if you have not done so already.)

ABP Ltd makes two products, X and Y, with the following cost patterns.

	Product X	Product Y
	£	£
Direct materials	27	24
Direct labour at £5 per hour	20	25
Variable production overheads at £6 per hour	3	6
	50	55

Production fixed overheads total £300,000 per month and these are absorbed on the basis of direct labour hours. Budgeted direct labour hours are 25,000 per month. However, the company has carried out an analysis of its production support activities and found that its 'fixed costs' actually vary in accordance with non volume-related factors.

Activity	Cost driver	Product X	Product Y	Total cost
				£
Set-ups	Production runs	30	20	40,000
Materials handling	Production runs	30	20	150,000
Inspection	Inspections	880	3,520	110,000
				300,000

Budgeted production is 1,250 units of product X and 4,000 units of product Y.

Required

Given that the company wishes to make a profit of 20% on full production costs calculate the prices that should be charged for products X and Y using:

(a) full cost-plus pricing;

(b) activity based cost-plus pricing.

1.9 SOLUTION

(a) The full cost and mark-up will be calculated as follows.

	Product X £	Product Y £
Variable costs	50.00	55.00
Fixed prod o/hds (£300,000/25,000 = £12 per direct labour hr)	48.00	60.00
	98.00	115.00
Profit mark-up (20%)	19.60	23.00
Selling price	117.60	138.00

(b) Using activity based costing, overheads will be allocated on the basis of cost drivers.

	X	Y	Total
Set ups (30:20)	24,000	16,000	40,000
Materials handling (30:20)	90,000	60,000	150,000
Inspections (880:3,520)	22,000	88,000	110,000
	136,000	164,000	300,000
Budgeted units	1,250	4,000	
Overheads per unit	£108.80	£41.00	

The price is then calculated as before.

	Product X £	Product Y £
Variable costs	50.00	55.00
Production overheads	108.80	41.00
	158.80	96.00
Profit mark-up (20%)	31.76	19.20
	190.56	115.20

Commentary

1.10 The results in (b) are radically different from those in (a). On this basis it appears that the company has previously been making a huge loss on every unit of product X sold for £117.60. If the market will not accept a price increase, it may be worth considering ceasing production of product X entirely. It also appears that there is scope for a reduction in the price of product Y, and this would certainly be worthwhile if demand for the product is elastic.

The pricing implications of activity based costing

1.11 Consider a business that produces a **large volume** standard product and a number of **variants** which are more refined versions of the basic product and sell in low volumes at a higher price. Such companies are common in practice in the modern business environment. In practice, also, such companies absorb fixed overheads on a conventional basis such as direct labour hours, and price their products by adding a mark up to full cost.

1.12 In the situation described, the **majority of the overheads** would be allocated to the **standard** range, and only a small percentage to the up-market products. The result would be that the profit margin achieved on the standard range would be much lower than that on the up-market range.

1.13 Thus the traditional costing and pricing system indicates that the firm might be wise to concentrate on its high margin, up-market products and drop its standard range. This is **absurd,** however. Much of the overhead cost incurred in such an organisation is the cost of support activities like production scheduling: the more different **varieties** of product there are, the higher the level of such activities will become. The cost of marketing and distribution also increase disproportionately to the volume of products being made.

1.14 The bulk of the overheads in such an organisation are actually the 'costs of complexity'. Their arbitrary allocation on the basis of labour hours gives an entirely **distorted** view of production line profitability; many products that appear to be highly profitable actually make a loss if costs are allocated on the basis of what activities cause them.

1.15 The problem arises with **marginal cost-plus** approaches as well as with absorption cost based approaches, particularly in a modern manufacturing environment, where a relatively small proportion of the total cost is variable. The implication in both cases is that conventional costing should be abandoned in favour of ABC.

The examiner and the ABC approach to pricing

1.16 The examiner provides an example of the **implications of adopting an ABC system** for determining prices as opposed to a traditional volume-related approach in 'Product costing/pricing strategy' (*ACCA Students' Newsletter*, August 1999). As well as providing numerical illustrations, the examiner lists the following **problems of applying an ABC system.**

- The selection of the relevant activities and cost drivers

- The collection of data to enable accurate cost driver rates to be calculated

- The problem of cost driver denominator level – similar to that in a traditional volume related system

- Achieving the required level of management commitment to the change

The examiner also mentions the problem of applying cost driver rates to products, which may require the **hierarchical approach** as covered in section 6 of chapter 3.

2 PRICING POLICY AND THE MARKET

2.1 In practice in the **modern world** there are many more influences on price than the cost of a product or service.

Influence	Explanation/Example
Price sensitivity	Sensitivity to price levels will vary amongst purchasers. Those that can pass on the cost of purchases will be the least sensitive and will therefore respond more to other elements of perceived value. For example, a business traveller will be more concerned about the level of service in looking for an hotel than price, provided that it fits the corporate budget. In contrast, a family on holiday are likely to be very price sensitive when choosing an overnight stay.
Price perception	Price perception is the **way customers react to prices**. For example, customers may react to a price increase by buying more. This could be because they expect further price increases to follow (they are 'stocking up').
Quality	This is an aspect of price perception. In the absence of other information, customers tend to **judge quality by price**. Thus a price rise may indicate improvements in quality, a price reduction may signal reduced quality.

Influence	Explanation/Example
Intermediaries	If an organisation distributes products or services to the market through independent intermediaries, such intermediaries are likely to deal with a range of suppliers and **their aims** concern their own profits rather than those of suppliers.
Competitors	In some industries (such as petrol retailing) pricing moves in unison; in others, price changes by one supplier may initiate a price war. **Competition is discussed in more detail below**.
Suppliers	If an organisation's suppliers notice a price rise for the organisation's products, they may seek a rise in the price for their supplies to the organisation.
Inflation	In periods of inflation the organisation may need to change prices to reflect increases in the prices of supplies, labour, rent and so on.
Newness	When a **new product is introduced for the first time** there are **no existing reference points** such as customer or competitor behaviour; pricing decisions are most difficult to make in such circumstances. It may be possible to seek alternative reference points, such as the price in another market where the new product has already been launched, or the price set by a competitor.
Incomes	If **incomes are rising, price** may be a **less important** marketing variable than product quality and convenience of access (distribution). When income levels are falling and/or unemployment levels rising, price will be more important.
Product range	Products are often interrelated, being complements to each other or substitutes for one another. The management of the pricing function is likely to focus on the profit from the whole range rather than the profit on each single product.
	For example, a very low price is charged for a **loss leader** to make consumers buy additional products in the range which carry higher profit margins (eg selling razors at very low prices whilst selling the blades for them at a higher profit margin).
Ethics	Ethical considerations may be a further factor, for example whether or not to exploit short-term shortages through higher prices.

Porter's Five Forces Model

2.2   Porter's model suggests the importance of **pressure from five competitive forces on price.**

(a) **Threat of new entrants** (which will be affected by barriers to entry and expected reaction from existing firms).

(b) **Threat of substitutes** (which will be determined by the level of innovation of existing producers, the ability of existing competitors to finance responses to the threat and the propensity of buyers to substitute).

(c) **Bargaining power of buyers** (which will be linked to the number of buyers).

(d) **Bargaining power of suppliers** (supplier power and the impact on costs being greater when there are fewer of them).

(e) **Rivalry between existing competitors** (the strength of rivalry being determined by number of competitors, market power, brand identity, producer differences cost structure and so on).

Product life cycle

2.3   A typical product has a life cycle of four stages.

(a) **Introduction**

The product is introduced to the market. Heavy **capital expenditure** will be incurred on product development and perhaps also on new fixed assets and building up stocks for sale. The product will begin to earn some revenue, but initially demand is likely to be small, the level being determined by the product's advantage on price or quality over rival products. Potential customers will be unaware of the product or service, and the organisation may have to spend further on **advertising** to bring the product or service to the attention of the market. Investment in distribution, after-sales warranties and so on should help to overcome customer resistance and any perception of recent lack of reliability or longevity of the product. We will consider the importance of focusing on customer satisfaction and identifying where we look at the performance pyramid view of business and balanced scorecard performance measurement system in chapter 17.

(b) **Growth**

The product gains a bigger market as demand builds up. Sales revenues increase and the product begins to make a profit. The initial costs of the **investment** in the new product are gradually **recovered**. Characteristics of this phase are reduced uncertainty about the product, repeat buyers, brand loyalty and a perception of price and/or quality advantages by consumers.

(c) **Maturity**

Eventually, the growth in demand for the product will slow down and it will enter a period of relative maturity. It will continue to be profitable. The need to retain existing customers or attract new ones will be important. The product may be **modified or improved**, as a means of sustaining its demand.

(d) **Saturation and decline**

At some stage, the market will have bought enough of the product and it will therefore reach 'saturation point'. Demand will start to fall. The rate of decline may depend on the degree of change in fashion and/or technological change, and the comparative price/quality advantages of emerging products. For a while, the product will still be profitable in spite of declining sales, but eventually it will become a **loss-maker** and this is the time when the organisation should decide to stop selling the product or service. Remember, however, that some mature products will **never decline**: staple food products are the best example.

The product life cycle is a relevant factor in the determining of product market strategies and the price/cost relationships which are factors in the pricing and profitability of a product (George Brown 'Product costing/pricing strategy', *ACCA Students' Newsletter*, August 1999).

BPP PUBLISHING

Boston Consulting Group (BCG) Portfolio matrix

2.4   The BCG portfolio matrix provides a method of positioning products through their life cycles in terms of market growth and market share.

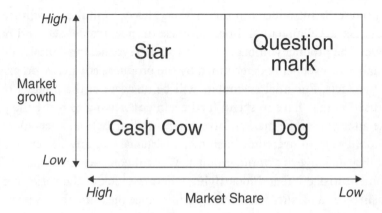

(a)   **Stars** are products with a **high share** of a **high growth market.** In the short term, items require investment in excess of the cash they generate in order to maintain their market position, but promise high returns in the future.

(b)   In due course, however, starts will become **cash cows,** with a **high share** of a **low growth** (mature) **market.** They require very little investment and generate high levels of cash income. The important strategic feature of cash cows is that they are already generating high cash returns, which can support the stars.

(c)   **Question marks** are competitive products with a **low share** of a **huge growth market.** They have the potential to become stars but a question mark hangs over their ability to achieve sufficient market retention to justify further investment.

(d)   **Dogs** are products with a **low share** of a low growth market. They should be allowed to die, or killed off.

2.5   The matrix must be managed so that an organisation's product range is balanced. Four basic strategies can be adopted.

(a)   **Build.** This involves increasing the market share, even at the expense of short-term profits. A 'build' strategy might be to turn a question mark into a star. A penetration pricing policy (see paragraph 2.9) and investment in stabilising quality and brand loyalty may be required.

(b)   **Hold.** This involves preserving market share and ensuring that cash cows remain cash cows. Additional investment in customer retention through competitive pricing and marketing may be required.

(c)   **Harvest.** This involves using funds to promote products which have the potential to become future stars or to support existing stars.

(d)   **Divest**. This involves eliminating dogs and question marks which are under performing.

Markets

2.6   The price that an organisation can charge for its products will be determined to a greater or lesser degree by the **market** in which it operates. Here are some familiar economic terms that might feature as background for a question or that you might want to use in a written answer.

KEY TERMS

- **Perfect competition**: many buyers and many sellers all dealing in an identical product. Neither producer nor user has any market power and both must accept the prevailing market price.

- **Monopoly**: one seller who dominates many buyers. The monopolist can use his market power to set a profit-maximising price.

- **Monopolistic competition**: a large number of suppliers offer similar, but not identical, products. The similarities ensure elastic demand whereas the slight differences give some monopolistic power to the supplier.

- **Oligopoly**: where relatively few competitive companies dominate the market. Whilst each large firm has the ability to influence market prices, the unpredictable reaction from the other giants makes the final industry price indeterminate. Cartels are often formed.

Competition

2.7 In **established industries** dominated by a few major firms, it is generally accepted that a price initiative by one firm will be countered by a price reaction by competitors. In these circumstances, prices tend to be **fairly stable**, unless pushed upwards by inflation or strong growth in demand.

2.8 If a rival **cuts its prices** in the expectation of increasing its market share, a firm has several options.

(a) It will **maintain its existing prices** if the expectation is that only a small market share would be lost, so that it is more profitable to keep prices at their existing level. Eventually, the rival firm may drop out of the market or be forced to raise its prices.

(b) It may maintain its prices but respond with a **non-price counter-attack**. This is a more positive response, because the firm will be securing or justifying its current prices with a product change, advertising, or better back-up services.

(c) It may **reduce its prices**. This should protect the firm's market share so that the main beneficiary from the price reduction will be the consumer.

(d) It may **raise its prices** *and respond with a* **non-price counter-attack**. The extra revenue from the higher prices might be used to finance an advertising campaign or product design changes. A price increase would be based on a campaign to emphasise the quality difference between the firm's and the rival's products.

Question 3

What technique might be used to relate prices to cost in the modern business environment?

Answer

The answer, of course, is **target costing,** which you met in Chapters 3 and 4. Price is determined by the market. Costs have to come below this price.

Market penetration pricing

2.9 This is a policy of **low prices** when the product is **first launched** in order to obtain sufficient penetration into the market. A penetration policy may be appropriate in the cases below.

(a) The firm wishes to **discourage new entrants** into the market.

(b) The firm wishes to **shorten the initial period** of the product's life cycle in order to enter the growth and maturity stages as quickly as possible.

(c) There are significant **economies of scale** to be achieved from a high volume of output.

(d) Demand is **highly elastic** and so would respond well to low prices.

2.10 Penetration prices are prices which aim to secure a substantial share in a substantial total market. A firm might therefore deliberately build **excess production capacity** and set its prices very low. As demand builds up the spare capacity will be used up gradually and unit costs will fall; the firm might even reduce prices further as unit costs fall. In this way, early losses will enable the firm to dominate the market and have the lowest costs.

Market skimming pricing

2.11 In contrast, market skimming involves charging **high prices** when a product is **first launched** and spending heavily on advertising and sales promotion to obtain sales. As the product moves into the later stages of its life cycle (growth, maturity and decline) progressively lower prices will be charged. The profitable 'cream' is thus skimmed off in stages until sales can only be sustained at lower prices.

2.12 The aim of market skimming is to gain **high unit profits** early in the product's life. High unit prices make it more likely that **competitors** will enter the market than if lower prices were to be charged.

2.13 Such a policy may be appropriate in the cases below.

(a) The product is **new and different**, so that customers are prepared to pay high prices so as to be one up on other people who do not own it.

(b) The strength of **demand** and the sensitivity of demand to price are **unknown**. It is better from the point of view of marketing to start by charging high prices and then reduce them if the demand for the product turns out to be price elastic than to start by charging low prices and then attempt to raise them substantially if demand appears to be insensitive to higher prices.

(c) High prices in the early stages of a product's life might generate **high initial cash flows**. A firm with liquidity problems may prefer market-skimming for this reason.

(d) The firm can identify **different market segments** for the product, each prepared to pay progressively lower prices. It may therefore be possible to continue to sell at higher prices to some market segments when lower prices are charged in others. This is discussed further below.

(e) Products may have a **short life cycle,** and so need to recover their development costs and make a profit relatively quickly. This too is discussed later.

Differential pricing

2.14 In certain circumstances the **same product** can be sold at different prices to **different customers**. There are a number of bases on which such discriminating prices can be set.

(a) **By market segment**. A cross-channel ferry company would market its services at different prices in England and France, for example. Services such as cinemas and hairdressers are often available at lower prices to old age pensioners and/or juveniles.

(b) **By product version**. Many car models have 'add on' extras which enable one brand to appeal to a wider cross-section of customers. The final price need not reflect the cost price of the add on extras directly: usually the top of the range model would carry a price much in excess of the cost of provision of the extras, as a prestige appeal.

(c) **By place**. Theatre seats are usually sold according to their location so that patrons pay different prices for the same performance according to the seat type they occupy.

(d) **By time**. This is perhaps the most popular type of price discrimination. Off-peak travel bargains, hotel prices and telephone charges are all attempts to increase sales revenue by covering variable but not necessarily average cost of provision. Railway companies are successful price discriminators, charging more to rush hour rail commuters whose demand is inelastic at certain times of the day.

2.15 Price discrimination can only be effective if a number of **conditions** hold.

(a) The market must be **segmentable** in price terms, and different sectors must show different intensities of demand. Each of the sectors must be identifiable, distinct and separate from the others, and be accessible to the firm's marketing communications.

(b) There must be little or **no** chance of a **black market** developing (this would allow those in the lower priced segment to resell to those in the higher priced segment).

(c) There must be little or **no** chance that **competitors** can and will undercut the firm's prices in the higher priced (and/or most profitable) market segments.

(d) The cost of segmenting and **administering** the arrangements should not exceed the extra revenue derived from the price discrimination strategy.

Exam focus point

Any of the topics discussed in Section 2 of this chapter could be relevant to the 'discussion' part of a Paper 9 question. Even if the question does not specifically mention 'pricing policy' or the 'market', you need to be aware of such considerations to demonstrate to the examiner that you possess common **business sense**.

2.16 Try the following question, which is intended to be typical of **Paper 9** in that it has a few 'tricks', but **looks more daunting than it is** if you keep your head and take care.

Question 4

Curltown Cinemas operates a chain of 30 cinemas. Standard admission price is £7 per person, but this is subject to certain discounts. Average attendance at a cinema per month on normal price days is 5,000 people, but this is expected to be subject to seasonal variation, as follows.

Month	J	F	M	A	M	J	J	A	S	•	N	D
%	+10	-2	0	+5	-5	-5	+10	+7	-4	-4	0	+12

In December, January, July and August audiences are made up of 60% under-14s, who pay half-price admission. For the rest of the year under 14s represent only 10% of the audience. One day per month all tickets are sold at a special offer price of £1, irrespective of the age of the customer. This invariably guarantees a full house of 200 customers.

Required

(a)   What is Curltown Cinemas' total revenue from cinema admissions for a year?

(b)   If Curltown puts up prices for over-14s (other than the £1 special offer price) to £8 what will its total revenue from cinema admissions be for the year?

(c)   Should the special offer be continued?

Answer

(a)   Like many Paper 9 questions, this is simply a matter of reading the question carefully and patiently tabulating the data – often (but not necessarily) using a **different layout** to the one given in the question. Note that you save yourself potential error if you convert percentages into decimals as you transfer the question information into your own table. Don't forget that there are 30 cinemas.

Month	Variation	Average no	Adjusted no	Full price	Revenue @ £7.00 £	Half price	Revenue @ £3.50 £
Jan	+0.10	5,000	5,500	0.4	15,400.00	0.6	11,550.00
Feb	-0.02	5,000	4,900	0.9	30,870.00	0.1	1,715.00
Mar	+0.00	5,000	5,000	0.9	31,500.00	0.1	1,750.00
Apr	+0.05	5,000	5,250	0.9	33,075.00	0.1	1,837.50
May	-0.05	5,000	4,750	0.9	29,925.00	0.1	1,662.50
Jun	-0.05	5,000	4,750	0.9	29,925.00	0.1	1,662.50
Jul	+0.10	5,000	5,500	0.4	15,400.00	0.6	11,550.00
Aug	+0.07	5,000	5,350	0.4	14,980.00	0.6	11,235.00
Sept	-0.04	5,000	4,800	0.9	30,240.00	0.1	1,680.00
Oct	-0.04	5,000	4,800	0.9	30,240.00	0.1	1,680.00
Nov	0.00	5,000	5,000	0.9	31,500.00	0.1	1,750.00
Dec	+0.12	5,000	5,600	0.4	15,680.00	0.6	11,760.00
					308,735.00		59,832.50

	£
Total normal price (£308,735.00 + £59, 832.50)	368,567.50
Special offer (12 × £1 × 200)	2,400.00
Total per cinema	370,967.50
Total per 30 cinemas	11,129,025.00

(b)   There is no need to work out **all** the numbers again at the new prices.

	£
Total as calculated above	11,129,025.00
Less: current adult normal price (£308,735 × 30)	(9,262,050.00)
Add: revised adult normal price (£308,735 ×30 ×8/7)	10,585,200.00
	12,452,175.00

(c)   If the income of £200 per cinema on the twelve special offer days is compared with an average of, say, £368,567.50/(365-12 days) = over £1,000, then it is clearly not worthwhile. The cinemas get average attendances of (5000 × 12)/365 = about 164 people in any case, even without special offers. (You could do rough calculations to estimate the overall loss of revenue per annum. Try it, making any **assumptions** you need, if you haven't done so, but not at the expense of written comments.)

However, the offer is a **loss-leader** which probably has other benefits. It will be liked by customers, and if the film they see is a good one they will recommend it to their friends. It may help to encourage the cinema-going habit amongst potential new regular customers. You may have thought of other relevant comments, either in favour of the policy or against it.

2.17   It is also worth considering **customer-specific costs** or **segment-specific costs**. Certain types of customer are more expensive to serve than others.

3 THE OPTIMUM PRICE/OUTPUT LEVEL

3.1 Some businesses enjoy a **monopoly** position in their market or something akin to a monopoly position, even in a competitive market. This is because they develop a unique marketing mix, for example a unique combination of price and quality, or a monopoly in a localised area.

3.2 The significance of a monopoly situation is as follows.

(a) The business has choice and flexibility in the prices it sets.

(b) Because the business has this freedom of choice in pricing, it will find that at **higher prices** demand for its products or services will be **less**. Conversely, at **lower prices**, demand for its products or services will be **higher**.

(c) There will be an **optimum** price/output level at which profits will be maximised.

Case example

A large public transport organisation might be considering an increase in bus fares or underground fares. The effect on total revenues and profit of the fares increase could be estimated from a knowledge of the demand for transport services at different price levels. If an increase in the price per ticket caused a large fall in demand (that is, if demand were price-elastic) total revenues and profits would fall; whereas a fares increase when demand is price-inelastic would boost total revenue and since a transport organisation's costs are largely fixed, would probably boost total profits too.

Deriving the demand curve

> **FORMULAE TO LEARN**
>
> When demand is linear the equation for the demand curve is:
>
> $P = a - bQ/\Delta Q$
>
> where P = the price
> Q = the quantity demanded
> a = the price at which demand would be nil
> b = the amount by which the price falls for each stepped change in demand
> ΔQ = the stepped change in demand
>
> The constant a is calculated as follows.
>
> $$a = \text{£(current price)} + \left(\frac{\text{Current quantity at current price}}{\text{Change in quantity when price is changed by £b}} \times \text{£b} \right)$$

3.3 This looks rather complicated in words, but it is very easy once the numbers are substituted. **Note that you are not given these formulae in the exam.**

3.4 EXAMPLE: DERIVING THE DEMAND CURVE

The current price of a product is £12. At this price the company sells 60 items a month. One month the company decides to raise the price to £14, but only 45 items are sold at this price. Determine the demand equation.

3.5 SOLUTION

Step 1. **Find the price at which demand would be nil**

Assuming demand is linear, each increase of £2 in the price would result in a fall in demand of 15 units. For demand to be nil, the price needs to rise from its current level by as many times as there are 15 units in 60 units (60/15 = 4) ie to £12 + (4 × £2) = £20.

Using the formula above, this can be shown as a = £12 + ((60/15) × £2) = £20

Step 2. **Extract figures from the question**

The **demand equation** can now be determined as P = a − bQ/ΔQ = 20 − 2Q/15

Step 3. **Check your equation**

We can check this by substituting £12 and £14 for P.

$$12 = 20 - (2 \times 60/15) = 20 - 8 = 12$$
$$4 = 20 - (2 \times 45/15) = 20 - 6 = 14$$

FORMULA TO LEARN

The equation can also be re-arranged as $Q = \dfrac{(a \times \Delta Q) - (\Delta Q \times P)}{b}$

Exam focus point

Deriving the demand formula came up in the **June 1995** exam in conjunction with spreadsheets. Make sure you do *both* of the following questions.

Question 5

The current price of a product is £30 and the producers sell 100 items a week at this price. One week the price is dropped by £3 as a special offer and the producers sell 150 items. Find an expression for the demand curve.

Answer

a	=	£30 + (100/50 × £3)	= £36		
P	=	36 − 3Q/50	or	Q	= (1,800 − 50P)/3

Check

27	= 36 − 3Q/50		150	= (1,800 − 50P)/3
3Q/50	= 9		50P	= 1,800 − 450
Q	= 150		P	= 27

Question 6

A model of the problem in question 4 has been set up on a spreadsheet as follows. All cells other than cell B2 are protected and locked and cannot be changed by the user.

	A	B	C	D	E	F
1				*Price*	*Volume*	*Profit*
2	**Specified price**	25			=B5	=B10
3				20	800	6400
4				21	750	6300
5	**Sales volume at this price**	=IF(((B19*B16)-(B16*B2))/B17>0, ((B19*B16)-(B16*B2))B17,0)		22	700	6160
6				23	650	5980
7		£		24	600	5760
8	Revenue	=B2*B5		25	550	5500
9	Costs	=-B8*0.6		26	500	5200
10	Profit	=SUM(B8:B9)		27	450	4860
11				28	400	4480
12				29	350	4060
13	**Variables**			30	300	3600
14	Current quantity	100		31	250	3100
15	Current price	30		32	200	2560
16	Change in Q	50		33	150	1980
17	b	3		34	100	1360
18	**Intermediate variable**			35	50	700
19	a	=B15+(B14/B16*B17)		36	0	0
20						

(a) Explain the meaning of the formulae in cells B19, B5, E2 and F2 (in that order).

(b) Give an example of a **controlled variable** and an **intermediate variable**, and explain what these terms mean.

(c) Does the spreadsheet show the optimum pricing policy, and if not how could it be amended? (*Hint:* look at the profit figures on the data table.)

Answer

This is a difficult exercise but one that should equip you well to cope with **spreadsheet questions in Paper 9.**

(a) **B19.** This calculates the value of the variable a in the demand formula. The variable a represents the price at which demand would be nil.

B5. The part of the formula that reads ((B19*B16) – (B16*B2))/B17 is equivalent to the expression for the demand formula that calculates Q. An IF function has been added to avoid nonsensical results where demand is less than nought. In other words, 'if Q is greater than 0 the value in B5 is Q, otherwise it is 0'.

E2 and F2. These are the 'headings' in the one-way data table in cells D2 to F19. When the data table function is used the cells in column E will show the sales volume at different price levels and those in column F the profit earned at each price level.

(b) The only **controlled variable** is B2, price. Management can set whatever price they like. The spreadsheet has been set up so that the user simply types in a trial price in cell B2 and the sales volume, revenue costs and profits all change to match.

The **intermediate variable** is in cell B19. This is calculated from the variables in cells B14 to B17 and is then used as input for the formula in cell B5.

(c) The highest profit shown is £6,400, but this is at the lowest price being considered, £20. It is probable that higher profits would be made at lower levels of price. The user could experiment by typing in lower figures in cell B2 and looking at the result in cell B10 to see if it is higher than £6,400. As it turns out, equal or higher profits can be made at prices of £19, £18 and £17. The price £18 is the best choice. The figures in column D could then be altered so that they show a wider spread of profits either side of the maximum figure. In the example below we have assumed that management want to know what price levels will give them a profit of over £5,000.

	A	B	C	D	E	F	G
1				*Price*	*Volume*	*Profit*	
2	**Specified price**	18			900	6,480.00	
3				9	1350	4,860.00	
4				10	1300	5,200.00	
5	Sales volume at this price	900		11	1250	5,500.00	
6				12	1200	5,760.00	
7		£		13	1150	5,980.00	
8	Revenue	16,200.00		14	1100	6,160.00	
9	Costs	(9,720.00)		15	1050	6,300.00	
10	Profit	6,480.00		16	1000	6,400.00	
11				17	950	6,460.00	
12				18	900	6,480.00	
13	**Variables**			19	850	6,460.00	
14	Current quantity	100		20	800	6,400.00	
15	Current price	30		21	750	6,300.00	
16	Change in Q	50		22	700	6,160.00	
17	b	3		23	650	5,980.00	
18	**Intermediate variable**			24	600	5,760.00	
19	a	36		25	550	5,500.00	
20				26	500	5,200.00	
21				27	450	4,860.00	
22							

Using the demand function

3.6 Suppose that we know that the demand function for a company's product is:

$$P = 5 - 0.002Q$$

where P is the unit price (in £) and Q is the volume of sales in units at price P. (This is the formula of the demand curve for the product.)

From the demand curve formula, we could establish the **total revenue function TR**. This is of course the number of units sold (Q) times the price at which they are sold (P).

$$TR \quad = P \times Q = (5 - 0.002Q) \times Q$$
$$= 5Q - 0.002Q^2$$

3.7 The **marginal revenue** function can be calculated from the total revenue function using differential calculus. This will be described later, but if you are not familiar with differential calculus, you will need to accept at this stage that the marginal revenue function in our example is:

$$MR = 5 - 0.004Q$$

where MR is the marginal revenue from an extra unit of sales at any given sales level Q.

3.8 The demand curve $P = 5 - 0.002Q$ and the marginal revenue curve $MR = 5 - 0.004Q$ can be shown on the same graph, as follows.

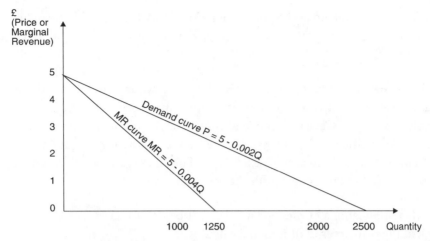

Note. Marginal revenue becomes zero at output of 1,250 units, and negative at higher volumes above 1,250. This is because total revenue is maximised at 1,250 units, and declines at higher volumes. Experiment with the TR formula if you don't believe this.

(a) At sales of 1,250 units, TR $= 1,250 \times [5 - (0.002)(1,250)] = £3,125$

(b) At sales of 1,251 units, TR is less: $1,251 \times [5 - (0.002)(1,251)] = £3,124.998$

These figures show how TR begins to fall beyond 1,250 units of sales.

Exam focus point

In the **December 1997** exam, candidates were provided with the price/demand function and had to use it to obtain information for a DCF analysis.

Profit maximisation

3.9 Microeconomic theory suggests that **as output increases,** the marginal cost per unit might rise (due to the law of diminishing returns) and whenever the firm is faced with a downward sloping demand curve, the **marginal revenue per unit will decline.**

Eventually, a level of output will be reached where the **extra cost** of making one extra unit of output is greater than the **extra revenue** obtained from its sale. It would then be unprofitable to make and sell that extra unit.

3.10 Profits will continue to be maximised only up to the output level where marginal cost has risen to be exactly equal to the marginal revenue.

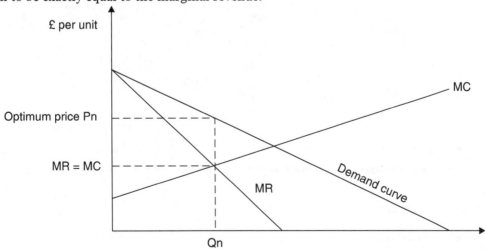

Profits are **maximised** at the point where **MC = MR**, ie at a volume of Qn units. If we add a demand curve to the graph, we can see that at an output level of Qn, the sales price per unit would be Pn.

3.11 It is important to make a clear distinction in your mind between the sales price and marginal revenue. In this example, the optimum price is Pn, but the marginal revenue is much less. This is because the 'additional' sales **unit** to reach output Qn has only been achieved by reducing the unit sales **price** from an amount higher than Pn for **all** the units to be sold, not just the marginal extra one. The increase in sales volume is therefore partly offset by a reduction in unit price; hence MR is lower than Pn.

3.12 Further applications of these principles will be described in a moment, but first we need to look at the principles of differential calculus.

Question 7

A firm operates in a market where there is imperfect competition, so that to sell more units of output, it must reduce the sales price of all the units it sells. The following data is available for prices and costs.

Total output Units	Sales price per unit (AR) £	Average cost of output (AC) £ per unit
0	-	-
1	504	720
2	471	402
3	439	288
4	407	231
5	377	201
6	346	189
7	317	182
8	288	180
9	259	186
10	232	198

The total cost of zero output is £600.

At what output level and price would the firm maximise its profits, assuming that fractions of units cannot be made?

Answer

Units	Price £	Total revenue £	Marginal revenue £	Total cost £	Marginal cost £	Profit £
0	0	0	0	600	-	(600)
1	504	504	504	720	120	(216)
2	471	942	438	804	84	138
3	439	1,317	375	864	60	453
4	407	1,629	311	924	60	704
5	377	1,885	257	1,005	81	880
6	346	2,076	191	1,134	129	942
7*	317	2,219	143	1,274	140	945
8	288	2,304	85	1,440	166	864
9	259	2,331	27	1,674	234	657
10	232	2,320	-11	1,980	306	340

* Profit is maximised at 7 units of output where MR is most nearly equal to MC.

Differential calculus

3.13 Differential calculus is a branch of mathematics which is used to calculate the **rate of change** in one variable with respect to changes in another variable. For example, it can be used to estimate the following.

(a) The rate of change in total revenue as sales volume is increased (the **marginal revenue** per unit at any level of output).

(b) The rate of change in total costs as sales and production volume is increased (the **marginal cost** per unit).

(c) The rate of **change in total profits** as sales volume is increased.

The rate of change is found by means of **differentiation**.

> **FORMULA TO LEARN**
>
> If we have a function $y = ax^n$, where x is the independent variable and y is the dependent variable, we can find the rate of change in y with respect to changes in x by **differentiating y** with respect to x. When $y = ax^n$ then $\dfrac{dy}{dx} = nax^{n-1}$

3.14 For example if:

(a) $y = 3x^4$, then $\dfrac{dy}{dx} = (4)(3)x^{4-1} = 12x^3$

(b) $y = 2x^2 + 5x$, then $\dfrac{dy}{dx} = (2)(2)x^{2-1} + (1)(5)x^{1-1} = 4x + 5$

The formula nax^{n-1} is applied to each *separate* expression in the equation.

(c) If there is a 'constant' value, this disappears on differentiation, so that if

$y = 6x^2 + 3x + 200$

$\dfrac{dy}{dx} = (2)(6)x^{2-1} + (1)(3)x^{1-1} = 12x + 3$

The fixed amount 200 does not appear in the expression of $\dfrac{dy}{dx}$.

3.15 EXAMPLE: MARGINAL COSTS

If total costs (C) of making a product are (in £) 10,000 + 5Q, where Q is the volume of production, the marginal cost per unit is found by differentiating C with respect to Q.

$\dfrac{dC}{dQ} = 5$

The marginal cost per unit is £5 for every unit produced. Put more simply, perhaps, the variable cost per unit is £5 at all volumes of output.

3.16 If the total costs of making a product are (in £):

$C = 15,000 + 2x + 0.08x^2$

where x is the volume of production, the marginal cost function is found by differentiating C with respect to x

$\dfrac{dC}{dx} = 2 + 0.16x$

In this example, the marginal cost per unit will increase as x gets bigger.

3.17 EXAMPLE: MARGINAL REVENUE

Glutton Ltd has estimated that its total revenue function is:

$$y = 300x - 0.1x^2$$

where y is total revenue and x is the volume of sales. The marginal revenue function is found by differentiating y with respect to x.

$$\frac{dy}{dx} = 300 - 0.2x$$

3.18 Avarice Ltd has estimated that the demand function for its product is

$$P = 6 - 0.003Q$$

where P is the unit price (in £) and Q is the volume of sales.

The total revenue is:

$$R = PQ = (6 - 0.003Q)Q = 6Q - 0.003Q^2.$$

The marginal revenue function is found by differentiating R with respect to Q.

$$MR = \frac{dR}{dQ} = 6 - 0.006Q.$$

3.19 EXAMPLE: PROFIT MAXIMISATION

D Ltd produces an item, the C, for which the estimated demand curve is:

$$P = 10 - 0.0001Q$$

where P is the unit price in £ and Q is the annual sales volume in units.

The variable cost of making and selling the C is £2 per unit and fixed costs are £110,000 per annum.

What is the profit-maximising price?

3.20 SOLUTION

Revenue $\quad$ R $\quad = PQ = (10 - 0.0001Q)Q = 10Q - 0.0001Q^2$

Marginal revenue MR $\quad = \dfrac{dR}{dQ} = 10 - 0.0002Q$

Costs $\quad$ C $\quad = 2Q + 110,000$

Marginal cost $\quad$ MC $\quad = \dfrac{dC}{dQ} = 2$

Profits are maximised when marginal cost is equal to marginal revenue.

$10 - 0.0002Q = 2$

$0.0002Q \quad = 8$

$Q \quad = 40,000$ units

Price P (in £) $= 10 - 0.0001Q = 10 - 4 = 6$

The profit maximising price is £6. At this price, the annual profit would be as follows.

		£
Sales	$(40,000 \times 6)$	240,000
Costs	$(110,000 + 40,000 \times 2)$	190,000
Profit		50,000

The examiner and price/demand relationships and pricing

3.21 The last section of the examiner's August 1999 *ACCA Students' Newsletter* article 'Product costing/pricing strategy' (reproduced at the end of this text), looks at three **ways in which the profit-maximum selling price can be determined.**

(a) **Visual inspection of a tabulation of data.**

(i) Work out the demand curve and hence the price and the total revenue at various levels of demand.

(ii) Calculate total cost and hence marginal cost at each level of clearance.

(iii) Finally calculate profit at each level of demand, thereby determining the price and demand on which profits are measured.

(b) **Graphical approach.** The diagrams below show that profits are maximised at the point where the vertical distance between the total revenue curve and the total costs curve is at a maximum (which is fairly obvious if you think about it since profits are maximised when the difference between cost and revenue in maximised). This profit-maximising demands levels also corresponds to the point at which the MC and MR curves intersect, as we would expect. Notice how the profit maximum price can be read off from the amend curve.

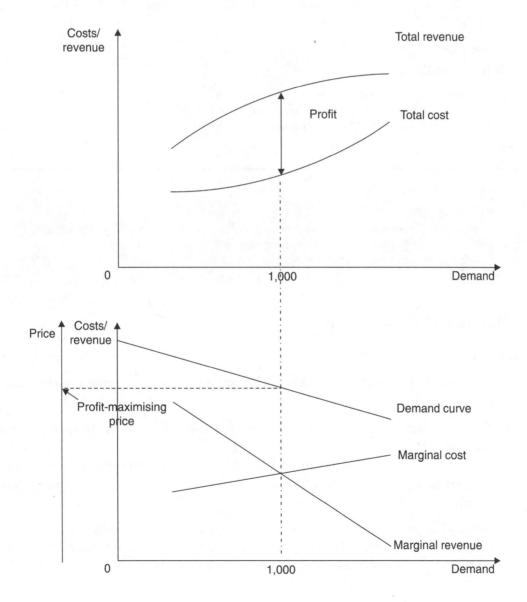

(c) **Differential Calculus**

Optimum pricing in practice

3.22 There are problems with applying the approach described above in practice for the following reasons.

(a) It assumes that the demand curve and total costs can be **identified with certainty**. This is unlikely to be so.

(b) It ignores the **market research costs** of acquiring knowledge of demand.

(c) It assumes the firm has **no production constraint** which could mean that the equilibrium point between supply and demand cannot be reached.

(d) It assumes the objective is **to maximise profits**. There may be other objectives.

(e) It assumes that **price is the only influence** on quantity demanded. We saw in Section 2 that this is far from the case.

Question 8

Work through Paragraph 3.20 and make yourself a step by step list of how to approach a profit maximisation problem.

Answer

Your answer should look like this.

Step 1: establish the mathematical relationship between P and Q
Step 2: establish the mathematical relationship between C and Q
Step 3: establish the function for total revenue

and so on.

Exam focus point

The calculation of the optimum price/output level using calculus came up in **December 1997**. The examiner has confirmed that a tabular approach (such as that adopted in Question 7) is acceptable as an alternative to calculus in pricing questions.

4 SPECIAL CASES IN PRICING

Special orders

4.1 A special order is a **one-off** revenue earning opportunity. These may arise in the following situations.

(a) When a business has a regular source of income but also has some **spare capacity** allowing it to take on extra work if demanded. For example a brewery might have a capacity of 500,000 barrels per month but only be producing and selling 300,000 barrels per month. It could therefore consider special orders to use up some of its spare capacity.

(b) When a business has **no regular source of income** and relies exclusively on its ability to respond to demand. A building firm is a typical example as are many types of sub-contractors. In the service sector consultants often work on this basis.

4.2 The reason for making the distinction is that in the case of (a), a firm would normally attempt to cover its longer-term running costs in its prices for its regular product. Pricing for special orders need therefore take no account of unavoidable fixed costs. This is clearly not the case for a firm in (b)'s position, where special orders are the only source of income for the foreseeable future.

4.3 Examination questions featuring pricing for special orders typically present a scenario in which a firm has to decide whether to bid for a contract.

New products

4.4 The role of the management accountant in new product pricing might be to estimate the cash flows and return on investment that would be expected, given a particular sales price, and estimates of sales demand.

4.5 **Discounted cash** flow techniques could be used to estimate whether a new product will yield a satisfactory return at the proposed selling price, and which combination of sales price and sales volume would yield the best return for a product over its life cycle. In examination questions you would have to be given suitable information about the timing of cash flows and the cost of capital.

4.6 The example that follows is a **simplified version of examination questions** that have been set on this topic.

4.7 EXAMPLE: NEW PRODUCT PRICING

Novo plc is about to launch a new product with a variable cost of £10 per unit. The company has carried out market research (at a cost of £15,000) to determine the potential demand for the product at various selling prices.

Selling price £	Demand Units
30	20,000
25	30,000
20	40,000

Its current capacity is for 20,000 units but additional capacity can be made available by using the resources of another product line. If this is done the lost contribution from the other product will be £35,000 for each additional 10,000 units of capacity.

Senior management have asked you to analyse this information in a way that helps them to decide on the product's launch price.

4.8 SOLUTION

Tabulation is the approach to use with a problem of this type.

Selling price £	Demand Units ('000)	Variable costs £'000	Opportunity costs £'000	Total costs £'000	Sales revenue £'000	Contribution £'000
30	20	200	-	200	600	400
25	30	300	35	335	750	415
20	40	400	70	470	800	330

The optimum price to maximise short-term profits is £25.

The main **drawbacks** of the approach described above are that it only considers a limited range of prices (what about charging £27.50?) and it takes no account of the uncertainty of forecast demand. However, allowance could be made for both situations by collecting more information.

Short-life products

4.9 A short-life product is one for which the demand is likely to cease a relatively short time after the product is launched. Examples include the following.

(a) Goods commemorating **special occasions**, like sporting events or state ceremonies

(b) Goods intended to **promote other products**, like T-shirts associated with a new film

(c) **'Limited editions'**, produced in very small numbers to give them a rarity value

(d) Goods which are of use for a **predetermined period**, after which a new version will be produced. Prime examples are **diaries and calendars**.

4.10 Such products have the characteristics of both special orders and new products. Short-life products are often **quite highly priced** so as to give the manufacturer a chance to recover his investment and make a worthwhile return.

4.11 However, the main problem with short-life products is deciding **how many** to produce in order that demand will be fully satisfied and no unsold stocks will be left over when demand ceases. (This even applies to some extent to limited editions: how 'limited' should they be?) There is no easy answer to this question unless the level of demand can be predicted with absolute certainty. Given that such products are often one-offs, this can be extremely difficult.

Exam focus point
Be prepared for questions that ask you to determine the optimum pricing and production strategy given a range of possibilities. The illustrative question for this chapter is a case in point.

Pricing for competitive advantage

4.12 Porter sites a number of strategies which an organisation can adopt with respect to its competitive position to provide competitive advantage.

(a) **Cost leadership**

    (i)   Cost-conscious approach to operations
    (ii)   Pursuit of technical advantages
    (iii) Acknowledged lowest costs in the industry
    (iv) Low costs $\neq$ cheap product philosophy
    (v)   Prices not necessarily low (but **can** lower prices if competition fierce)

(b) **Differentiation**

    (i)   Multiple products each branded and promoted
    (ii)   Competition must overcome brand loyalty through price cutting
    (iii) Adds attributes valued by the customer and for which the customer will pay
    (iv) Aims to maximise profit gap between price and cost

(c) **Focus (niche)**

    (i)   Focus on cost and differentiating factors in response to customer needs in a specific market segment

    (ii)   Higher profits in the short term

Pricing internal services

Knowledge brought forward from Paper 8

Costing and pricing internal services

The price charged to user departments for the use of internal services could be based on any of the following costs.

- **No charge at all**. Costs will be apportioned on an arbitrary basis between production departments (absorption costing) or charged against profit as a period charge (marginal costing), without any attempt to recognise that some departments might be using services more than others.

- **Total actual cost**. Charge to the user departments will be ((total actual cost/total activity) × work done for user department). User departments will be charged for any overspending and inefficiency in the service departments and charges will depend on workload in service departments, making it difficult for the user departments to plan and control costs.

- **Standard absorption cost**. Charge is based on a standard, predetermined cost for the service. User departments are *not* penalised for either overspending and inefficiency or under capacity in the service department. The standard costs must be reviewed regularly and frequently (so that user departments do not get a false impression of the cost of the service), however, and there is also a problem in deciding on the standard activity level.

- (Standard or actual) **variable cost.** User departments are charged for the extra costs incurred by using more of the service, but they would be under a false impression as to the true full cost of the service. If actual variable costs are used, there would be no control of overspending and inefficiency in the service department because it would simply 'pass on' its overspending in higher charges to the user department. If standard variable cost is used, the standard must be reviewed regularly.

- **Opportunity cost**. This is appropriate if the service department is working at full capacity and is also providing services outside the company, so that profit is forgone every time the service department provides a service internally. The difficulty with this method is establishing the opportunity cost.

- **External cost**. The service department is thus treated as a profit centre. User departments have the opportunity to compare internally-provided service quality with that offered by an external source.

Exam focus point

The advantages of various charge bases featured in a question in the **December 1998** exam.

BPP PUBLISHING

Chapter roundup

- Traditional ideas suggest that pricing is **cost-based** (full cost-plus, marginal cost-plus etc)

- **Activity based costing** provides an opportunity for organisations that use cost-based pricing to gain a greater understanding of their costs and so correct pricing anomalies that derive from the distorted view given by conventional volume-related costing.

- Pricing is **influenced by many factors** other than cost: consumer preferences, competitors' actions and the nature of the product itself all have wide implications.

- **Porter's Five Forces Model** suggests the importance of pressure from five competitive forces on price.

  - Rivalry between existing competitors
  - Threat of substitutes
  - Bargaining power of suppliers
  - Threat of new entrants
  - Bargaining power of buyers

- The **BCG portfolio matrix** classifies products as stars, cash cows, question marks and dogs.

- **Market penetration** pricing sets **low** prices when a product is first considered. **Market skimming** pricing sets high prices.

- **Different prices** can be charged for the same product where consumer surplus exists, but this can be very difficult to implement in practice because it relies for success upon the continued existence of certain market conditions.

- Calculations can be performed to determine an **optimum price/output level** using differential **calculus**. Alternatively tabulation or a graphical approach can be adopted.

- **Special orders** require a relevant cost approach to the calculation of the tender price.

- **New products** that are expected to have a long life will require management accounting techniques like discounted cash flow and risk analysis.

- **Short-life products** should be priced using relevant costs and risk analysis where possible. Accurately predicting demand is vital in such situations.

- Pricing strategies for competitive advantage include, **cost leadership, product differentiation and niche marketing.**

- The price charged to user departments for using **internal services** may be based on a number of costs.

Quick quiz

1   How important is pricing? (see paras 1.2 - 1.3)

2   Why might traditional approaches to pricing lead to bad decisions? (1.12 - 1.16)

3   Give eight examples of influences on price other than cost. (2.1)

4   What is the product life cycle? (2.3)

5   What are the characteristics of a product classifies by the BCG portfolio matrix as a question mark? (2.4)

6   How might a firm respond to a price cut by a competitor? (2.8)

7   When is a market skimming policy appropriate? (2.13)

8   When can discriminating prices be set? (2.15)

9   What is the formula for the demand curve? (3.3)

10 What is the significance of the point where MC = MR? (3.10)

11 Why is optimum pricing difficult to achieve in practice? (3.22)

12 Give two examples of short-life products (4.9)

Question to try	Level	Marks	Time
9	Exam standard	25	45 mins

Part D

Accounting control systems and standard costing

Chapter 10

BUDGETING

Chapter topic list	Syllabus reference
1 Control systems	3(a)
2 Budgetary control	3(a)
3 Human behaviour and budgetary planning and control	1(a), 1(c), 3(a)
4 Alternative approaches to budgeting	1(a), 1(c), 3(a)
5 TQM and ABB	1(a), 1(c), 3(a)

Introduction

In this chapter we introduce the topic of budgeting, one that you should have studied in some depth already for Paper 8

The background of systems and control theory is quite important for Paper 9: in particular questions have often come up on **feedforward control**, especially in connection with planning and operational variances (see Chapter 13). Likewise behavioural aspects and alternative approaches such as ZBB have featured in exam questions, so it is worth reminding yourself of the key points.

The final section of this chapter is perhaps the most important because it links up with material on ABC, TQM etc.

Core areas of the syllabus identified by the examiner and covered in this chapter: **possible dysfunctional impacts of standards and variances; alternative approaches to budgeting such as incremental budgets, ZBB, ABB and rolling budgets;** the **impact of links between budgets and JIT, activity-based ideas and a total quality philosophy.**

---

1   CONTROL SYSTEMS

1.1   We have mentioned 'control' and 'control systems' frequently in the preceding pages without explaining in detail what these terms mean. However, your syllabus requires you to have some understanding of **control theory** and you may be expected to use or explain some of the terminology of control theory and systems theory.

Knowledge brought forward from Papers 5 and 8

Systems theory

- The word **system** is impossible to define satisfactorily (the tax 'system', the respiratory 'system', the class 'system'). Basically it means something that **connects things up.**

- A **closed system** is isolated and shut off from the environment, is unaffected by the environment and cannot influence the environment.

- An **open system** is connected to and interacts with the environment and is influenced by it.

- All **social systems**, for example organisations, are **open** systems.

- Every system can be broken down into **sub-systems** which can be differentiated from each other by function, space or time.

> **KEY TERM**
>
> **Control**, in a business sense, is the process of guiding organisations into viable patterns of activity in a changing environment.
>
> More simply, the aim of a control system is to *make sure that the right things get done.*

Why bother with control?

1.2 A system such as a business organisation must be controlled to **keep it steady** or **enable it to change** safely.

1.3 Control is required because **unpredictable disturbances** arise and enter the system, so that **actual results** (outputs of the system) deviate from the **expected results** or goals.

1.4 Examples of disturbances in a business system would be the entry of a powerful new **competitor** into the market, an unexpected **rise in costs**, a decline in **quality** standards or the tendency of **employees** to stop working in order to chatter or gossip.

1.5 To have a control system, there has to be a plan, standard, budget, rule book or any other sort of target or **guideline** towards which the system as a whole should be aiming.

1.6 Control is dependent on the receipt and processing of **information**, both to plan in the first place and to compare actual results against the plan, so as to judge what control measures, if any, are needed.

Feedback

> **KEY TERM**
>
> **Feedback** is information about actual achievements. In a business organisation, it is information about actual results, produced from within the organisation (for example management accounting control reports) with the purpose of helping with control decisions.

1.7 A feature of feedback is that it is information that is gathered by measuring the **outputs** of the system itself. It has an 'internal' source, as distinct from 'environmental' information, which comes from outside the system.

1.8 Some form of internally generated feedback is essential if there is to be any effective control within an organisation, and the **most common types of control system** in businesses, such as budgetary control and stock control systems, are **all based on feedback** cycles.

Negative feedback

> **KEY TERM**
>
> **Negative feedback** is information which indicates that the system is deviating from its planned or prescribed course, and that some re-adjustment is necessary to bring it back on course. This feedback is called 'negative' because control action would seek to reverse the direction or movement of the system back towards its planned course.

1.9   Negative feedback gives rise to attempts to change the direction of the actual movement of the system to bring it **back into line** with the plan.

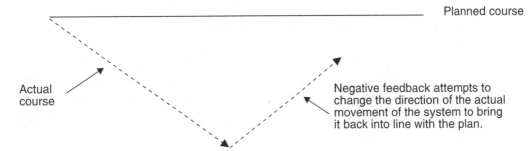

Planned course

Actual course

Negative feedback attempts to change the direction of the actual movement of the system to bring it back into line with the plan.

1.10 Thus, if the budgeted sales for June and July were £100,000 in each month, whereas the report of actual sales in June showed that only £90,000 had been reached, this negative feedback would indicate that control action was necessary to raise sales in July to £110,000 in order to get back on to the planned course.

Positive feedback

> **KEY TERM**
>
> **Positive feedback** results in control action which causes actual results to maintain (or increase) their path of deviation from planned results. This contrasts with negative feedback, which attempts to *reverse* the deviation and bring actual results back on to the prescribed course.

1.11 Suppose that a company budgets to produce and sell 100 units of product each month, maintaining an average stock level of 40 units. If actual sales exceed the budget, and show signs of sustained growth, it will obviously be in the company's interests to produce and sell as much as possible (provided additional output earns extra contribution to profit).

   (a) Feedback in the first month might show that sales are above budget, selling costs are a little higher than budget and that stocks have been run down to meet demand.

   (b) Action should attempt to increase sales (in other words, to promote the deviation of actual results from the plan) even if this requires extra selling costs for advertising or sales promotion, maintaining the 'adverse' deviation of actual costs from budget.

   Additional production volumes would be required, although initially some extra sales might be made out of remaining stocks (resulting in further deviations from the production and finished goods stocks budgets).

Planning and control

1.12 Feedback is important, but there are **four necessary conditions** that must be satisfied before any process can be said to be controlled. These will help us to put control into a wider context still.

   (a) **Objectives** for the process being controlled must exist, for without an aim or purpose control has no meaning.

   (b) The output of the process must be **measurable** in terms of the dimensions defined by the objectives.

(c) A **predictive model** of the process being controlled is required so that causes for the non-attainment of objectives can be determined and proposed corrective actions evaluated.

(d) There must be a **capability of taking action** so that deviations of attainment from objectives can be reduced.

1.13 Note that control involves more than just measuring results and taking corrective action. Control in its broadest sense also embraces the **formulation of objectives** - deciding *what are* the 'right things' that need to be done in the first place -as well as monitoring their attainment by way of feedback.

Feedforward control

> ### KEY TERM
>
> **Feedforward control** describes a control system in which deviations in the system are anticipated in a forecast of future results, so that 'corrective action' can be taken in advance of any deviations actually happening.

1.14 Some simple **examples** of feedforward control are as follows.

(a) The control over the completion time of projects, using **critical path analysis**. Delays that might postpone the completion of the project are identified in advance, and corrective action taken as necessary.

(b) **Cash budgets,** prepared regularly, where future cash flows and cash balances are checked to make sure that the organisation will have available the cash resources that it needs, without overstepping its borrowing facility limits.

1.15 More generally, feedforward control is the fulfilment of the first condition for control - putting the **objectives** in place - or, in conventional terms, **'planning'**. Thus control encompasses both the activity of planning and of ensuring conformity to plan including, if necessary, the generation of new plans.

The Paper 9 examiner and feedforward control

1.16 As George Brown points out in an article in the ACCA *Students' Newsletter*:

> 'It is increasingly argued that [the] feedback control routine is of limited value since it is focusing on what has **already occurred**. The effort involved in identifying deviations from plan is only relevant if such deviations may be identified as controllable and if feedback information can be used as the basis for feedforward control'
>
> (G Brown, 'A Feedback and Feedforward Control Model', *ACCA Students' Newsletter,* November 1992).

> **Exam focus point**
> Feedforward control has featured in several exam questions for example in **June 1994, June 1995, December 1995 and December 1999**

1.17 **Computer technology** and increasingly sophisticated management information systems have widened the scope for the use of this budgetary control technique. **Forecasting**

models can be constructed which enable regular revised forecasts to be prepared about what is now likely to happen in view of changes in key variables such as sales demand.

1.18 If regular forecasts are prepared, managers will have both the current forecast and the master budget to guide their action. The master budget, which is the **original plan**, may **not** be **achievable** in view of the changing circumstances. The current forecast indicates what is expected to happen in view of these new circumstances.

1.19 **Control comparisons** which are then possible are as follows.

(a) **Current forecast v budget**: what action must be taken to get back to the budget plan, given the differences between the current forecast and the budget? Is any control action worthwhile?

(b) If **control action** is planned, the current forecast will need to be amended to take account of the effects of the control action and a **revised forecast** prepared. The next comparison should then be: **revised forecast v budget** to determine whether the budget plan is now expected to be achieved.

(c) A comparison of **current forecast v revised forecast** will show what the expected effect of the control action will be.

The predictive model

1.20 The third item the list of conditions for effective control – the **predictive model** – presents problems in practice

1.21 It is **not possible** in practice for an organisation to construct a **satisfactory predictive model** of the process being controlled for two reasons.

(a) Because an organisation is an open system which is connected to and interacts with its environment. That environment is the world at large and it is chiefly characterised by **change**. Attempts have to be made to forecast what will happen in the future, but in most situations such attempts are beset with **uncertainty**.

(b) Because organisations are made up of **individuals**, who are themselves 'sub-systems', and who cannot be relied upon to react predictably in response to efforts to direct their behaviour towards a particular end.

Programmed and non-programmed decisions

> **KEY TERMS**
>
> A **programmed decision**, as the name implies, is one whose outcome can be predicted, and relied upon to turn out as expected (think of a computer 'program').
>
> A **non-programmed decision** is subject to uncertainty about its outcome.

1.22 This book follows the classic academic work on management accounting control (by Emmanuel *et al* and on your Paper 9 reading list).

(a) Our discussion of **programmed** activities focuses on **budgetary control** (a budget being a sort of 'program') and **standard costing**.

(b) Our discussion of **non-programmed** activities concentrates on the complexity of **performance measurement** (of both business units and managers) in the most uncertain of operating environments, the multi-divisional organisation structure.

Question 1

Write *your own* explanation of each of the following terms, and give an example.

(a) Open system
(b) Positive feedback

(c) Feedforward control
(d) Programmed decisions

Don't neglect this because it is typical of a **real exam question.**

If you cannot write your own explanation, find ours and write that down. Then try to think of *your own* example to illustrate the meaning of each term.

2   BUDGETARY CONTROL

KEY TERMS

A **budget** is a 'plan expressed in money. It is prepared and approved prior to the budget period and may show income, expenditure, and the capital to be employed' (CIMA, *Official Terminology*).

A budget is what the organisation wants to happen, as opposed to a forecast, which is what is likely to happen.

Knowledge brought forward from Paper 8

Budgeting is a multi-purpose activity. Some reasons why budgets are used are given below.

- As a **planning** aid.
- To **communicate** ideas and plans to everyone affected by them.
- To **co-ordinate** the activities of different departments or sub-units of the organisation.
- To provide a framework for **responsibility accounting**.
- To establish a system of **control**.
- To **motivate** employees to improve their **performance**.

A budget, since it has different purposes, might mean different things to different people.

- As a **forecast** of the most likely future for the organisation, it helps managers to plan.

- As a means of **allocating resources**, it can be used to decide the resources needed (labour and so on) and how many should be given to each area of the organisation.

- As a **yardstick** against which to compare actual performance, it indicates where and when **control** action may be necessary.

- As a **target** for achievement, a budget might be a means of motivating the workforce to greater personal accomplishment; another aspect of control.

Question 2

Given the following information about a firm, what difficulties do you suspect may arise in the co-ordination of its activities? (No calculations are required.)

	Product X	Product Y
Market demand	150,000 units	250,000 units
Selling price	£4 per unit	£4 per unit

Production capacity (overall)	375,000 units
Capital expenditure requirements for the coming year	£110,000 (3 projects)
Average working capital required	£100,000 per 30,000 units
Cash collection trend	10% month 1; 20% month 2; 40% month 3; balance thereafter
Current overdraft	£40,000
Maximum overdraft facility	£75,000

Answer

Product X and product Y sales managers will compete for production time. Capacity is inadequate to meet the full demand. All departments will compete for working capital and given the slowness of cash collection the overdraft facility may be exceeded without careful planning. Capital expenditure may have to be delayed, but this might hamper the ability of production to produce to meet demand.

Budgetary control

2.1 Suppose that a director tells a manager that he expects him to produce 100 units a day. On a particular day only 75 units are produced. When asked why, the manager says that production had to stop because a machine keeps breaking down. The director authorises the manager to buy a new machine. This is **budgetary control** in miniature.

> **KEY TERM**
>
> **Budgetary control** is 'the establishment of budgets relating the responsibilities of executives to the requirements of a policy, and the continuous comparison of actual with budgeted results, either to secure by individual action the objectives of that policy or to provide a basis for its revision' (CIMA).

2.2 The main uses of budgetary control are as follows.

(a) To define the **objectives** of the organisation as a whole
(b) To reveal by how much **actual results** have exceeded or fallen short of the budget
(c) To indicate why actual results **differ** from those budgeted
(d) As a basis for the **revision** of the current budget/preparation of future budgets
(e) To ensure that **resources** are used as efficiently as possible
(f) To see how well the activities of the organisation have been **co-ordinated**
(g) To provide some **central control** where activities are decentralised

3 HUMAN BEHAVIOUR AND BUDGETARY PLANNING AND CONTROL

3.1 An important feature of control in business is that control is exercised by managers over **people**. Their attitude and response to budgetary planning and control will affect the way in which it operates.

Conventional and newer ideas

3.2 A great deal has been written about the human behavioural factors at work in budgetary planning and control and the following brief history may help you to shift knowledge acquired earlier into a **more modern** perspective. Interest in the topic was stimulated by an article written in 1953 by Chris Argyris ('Human problems with budgets'). Argyris identified the following four perspectives.

Perspective	Comment
Pressure device	The budget is seen as a **pressure device**, used by management to force 'lazy' employees to work harder. The intention is to improve performance, but the unfavourable reactions of subordinates against it 'seems to be at the core of the budget problem'.
Budget men want to see failure	The **accounting department** is usually responsible for actual/ budget comparisons. Accountants are therefore **budget men**. Their success is to find significant adverse variances, and identify the managers responsible. The success of a 'budget man' is the **failure of another manager** and this failure causes loss of interest and declining performance. The accountant, on the other hand, fearful of having his budget criticised by factory management, obscures his budget and variance reporting, and deliberately makes it difficult to understand.
Targets and goal congruence	The budget usually sets **targets** for each department. Achieving the target becomes of paramount importance, regardless of the effect on other departments and overall company performance. This is the problem of **goal congruence**.
Management style	Budgets are used by managers to express their character and patterns of leadership on subordinates. Subordinates, resentful of their leader's **style**, blame the budget rather than the leader.

Management styles

3.3 The final point was developed by Hopwood in another influential study, *Accounting and Human Behaviour* (1974). Hopwood identifies three distinct supervisory styles.

Supervisory style	Hopwood says …
Budget-constrained style	'The manager's performance is primarily evaluated upon the basis of his ability to continually **meet the budget** on a short-term basis . . . stressed at the expense of other valued and important criteria and the manager will receive unfavourable feedback from his superior if, for instance, his actual costs exceed the budgeted costs, regardless of other considerations.'
Profit-conscious style	'The manager's performance is evaluated on the basis of his ability to **increase the general effectiveness** of his unit's operations in relation to the long-term purposes of the organisation'. '
Non-accounting style	'The budgetary information plays a **relatively unimportant** part in the superior's evaluation of the manager's performance.'

Knowledge brought forward from Paper 8

Budgets can be set from the **top down** (imposed) or from the **bottom up** (participatory).

- **Imposed budgets** can be effective.

  - During difficult economic conditions
  - If operational managers lack budgeting skills
  - If the organisation's units need very precise co-ordination
  - In very small businesses
  - In newly-formed organisations

- Imposed budgets may be more effective at incorporating **overall strategy** into operational plans.

- Imposed budgets may be **resented**. Operational managers may resent them or even go against them if they think they are unfair.

- **Participative budgets** are developed by lower-level managers, on the basis of what they think is achievable and the resources they need, and then submitted for approval to more senior managers.

- Participative budgets can be effective in the opposite set of circumstances to imposed budgets. Lower level managers have a clearer idea of the needs and limitations of their units. They are more likely to be committed to targets they set themselves.

- Participative budgets take longer to prepare and co-ordinate with other units' budgets and strategic plans. They risk **budgetary slack**.

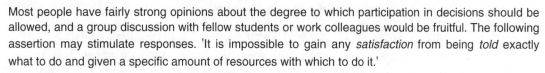

Question 3

Most people have fairly strong opinions about the degree to which participation in decisions should be allowed, and a group discussion with fellow students or work colleagues would be fruitful. The following assertion may stimulate responses. 'It is impossible to gain any *satisfaction* from being *told* exactly what to do and given a specific amount of resources with which to do it.'

Discuss!

Contingency theory

3.4 Some researchers have argued that the **context** in which budgetary control is used is as important as the style in which it is implemented and used. This is known as **contingency theory.**

> 'The contingency approach to management accounting is based on the premise that there is no universally appropriate accounting system applicable to all organisations in all circumstances. Rather a contingency theory attempts to identify specific aspects of an accounting system that are associated with certain defined circumstances and to demonstrate an appropriate matching'
> (Emmanuel, Otley and Merchant).

3.5 The major factors that have been identified are classified by Emmanuel *et al* as follows.

(a) **The environment**. For example:

- Its degree of predictability
- The degree of competition faced
- The number of different product markets faced
- The degree of hostility exhibited by competing organisations

(b) **Organisational structure**. For example:

- Size
- Interdependence of parts

- Degree of decentralisation
- Availability of resources

(c) **Technology**. For example:

- The nature of the production process
- The routineness/complexity of the production process
- How well the relationship between ends and means is understood
- The amount of variety in each task that has to be performed

Subsequent developments

3.6 Contingency theory has been **criticised** because it does little more than identify an array of contingent variables and describe what systems exist: it does not put forward suggestions as to how accounting systems could be **improved** by demonstrating what systems work well in what circumstances.

Corporate aspirations and internal conflict

3.7 A budget is meant to be formulated so as to achieve the overall **objectives** of the organisation, at least within the short term. However, organisational objectives are very **rarely clearly defined** (and one organisation is likely to have a number of different objectives anyway). Different managers will perceive their objectives differently, and so the budget demands of managers will frequently be **incompatible**.

3.8 The conflicting demands of different departments are accentuated by:

- The **lack of social interaction** between people in different departments
- The different and often **conflicting sources of information** for each department
- Different, or even competing, **reward structures**

Expectations and aspirations

3.9 As targets, budgets can motivate managers to achieve a high level of performance. But **how difficult** should targets be? And how might people react to targets of differing degrees of difficulty in achievement?

(a) There is likely to be a **demotivating** effect where an **ideal standard** of performance is set, because adverse efficiency variances will always be reported.

(b) A **low standard** of efficiency is also **demotivating**, because there is no sense of achievement in attaining the required standards. If the budgeted level of attainment is too 'loose', targets will be achieved easily, and there will be no impetus for employees to try harder to do better than this.

(c) A budgeted level of attainment could be the **same as** the level that has been achieved **in the past**. Arguably, this level will be too low. It might encourage **budgetary slack**.

3.10 Academics have argued that each individual has a **personal 'aspiration level'**. This is a level of performance, in a task with which the individual is familiar, which the individual undertakes for himself to reach. However, individual aspirations may be much higher or much lower than the organisation's aspirations. If they are **not realistic** they are of no use for planning and decision making.

3.11 The solution might therefore be to have **two budgets**.

(a) A budget for **planning and decision making** based on reasonable expectations

(b) A budget for **motivational purposes,** with more difficult targets of performance (ie targets of an intermediate level of difficulty)

These two budgets might be called an **expectations budget** and an **aspirations budget** respectively.

> ### Exam focus point
> Two tables provided in a **June 1998** exam question provided illustrations (in terms of units of output) of the results of two separate studies linking targets, aspiration levels and achievement. In the light of this data, candidates were required to discuss the theory that individual performance is likely to be related to the individual's aspiration level and the timing and level of the target set.

Question 4

Given the problems of accommodating personal motivations within a budgeting system on the one hand, and the difficulties of defining organisational goals by means of budgeting on the other, should budgeting even attempt to address these issues? Can you suggest another way of tackling the problem?

Answer

There is room here for a variety of views. Is the real problem one of communication (in which case accountants have a good deal to answer for)? It is more likely, however, that the budget is the wrong medium for the message. Many organisations have adopted **mission statements** to communicate their corporate aims and have successfully set about changing attitudes by encouraging philosophies like **total quality management**. This is further discussed below.

4 ALTERNATIVE APPROACHES TO BUDGETING

Incremental budgeting

4.1 The term **incremental budgeting** is often used, not to describe an incremental cost versus incremental benefit approach to budgeting, but for the more traditional approach of setting a budget which is based on the **current year's** results plus an **extra amount** (an 'increment') for estimated growth or inflation next year.

4.2 Traditional incremental budgeting will be sufficient only if current operations are as effective, efficient and economical as they can be, without any alternative courses of action available to the organisation.

4.3 However, the planning process should take account of **alternative options,** and look for **ways of improving performance**: this is something that traditional incremental budgeting simply does not do.

4.4 Although administratively an incremental budget is fairly easy to prepare, it encourages **slack and wasteful spending** to creep into budgets and to become a normal feature of actual spending.

Exam focus point
You might be asked in your examination to compare the merits of newer approaches discussed below with traditional incremental budgeting, or to suggest what the weaknesses of traditional incremental budgeting might be. In the **June 1998** exam, candidates had to discuss the impact of modern developments on the way in which budgets are prepared compared to budget preparation under an incremental budgeting system.

Zero-base budgeting

4.5 The principle behind zero-base budgeting is that the budget for each cost centre should be **made from 'scratch'** (a 'zero base'). It starts from the basic premise that the budget for next year is zero; every process or expenditure then has to be justified in its entirety in order to be included in the next year's budget.

4.6 In zero-base budgeting, there should be a positive attempt to **eliminate inefficiency and slack** from current expenditure, not merely to prevent future cost increases. ZBB rejects the idea that next year's budgeted activities should assume that last year's activities will continue at the same level or volume, and that next year's budget can be based on last year's costs plus an extra amount for expansion and inflation.

4.7 The basic approach of zero-base budgeting has five steps.

Step 1. Managers within the organisation are asked to specify the **decision units** within their area of authority (programmes of work or capital expenditure programmes or areas of activity which can be individually evaluated).

Step 2. Each of the separate decision units is described in a **decision package** (a document which identifies and describes the specific activity in such a way that management can evaluate it and rank it in order of priority against other activities).

Step 3. Each decision package is evaluated and **ranked** by cost benefit analysis.

Step 4. Activities which would cost more than they are worth (in qualitative or quantitative terms) should be **dropped**.

Step 5. **Resources** in the budget are then **allocated** according to the funds available and the evaluation and ranking of the competing packages.

4.8 Packages involving small expenditures can be dealt with by junior managers but senior managers must make decisions involving larger amounts of expenditure. The ZBB process must, however, **run through the entire management structure.**

4.9 There are two types of decision package.

(a) **Mutually exclusive packages.** Each of these contains an alternative method of getting the same job done. The best option among the packages must be selected by cost benefit analysis and the other packages are then discarded.

(b) **Incremental packages.** These divide one aspect of work or activity into different levels of effort. The 'base' package will describe the minimum amount of work that must be done to carry out the activity and the other packages describe what additional work could be done, at what cost and for what benefits.

Question 5

Obtain your bank statements and credit card statements for the last three months, say, and identify as much of the expenditure as you can in as precise detail as possible.

(a) Identify the decision units ('accommodation', 'travel', 'food and drink', 'saving' etc).
(b) Identify mutually exclusive activities (eating out or in, driving to work or taking the bus etc).
(c) Identify 'incremental packages' (activities that you might spend more on if funds were available).
(d) Draw up a base package for these activities and several incremental packages.

What proportion of your total income do you spend per month on discretionary activities?

Uses of ZBB

4.10 Some particular uses of ZBB are as follows.

(a) Budgeting for **discretionary cost items,** such as training costs. The priorities for spending money could be established by ranking activities and alternative levels of spending or service can be evaluated on an incremental basis. For example, is it worth spending £2,000 more to increase the numbers trained on one type of training course by 10%? If so, what priority should this incremental spending on training be given, when compared with other potential training activities?

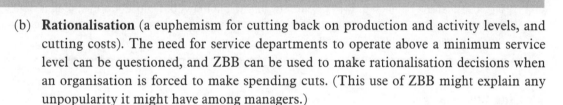

Exam focus point

An explanation of how recognition of the committed, engineered and discretionary nature of planned expenditure may help in the formulation of a budget plan which will provide the desired annual profit was required in the **December 1999** exam. See chapter 12 for details of engineered costs.

(b) **Rationalisation** (a euphemism for cutting back on production and activity levels, and cutting costs). The need for service departments to operate above a minimum service level can be questioned, and ZBB can be used to make rationalisation decisions when an organisation is forced to make spending cuts. (This use of ZBB might explain any unpopularity it might have among managers.)

Advantages of ZBB

4.11 If it can be applied, the advantages of zero-base budgeting are as follows.

(a) It provides a budgeting and planning tool for management which **responds to changes** in the business environment; obsolete items of expenditure and activities are identified and ceased.

(b) It obliges an organisation to look very closely into its **cost behaviour** patterns in order to decide the effect of alternative courses of action.

(c) It should result in a more efficient **allocation of resources**.

(d) It adds a psychological impetus to employees to **avoid wasteful expenditure**.

(e) The **documentation** required makes a co-ordinated, in-depth knowledge of an organisation's operations available to all management.

Disadvantages of ZBB

4.12 The most serious drawback to ZBB is that it requires a lot of management **time** and paperwork (though computers help with this), and managers must be **trained** in ZBB techniques in order that they can apply them sensibly and properly. The organisation's **information systems** must also be capable of providing suitable incremental cost and incremental benefit analysis.

4.13 Zero-base budgeting requires the extensive involvement of managers and it will therefore **not be appropriate** in an organisation structure that is not conducive to participation in budgeting.

4.14 Frequently the disadvantages of the full version of ZBB will outweigh the benefits, but the approach is self-evidently preferable to traditional incremental budgeting and many organisations have adopted **less complex versions** of the ZBB approach.

Question 6

An organisation used ZBB last year to prepare its budget and is now as efficient, effective and economical as it can possibly be. A manager has put it to the board that in view of this a further round of ZBB this year would itself be a wasteful activity and that the time could be more profitably spent on other matters. She proposes taking this year's results as the basis for next year's budget and adjusting the figures to allow for planned growth plus inflation at the rate currently indicated by the Retail Price Index, or other more appropriate indices where these are available.

The board has asked you for your opinion.

Answer

Provided that the organisation is indeed already as efficient, effective and economical as possible, and provided that the planned growth or other factors will not have an impact on this, then it would seem perfectly reasonable to use the proposed incremental approach in this case. In practice the conditions described will rarely apply, of course.

Rolling budgets

KEY TERM

A **rolling budget** is 'a budget continuously updated by adding a further period, say a month or quarter and deducting the earliest period.' Such procedures are 'Beneficial where future costs and/or activities cannot be forecast reliably.' (CIMA, *Official Terminology*)

4.15 Rolling budgets are an attempt to prepare targets and plans which are **more realistic and certain**, particularly with a regard to price levels, by shortening the period between preparing budgets.

4.16 Instead of preparing a **periodic budget** annually for the full budget period, there would be budgets every one, two, three or four months. Each of these budgets would plan for the next twelve months so that the current budget is extended by an extra period as the current period ends: hence the name **rolling** budgets.

Advantages of rolling budgets

4.17 They may be advantageous in **larger businesses** operating in **unstable environments**.

    (a) They reduce the element of **uncertainty** in budgeting because it is easier to predict what will happen in the short-term.

    (b) Planning and control will be based on a **recent plan** which is **more realistic** than a fixed annual budget that might have been made many months ago.

    (c) There will always be a budget which **extends for several months ahead.**

    (d) They force managers to reassess the budget regularly, and to produce budgets which are **up to date** in the light of current events and expectations.

    (e) Realistic budgets are likely to have a **better motivational influence** on managers.

Disadvantages of rolling budgets

4.18 In an organisation where the finance function is not fully developed or has limited time available, the **disadvantages** of rolling budgets can outweigh any benefits.

    (a) They involve more **time, effort and money** in budget preparation, although computers and spreadsheets help considerably.

    (b) Frequent budgeting might have an off-putting effect on **managers** who doubt the value of preparing one budget after another at regular intervals.

    (c) If the business's environment is fairly **stable**, routine updating of the budget may be **unnecessary**. Instead the annual budget could simply be **updated** whenever changes become foreseeable. A budget might be updated once or twice during the course of the year.

Exam focus point

A question in the **June 1997** exam is a wonderful example of the differences between Paper 8 and Paper 9 questions. Rather than describe rolling budgets, flexible budgets and planning and operational variances (as might be expected in Paper 8), candidates had to discuss how they helped with planning and control. You must be able to **apply your knowledge** in Paper 9.

---

5   TQM AND ABB

Conventional budgeting in a changing environment

5.1 Surveys suggest that very few senior managers believed that conventional budget, cost centre and variance reporting is a 'very effective' control mechanism. Traditional budgetary control is seen as a **costly and burdensome** routine, reinforcing **bad practice** and **constraining response** in a rapidly changing commercial environment.

5.2 There are a number of reasons for this, including the following.

    (a) People prefer to be **in control**, and dislike **being** controlled. **Control has become constraint**, suffocating managerial initiative and running completely counter to the empowering philosophy of total quality and continuous improvement.

    (b) The process of negotiation and adjustment that follows the initial budget proposals results in individual departmental budgets that **bear little relation to the strategy** that gave rise to the original proposals.

(c) Budgets are often expressed in **financial terms** using established ledger headings, which is convenient for the finance function but of limited use for departmental managers. **Non-financial measures** are the exception rather than the rule.

(d) Managers are inclined to reduce department budgets crudely. The errors that ensue and their correction in other parts of the organisation costs more overall than is saved by the original reduction.

Total Quality Management and budgeting

5.3 As you know, total quality management is an organisational philosophy with two main themes, get it right first time and continuous improvement.

5.4 Where such a philosophy is adopted this has a number of implications for the use of budgeting and budgetary control.

(a) **Negative feedback** is a clear indication that the operation in question is falling short of the required target, assuming that '**not getting it right**' means failing to meet the budget.

(b) **Positive feedback** indicates that there is further potential for **improvement**: feedforward control action should be taken to encourage this in future periods.

5.5 The TQM approach has the potential to eliminate many of the unfortunate **behavioural** consequences of traditional budgetary control. It attempts to appeal to everybody's **innate desire to do better** and turns this into a corporate mission. Ideally where such an organisational culture has taken hold, the budgetary control system will be viewed by managers as part of the organisation's overall quality control system.

5.6 The **management accountant** can contribute here by being aware of the general movement within the organisation and taking a contingent approach, redesigning management reports in a **style and language** that is compatible with the philosophy. Far from usurping the role of budgets as the means of controlling performance, the TQM movement may offer budgetary control a new role as a key part of a more radical and broadly-based attempt to **change attitudes** and achieve goal congruence.

Activity based budgeting

5.7 **Activity based budgeting (ABB)** has been proposed by a number of writers.

5.8 Implementing ABC leads to the realisation that the **business as a whole** needs to be **managed** with far more reference to the behaviour of activities and cost drivers identified. For example, traditional budgeting may make managers 'responsible' for activities which are driven by factors beyond their control: the **personnel department** cost of setting up new employee records is driven by the number of new employees required by managers **other than the personnel manager.**

5.9 ABB involves defining the activities that underlie the financial figures in each function and using the **level of activity** to decide how much resource should be **allocated**, how well it is being **managed** and to **explain variances** from budget.

Business Process Re-engineering (BPR)

5.10 Some writers link ABB to what is known as **Business Process Re-engineering (BPR)** - re-organising a business according to the **processes** it performs rather than the functions it performs (for example a sale is a process that is traditionally handled not only by 'sales' people, but also by accounts people, warehousing people and so on).

5.11 BPR is closely linked with ideas like TQM and employee empowerment, and ABB may quite legitimately be seen as **one of the tools of BPR**. In some circumstances ABB may be the initiative that prompts a wide ranging examination of business processes.

The Paper 9 examiner and ABB

5.12 Other writers, including the **Paper 9 examiner** (*ACCA Students' Newsletter*, March 1994), treat ABB as a complete **philosophy** in itself and attribute to it all the good features of strategic management accounting, zero base budgeting, total quality management, and other ideas. For example, it has been claimed that, using ABB:

(a) different **activity levels** will provide a foundation for the 'base' package and incremental packages of **ZBB**;

(b) it will ensure that the organisation's overall **strategy** and any actual or likely changes in that strategy will be taken into account, because it attempts to manage the business as the **sum of its interrelated parts**;

(c) **critical success factors** will be identified and performance measures devised to monitor progress towards them. (A critical success factor is an activity in which a business **must** perform well if it is to succeed);

(d) because concentration is focused on the **whole of an activity**, not just its separate parts, there is more likelihood of **getting it right first time**. For example what is the use of being able to **produce** goods in time for their despatch date if the budget provides insufficient resources for the distribution manager who has to **deliver** them?

PUBLISHING

Chapter roundup

- The main purpose of studying control theory is to become familiar with **terminology** that can usefully be applied in business situations.

- Control in the broad sense encompasses both **planning** and **ensuring conformity to plan** (by making new plans if necessary).

- **Predictability** is the biggest problem in control. A situation may be programmed (outcomes ought to be as expected) or non-programmed (outcomes are uncertain).

- **Budgetary control** recognises that business organisations are dynamic, especially when feedforward control is used to anticipate future threats to the achievement of the plan or opportunities to achieve it more efficiently.

- The **behavioural** issues in budgeting include the different management styles, the question of participation and the conflict between personal and corporate goods.

- **Zero base budgeting** is preferable to incremental budgeting. **Rolling budgets** may be useful for larger businesses in an unstable environment.

- **New ideas** in management (such as BPR, TQM and JIT) and in management accounting (such as ABC) are **likely to have an impact on budgeting**, and so is the highly competitive and fast-moving environment in which most businesses now operate.

Quick quiz

1   Why bother with control? (see para 1.2 - 1.3)

2   What four conditions are necessary for a process to be controlled? (1.12)

3   What is feedforward control? (1.14)

4   What is a non-programmed decision? (1.22)

5   What are the uses of budgetary control? (2.2)

6   What are the main contingent factors? (3.5)

7   What are the steps in ZBB? (4.7)

8   What are the advantages of ZBB? (4.11)

9   What are the disadvantages of rolling budgets? (4.18)

10   What are the implications of TQM for a budgetary control system? (5.4, 5.5)

11   What four claims does the Paper 9 examiner make for activity based budgeting? (5.12)

Question to try	Level	Marks	Time
10	Exam standard	20	36 mins

Chapter 11

STANDARD COSTING AND VARIANCES

Chapter topic list	Syllabus reference
1 Flexible budgeting	3(b)
2 Standard costing	3(b)
3 Variances	3(b)
4 Interpretation of variances	3(b)
5 Standard costing in the modern environment	3(b)

Introduction

We combine our coverage of budgeting with the topics of standard costing and variances in this book because that is what **Paper 9 questions** tend to do.

The early parts of this chapter remind you of a few basic issues and techniques and will help you to sharpen up your skills if they are a bit rusty. Then we move on to areas that are of special interest to the Paper 9 **examiner**, such as variance trends and TQM.

In the next two chapters we concentrate on more complicated techniques that you may have to use or describe in budgeting/standard costing questions in the exam.

Core areas of the syllabus identified by the examiner and covered in this chapter: **the role of standard costing in modern business**.

1 FLEXIBLE BUDGETING

> **KEY TERMS**
>
> A **fixed budget** is one that is not adjusted to the actual volume of output or level of activity attained in a period. This is most unrealistic because the actual level will almost certainly be different from the level of activity originally planned.
>
> A **flexible budget**. however, recognises this uncertainty. It is designed to change so as to relate to the actual volumes of output.

1.1 Flexible budgets may be used in one of two ways.

Planning

1.2 At the **planning** stage when budgets are set, to reduce the effect of uncertainty. For example, suppose that a company expects to sell 10,000 units of output during the next year. A master budget (the fixed budget) would be prepared on the basis of this expected volume. However, if the company thinks that output and sales might be as low as 8,000 units or as high as 12,000 units, it may prepare contingency flexible budgets, at volumes of say, 8,000, 9,000, 11,000 and 12,000 units.

1.3 The **advantages** of planning with flexible budgets include:

(a) finding out well in advance the **costs** of lay-off pay, idle time and so on if **output falls short** of budget;

(b) deciding whether it would be possible to find **alternative uses** for spare capacity if **output falls short** of budget;

(c) estimating the **costs** of overtime or sub-contracting work if sales **volume exceeds the fixed budget** estimate, and finding out if there is a **limiting factor** which would prevent high volumes of output and sales being achieved.

1.4 It has been suggested, however, that since many cost items in modern industry are fixed costs, the value of flexible budgets in **planning** is dwindling. For example:

(a) in many manufacturing industries, **plant costs** (depreciation, rent and so on) are a very large proportion of total costs, and these tend to be fixed costs;

(b) **wages costs** also tend to be fixed, because employees are generally guaranteed a basic wage for a working week of an agreed number of hours;

(c) with the growth of **service industries,** fixed salaries and overheads will account for most costs, direct materials being only a relatively small proportion.

Exam focus point

Twelve fairly easy marks were available in the **December 1998** exam for preparing a flexible budget.

Control

1.5 Flexible budgets are also used 'retrospectively' at the end of each month (control period) or year, to compare actual results achieved with the results that would have been expected if the actual circumstances had been known in advance. Flexible budgets are an essential factor in **budgetary control** and **variance analysis.**

2 STANDARD COSTING

KEY TERM

A **standard cost** is a carefully predetermined estimated unit cost. Note each element of this definition well: they are all important.

Its main uses are providing bases for performance measurement, control by exception reporting, valuing stock and establishing selling prices.

Exam focus point

The relevance of standard costs and variances in the application of target costing, backflush accounting and transfer pricing had to be discussed in the **December 1998** exam, while the value of standard specifications in product pricing and target costing was examined in **December 1999.**

Budgets and standard costs

2.1 All standard costs consist of two elements: a physical quantity or length of time, and a monetary amount. An example of a **standard cost** record for a **unit** of a product (where absorption costing or ABC is used) is as follows. (Worry a great deal about how much you know if you could not have drawn up a standard cost record such as this yourself!)

PRODUCT: THE SPLODGET, NO 12345

		£	£
Direct materials			
A	6 kg at £2 per kg	12	
B	2 kg at £3 per kg	6	
C	1 litre at £4 per litre	4	
Others		2	
			24
Direct labour			
Grade I	3 hours at £4 per hour	12	
Grade II	5 hours at £5.40 per hour	27	
			39
Variable production overheads 8 hours at £1			8
Fixed production overheads 8 hours at £3 per hour			24
Standard full cost of production			95

2.2 In practice, the terms '**standard cost**' and '**budgeted cost**' might be used interchangeably. Whereas it is possible to have budgeting without standard costs, it is not possible to have a standard cost system without a total cost budgeting system.

> ### Exam focus point
> The examiner has confirmed (1999) that more discussion questions can be expected on standard costing. In the light of this we strongly recommend that you study in detail his article 'Standard costing - a status check' (*ACCA Students' Newsletter*, March 1999), covers a wide range of standard costing discussion topics. We have included the most important aspects of the article as appropriate in this and the following chapters.
>
> In the article, George Brown looks at the development of standard costing from when it was first used in the early part of the twentieth century to its role in the modern business environment. We will leave you to read for yourself this historical perspective - it may not be tested in the exam but it will provide very useful background knowledge.

Standard costs, budgetary control and variances

2.3 Standard costing and budgetary control are interlinked items. Once standard costs have been determined it is relatively easy to **compute budgets** for production costs and sales and, when actual figures differ from expected standards, to calculate **variances**, to provide a basis for control reporting.

> ### Exam focus point
> Questions that ask you to do this are the commonest sort of budgeting questions in paper 9.

2.4 A standard cost is an **average expected unit cost**. It is set using the best available estimates and it cannot be expected in practice that actual results will conform to standard. Variances should therefore be **expected to fluctuate** randomly within normal limits. Such random fluctuations need no investigation and **tolerance limits** are set (investigate only those variances which exceed £x or y% of standard cost).

Installing a standard cost system

2.5 Standard costing is appropriate in any situation where the same resources are used **over and over again** in the same way. It is therefore particularly appropriate for manufacturing businesses producing **large numbers of identical items**, especially where the same operations are combined in different ways to produce different products. It also has applications in service businesses that involve repetitive operations.

2.6 Installing a standard costing system entails designing an **information system** that can collect and analyse details about activities in such a way that the standards can be set and applied. In effect this means collecting quantitative data about the use of resources.

The advantages and disadvantages of standard costing

2.7 **Advantages**

(a) Carefully planned standards are an aid to **more accurate budgeting**.

(b) Standard costs provide a **yardstick** against which actual costs can be measured.

(c) The setting of standards involves determining the **best materials and methods** which may lead to economies.

(d) A target of **efficiency** to reach is set for employees and **cost-consciousness** is stimulated.

(e) Variances can be calculated which enable the principle of '**management by exception**' to be operated. Only the variances which exceed acceptable tolerance limits need to be investigated by management with a view to control action.

2.8 **Disadvantages**

(a) It is **difficult to set** accurate standards.
(b) The collection and analysis of the necessary data may be very **time-consuming**.
(c) Standards may be seen as a **pressure device**.

Exam focus point

Five marks were available in the **December 1997** exam for suggesting possible dysfunctional consequences of focusing on the minimisation of an adverse material price variance.

The Paper 9 examiner and standard costs

2.9 George Brown, 'Planning and operational variances in a service business', *ACCA Students' Newsletter*, April 1995, gives the following **aims** for standard costing and variance analysis.

(a) To provide data which is relevant to management for **feedback control** purposes, to show where deviations from plan have arisen and to point towards areas where corrective action may be taken.

(b) To show which deviations from plan are **controllable** and which are non-controllable, and to value variances on a basis which is related to the level at which they are controllable.

(c) To determine the **cause** of a controllable deviation from plan and to attempt to minimise any adverse effect on costs and profit.

(d) To determine which variances are due to **planning** factors and which to **operational** factors.

(e) To provide a basis for **feedforward control** action.

Question 1

What are the problems associated with using current price or average expected price/estimated mid-year price as the standard material price in times of inflation?

Answer

If the current price were used in the standard, the reported price variance would become adverse as soon as prices go up, which might be very early in the year. If prices go up gradually rather than in one big jump, it would be difficult to select an appropriate time for revising the standard.

If an estimated mid-year price were used, price variances should be favourable in the first half of the year and adverse in the second half, again assuming that prices go up gradually. Management could only really check that in any month, the price variance did not become excessively adverse (or favourable) and that it switched from being favourable to adverse around month six and not sooner.

Question 2

(a) In a TQM environment, which types of performance standard are acceptable?
(b) Which performance standards are thought to be the best basis for budgeting?

Answer

(a) Employees should not be satisfied with anything less than ideal performance.

(b) Current or attainable (since they represent the level of productivity which management can realistically plan for).

3 VARIANCES

3.1 Variances are the differences between actual results and expected results. Expected results are the standard costs and standard revenues.

3.2 Basic variance analysis such as this should be second nature to you by this stage, but many students hate the subject and others may be a little rusty, so the following notes may be helpful. Read through the notes and then try Questions 3, 4, and 5.

Exam focus point

The examiner has confirmed that he does not envisage a full computational question on standard costing but that you may be required to calculate specific variances as part of an overall analysis and discussion of the topic.

Knowledge brought forward from Paper 8

Variances

- The ***selling price variance*** is a measure of the effect on expected profit of a different selling price to the standard selling price. It is calculated as the difference between the standard revenue from the actual quantity of goods sold and the actual revenue.

- The ***sales volume variance*** is the difference between the actual units sold and the budgeted quantity, valued at the standard profit or contribution per unit. In other words, it measures the increase or decrease between standard and actual profit or contribution as a result of the sales volume being higher or lower than budgeted.

- **Price, rate and expenditure variances** measure the difference between the actual amount of money paid and the amount of money that should have been paid for the actual quantity of materials or the actual number of hours of labour or variable overheads used. Note that if materials are valued at standard cost, the materials price variance is calculated on purchases in the period but if they are valued at actual cost the variance is calculated on materials used in production in the period.

- **Usage and efficiency variances** are *quantity* variances. They measure the difference between the actual physical quantity of materials used or hours taken and the quantities that should have been used or taken for the actual volume of production. These physical differences are converted into money values by applying the appropriate standard cost.

- The **idle time variance** is the hours of idle time valued at the standard rate per hour.

Exam focus point

An easy four marks were available in the **December 1997** exam for calculating material and variable overhead variances, the variable overhead being a conversion process.

Question 3

WIB Ltd has budgeted to sell 1,300 units of product CBB in period 13 at a selling price of £22, the budgeted standard full cost of production being £12. In fact, 1,250 units were sold at a price of £24.50 each.

Required

Calculate the selling price variance and the sales volume profit variance.

Answer

(a)

	£
Revenue from 1,250 units should have been (× £22)	27,500
but was (× £24.50)	30,625
Selling price variance	3,125 (F)

(b)

Budgeted sales volume	1,300 units
Actual sales volume	1,250 units
Sales volume profit variance in units	50 units (A)
× standard profit margin per unit (× £(22 −12))	× £10
Sales volume profit variance in £	£500 (A)

Question 4

The following standard costs apply in a business that manufactures a single product.

Standard weight to produce one unit	12 kgs	Standard hours to produce one unit	10
Standard price per kg	£9	Standard rate per hour	£4

Actual production and costs for one accounting period (when output was 290 units) were as follows.

Material used	3,770 kgs	Hours paid for	2,900
Material cost	£35,815	Wages paid	£11,571
Hours actually worked	2,755		

Required

Calculate relevant material and labour variances.

Answer

	£
3,770 kgs should cost (× £9)	33,930
but did cost	35,815
Material cost variance	1,885 (A)
290 units should use (× 12 kgs)	3,480 kgs
but did use	3,770 kgs
Material usage variance in kgs	290 kgs (A)
× standard cost per kg	× £9
Material usage variance in £	£2,610 (A)
2,900 hours should cost (× £4)	11,600
but did cost	11,571
Labour rate variance	29 (F)
290 units should take (× 10 hrs)	2,900 hrs
but did take	2,755 hrs
Labour efficiency variance in hrs	145 hrs (F)
× standard rate per hour	× £4
Labour efficiency variance in £	£580 (F)
Idle time variance: (2,900 − 2,755) hrs × £4	£580 (A)

Question 5

Basic Analysis Ltd produces and sells one product only, the Verintz, the standard cost for one unit being as follows.

	£
Direct material A - 10 kilograms at £20 per kg	200
Direct material B - 5 litres at £6 per litre	30
Direct wages - 5 hours at £6 per hour	30
Fixed production overhead	50
Total standard cost	310

The fixed overhead included in the standard cost is based on an expected monthly output of 900 units.

During April 19X3, 800 units were produced and the actual results were as follows.

Material A	7,800 kg used, costing £159,900
Material B	4,300 units used, costing £23,650
Direct wages	4,200 hours worked for £24,150
Fixed production overhead	£47,000

Required

(a)   Calculate price and usage variances for each material.
(b)   Calculate labour rate and efficiency variances.
(c)   Calculate fixed production overhead expenditure and volume variances

Answer

(a)

		£
7,800 kgs should have cost (× £20)		156,000
but did cost		159,900
Price variance - A		3,900 (A)

800 units should have used (× 10 kgs)		8,000 kgs
but did use		7,800 kgs
Usage variance in kgs		200 kgs (F)
× standard cost per kilogram		× £20
Usage variance in £ - A		£4,000 (F)

		£
4,300 units should have cost (× £6)		25,800
but did cost		23,650
Price variance - B		2,150 (F)

800 units should have used (× 5 l)		4,000 l
but did use		4,300 l
Usage variance in litres		300 (A)
× standard cost per litre		× £6
Usage variance in £ - B		£1,800 (A)

(b)

		£
4,200 hours should have cost (× £6)		25,200
but did cost		24,150
Rate variance		1,050 (F)

800 units should have taken (× 5 hrs)		4,000 hrs
but did take		4,200 hrs
Efficiency variance in hours		200 hrs (A)
× standard rate per hour		× £6
Efficiency variance in £		£1,200 (A)

(c)

		£
Budgeted expenditure (£50 × 900)		45,000
Actual expenditure		47,000
Fixed overhead expenditure variance		2,000 (A)

		£
Budgeted production at standard rate (900 × £50)		45,000
Actual production at standard rate (800 × £50)		40,000
Fixed overhead volume variance		5,000 (A)

4 INTERPRETATION OF VARIANCES

Trend, materiality and controllability (and the Paper 9 examiner)

4.1 The point of comparing flexed budget and actual figures is to see what corrective action, if any, is needed to ensure that the plan will be successfully completed. Thus every variance needs to be considered to see whether it should prompt control action.

4.2 Three important points should be kept in mind.

(a) **Materiality**

Small variations in a single period are bound to occur occasionally and are **unlikely to be significant**. Obtaining an 'explanation' is likely to be time-consuming and irritating for the manager concerned. The explanation will often be 'chance', which is not helpful. Further investigation is not worthwhile.

(b) **Trend**

Small variations that occur consistently may need more attention. As the **examiner** comments in an article in the *ACCA Students' Newsletter* (November 1992):

'Variance trend is more important than a single set of variances for one accounting period. Trend analysis provides information which gives an indication as to whether a variance is fluctuating within acceptable control limits or is moving into an out of control situation'.

In the second of his 'Control information and standard process costs' articles (*ACCA Students' Newsletter,* December, 1995), the **examiner** again commented on the usefulness of a trend of variances rather than one period variances. Trend is discussed further below.

(c) **Controllability**

Controllability must also influence the decision whether to investigate further. If a central decision is made to award all employees a 10% increase in salary, staff costs in A division will increase by this amount and the variance is not controllable by A division's manager. Uncontrollable variances call for a **change in the plan**, not an investigation into the past.

> **Exam focus point**
> The issue of **controllability** was examined in the **December 1997** exam.

Variance trend

4.3 If, say, an efficiency variance is £1,000 adverse in month 1, the obvious conclusion is that the process is **out of control** and that corrective action must be taken. This may be correct, but what if the same variance is £1,000 adverse every month? The **trend** indicates that the process is **in control** and the standard has been wrongly set.

4.4 Suppose, though, that the same variance is consistently £1,000 adverse for each of the first six months of the year but that production has steadily fallen from 100 units in month 1 to 65 units by month 6. The variance trend in absolute terms is constant, but relative to the number of units produced, efficiency has got steadily worse.

4.5 EXAMPLE: VARIANCE TREND

One unit takes ten hours to produce. The standard labour cost is £5 per hour. In period 1, 100 units are produced in 1,200 hours. In period 6, 65 units are produced in 850 hours. What is the best way of presenting this information to management?

4.6 SOLUTION

The labour efficiency variance can be calculated in the normal way.

	Period 1		*Period 6*
	Hours		Hours
100 units should take	1,000	65 units should take	650
but did take	1,200	but did take	850
Efficiency variance in hours	200	Efficiency variance in hours	200
× standard rate per hour	× £5	× standard rate per hour	× £5
	£1,000		£1,000

The absolute measures, whether in hours or pounds, do not convey what is happening at all. What is needed is a **relative measure**.

(a) In **physical** terms, one unit takes 12 hours to make in period 1, but more than 13 hours (850/65) in period 6.

(b) In **monetary** terms the variance can be related to standard cost and expressed as a percentage. In period 1 £1,000 represents 20% of the standard cost for 100 units of £5,000. In period 6 £1,000 represents over 30% of the standard cost for 65 units of £3,250.

Conclusions

4.7 (a) Single period variances are not necessarily a good indication of whether or not a process is in control.

(b) Absolute measurement may disguise some of the significance of a variance. It is helpful to supplement this information by measurement over time in percentage terms against an appropriate base.

Exam focus point

A question that asked you to highlight variance trends and comment on them featured in the **June 1994** exam.

Question 6

The standard cost of a material is £15 per kg and the standard usage for one unit is 10 kg. In the first six months of the year actual usage and costs have been as follows.

	Output Units	Usage kg	Cost £
January	30	300	4,800
February	40	425	6,800
March	35	385	6,160
April	42	465	6,975
May	38	420	6,300
June	40	435	6,525

Required

Calculate the price and usage variances both in absolute terms and in percentage terms. Comment on the trend as revealed by each method.

Answer

	Price variance £		%	Usage variance £		%
January	300	(A)	$6^2/_3$	-		0
February	425	(A)	$6^2/_3$	375	(A)	6.25
March	385	(A)	$6^2/_3$	525	(A)	10.0
April	-		0	675	(A)	10.7
May	-		0	600	(A)	10.5
June	-		0	525	(A)	8.75

The percentages are based on standard cost or usage.

For the price variance the absolute variances indicate that suppliers were charging more than had been anticipated but the price appears to be fluctuating. The percentage measures show that there was a temporary blip of a constant amount in the first quarter. Perhaps a bulk discount was not being claimed, and corrective action was taken in April.

For the usage variance there is less to choose between the two methods. The process seems to have gone out of control in February but corrective action seems to be bringing it gradually back under control. Both absolute measures and percentage measures show this, but the percentage measures more clearly indicate that the control action is working (compare June and March).

Management signals

4.8 Variance analysis is a means of assessing performance, but it is only a method of **signalling** to management areas of possible weakness where control action might be necessary. It does not provide a ready-made **diagnosis** of faults, nor does it provide management with a ready-made indication of what action needs to be taken. It merely highlights items for possible investigation.

4.9 As you should know from your previous studies, individual variances should **not be looked at in isolation**. As an obvious example, a favourable sales price variance is likely to be accompanied by an adverse sales volume variance: the increase in price has caused a fall in demand. We now know in addition that sets of variances should be scrutinised for a number of successive periods if their full significance is to be appreciated.

4.10 Here are some of the **signals** that may be extracted from variance **trend** information.

(a) Materials price variances may be favourable for a few months, then adverse for the next few months and so on. This could indicate that prices are **seasonal** and perhaps stock could be built up in cheap seasons, if not inconsistent with JIT policy.

(b) Regular, perhaps fairly slight, increases in adverse price variances usually indicate the workings of general **inflation**. If desired, allowance could be made for general inflation when flexing the budget.

(c) Rapid large increases in adverse price variances may suggest a sudden **scarcity** of a resource. It may soon be necessary to seek out cheaper substitutes.

(d) Gradually improving labour efficiency variances may signal the existence of a **learning curve,** or the **motivational** success of a productivity bonus scheme. In either case opportunities should be sought to encourage the trend.

(e) Worsening trends in machine running expenses may show up that **equipment is deteriorating** and will soon need repair or even replacement.

4.11 These are just a few examples. Note that in each case it is suggested that the variance trend be used as **feedforward control** information, anticipating future problems before they occur. Use this term if you can, because the **examiner** loves it!

Question 7

After examining the monthly variance reports for SP (Products) Ltd for the past six months you have identified the following trends.

Variance	*Trend*
Sales volume	Improving
Sales price	Sudden fall, now constant
Materials price	Constant, then improving
Materials usage	Worsening
Labour rate	Constant
Labour efficiency	Worsening
Variable overhead rate	Sudden fall, now constant
Variable overhead efficiency	Fluctuating

What might be happening in this business, and how is it reflected in the variance report?

Answer

A variety of answers is possible. Try to interpret each trend sensibly, bearing in mind the other trends. One interpretation (in outline) is that the company has tried to increase market share by going downmarket. You may have an equally good - and hopefully more detailed - answer.

Uncertainty in variance analysis

4.12 Horngren identifies seven principal sources of variances, most of which ultimately derive from the fact that it is not possible to know what is going to happen in advance.

Exam focus point

Candidates had to consider the **impact of total variances** (as opposed to individual components such as materials price and usage variances) in the **December 1997** exam.

Principal sources of variances	Comments
Inefficiencies in operations	Such problems as spoilage and idle time will be very familiar from typical examination questions on variances.
Inappropriate standards (or targets)	This is a problem arising from deficiencies in *planning*. If not enough time and resources are devoted to setting accurate standards in the first place, and if they are not kept up to date, subsequent performance is highly likely to deviate from what was expected.
Mis-measurement of actual results	Scales may be misread, the pilfering or wastage of materials may go unrecorded, items may be wrongly classified (as material X3 say, when material X8 was used in reality), or employees may make 'cosmetic' adjustments to their records to make their own performance look better than it really was.
Implementation breakdown	By this Horngren means that for a variety of causes employees will not always implement the plan in the way that was intended, such as purchasing materials at a lower than budgeted price, causing quality problems. Such problems may arise whether employees act with the best intentions or whether they deliberately take their own course because they do not agree with the plan. They may also be caused by poor communication or inadequate training.
Parameter prediction error	This is another aspect of faulty *planning*. As Horngren says, 'Planning decisions are based on predictions of future costs, future selling prices, future demand, and so on. In many cases there will be a difference between the actual value and the predicted value.' Such differences are not only due to uncertainty about the future: the prediction may not have taken proper account of conditions existing at the time when it was made, like a recently agreed pay rise, or an agreement to increase wages in three months time.

Principal sources of variances	Comments
Inappropriate decision models	Again this is well explained by Horngren. 'Variances can arise when the chosen decision model fails to capture important aspects affecting the decision... The solution to a linear programming model can be used when setting standards for direct material purchase prices. These standards, however, may be inappropriate if the LP solution is not feasible because the LP model fails to recognise a constraint on labour availability or storage capacity.' (It is the relationship between the variables that causes the problem here, not the failure to predict accurately.)
Randomness of operating processes	A standard is an *average* figure: it represents the mid-point of a range of possible values and so individual measurements will deviate *un*predictably within this predicable range.

Exam focus point

Although Horngren's book is not on the official reading list, these terms have been used in exam questions set by this examiner in the past and you could find them a useful framework for the written part of a question.

Staff and management and variance analysis

4.13 Standard costing and variance analysis have an impact on **people** and so inevitably, people's **attitudes** may be the true cause of a variance.

(a) Standards are targets to aim at and depending upon how well they are set they may **motivate or demotivate** the staff and managers who are expected to achieve them.

(b) **Participation** in setting standards *may* make staff more committed to them.

(c) Variance reports should be intended to help the managers concerned. Management accountants need to be aware that badly presented information of this type may be construed as **judgement and criticism** and be counter-productive.

5 STANDARD COSTING IN THE MODERN ENVIRONMENT

Standard costing and new technology

5.1 Standard costing has traditionally been associated with labour-intensive operations, but it can be applied to capital-intensive production too. With the shift to an '**advanced manufacturing technology**' environment we have seen the following.

(a) The introduction of robotics.
(b) The introduction of flexible manufacturing systems (FMS).
(c) Computer aided design/computer aided manufacture (CADCAM) systems.
(d) Job flexibility, with workers able to move from one aspect of work to another.

5.2 It is quite possible that with advanced manufacturing technology variable overheads are incurred in relation to machine time rather than labour time, and **standard costs should reflect this** where appropriate.

5.3   With **CADCAM** systems, the planning of manufacturing requirements can be computerised, so that standard costs can be constructed by computer, saving administrative time and expense while providing far **more accurate standards**.

Standard costing and new philosophy

5.4   It has been argued that traditional variance analysis is unhelpful and **potentially misleading** in the modern organisation, and can make managers focus their attention on the wrong issues, for example **over-producing** and stockpiling finished goods, because higher production volumes mean that overheads are spread over more units. Here are two examples.

(a) **Efficiency variance**. Adverse efficiency variances should be avoided, which means that managers should try to prevent idle time and to keep up production. In a TQM environment using just-in-time manufacturing, action to eliminate idle time could result in the manufacture of unwanted products that must be held in store and might eventually be scrapped. Efficiency variances could focus management attention on the wrong problems.

(b) **Materials price variance**. In a JIT environment, the key issues with materials purchasing are supplier reliability, materials quality, and delivery in small order quantities. Purchasing managers shouldn't be shopping around every month looking for the cheapest price. Many JIT systems depend on long-term contractual links with suppliers, which means that material price variances are not relevant for control purposes.

5.5   One of the central themes of the **examiner's article** 'Standard costing - a status check' (*ACCA Students' Newsletter*, March 1999)is the **role of standards and variances in the modern business environment**.

> 'The rate of change in product type and design due to technological improvement, customer requirements and increased competition has led to rapid change in how businesses operate. The need to respond to customer demands for speedy availability of products, shortening product life cycles and higher quality standards has contributed to a number of changes in the way businesses operate...just-in-time systems...total quality programmes.....greater emphasis on the value chain.....accurate product costing and pricing information......improved speed and flexibility of information availability...'

5.6   **Standard costing,** on the other hand, is most appropriate in a stable, standardised and repetitive environment and one of the main objectives of standard costing is to ensure that processes conform to standards, that they do not vary, and that variances are eliminated. This may seem **restrictive and inhibiting in the business environment of the late 1990s**. (In fact, in the article referred to above, the examiner attempts to show that concerns about the restrictive and inhibiting nature of standard costing have been raised since it was first used and that efforts have continuously been made (such as planning and operating variances) to redesign standards and variances to maintain their relevance in an environment of change.)

5.7   Standard costing concentrates on **quantity** and ignores other factors contributing to effectiveness. In a **total quality environment**, however, quantity is not an issue; quality is. Effectiveness in such an environment therefore centres on high quality output (produced as a result of high quality input and the elimination of non-value adding activities) and the cost of failing to achieve the required level of effectiveness is measured not in variances, but in terms of **internal and external failure costs**, neither of which would be identified by a traditional standard costing analysis.

5.8 Standard costing systems might measure, say, **labour efficiency** in terms of individual tasks and level of **output.** In a total quality environment, labour is more likely to be viewed as a number of **multi-task** teams who are responsible for the completion of a part of the production process. The effectiveness of such a team is more appropriately measured in terms of **re-working** required, **returns** from customers, **defects** identified in subsequent stages of production and so on.

Can standard costing and TQM co-exist?

5.9 Arguably, there is little point in running both a total quality management programme and a standard costing system simultaneously.

(a) Predetermined standards are at odds with the philosophy of **continual improvement** inherent in a total quality management programme.

(b) Continual improvements are likely to alter methods of working, prices, quantities of inputs and so on, whereas standard costing is most appropriate in a stable, standardised and repetitive environment.

(c) Material standards costs often incorporate a planned level of scrap. This is at odds with the TQM aim of **zero defects** and there is no motivation to 'get it right first time'.

(d) Attainable standards, which make some allowance for wastage and inefficiencies are commonly set. The use of such standards conflicts with the **elimination of waste** which is such a vital ingredient of a TQM programme

(e) Standard costing control systems make individual managers **responsible** for the variances relating to their part of the organisation's activities. A TQM programme, on the other hand, aims to make **all personnel** aware of, and responsible for, the importance of supplying the customer with a quality product.

Exam focus point

Questions set in the **June 1996** and **December 1997** exams asked about the relevance of standard costing in the light of newer philosophies. The role of standard costing and variance analysis was the topic of a **June 1999** question.

Our answer to Question 8 below hints that a case could be made for defending standard costing. **Alternative answers** are possible with some written questions: there are not necessarily right and wrong conclusions, so long as you demonstrate your knowledge in arriving at them.

Question 8

One of the basic tenets of total quality management is 'get it right first time'. Is variance reporting a help or a hindrance in this respect?

Answer

In theory it should not be of any relevance at all, because variances will not occur. In practice an organisation will not get everything right first time and variance reporting may still draw attention to areas for improvement - **if the standard and 'being right' are the same thing.**

5.10 George Brown's article ('Standard costing - a status check' *ACCA Students' Newsletter,* March 1999), details two surveys ((Puxty and Lyall (1989) and Drury *et al* (1993)) which confirmed the **continued wide use of standard costing systems**. Drury *et al,* for instance, showed that 76% of the responding organisations operated a standard costing system.

5.11 The article goes on to consider the role in modern business of standards and variances.

(a) **Planning**. Even in a TQM environment, budgets will still need to be quantified. For example, the planned level of prevention and appraisal costs needs to be determined. Standards, such as returns of a particular product should not exceed 1% of deliveries during a budget period, can be set.

(b) **Control**. Cost and mix changes from plan will still be relevant in many processing situations.

(c) **Decision making**. Existing standards can be used as the starting point in the construction of a cost for a new product.

(d) **Performance measurement**. If the product mix is relatively stable, performance measurement may be enhanced by the use of a system of planning and operational variances.

(e) **Product pricing**. Target costs may be compared with current standards, and the resulting 'cost gap' investigated with a view to reducing it or eliminating it using techniques such as value engineering.

(f) **Improvement and change**. Variance trends can be monitored over time.

(g) **Accounting valuations**. Although the operation of a JIT system in conjunction with backflush accounting will reduce the need for standard costs and variance analysis, standards may be used to value residual stocks and the transfers to cost of sales account.

Chapter roundup

- A good deal of this chapter is likely to have been familiar from your earlier studies. Make sure you have done all the questions in Sections 1 and 2 to conquer any fear you may have of variances before moving on to more difficult problems.

- Note the **examiner's comments** on the aims of standard costing and variance analysis.

- Be clear in your mind about the link between budgeting and standard costing.

- **Immaterial** variances are to be expected; **uncontrollable** variances are to be accounted for in the plan.

- Variances should not be interpreted in isolation: the **trend** is frequently more revealing. This information provides signals for action.

- Variances may have a variety of **sources**. The process of standard setting is as much a victim of **uncertainty** as the process of implementing standards by carrying out operations

- The role of **standard costing** in the **modern environment** is open to question.

Quick quiz

1   What are the advantages of planning with flexible budgeting? (see para 1.3)

2   What is a standard cost and what is it used for? (2.1)

3   What are the aims of standard costing and variance analysis? (2.9)

4   What does an efficiency variance measure? (3.2)

5   Why is variance trend important? (4.3)

6   What signals might a variance trend give to management? (4.10)

7   List seven sources of variances. (4.12)

8   How might a modern environment affect standard costing? (5.1 - 5.3)

9   How might a modern environment undermine standard costing? (5.4 - 5.9)

Question to try	Level	Marks	Time
11	Exam standard	15	27 mins

BPP
PUBLISHING

Chapter 12

PAPER 9 TECHNIQUES FOR BUDGETING AND STANDARD COSTING

Chapter topic list		Syllabus reference
1	Paper 9 techniques	2(a), 3(a)
2	Layouts required	2(a), 3(a)
3	Variances and the Paper 9 exam	2(a), 3(a)
4	Investigation of variances	2(a), 3(a)
5	Cost analysis techniques	2(a), 3(a)
6	Forecasting techniques	2(a), 3(a)
7	Learning curve theory	2(a), 3(a)
8	Budgets and probability	2(a), 3(a)

Introduction

In this chapter we look at a selection of calculations, requirements and techniques, many of which are drawn directly from budgeting and standard costing questions set by the **Paper 9 examiner**, to give you a better idea of what to expect in the exam. We also review a number of techniques that you have studied in the past, which may feature either in written questions ('how is this technique used ... ') or involve calculations.

Sections 3, 7 and 8 are particularly important.

Core areas of the syllabus identified by the examiner and covered in this chapter: use of budgeting techniques such as the **learning curve**; **forecasting**; use of **probabilities**.

1   PAPER 9 TECHNIQUES

1.1   In Paper 9 questions you will **not be asked** to calculate, say, cash budgets or materials usage variances, or at least not in the ways that are familiar from your previous studies.

1.2   Instead you **will be asked** to do tasks like these.

   (a) **Work backwards** from the final results, given in the question, to get a certain figure.

   (b) Present your answer as **percentages** or **indices** rather than monetary amounts.

   (c) Show how the final results **would have looked** if X costs were 10% higher, Y costs were a certain percentage (which you have to calculate from other information) lower, and revenues were forecast according to the **most optimistic** rather than the **least optimistic** forecast (again, you would have to calculate the input figures from information given elsewhere in the question).

1.3 Examples of the **calculations** and **explanations** needed for these and other requirements are given in the sections that follow.

> **Exam focus point**
> Many of the examples in this chapter are derived directly from questions set by the Paper 9 examiner.

2 LAYOUTS REQUIRED

2.1 The first problem you encounter with any requirement is deciding how the final answer should look. Here is a selection of possible problems you may face.

Prepare a budgeted profit and loss statement

2.2 You may be **given a specific layout** to use. For instance a question may present you with a spreadsheet with some of the cells blank and ask you to fill in the missing numbers based on the other information given in the question or shown on the spreadsheet.

2.3 An example is shown below. There is nothing difficult about this layout in itself: it is just unusual to see it presented as a spreadsheet. Candidates were required to prepare their own version (not in spreadsheet form), simply copying the headings and layout and filling in the figures, as indicated by blank boxes.

	A	B	C	D	E	F
25	*Output section*					
26						
27						
28				*Budgeted profit and loss statement*		
29				£		£
30	Revenue from X					☐
31						
32	Profit from Y					☐
33						
34	Fees received					☐
35						
36	**Total income**					☐
37						
38						
39	Fees paid (net)			☐		
40						
41	Commission paid to Q			☐		
42						
43	Commission paid to P			☐		
44						
45	Sundry fixed costs			☐		
46						
47	**Total cost**					☐
48						
49	**Net profit or loss**					☐

Specific instructions

2.4 Sometimes the instructions you are given are very specific. Here, for instance, is a slightly adapted requirement for one of the questions in the **Paper 9 pilot paper**.

> Prepare a budget summary for the coming year which details the following for each product.
>
> (i)   Fixed and variable costs by machine operation (per unit and in total)
> (ii) Contributions earned per unit and in total for each product.
> (iii) Net profit or loss per unit and in total for each product.

2.5 Note that your budget summary should include **each product,** everything should be analysed both in **total** and in terms of individual **units of product**, and the answer should include certain specific **row headings**. Here is how it might have looked.

X LTD
STATEMENT OF BUDGETED PROFIT FOR 20X5

| | Product A X,000 units | | Product B Y,000 units | |
Sales volume	£ unit	Total £'000	£ unit	Total £'000
Sales revenue	X	X	X	X
Variable costs				
Direct materials	X	X	X	X
Conversion costs				
Type P	X	X	X	X
Type Q	X̲	X̲	X̲	X̲
Total variable costs	X̲	X̲	X̲	X̲
Contribution	X	X	X	X
Fixed costs				
Type P	X	X	X	X
Type Q	X̲	X̲	X̲	X̲
Total fixed costs	X̲	X̲	X̲	X̲
PROFITS	X̲	X̲	X̲	X̲

Question 1

Match up each of the headings and columns in the table above with the Paper 9 requirements (Paragraph 2.4). This will give you some practice at reading questions carefully.

What is missing from the above outline answer (apart from the figures)?

Answer

Whoever did this answer has forgotten to draw the markers attention to his or her **workings** (W1, W2, etc)! See Chapter 6 if you have forgotten about these. Don't forget that workings and good layout represent your **EASY MARKS**, the ones that will get you comfortably through the exam.

Less specific instructions

2.6 The previous example is about the fullest statement that you might are likely to be asked to prepare. If the instructions are **less specific**, as they usually will be, deciding on layout is a three-step process.

Step 1. **Re-read the question** to make sure you have not missed a specific requirement.

Step 2. Read the **rest of the requirements** to see if you can spot that a particular layout will be helpful. If you were initially inclined to give **totals** only for part (a) of a question but spot that a part (c) of the question is talking in terms of **unit-by-unit** analysis, then it is probably better to do both units and totals for part (a).

Step 3. Have something along the following lines in mind as a **skeleton**. There will be more or less rows and columns, depending on the information in the question and the requirement (eg you may only be required to go down as far as contribution).

??? COMPANY PLC
BUDGET FOR ??? AND ???, 20X2

	(Quarter 1, Product ZX or whatever)		(Quarter 2, Product PQ or whatever)	
	£	£	£	£
Turnover (or Revenue) (W1)		X		X
Conversion costs				
Cost 1 (W2)	X		X	
Cost 2 (W3)	X		X	
	X		X	
	X		X	
Contribution	X		X	
Fixed costs				
Type A (W4)	X		X	
Type B (W5)	X		X	
	XX	X	XX	X
Profit		X		X

Operating statements

2.7 You have met these before. They have sometimes been required in Paper 9 questions, though invariably in connection with **planning and operational** variances, covered in the next chapter.

2.8 Here is a reminder of the general format using absorption costing (or ABC), which reconciles **budgeted profit** to **actual profit**. The figures are for illustration only.

AK LTD - OPERATING STATEMENT JUNE 20X7

	£	£
Budgeted profit		30,600
Sales variances: Price	(1,400) (A)	
Volume	(1,500) (A)	
		(2,900) (A)
Actual sales minus the standard cost of sales		27,700

Cost variances	(F) £	(A) £	
Material price		(600)	
Material usage	500		
Labour rate	200		
Labour efficiency	3,400		
Labour idle time		(1,000)	
Variable overhead expenditure		(200)	
Variable overhead efficiency	510		
Fixed overhead expenditure		(4,560)	
Fixed overhead efficiency	6,290		
Fixed overhead capacity		(8,140)	
	10,900	(14,500)	(3,600) (A)
Actual profit before sales/admin costs			24,100
Sales and administration costs			(18,000)
Actual profit, June 20X7			6,100

Check		£	£
Sales		9,800	95,600
Materials		16,800	
Labour		2,600	
Variable overhead		42,300	
Fixed overhead		18,000	
Sales and administration			
			(89,500)
Profit			6,100

Standard marginal costing and variance calculation

2.9 If an organisation uses standard marginal costing there will be two differences in the way that variances are calculated and operating statements are prepared.

(a) Since fixed overheads are not absorbed into production costs, there will be **no fixed production overhead volume variance**. There will, however, be a fixed overhead *expenditure* variance.

(b) The **sales volume margin variance** will normally be valued at standard **contribution** margin, not standard profit margin.

2.10 The **other variances are unchanged**, therefore an operating statement might appear as shown on the next page.

2.11 The profit here happens to be the same as the profit calculated by standard absorption costing because there were no changes in stocks.

AK LTD – OPERATING STATEMENT JUNE 20X7

	£	£
Budgeted profit before sales and administration costs		30,600
Budgeted fixed production overhead		37,740
Budgeted contribution		68,340
Sales variances: volume	3,350 (A)	
Price	1,400 (A)	
		4,750 (A)
Actual sales minus standard variable cost of sales		63,590

Variable cost variances	(F)	(A)	
		(600)	
Material price	500		
Material usage	200		
Labour rate	3,400		
Labour efficiency		(1,000)	
Labour idle time		(200)	
Variable overhead expenditure	510		
Variable overhead efficiency	4,610	(1,800)	2,810 (F)
			66,400

Actual contribution		37,740	
Budgeted fixed production overhead	4,560 (A)	
Expenditure variance		42,300
Actual fixed production overhead		24,100
Actual profit before sales and administration costs		18,000
Sales and administration costs		6,100
Actual profit		

> **Exam focus point**
> As already mentioned, you are unlikely to get a question in a Paper 9 exam that asks you to **prepare** straightforward operating statements, but you could get question that asks you to **explain** one that was given to you or one that introduced some twist to the basic idea.

3   VARIANCES AND THE PAPER 9 EXAM

3.1   Be prepared to calculate some **unfamiliar variances** in your Paper 9 exam. The examiner has a fertile imagination in this area, as his articles in the *ACCA Students' Newsletter* testify. Here are some tips based on some recent past questions.

> **KEY TERMS**
>
> A **standard hour** of output is the amount that workers ought to produce in an hour. Thus it might take a slow worker an hour and a half of productive time to produce a 'standard hour' of output.
>
> **Gross hours** is a term used by the examiner to mean all the time paid for. In other words, gross hours = productive hours plus non-productive hours.

> **Exam focus point**
> Conversion process variances had to be calculated in terms of standard hours in the **December 1997** exam.

Productivity variances

3.2 A **productivity variance** is calculated as follows.

Standard hours of output	X hrs
Productive hours	(X) hrs
Productivity variance in hours	X hrs
× 'standard cost of production per hour'	× £X
Productivity variance	£X

The '**standard cost of production per hour**' is explained below.

Idle time variances

3.3 The Paper 9 examiner is fond of scenarios in which **idle time is budgeted for in advance** (because he feels this is what happens in practice), and this makes idle time more difficult to deal with than usual. The following is based on an article by the examiner in the June 1991, *ACCA Students' Newsletter* ('Cost control information - an illustrative study').

3.4 EXAMPLE: IDLE TIME IN THE BUDGET

Bruno Ltd's budget for April 1995 includes total budgeted machine time of 5,000 hours, and budgeted output of 18,525 units. Due to inevitable delays for set-ups, idle time of 5% is allowed. Total budgeted costs for the month are £44,460. In practice in April 1995 actual machine hours were 6,000, of which 800 were idle hours.

Required

Calculate the idle time variance.

3.5 SOLUTION

	Hours
Hours available for production were (6,000 – 800)	5,200
but should have been (95% × 6,000)	5,700
Idle time variance in hours	500
Standard production per productive hour (18,525 ÷ (5,000 × 95%))	3.9 units
Units lost because of excess idle time (500 × 3.9)	1,950 units
× standard cost per unit (£44,460 ÷ 18,525)	× £2.40
Variance	£4,680

This approach to idle time does not, to our knowledge, appear outside the work of the examiner, but **you have been warned**.

Exam focus point
Questions in **December 1994** and **June 1995** featured these techniques.

Rate per hour

3.6 You might be given the rate per hour in a **variety of forms**. for example for a machine whose running costs are £60 per hour and which typically incurs 5% non-productive time the wording and figures might be:

'Standard cost of *machine time*' Or 'Standard machine cost per gross hour'	£60
'Standard cost of *production*' Or 'Cost of idle time'	£63.16 (ie £60 ÷ 0.95)

3.7 Note that the **productivity** and **idle time** variances described above should be **valued** at the **standard cost of production**. It might be helpful to think of this in terms of minutes only. For every 60 minutes that the machine is run, only 57 minutes $(60 \times (100 - 5)\%)$ of output is obtained due to warming up time or whatever. To get 60 minutes of output (a standard hour) would take $60 \div (100 - 5)\% = 63.16$ minutes. (*Check*: $63.16 \times 0.95 = 60$.)

Variances as percentages

3.8 The Paper 9 examiner is sometimes very kind! For instance he might give you a figure for **total budgeted** costs and **total actual** costs and a breakdown of each cost in **percentage form** 'Materials 8% (Budget), 9% (Actual) ...' and so on. To calculate the variance, all you have to do is **apply** each budgeted and actual percentage to each budgeted and actual cost and subtract one from the other.

Question 2

Total estimated costs for a period are £100,000 and this is broken down as Materials 40%, Machine costs 45%, Wages 15%. Actual costs turned out to be £115,000, broken down as Materials 37%, Machine costs 50%, Wages 13%. Draw up a variance statement comparing actual performance with budgeted performance.

Answer

	Budget £	Actual £	Variance £
Materials	40,000	42,550	2,550 (A)
Machine costs	45,000	57,500	12,500 (A)
Wages	15,000	14,950	50 (F)
	100,000	115,000	15,000

Exam focus point

This technique featured in a question in the **December 1996** exam.

Variance trends as percentages

3.9 Money amounts are sometimes uninformative and to judge variance **trends** it may be more useful to consider variances in percentage terms. As a rule (unless told otherwise) the **variance** (in money/hours/kg or whatever) would be divided by the **standard amount** (in money/hours/kg or whatever) and the result expressed as a percentage. For example, the excess idle time variance as a percentage can be expressed as follows.

$$\frac{\text{Excess idle time}}{\text{Expected idle time}} \times 100 \%$$

4 INVESTIGATION OF VARIANCES

In or out of control?

4.1 Because standard costs are only **estimates** of average costs, it would be incorrect to treat them as being rigid. A distinction can be made between variances that are 'in control' and those that are 'out of control'. Only variances that are **out of control** should be reported as being worthy of investigation.

4.2 Variances that are '**in control**' would be of three types.

(a) **Normal variations** around the average cost, with variations above and below the average (adverse and favourable variances) cancelling each other out over time.

(b) **Minor operational variances** which are too small to justify the cost of investigation and control action. Small variances might 'sort themselves out' in time, and only if they persist and grow larger should investigative action be worthwhile.

(c) A **minor planning error** in the standard cost for the year.

4.3 There are different ways of establishing 'rules' for deciding **whether or not to investigate** a variance.

Rule of thumb

4.4 This means simply **deciding a limit**. If the size of a variance is within the limit, it should be considered immaterial. Only if it exceeds the limit is it considered materially significant, and worthy of investigation. (This method is sometimes called the 'materiality significance model or the 'heuristic method', making it sound more scientific.)

Control charts

4.5 By marking control limits (set using statistical theory) and variances on a chart, investigation would be signalled not only when a particular variance exceeds the control limit, but also when the **trend** of variances shows a progressively worsening movement in actual results even though the variance in any single control period has not yet overstepped the control limit.

Statistical decision theory

4.6 Whether a variance is worth investigating also depends on the **expected costs** of investigation and control, and the **expected benefits** from control action.

Step 1. The **cost** of investigation of a variance, **I**, should be computed.

Step 2. The **net benefits** from control action, B – C, should be assessed, where **B** are the benefits from control action and **C** are the costs of taking control action.

Step 3. The **probability, p**, that the process is **out of control** and corrective action can be taken to remedy the situation. Variances are said to be controllable. It follows that the probability that the process is not out of control is **(1–p)**.

If the process is not out of control, it is *in control* and variances are due to random fluctuations around the expected outcome. Such variances are said to be **uncontrollable.**

4.7 The decision to be made can be shown as a **decision tree**.

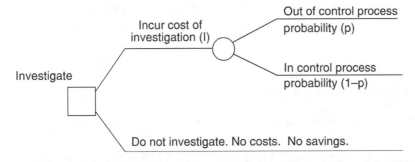

FORMULA TO LEARN

A variance should be investigated if the expected value of the benefits exceeds the expected value of the costs, that is, if:

$$pB \geq I + pC$$

where   p   is the probability that the process is out of control;
          B   is the benefits from control action when the process is out of control;
          I   is the cost of investigating the cause of a variance;
          C   is the cost of control action when the process is out of control.

Alternatively, the formula could be stated thus: a variance should be investigated if $p(B - C) \geq I$.

4.8 EXAMPLE: SINGLE PERIOD COST BENEFIT APPROACH

In August an adverse materials usage variance of £1,250 was reported. The cost of investigating the process would be £250, and the cost of corrective action, if the variance proves to be controllable, would be £300. It is estimated that the savings which would be earned from correcting the variance, if it were controllable, would be £950. The probability that the process is in control, based on past experience, is 0.4.

Should the variance be investigated?

4.9 SOLUTION

The cost of investigation, I, would be £250. The net benefit of control action (B-C), if the variance is controllable, would be £(950 – 300) = £650.

The probability that the process is out of control is $1 - p = 0.6$ and therefore the expected value of benefits from investigation is $p(B - C) = 0.6 \times £650 = £390$.

Since the EV of benefits (£390) exceeds the cost of investigation (£250) the variance **should be investigated.**

4.10 Note, however, the following points.

(a) The expected benefits from control action (B – C) do not equal the size of the original variance, £1,250 (A).

(b) In situations where the inefficiency will be repeated, (B – C) should strictly be defined as the PV of the costs that will be incurred in the future if an investigation is not made now. In other words, the benefits of investigation and control are the savings of costs in several future periods, **discounted** to a present value.

(c) Controllable variances should only need to be identified **once** for management to do something about them. Once they are corrected the organisation should 'get it right first time' in future.

Variations in the cost/benefit decision tree

4.11 The decision tree illustrated above can be varied to allow for two other factors.

Different types of variance

4.12 Some variances will occur **once only**, or perhaps once or twice, whereas others might continue **month after month**. In these cases, a distinction can be made between the outcome for each type of variance of a decision whether or not to investigate the variance.

4.13 Suppose that a company believes that variances can be categorised into three types.

Type 1. **Controllable variances**, which are costing the company on average £200 per month, so long as control action is not taken.

Type 2. **Short-term self-correcting variances** that will only occur once, in one month, and then never recur.

Type 3. **Uncontrollable variances**, which are reducing the company's budgeted profits by £150 per month on average.

The probability of a variance belonging to types 1, 2 or 3 are 50%, 20% and 30% respectively. A decision tree of the consequences of not taking control action would be as follows.

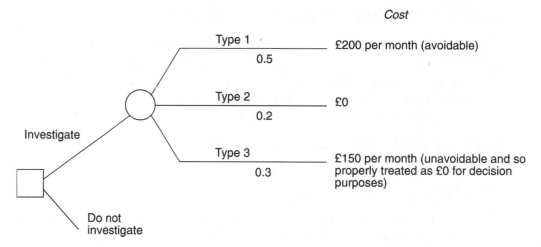

Not responding

4.14 The second factor that can be built into a decision tree is that **control action might not work**. For example, a company might find on investigation that 60% of the reported variances are controllable. However, when control action is taken, only 80% respond to treatment to eliminate the fault. Then, consider the two factors below.

(a) Investigation costs £80 on average, and control action costs £100 on average.

(b) If control action is not taken on a controllable variance, it will cost the organisation £200 per month in lost profits.

4.15 A decision tree would look like this.

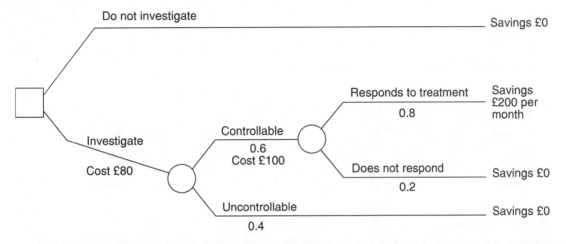

Exam focus point
This type of tree featured in a question in the **December 1994** exam.

Cost benefit approach: disadvantages

4.16 The costs and benefits approach has the appeal of being the most **financially aware** investigation method, but it does have some severe disadvantages.

(a) It assumes that the probabilities, costs and benefits can all be **identified** and **quantified** accurately.

(b) It assumes that the costs of investigation and correction are **constant**, which might presuppose that the **cause** of a variance is the same every time and does not allow for the process of **learning** from mistakes.

5 COST ANALYSIS TECHNIQUES

5.1 **Cost estimation** is a term used to describe the measurement of historical costs with a view to providing estimates on which to base future expectations of cost. For your examination, you might be expected to assess the merits and weaknesses of various methods of estimating costs and apply one or more of these methods in practice.

5.2 Historical costs can be assumed to have a '**mixed cost**' behaviour pattern. Mixed costs can be separated into their fixed and variable elements, using a variety of techniques. Some techniques are more sophisticated than others, and are therefore likely to be more reliable, but in practice, the simpler techniques are more commonly found and might give estimates that are accurate enough for their purpose. The techniques are dealt with in order of complexity in the following paragraphs.

BPP PUBLISHING

Engineered costs

5.3 By this method (also called the 'account classification method') expenditure items are classified as **fixed, variable** or **semi-variable**. This allows managers to determine the **inputs** required for a given level of **output**.

5.4 This, in rough terms, is how the direct cost items (materials and labour costs) might be built-up when a **budgeted direct cost per unit** of output is estimated. The technique depends on subjective judgement and skill and realism in estimating costs, and so only an approximate accuracy can be expected from its use.

Exam focus point

A question in the **June 1997 exam** asked how strategic management accounting could help with decision making through the use of engineered costs (amongst other things). Clearly any sort of planning is facilitated through better understanding of what resources are needed.

High-low method

5.5 The high low method involves reviewing records of production in previous periods and selecting the two with the **highest and lowest volume of output**. The difference between the total costs of the two periods is assumed to be the total variable cost of the extra units produced. For example, if the highest level of output were 8,000 units and the lowest 6,000, then the difference between the total costs for these two periods would equal the variable cost of 2,000 units. This allows the variable cost per unit to be calculated and, by substitution, the total fixed costs can be found. You should remember this method from earlier studies, so try a question.

Question 3

A company has recorded the following total costs during the last five years.

Year	Output volume Units	Total cost £	Average price level index
19X0	65,000	145,000	100
19X1	80,000	179,000	112
19X2	90,000	209,100	123
19X3	60,000	201,600	144
19X4	75,000	248,000	160

What costs should be expected in 19X5 if output is 85,000 units and the average price level index is 180? (In other words do not ignore inflation!)

Answer

Price levels should be adjusted to a common basis, say index level 100.

(a)

	Output Units	Total cost £	Cost at price level index = 100 £
High level	90,000	209,100 × 100/123 =	170,000
Low level	60,000	201,600 × 100/144 =	140,000
Variable cost	30,000		30,000

Variable cost per unit = £30,000/30,000 = £1

(b) Substituting

	£
Total cost of 90,000 units (Index 100)	170,000
Variable cost of 90,000 units (× £1)	90,000
Fixed costs (Index 100)	80,000

(c)   Costs in 19X5 for 85,000 units will be:

	£
Variable costs (Index 100)	85,000
Fixed costs (Index 100)	80,000
Total costs (Index 100)	165,000

At 19X5 price levels (index 180) = £165,000 × 180/100 = £297,000

5.6   The major **drawback** to the high-low method is that **only two historical cost records** from previous periods are used in the cost estimation. Unless these two records are a reliable indicator of costs throughout the relevant range of output, which is unlikely, only a 'loose approximation' of fixed and variable costs will be obtained. The **advantage** of the method is its relative **simplicity**.

Linear regression analysis (least squares method)

5.7   This is a statistical method of estimating fixed and variable costs using historical data from a number of previous accounting periods.

> ### Exam focus point
> A question in **June 1995** asked how linear regression (amongst other techniques) could be useful for budgeting. Detailed technical description of the technique was **not** required.

5.8   Linear regression analysis is used to derive a **linear cost function y = a + bx** where:

y, the dependent variable	=	total cost
x, the independent variable	=	the level of activity
a	=	the fixed cost
b	=	the variable cost per unit of activity

5.9   Historical data is collected from previous periods, and adjusted to a common price level to remove inflationary differences, so that a number of 'readings' exist for **output volumes (x)** and their **associated costs (y)**. The aim is to provide estimates of **fixed costs** (a) and **unit variable costs** (b) using these readings for x and y.

The conditions suited to the use of linear regression analysis

5.10 Linear regression analysis is an **alternative** technique to the **high-low method**, and it would be used when:

(a)   the high-low method is thought to be too **unreliable** so that it might produce serious inaccuracies in the estimate of costs;

(b)   there is a **sufficient number of historical records** of cost at different activity levels to make it capable of providing a more reliable estimate of costs.

5.11 The **conditions** which should apply if linear regression analysis is to be used to estimate costs are as follows.

(a)   A **linear** cost function should be assumed.

(b)   There should be a **wide spread of activity levels** in the historical data used so that it covers the full normal range of business activity.

(c) The historical data for cost and output should be adjusted to a **common price level** (to overcome cost differences caused by inflation) and the historical data should also be **representative of current conditions** (ie current technology, current efficiency levels, current operations (products made)).

Multiple regression analysis

5.12 Unlike the techniques so far described multiple regression analysis recognises that **several different factors**, not just one, can affect costs. For example, total costs in a factory might be affected by the volume of output, the time of year, the size of batches, labour turnover, the age of machinery, and so on.

5.13 The **disadvantage** of multiple regression analysis is its relative complexity: a computer program would be needed to derive an estimation of the cost function. However, provided that past costs are a reliable guide to estimating future expected costs (if the use of historical data to predict the future is valid) multiple regression is likely to produce **more accurate estimates**. It should provide **better information** and its users can have more confidence in its cost predictions than with other methods.

Question 4

Why should we want to analyse costs into fixed and variable components?

Answer

A knowledge of cost behaviour is fundamental to **planning**, where costs at various levels of activity help to determine what the organisation can and cannot attempt.

It is fundamental to **control**, because if the level of activity is not the expected level it is less meaningful to compare actual results with the budget without making allowance for this.

In **decision making** a knowledge of what costs will change as a result of a decision and which will remain the same is essential, because costs that will never be affected by the decision do not need to be considered when making it.

6 FORECASTING TECHNIQUES

6.1 There are a number of different forecasting techniques which can be used for **budgeting and longer-term strategic planning**. Some of the techniques are mathematical and quantitative; others are based on human judgement.

6.2 The mathematical techniques usually take **historical records** as data which can be **analysed and extrapolated** to make forecasts. On the whole, however, the usefulness of historical records for forecasting decreases as the forecast period increases in length.

Long-term forecasting: scenario building (the Delphi model)

6.3 For long-term planning, forecasts will be needed about what the future state of an industry, its markets or its technology might be in a few years' time. **Scenario building** is a term used to describe the process of **identifying alternative futures** and predicting what might happen.

6.4 The **Delphi model** or technique is one method of scenario building, in which a **group of experts** are asked individually to provide their views about what will happen in the future (for example technological breakthroughs, changes over time and so on).

Econometric models

6.5 A variety of **forecasting models** might be used by an organisation. One type of model used for both short-term and medium-term forecasting is an econometric model. (**Econometrics** is the study of economic variables and how they are interrelated, using a computer model.)

6.6 Econometric models can be used to obtain information about economic developments which might be important for an organisation's future plans, such as:

- The likely rate of cost **inflation**
- The likely level of **interest rates**
- The expected **growth in the economy** and **consumer demand**
- Expected movements in **foreign exchange rates**

Short-term forecasts

6.7 Short-term forecasts are forecasts of sales, costs or resource requirements and so on for up to **about one year ahead**. They are usually prepared by extrapolating historical data, on the assumption that future operating trends and characteristics will, in the short term at least, be a continuation of recent trends and current operating characteristics.

6.8 Extrapolation is the technique of determining a projection by statistical means. It is usually done by some form of **time series analysis,** that is, by calculating how sales, costs and so on are likely to vary over time.

> **Exam focus point**
>
> None of the above forecasting techniques (which you studied for Paper 8) have appeared in Paper 9 exams to date. However, candidates have been asked to prepare forecasts in the sense that **budgets** are forecasts and **investment appraisal** is a type of forecasting.
>
> In **June 1999**, candidates had to manipulate a forecasting model which was provided in the question. This simply involved substituting values of variables into the model.

7 LEARNING CURVE THEORY

7.1 Whenever an individual starts a job which is **fairly repetitive** in nature, and provided that his speed of working is not dictated to him by the speed of machinery (as it would be on a production line), he is likely to become **more confident and knowledgeable** about the work as he gains experience, to become **more efficient**, and to do the work **more quickly**.

7.2 **Eventually**, however, when he has acquired enough experience, there will be nothing more for him to learn, and so **the learning process will stop**.

> **KEY TERM**
>
> **Learning curve theory** applies to these situations, where the work force as a whole improves in efficiency with experience. The learning effect or learning curve effect describes the speeding up of a job with repeated performance.

BPP
PUBLISHING

Where does learning curve theory apply?

7.3 Labour time should be expected to get shorter, with experience, in the production of items which exhibit any or all of the following features.

- Made largely **by labour effort** (rather than by a **highly mechanised** process)
- Brand **new** or relatively **short-lived** (learning process does not continue indefinitely)
- **Complex** and made in **small quantities** for **special orders**

The learning rate: cumulative average time

7.4 In learning theory the **cumulative average time per unit** produced is assumed to **decrease** by a **constant percentage** every time **total output** of the product **doubles**.

7.5 For instance, where an 80% learning effect occurs, the cumulative average time required per unit of output is reduced to 80% of the previous cumulative average time when output is doubled.

(a) By **cumulative average time**, we mean the average time per unit for all units produced so far, back to and including the first unit made.

(b) The **doubling** of output is an important feature of the learning curve measurement.

7.6 Don't worry if this sounds quite **hard to grasp** in words, because it **is** hard to grasp (until you've learned it!). It is best explained by a numerical example.

7.7 EXAMPLE: AN 80% LEARNING CURVE

The first unit of output of a new product requires 100 hours. An 80% learning curve applies. The production times would be as follows.

Number of units produced	Cumulative avg time required per unit		Total time required		Incremental time for additional units	
1		100.0	(× 1)	100.0		
2★	(80%)	80.0	(× 2)	160.0	60.0	(for 1 extra unit)
4★	(80%)	64.0	(× 4)	256.0	96.0	(for 2 extra units)
8★	(80%)	51.2	(× 8)	409.6	153.6	(for 4 extra units)

★ Output is being **doubled** each time.

7.8 This effect can be shown on a **graph**, as a learning curve either for **unit times** or **cumulative total times or costs**.

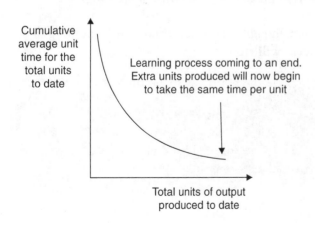

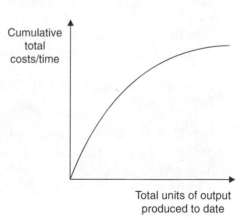

The curve and the formula

7.9 The curve on the left becomes horizontal once a sufficient number of units have been produced. At this point the learning effect is lost and production time should become a constant standard, to which a standard efficiency rate may be applied.

FORMULA TO LEARN

The formula for the learning curve is $y = ax^b$

where   **y** is the cumulative average time per unit
   x is the number of units made so far
   a is the time for the first unit
   b is the learning factor. With an 80% learning curve, b = -0.322.

(*Note*. 'b' may be taken from the logarithm of 0.8 divided by the logarithm of 2.)

Exam focus point
This formula was **given** in the **June 1996** and **June 1999** exam questions on learning curve theory.

7.10 EXAMPLE: THE LEARNING CURVE FORMULA

Captain Kitts Ltd has designed a new type of sailing boat, for which the cost and sales price of the first boat to be produced has been estimated as follows:

	£
Materials	5,000
Labour (800 hrs × £5 per hr)	4,000
Overhead (150% of labour cost)	6,000
	15,000
Profit mark-up (20%)	3,000
Sales price	18,000

It is planned to sell all the yachts at full cost plus 20%. An 80% learning curve is expected to apply to the production work. A customer has expressed interest in buying the yacht, but thinks £18,000 is too high a price to pay. He might want to buy 2, or even 4 of the yachts during the next six months. He has asked the following questions.

(a) If he paid £18,000 for the first yacht, what price should be paid later for a second?

(b) Could Captain Kitts Ltd quote the same unit price for two yachts, if the customer ordered two at the same time?

(c) If the customer bought two yachts now at one price, what would be the price per unit for a third and a fourth yacht, if he ordered them separately later on?

(d) If they were all ordered now, could Captain Kitts Ltd quote a single unit price for four yachts and eight yachts.

Assuming that there are no other prospective customers for the yacht, how would these questions be answered?

BPP PUBLISHING

7.11 SOLUTION

Number of yachts		Cumulative average time per yacht Hours		Total time for all yachts to date Hours		Incremental time for additional yachts Hours
1				800.0		800.0
2	(× 80%)	640.0	(× 2)	1,280.0	(1,280 – 800)	480.0
4	(× 80%)	512.0	(× 4)	2,048.0	(2,048 – 1,280)	768.0
8	(× 80%)	409.6	(× 8)	3,276.8	(3,276.8 – 2,048)	1,228.8

(a) *Separate price for a second yacht*

	£
Materials	5,000
Labour (480 hrs × £5)	2,400
Overhead (150% of labour cost)	3,600
Total cost	11,000
Profit (20%)	2,200
Sales price	13,200

(b) *A single price for the first two yachts*

	£
Materials cost for two yachts	10,000
Labour (1,280 hrs × £5)	6,400
Overhead (150% of labour cost)	9,600
Total cost for two yachts	26,000
Profit (20%)	5,200
Total sales price for two yachts	31,200
Price per yacht (÷2)	£15,600

(c) *A price for the third and fourth yachts*

	£
Materials cost for two yachts	10,000
Labour (768 hours × £5)	3,840
Overhead (150% of labour cost)	5,760
Total cost	19,600
Profit	3,920
Total sales price for two yachts	23,520
Price per yacht (÷2)	£11,760

(d) *A price for the first four yachts together and for the first eight yachts together*

		First four yachts £		First eight yachts £
Materials		20,000		40,000
Labour	(2,048 hrs)	10,240	(3,276.8 hrs)	16,384
Overhead (150% of labour cost)		15,360		24,576
Total cost		45,600		80,960
Profit (20%)		9,120		16,192
Total sales price		54,720		97,152
Price per yacht	(÷4)	£13,680	(÷8)	£12,144

Question 5

Bortamord Ltd anticipates that a 90% learning curve will apply to the production of a new item. The first item will cost £2,000 in materials, and will take 500 labour hours. The cost per hour for labour and variable overhead is £5.

You are required to calculate the total cost for the first unit and for the first 8 units.

Answer

	Units		Cumulative average time per unit Hours		Total time for all units produced to date Hours
	1		500.0		500
(double)	2	(90%)	450.0	(× 2)	900
(double)	4	(90%)	405.0	(× 4)	1,620
(double)	8	(90%)	364.5	(× 8)	2,916

	Cost of 1st unit £		Cost of 1st 8 units £
Materials	2,000		16,000
Labour and variable o/hd (500 hrs)	2,500	(2,916 hours)	14,580
	4,500		30,580
Average cost/unit	4,500		3,822.50

The relevance of learning curve effects in management accounting

7.12 You should have realised by now that where the learning curve effect applies, there are important consequences for **budgeting, standards costs, pricing** and so on.

> ### Exam focus point
> A written question in **June 1995** asked about the relevance of the learning curve in budgetary planning. Its relevance and limitations (see Paragraph 7.14) were examined in **June 1999**.

7.13 A number of considerations should be borne in mind.

(a) **Sales projections, advertising expenditure and delivery date commitments.** Identifying a learning curve effect should allow an organisation to plan its advertising and delivery schedules to coincide with expected production schedules. Production capacity obviously affects sales capacity and sales projections.

(b) **Budgeting with standard costs.** Companies that use standard costing for much of their production output cannot apply standard times to output where a learning effect is taking place. This problem can be overcome in practice by:

  (i) establishing **standard times** for output, once the learning effect has worn off or become insignificant; and

  (ii) introducing a '**launch cost**' budget for the product for the duration of the learning period.

(c) **Budgetary control.** When learning is still taking place, it would be unreasonable to compare actual times with the standard times that ought eventually to be achieved when the learning effect wears off. **Allowance should be made** accordingly when interpreting labour efficiency variances.

(d) **Cash budgets.** Since the learning effect reduces unit variable costs as more units are produced, it should be allowed for in **cash flow projections**.

(e) **Work scheduling and overtime decisions.** To take full advantage of the learning effect, **idle production time** should be avoided and work scheduling/overtime decisions should pay regard to the expected learning effect.

(f) **Pay.** Where the workforce is paid a **productivity bonus,** the time needed to learn a new production process should be allowed for in calculating the bonus for a period.

BPP PUBLISHING

(g) **Recruiting new labour.** When a company plans to take on new labour to help with increasing production, the learning curve assumption will have to be reviewed.

(h) **Market share.** The significance of the learning curve is that by increasing its share of the market, a company can benefit from shop-floor, managerial and technological 'learning' to achieve **economies of scale**.

Limitations of learning curve theory

7.14 The limited use of learning curve theory is due to several factors.

(a) The learning curve phenomenon is **not always present**.

(b) It assumes **stable conditions** at work which will **enable learning to take place**. This is not always practicable, for example because of **labour turnover**.

(c) It must also assume a certain degree of **motivation** amongst employees.

(d) Breaks between repeating production of an item must not be too long, or workers will '**forget**' and the learning process will have to begin all over again.

(e) It might be difficult to **obtain accurate data** to decide what the learning curve is.

(f) **Workers might not agree** to a gradual reduction in production times per unit.

(g) **Production techniques might change,** or product design alterations might be made, so that it takes a long time for a 'standard' production method to emerge, to which a learning effect will apply.

8   BUDGETS AND PROBABILITY

KEY TERM

Probabilistic budgeting assigns probabilities to different conditions (most likely, worst possible, best possible) to derive an EV of profit. A standard deviation of the EV of profit can also be calculated as a measurement of risk. Management can then select, from among the alternatives which are being considered, the budget strategy which offers the 'best combination' of expected profit and risk.

8.1 A company, for example might make the following estimates of profitability for a given budget strategy under consideration:

	Profit/(loss)	*Probability*
	£'000	
Worst possible outcome	(220)	0.3
Most likely outcome	300	0.6
Best possible outcome	770	0.1

8.2 The EV of profit would be calculated as follows:

	Probability	*Profit*	*Expected value*
		£'000	*£'000*
Worst possible	0.3	(220)	(66)
Most likely	0.6	300	180
Best possible	0.1	770	77
Expected value of profits			191

8.3 Simple probabilistic income budgeting is not confined to a 'worst possible, most likely and best possible' analysis. For example, if the only uncertain elements in a budget are sales volume and unit variable costs, a probability tree analysis might be as follows:

Sales volume	Selling price £10 Variable cost per unit	Total contribution £	Joint probability	EV of contribution £
6,000 units 0.2	£4 0.5	36,000	0.10	3,600
	£5 0.5	30,000	0.10	3,000
8,000 units 0.5	£5 0.4	40,000	0.20	8,000
	£6 0.6	32,000	0.30	9,600
10,000 units 0.3	£6 0.3	40,000	0.09	3,600
	£7 0.7	30,000	0.21	6,300
				34,100

> **Exam focus point**
> A written question in **June 1995** asked how probabilities could be used in budgetary planning. Questions in **June 1994**, **June 1998** and **December 1988** followed the 'best, most likely and worst' pattern.

8.4 EXAMPLE: A PROBABILISTIC BUDGET

PIB Ltd has recently developed a new product, and is planning a marketing strategy for it. A choice must be made between selling the product at a unit price of either £15 or £17. Estimated sales volumes are as follows.

At price of £15 per unit		At price of £17 per unit	
Sales volume	*Probability*	*Sales volume*	*Probability*
Units		Units	
20,000	0.1	8,000	0.1
30,000	0.6	16,000	0.3
40,000	0.3	20,000	0.3
		24,000	0.3

(a) Sales promotion costs would be £5,000 at a price of £15 and £12,000 at a price of £17.

(b) Material costs are £8 per unit.

(c) Labour and variable production overhead costs will be £5 per unit up to 30,000 units and £5.50 per unit for additional units.

(d) Fixed production costs will be £38,000.

The management of PIB Ltd wish to allow for the risk of each pricing decision before choosing £15 or £17 as the selling price. They are considering the use of the formula 'desirability = WP + 2(EV)' to measure the 'desirability' value of each alternative, where WP is the worst possible outcome of profit and EV is the expected monetary value of profits.

Required

Determine which sales price would be preferred if the management selected the alternative which:

(a) Minimised the worst possible outcome of profit

(b) Maximised the best possible outcome of profit

(c) Maximised the desirability value (which attempts to balance the separate considerations of profit maximisation and risk minimisation)

8.5 SOLUTION

The unit contribution will be as follows:

	Price per unit	
	£15	£17
Up to 30,000 units	£2	£4
Above 30,000 units	£1.50	N/A

Sales price £15:

Units of sale '000	Unit contb'n £	Total contb'n £'000	Fixed costs £'000	Profit £'000	Probability	EV of profit £'000
20	2	40	43	(3)	0.1	(0.3)
30	2	60	43	17	0.6	10.2
40	30 @ £2 10 @ £1.50	75	43	32	0.3	9.6
						19.5

Sales price £17:

Units of sale '000	Unit contb'n £	Total contb'n £'000	Fixed costs £'000	Profit £'000	Probability	EV of profit £'000
8	4	32	50	(18)	0.1	(1.8)
16	4	64	50	14	0.3	5.2
20	4	80	50	30	0.3	9.0
24	4	96	50	46	0.3	13.8
						25.2

(a) The price which minimises the worst possible outcome is £15 (with a worst-possible loss of £3,000).

(b) The price which maximises the best possible outcome is £17 (with a best-possible profit of £46,000).

(c) Desirability formula

   (i)   *Price £15* (in £'000) Desirability = (3) + 2(19.5) = 36.0
   (ii) *Price £17* (in £'000) Desirability = (18) + 2(25.2) = 32.4

Using this formula, a price of £15 would be preferred.

Chapter roundup

*   **Budget statement layouts** in Paper 9 questions vary from **spreadsheet-type** presentations that you have to **interpret** to conventional 'Sales less costs' statements that you have to **prepare**. It is important to present the information in the way instructed in the question.

*   Variances may be presented in the form of an operating statement. You are more likely to have to **interpret** one and perhaps **fill in the gaps** than prepare a full statement from scratch.

*   Paper 9 variance questions have featured some unusual approaches to **idle time** and **productivity** and some special terminology that you should learn. Variances or trends in variances are sometimes expressed as **percentages**.

*   Variance investigation may be a matter of following a **rule of thumb** or it may involve drawing **control charts** using statistical theory. **Statistical decision theory** says that a variance should be investigated if the expected value of the benefits exceeds the expected value of the costs.

*   **Cost analysis** may be carried out by the engineering method, the high-low method, by linear regression analysis or by multiple regression analysis.

*   **Forecasting** may be done by means such as the Delphi model, econometric models, or extrapolation and time series analysis. In paper 9 forecasting is more likely to involve, say, preparing a **budget** in conditions of uncertainty or appraising an **investment**.

*   **Learning curve theory** may be useful for forecasting production time and labour costs in certain circumstances, although the method has many limitations.

*   **Uncertainty** can be allowed for in budgeting by means of probabilistic budgeting, which generally looks at most likely, worst possible and best possible scenarios.

Quick quiz

1   How should you decide how to lay out an answer to a question? (see para 2.6)

2   How is a productivity variance calculated? (3.2)

3   What is unusual about idle time in Paper 9 questions? (3.3)

4   What are four ways of expressing the rate per hour of machine time? (3.7)

5   Explain three steps to decide whether it is worth investigating a variance. (4.6)

6   When might linear regression be used? (5.10, 5.11)

7   Where does learning curve theory apply? (7.3)

8   What does cumulative average time mean? (7.5)

9   In what ways may the learning curve be helpful in management accounting? (7.13)

10 What is probabilistic budgeting? (8.1)

Question to try	Level	Marks	Time
12	Exam standard	20	36 mins
13	Exam standard	25	45 mins

Chapter 13

ADVANCED VARIANCE ANALYSIS

Chapter topic list	Syllabus reference
1 Mix and yield variances	3(b)
2 Planning and operational variances	3(b)
3 Calculating planning and operational variances	3(b)
4 Operating statements with planning and operational variances	3(b)

Introduction

We begin this chapter with a brief visit to the topic of **mix and yield variances**, one that you have studied before, but one that comes up occasionally because it provides a good test of a deep understanding of variance calculations.

The remainder of the chapter is devoted to **planning and operational variances**, a very **frequently examined topic**. Planning and operational variances may seem confusing if you do not have a really good grasp of the conventional approach and so, before you go any further, make sure that you understand everything that we covered in Chapter 11. Go back over any areas you are unsure about. Only when you are happy that you have mastered the basics should you begin this chapter.

Core areas identified by the examiner and covered in this chapter: **alternative approaches to standards and variances**.

1   MIX AND YIELD VARIANCES

Exam focus point

Different experts have recommended different approaches to mix and yield variances. Queries put to the examiner indicate that candidates will not be penalised for using alternative approaches. The methods shown below are detailed in the main academic text on the reading list by Colin Drury.

Materials mix and yield variances

1.1   When a product requires two or more raw materials in its make-up, it is often possible to sub-analyse the materials usage variance into a materials mix and a materials yield variance. You have met these before, but they sometimes cause difficulty and they have featured in questions set by the **Paper 9 examiner**, so this reminder may be useful.

KEY TERMS

A **yield variance** is the total usage variance at the standard mix price.

A **mix variance** evaluates whether the actual blend of materials is more or less expensive than standard.

Together, these add up to the usage variance, which considers materials separately and not as part of a mix.

1.2 EXAMPLE: MATERIALS USAGE, MIX AND YIELD VARIANCES

A company manufactures a chemical, Dymanite, using two compounds, Flash and Bang. The standard materials usage and cost of one unit of Dymanite are as follows.

		£
Flash	5 kg at £2 per kg	10
Bang	10 kg at £3 per kg	30
		40

In period 7, 80 units of Dymanite were produced from 500 kg of Flash and 730 kg of Bang.

Required

Calculate the materials usage, mix and yield variances.

1.3 SOLUTION

Usage variance (for 80 units of Dynamite)

	Actual usage Kg	Standard (expected) usage kg	Usage variance kg	Usage variance £
Flash	500	400	100 (A)	200 (A)
Bang	730	800	70 (F)	210 (F)
Total usage variance				10 (F)

The total usage variance of £10 (F) can be analysed into mix and yield variances.

Mix variance

Step 1. Decide how the **total quantity** of materials used (500 kg + 730 kg) should have been **divided** between Flash and Bang. This is what is meant by calculating the **standard mix** of the actual quantity of materials used.

		kg
Standard mix:	1/3 Flash	410
	2/3 Bang	820
Total quantity used (500 + 730)		1,230

Step 2. The **individual differences** between what should have been used in the mix and what was actually used should be converted into money values at **individual standard costs**. This gives the mix variance.

	Actual mix kg	Standard mix kg	Difference kg *	Mix variance £
Flash	500	410	90 (A) × £2	180 (A)
Bang	730	820	90 (F) × £3	270 (F)
	1,230	1,230	0	90 (F)

* When actual use exceeds standard use, the variance is adverse.

Note also that the total mix variance in quantity is 0. This must always be the case, because of what the mix variance means. Favourable quantity variances for one material counterbalance adverse quantity variances for others. The favourable money variance is due to the greater use in the mix of the relatively cheap Flash.

Yield variance

This is the usage variance in total for **all materials together** valued at average standard cost.

Step 1. Work out the total amount of materials required for one unit and the total cost.

	kg		£
Each unit of Dymanite requires	5	Flash, cost	10
	10	Bang, cost	30
	15	In total, cost	40

Step 2. **Average standard cost** per kilogram = £40/15 = £2.67

Step 3. Work out the **difference** between actual and standard materials requirements and value it at average standard cost.

Actual: 80 units of Dymanite required	1,230 kgs
Standard: 80 units should require (☐15 kgs)	1,200 kgs
Yield variance in kgs	30 kgs (A)
× average standard cost per kilogram	× £2.67
Yield variance	£80 (A)

In this example the mix of materials actually used consisted of a cheaper blend of materials than standard, but the output yield from the total materials used was less than standard. The mix variance (£90(F)) and yield variance (£80(A)) together add up to the usage variance (£10(F)).

Question 1

The standard materials cost of product D456 is as follows.

		£
Material X	3 kg at £2 per kg	6
Material Y	5 kg at £3.60 per kg	18
		24

During period 2, 2,000 kg of material X costing £4,100 and 2,400 kg of material Y costing £9,600 were used to produce 500 units of D456.

Required

Calculate the price, mix and yield variances.

Answer

(a)

		£
2,000 kg of X	should cost (× £2)	4,000
	did cost	4,100
Material X price variance		100 (A)

(b)

		£
2,400 kg of Y	should cost (× £3.6)	8,640
	did cost	9,600
Material Y price variance (× 0.4)		960 (A)

(c)

Material	Actual mix	Standard mix	Mix variance		
	kg	kg	kg		£
X	2,000	(3) 1,650	350(A)	(×2)	700 (A)
Y	2,400	(5) 2,750	350(F)	(×3.6)	1,260 (F)
	4,400	4,400	-		560 (F)

(d) Average standard price per kg of material   = £24/8 = £3 per kg

500 units of D456 should use (× (3 + 5))	4,000 kg
but did use	4,400 kg
Total usage (yield) variance	400 kg (A)
× standard (average) price per kg	× £3
Yield variance in £	£1,200 (A)

Labour mix variances

1.4 A labour mix variance can be calculated when more than one type or grade of labour is involved in making a product. The approach is basically the same as for materials mix and yield variances except that hours and wage rates are used instead of physical quantity and cost. The terms used may also be different.

- The **mix** variance might be called the **team composition** variance
- The **yield** variance might be called the **team productivity** variance.

Sales mix and quantity variances

1.5 If a company sells more than one product, it is possible to analyse the overall sales volume (profit) variance into a sales mix variance and a sales quantity variance.

(a) The **sales mix variance** is calculated in a similar way to the materials mix variance.

(b) The **sales quantity variance** is the difference between actual sales quantity in the budgeted proportions and the original budgeted sales quantity, normally valued at the standard contribution margin.

1.6 EXAMPLE: SALES MIX AND QUANTITY VARIANCES

JD Ltd makes and sells two products, coded BF and GD. The budgeted sales and profit are as follows.

	Sales Units	Revenue £	Costs £	Contribution £	Contribution per unit £
BF	400	8,000	6,000	2,000	5
GD	300	12,000	11,100	900	3
				2,900	

Actual sales were 280 units of BF and 630 units of GD.

The company management is able to control the relative sales of each product through the allocation of sales effort, advertising and sales promotion expenses. Calculate the sales margin volume, sales mix and sales quantity variances.

1.7 SOLUTION

When we look at the sales figures in this example it is apparent that a bigger proportion than budgeted of the less profitable GD has been sold

Step 1. A **sales volume variance** is calculated for each separate product in the usual way and valued at the standard contribution margin.

	BF	GD
Budgeted sales	400 units	300 units
Actual sales	280 units	630 units
Sales volume variance	120 units (A)	330 units (F)
× standard margin per unit	× £5	× £3
	£600 (A)	£990 (F)
Total sales margin volume variance		£390 (F)

Step 2. To calculate the **sales mix variance**, take the **actual total of sales** and **convert** this total into a **standard mix**, on the assumption that sales should have been in the **budgeted proportions** or mix.

The **difference** between **actual** sales and '**standard mix**' sales for each individual product is then valued at the standard contribution margin.

	Actual mix of sales	*Standard mix*	*Mix variance*	*Std margin per unit*	*Mix variance*
	Units	Units	Units	£	£
BF	280	(4) 520	240 (A)	5	1,200 (A)
GD	630	(3) 390	240 (F)	3	720 (F)
Actual total	910	910			480 (A)

The sales mix variance is £480 adverse, ie the standard profit would have been £480 higher if the 910 units sold had been in the standard mix of 4:3.

Step 3. The **sales quantity variance** compares **standard v budget**. It is the difference between the **actual** sales quantity **in the standard mix** and the **budgeted sales** quantity, valued at the standard contribution margin.

	Standard mix	*Budgeted sales*	*Quantity variance*	*Standard margin*	*Sales margin variance*
	Units	Units	Units	£	£
BF	520	400	120 (F)	5	600 (F)
GD	390	300	90 (F)	3	270 (F)
	910	700			870

Summary

	£
Sales mix variance	480 (A)
Sales quantity variance	870 (F)
Sales volume variance	390 (F)

Question 2

Think of a way of working out the *total* sales mix and quantity variances without working out the individual variances.

Answer

Total volume variance	= £((280 − 400) × 5) + £((630 − 300) × 3) = −£600 + £990 = £390 (F)
Budgeted weighted average contribution per unit	= (400/700 × £5) + (300/700 × £3) = £4.143
Quantity variance	= £4.143 × ((280 + 630) − (400 + 300)) = £4.143 × 210 = £870 (F)
Mix variance (balance)	= £(870 − 390) = £480 (A)

We recommend the approach shown in the main body of the text, since this covers all eventualities. The **Paper 9 examiner** has been somewhat unpredictable in what he does and does not consider examinable in this area, but he takes the attitude that **valid approaches will score marks**.

Valuing the sales mix and materials mix variances

1.8 In 'Standard costing - a status check' (*ACCA Students' Newsletter'*, March 1999), the examiner mentions Horngren and Foster's use of weighted average contribution rather than an individual product contribution approach for such valuations.

> 'The argument was that the weighted average approach gives a more consistent set of signals to management. For example, where actual product mix is such that **less** of a product earning a contribution per unit which is **lower** than the budgeted weighted average is sold, the mix variance reported for that product will be **favourable**. This is argued as correct since it indicates a swing towards more profitable products.'

The examiner goes on to explain that a similar argument can be applied to materials mix variances.

Note that an adverse variance is reported if the individual product contribution is used.

Valuing sales volume variances

1.9 In the example above we use **contribution** as the valuation base, but this is not the only possible approach. The base used depends on **what information management want**. Information should be presented in a way that is understandable to its users: if they are used to an absorption costing system they will prefer reporting in terms of profit; if they are used to marginal costing it should be presented in terms of contribution.

(a) If managers are most interested in **turnover** it will be useful to have an analysis of the overall impact on turnover (unit sales of 4,000 fewer extra units give rise to a decrease in turnover of £180,000), and of the breakdown by individual product.

(b) If they are most concerned with the bottom line figure, the variances in terms of **profit** will be most useful.

(c) For decision-making purposes, valuation according to **contribution** is the option to choose, because this only includes cash flows that will change as a result of any decision. Fixed costs are sunk costs and not relevant.

1.10 Arguably the most meaningful information is provided by **not valuing** the volume variance or sub-variances at all, but expressing them in **non-financial terms** (here number of units sold), although in 'Standard costing - a status check', the examiner commented that it may be argued that the contribution approach is of most use for planning and decision making since the valuation most closely approximates to the cash flow impact of the variance.

1.11 Alternatively, if managers are interested in **market share**, none of the above information of much value. Managers would need to be told the **percentage** of the overall market and of the markets for individual products that was taken during the period.

> **Exam focus point**
> The possibility of using other valuation bases was the subject of a question in **June 1995**. Incidentally this question also used the term 'individual model variances', which is not a special type of variance, as some candidates apparently thought, but simply means variances for individual models of the product in question as opposed to variances that lump all products together.

The relevance of mix and yield variances

1.12 **Materials** mix and yield variances have no meaning, and should never be calculated, unless they are a guide to **control action**. They are only appropriate in the following situations.

(a) Where **proportions** of materials in a mix are **changeable** and **controllable**.

(b) Where the usage variance of individual materials is of limited value because of the variability of the mix, and a combined yield variance for all the materials together is **more helpful for control**.

1.13 It would be totally **inappropriate** to calculate a mix variance where the materials in the 'mix' are **discrete** items. A chair, for example, might consist of wood, covering material, stuffing and glue. These materials are separate components, and it would not be possible to think in terms of controlling the proportions of each material in the final product. The usage of each material must be controlled separately.

1.14 **Sales** mix and quantity variances would likewise only be meaningful where management can **control** the proportions of the products sold.

2 PLANNING AND OPERATIONAL VARIANCES

> **KEY TERMS**
>
> A **planning variance** compares original standard cost with a revised standard cost that should and would have been used if planners had known what was going to happen in advance. Planning variances are sometimes called **revision variances**.
>
> An **operational variance** (or an **operating variance**) compares actual cost with the revised standard cost.
>
> **Ex ante** means original budget/standard.
>
> **Ex post** means revised budget/standard.

2.1 Planning and operational variances are based on the principle that variances ought to be reported by taking as the main starting point, not the original standard, but a standard which can be seen, in **hindsight**, to be the optimum that should have been achievable.

2.2 Exponents of this approach argue that the monetary value of variances ought to be a realistic reflection of what the **causes** of the variances have cost the organisation.

2.3 The cause of a total variance might be one or both of the following.

(a) Adverse or favourable **operational** performance
(b) Inaccurate **planning**, or faulty standards

2.4 Planning variances are sometimes called **opportunity cost** variances because they represent a missed opportunity to devise a more profitable plan.

The Paper 9 examiner, feedback and feedforward control

2.5 The traditional approach to variance analysis has a number of **drawbacks**, compared with the planning and operational variance approach. These drawbacks are summarised as follows by the Paper 9 **examiner**, George Brown:

'1. The **cost implication** of the variances may be **incorrect** if the standard price and performance levels are inaccurate.

2. The variance analysis will not show which deviations from plan are **controllable** and which are **non-controllable**.

3. The variance **trend** may not be clearly monitored from one period to another.

4. The analysis does not facilitate the provision of **feedforward control** information.'

(*ACCA Students Newsletter,* November 1992). As the examiner says, a system of planning and operational variances can help to overcome each of these problems.

Question 3

Planning and operational variances have clear advantages in cases 1 and 2 above. How can a system of planning and operational variances help with points 3 and 4?

Answer

Trends in *operational* performance may be hidden because of planning factors. This in turn means that there will be no early warning system to alert management to the need to take control action to anticipate future problems. Alternatively attempts may be made to 'correct' operational problems that do not exist.

2.6 In an article in the April 1995 edition of the *ACCA Students' Newsletter* (George Brown, 'Planning and operational variances in a service business'), the Paper 9 **examiner** expands on the role of planning and operational variances in **feedback control** and **feedforward control**.

> '**Feedback control** is enhanced where a system of planning and operational variance analysis is implemented. Planning and operational variance analysis segregates those variances which are deemed to represent permanent changes to the original plan and are hence non-controllable items. Such planning variances are then built into revised (ex-post) standards. The revised standards are compared with actual results to give a set of operational variances which should be the focus of any investigation and corrective action. Operational variances are non-permanent in nature. They are likely to respond to control action unless they are due to random non-controllable events.
>
> Planning and operational variance analysis also enhances the application of **feedforward control**. Feedforward control is where the desired outcome is compared with that which it is estimated will occur if the current plan is implemented. Where any deviation exists between the desired outcome and the current plan, corrective action may be implemented in order to achieve the desired outcome. Planning and operational variance analysis aids the quantification of future planned changes and whether they are likely to result in the desired outcome. The forward plan can be compiled using the revised (ex-post) standards as its base with further adjustments to allow for estimated improvements through control action which will eliminate part of the operational variances which currently exist.'

2.7 To summarise this, the calculation of planning and operational variances helps managers:

*   Focus on deviations from plan that are controllable (**feedback control**)

*   Incorporate into the ongoing plan the new actual conditions (**feedforward control**) that will determine what is achievable in the future

Other uses

2.8 Planning and operational variances might also be useful in circumstances where one department, such as a computing department, **charges** other departments for using its services (**transfer pricing).**

2.9 In this situation disputes can sometimes arise about other departments subsidising the **inefficiencies** of the service department. Transfer prices can be revised on the basis of planning and operational variances as a way of avoiding this.

(a) Changes in the transferring department's costs that are beyond its control will be reported as **planning variances** and reflected in a revised transfer price.

(b) Operational inefficiencies in the transferor division will be reported as **operational variances** and the consequences will not be passed on.

Disadvantages

2.10 The limitations of planning and operational variances, which must be overcome if they are to be applied in practice, are as follows.

(a) The difficulties in **deciding in hindsight** what the realistic standard should have been. Some independent yardstick must be available, such as official commodity prices for certain raw materials.

It becomes easy to **justify all the variances** as being due to bad planning by revising the budget to make it congruent with actual performance during the period, so no operational variance will be thrown up. (This problem should be avoided if planning and operational variances are regarded as a **feedforward control** device.)

(b) Establishing realistic revised standards and analysing the total variance into planning and operational variances can be **time consuming**, even with a spreadsheet.

(c) Managers may be **resistant** to the very idea of variances and refuse to see the virtues of the approach. Careful presentation and explanation will be required until managers are used to the concepts.

Exam focus point
The value of planning and operational variances featured in Paper 9 questions in **June 1994, June 1995, December 1995, June 1997, June 1999** and **December 1999**.

3 CALCULATING PLANNING AND OPERATIONAL VARIANCES

Exam focus point
A question in the **June 1994** exam asked you to **explain** in words what calculations would be done, so follow this section closely.

3.1 We will begin by looking at how to split a total cost variance into its planning and operational components.

3.2 EXAMPLE: TOTAL COST PLANNING AND OPERATIONAL VARIANCES

At the beginning of 19X0, WB Ltd set a standard marginal cost for its major product of £25 per unit. The standard cost is recalculated once each year. Actual production costs during August 19X0 were £304,000, when 8,000 units were made. With the benefit of hindsight, the management of WB Ltd realises that a more realistic standard cost for current conditions would be £40 per unit. The planned standard cost of £25 is unrealistically low.

Required

Calculate the planning and operational variances.

3.3 SOLUTION

With the benefit of hindsight, the realistic standard should have been £40. The variance caused by favourable or adverse **operating** performance should be calculated by comparing actual results against this realistic standard.

	£
Revised standard cost of actual production (8,000 × £40)	320,000
Actual cost	304,000
Total **operational** variance	16,000 (F)

The variance is favourable because the actual cost was lower than would have been expected using the revised basis.

The **planning** variance reveals the extent to which the original standard was at fault.

		£
Revised standard cost	8,000 units × £40 per unit	320,000
Original standard cost	8,000 units × £25 per unit	200,000
Total **planning** variance		120,000 (A)

It is an adverse variance because the original standard was too optimistic, overestimating the expected profits by understating the standard cost. More simply, it is adverse because the revised cost is much higher than the original cost.

	£
Planning variance	120,000 (A)
Operational variance	16,000 (F)
Total	104,000 (A)

3.4 If traditional variance analysis had been used, the total cost variance would have been the same, but all the 'blame' would appear to lie on operating inefficiencies.

	£
Standard cost of 8,000 units (× £25)	200,000
Actual cost of 8,000 units	304,000
Total cost variance	104,000

Question 4

Suppose a budget is prepared which includes raw materials costs per unit of product of 2 kg of copper at £1 per kg. Due to a rise in world prices for copper during the year, the average market price of copper rises to £1.50 per kg. During the year, 1,000 units were produced at a cost of £3,250 for 2,200 kg of copper.

Required

Calculate total planning and total operational variances.

Answer

Operational variance

	£
Actual cost (for 1,000 units)	3,250
Revised standard cost (for 1,000 units)	
(2,000 kg × £1.50)	3,000
Total operational variance	250 (A)

Planning variance

	£
Revised standard cost (1,000 × 2 kg × £1.50)	3,000
Original standard cost (1,000 × 2 kg × £1)	2,000
Total planning variance	1,000 (A)

Explain **in words** why these variances are adverse, to make sure you understand this.

Operational price and usage variances

3.5 So far we have only considered planning and operational variances in total, without carrying out the usual two-way split. In **Question 4**, for instance, we identified a **total** operational variance for materials of £250 without considering whether this operational variance could be split between a **usage** variance and a **price** variance.

3.6 This is not a problem so long as you retain your grasp of knowledge you already possess. You know that a **price** variance measures the difference between the actual amount of money paid and the amount of money that should have been paid for that quantity of materials (or whatever). Thus, in our example:

	£
Actual price of actual materials (2,200 kg)	3,250
Revised standard price of actual materials (£1.50 × 2,200 kg)	3,300
Operational price variance	50 (F)

The variance is favourable because the materials were acquired more cheaply than would have been expected.

3.7 Similarly, a **usage** variance measures the difference between the actual physical quantity of materials used or hours taken and the quantities that should have been used or taken for the actual volume of production. Those physical differences are then converted into money values by applying the appropriate standard cost.

3.8 We are calculating operational variances, so we are not interested in planning errors. This means that the **appropriate** standard cost is the **revised** standard cost of £1.50.

Actual quantity should have been	2,000 kgs
but was	2,200 kgs
Operational usage variance in kgs	200 kgs (A)
× revised standard cost per kg	× £1.50
Operational usage variance in £	£300 (A)

3.9 The two variances of course reconcile to the total variance as previously calculated.

	£
Operational price variance	50 (F)
Operational usage variance	(300) (A)
Total operational variance	250 (A)

Operational variances for labour and overheads

3.10 The same argument applies to the calculation of operational variances for labour and overheads, and the examples already given should be sufficient to enable you to do Question 5.

Question 5

A new product requires three hours of labour per unit at a standard rate of £6 per hour. In a particular month the budget is to produce 500 units. 540 units were actually produced, and 1,700 hours were actually worked, costing £10,500.

Within minutes of production starting it was realised that the job was extremely messy and the labour force could therefore claim an extra 25p per hour in 'dirty money'.

Required

Calculate planning and operational variances in as much detail as possible.

Answer

Keep calm and calculate the *total* variance in the normal way to begin with. Then you will understand what it is that you have to analyse. Next follow through the workings shown above, substituting the figures in the exercise for those in the example.

	£
Total labour variance	
540 units should have cost (× 3 hrs × £6)	9,720
but did cost	10,500
	780 (A)
Planning variance	£
Revised standard cost (540 × 3 hrs × £6.25)	10,125
Original standard cost (540 × 3 hrs × £6.00)	9,720
	405 (A)
Operational rate variance	£
Actual cost of actual units	10,500
Revised cost of actual units (1,700 × £6.25)	10,625
	125 (F)
Operational efficiency variance	
540 units should have taken (× 3 hrs)	1,620 hrs
but did take	1,700 hrs
Operational efficiency variance in hours	80 hrs
× revised standard rate per hour	× £6.25
Operational efficiency variance in £	£500 (A)

Planning variances and sub-variances

3.11   In the examples described so far, there has only been one 'planning error' in the standard cost. When **two planning errors** occur, there may be some difficulty in deciding how much of the total planning variance is due to each separate error.

3.12   EXAMPLE: TWO PLANNING ERRORS

For example suppose that a company estimates that the standard direct labour cost for a product should be 4 hours × £5 per hour. Actual production of 1,000 units took 6,200 hours at a cost of £23,800. In retrospect, it is realised that the standard cost should have been 6 hours × £4 per hour = £24 per unit.

Required

Calculate the planning and operational variances.

3.13   SOLUTION

(a)   *Operational variances*

(i)	1,000 units should take (× 6 hours)	6,000 hrs
	but did take	6,200 hrs
	Efficiency variance in hours	200 hrs (A)
	× revised standard cost per hour	× £4 (A)
	Efficiency variance in £	£800 (A)
		£
(ii)	6,200 hours should cost (× £4)	24,800
	but did cost	23,800
	Rate variance	1,000 (F)

	£
(iii) *Check:*	
Actual costs	23,800
Revised standard cost (1,000 units × £24)	24,000
Total operational variance (800 (A) + 1,000 (F))	200 (F)

(b) *Planning variance*

	£
Revised standard cost 1,000 units × 6 hours × £4	24,000
Original standard cost 1,000 units × 4 hours × £5	20,000
Planning variance	4,000 (A)

Commentary

3.14 Within the total planning variance, there are two separate variances.

(a) A **planning efficiency** variance of 1,000 units × (6 – 4) hours or 2,000 hours (A).
(b) A **planning rate variance** of £1 per hour (F).

3.15 Putting a value to these sub-variances can be done in **either of two ways.**

		£
(a) Planning efficiency variance	2,000 hours (A) × original price of £5	10,000 (A)
Planning rate variance	£1 per hour (F) × revised standard efficiency of 6,000 hours	6,000 (F)
Total		4,000 (A)

		£
(b) Planning efficiency variance	2,000 hours (A) × revised rate of £4	8,000 (A)
Planning rate variance	£1 per hour (F) × original efficiency of 4,000 hours	4,000 (F)
Total		4,000 (A)

3.16 Since the analysis can be done either way, it is doubtful whether there is much value in splitting the total planning variance. However, this point was **examinable** in **December 1999** and is worth learning. The following question provides an example of when there may be some point in carrying out the analysis.

Question 6

The standard materials cost of a product is 3 kg × £1.50 per kg = £4.50. Actual production of 10,000 units used 28,000 kg at a cost of £50,000. In retrospect it was realised that the standard materials cost should have been 2.5 kg per unit at a cost of £1.80 per kg (so that the *total* cost per unit was correct).

Required

Calculate the planning and operational variances in as much detail as possible, giving alternative analyses of planning variances.

Answer

As always, calculate the *total* materials variance first, to give you a point of reference. Then follow through the workings above.

Total materials variance	£
10,000 units should have cost (× £4.50)	45,000
but did cost	50,000
	5,000 (A)

Operational price variance	£
28,000 kg should cost (× £1.80)	50,400
but did cost	50,000
	400 (F)

Operational usage variance

10,000 units should use (× 2.5 kgs)	25,000 kgs
but did use	28,000 kgs
	3,000 kgs (A)
× standard rate per kg	× £1.80
	£5,400 (A)

Planning variance

Either	£
Planning price variance (5,000 kgs (F) × £1.50)	7,500 (F)
Planning usage variance (£0.30(A) × 25,000 kgs)	7,500 (A)
	-

or	£
Planning price variance (5,000 kgs (F) × £1.80)	9,000 (F)
Planning usage variance (£0.30 (A) × 30,000 kgs)	9,000 (A)
	-

> **Exam focus point**
> Planning and operational price and usage variances had to be calculated in the **December 1999** exam.

Planning and operational sales variances

3.17 Our final calculations in this chapter deal with planning and operational **sales** variances.

3.18 EXAMPLE: PLANNING AND OPERATIONAL VARIANCES AND SALES VOLUME

Dimsek Ltd budgeted to make and sell 400 units of its product, the jole, in the four-week period no 8 in 19X2, as follows.

	£
Budgeted sales (100 units per week)	40,000
Variable costs (400 units × £60)	24,000
Contribution	16,000
Fixed costs	10,000
Profit	6,000

At the beginning of the second week, production came to a halt because stocks of raw materials ran out, and a new supply was not received until the beginning of week 3. As a consequence, the company lost one week's production and sales. Actual results in period 8 were as follows.

	£
Sales (320 units)	32,000
Variable costs (320 units × £60)	19,200
Contribution	12,800
Fixed costs	10,000
Actual profit	2,800

In retrospect, it is decided that the optimum budget, given the loss of production facilities in the third week, would have been to sell only 300 units in the period.

Required

Calculate appropriate planning and operational variances.

3.19 SOLUTION

The **planning** variance compares the revised budget with the original budget.

Revised sales volume, given materials shortage	300 units
Original budgeted sales volume	400 units
Planning variance in units of sales	100 units(A)
× standard contribution per unit	× £40
Planning variance in £	£4,000 (A)

Arguably, running out of raw materials is an **operational** error and so the loss of sales volume and contribution from the materials shortage is an opportunity cost that could have been avoided with better purchasing arrangements. The operational variances are variances calculated in the usual way, except that actual results are compared with the revised standard or budget. There is a sales volume variance which is an operational variance, as follows.

Actual sales volume	320 units
Revised sales volume	300 units
Operational sales volume variance in units	20 units (F)
(possibly due to production efficiency or marketing efficiency)	
× standard contribution per unit	× £40
	£800 (F)

3.20 These variances can be used as **control information** to reconcile budgeted and actual profit.

	£	£
Operating statement, period 8		
Budgeted profit		6,000
Planning variance	4,000 (A)	
Operational variance - sales volume	800 (F)	
		3,200 (A)
Actual profit in period 8		2,800

3.21 In this example sales volume variances were valued at **contribution** forgone, and there were no fixed cost volume variances. This is because contribution forgone, in terms of lost revenue or extra expenditure incurred, is the nearest equivalent to **opportunity cost** which is readily available to management accountants (who assume linearity of costs and revenues within a relevant range of activity).

Question 7

KSO Ltd budgeted to sell 10,000 units of a new product during 19X0. The budgeted sales price was £10 per unit, and the variable cost £3 per unit. Although actual sales in 19X0 were 10,000 units and variable costs of sales were £30,000, sales revenue was only £5 per unit. With the benefit of hindsight, it is realised that the budgeted sales price of £10 was hopelessly optimistic, and a price of £4.50 per unit would have been much more realistic.

Required

Calculate planning and operational variances.

Answer

The only variances are selling price variances.

Planning (selling price) variance

	Volume	Sales price	Variable cost	Total
	Units	£	£	£
Revised budget	10,000	4.50	3	15,000
Original budget	10,000	10.00	3	70,000
Planning variance		5.50 (A) per unit		55,000 (A)

The original variance was too optimistic and so the planning variance is an adverse variance.

Operational (selling price) variance

	£
Actual sales (10,000 × £5)	50,000
Revised sales (10,000 × £4.50)	45,000
Operational (selling price) variance	5,000 (F)

The total difference between budgeted and actual profit is therefore analysed as follows.

	£
Operational variance (selling price)	5,000 (F)
Planning variance	55,000 (A)
	50,000 (A)

4 OPERATING STATEMENTS WITH PLANNING AND OPERATIONAL VARIANCES

4.1 The **format** of an operating statement that includes planning and operational variances should be tailored to the **information requirements** of the managers who receive it.

4.2 Senior management reviewing performance as a whole may find a layout that **identifies all of the planning variances together** and then all of the operational variances, to be the most illuminating. The difference due to planning is the responsibility of the planners, and the remainder of the difference is due to functional managers.

The Paper 9 examiner and operating statements

4.3 Here is a layout slightly adapted from George Brown's April 1995 article in the *Student's Newsletter*. (It also appeared in a **question** set by him under the old syllabus.)

OPERATING STATEMENT PERIOD 1

	£	£
Original budget contribution		X
Planning variances		
Material usage	X	
Material price	X	
Machine efficiency	X	
Machine idle time	X	
Machine expenditure	X	
Sales price	X	
		X
Revised budget contribution		X
Sales volume variance: due to		
Capacity utilisation	X	
Productivity	X	
Idle time	X	
		X
Revised standard contribution from sales achieved		X
Operational variances	X	
Sales price	X	
Material usage	X	
Material price	X	
Machine efficiency	X	
Machine idle time	X	
Machine expenditure	X	
		X
Actual contribution		X
Less: additional fixed costs		X
Actual margin		X

Question 8

This question is based on one set in **December 1995**.

Budgeted costs for a period include the following.

Cost 1	£8,000	(80% variable, 20% fixed)
Cost 2	£10,000	(60% fixed, 40% variable)
Cost 3	£5,000	(100% fixed)

In hindsight it is realised that budgeted cost 1 variable costs should have been set 4% higher; cost 2 fixed costs should have reflected an increase of £2,000 from the beginning of the period; and cost 3 fixed costs should have been set 7% lower.

An extract from the operating statement for the period is as follows.

		£
Budgeted contribution		X
Revision variances		256 (A)
Revised budget contribution		X
Less: fixed costs		
Original budget	X	
Revision variances	1,650 (A)	
		X
Revised budget profit		X

Required

Show how the revision variance figures were calculated and whether they are favourable or adverse.

Answer

	Total	Variable	Fixed
	£	£	£
Cost 1 (8:2)	8,000	6,400	1,600
Cost 2 (4:6)	10,000	4,000	6,000
Cost 3	5,000	-	5,000

Variable cost variances: cost 1 (£6,400 × 0.04) = £256 (A)

		£
Fixed cost revision variances:	cost 2	(2,000) (A)
	cost 3 (5,000 × 0.07)	350 (F)
		(1,650) (A)

More Paper 9 tricks

4.4 The next example demonstrates in a simplified form several of the more difficult points illustrated in the examiner's article in the April 1995 *ACCA Students' Newsletter*.

Exam focus point

These points were also examined in the **December 1995** exam.

4.5 EXAMPLE: WHAT IS CONTROLLABLE?

Proactive Provisions Ltd and Reactive Provisions Ltd are two fast food companies who have hot dog stalls at opposite ends of the local football ground. Coincidentally both companies prepare identical budgets for the first half of the coming season.

Capacity crowd	12,000 per match at each end
Number of matches to be played	10
Costs (all variable) assuming capacity crowds	£48,000 for the half season
Expected crowd	10,000 per match at each end
Number of hot-dogs purchased per person per match(average)	1
Selling price of hot dogs	£0.99 each

The day before the beginning of the season the Hot Dog Stall Association announces a new levy related to sales which will cause overall costs to rise by 7.5%.

The actual figures for the half season were as follows.

Average actual attendance per match at each end	9,400
Actual sales for both companies	9,400 hot dogs
Actual costs for both companies	£39,000

Otherwise all figures were as budgeted.

Both companies now prepare operating statements. Proactive does so on the basis that it **has some control** over the level of sales. Reactive does so on the assumption that sales are a function of attendance at matches, over which it has no control. The operating statements are shown below. Adverse variances are in brackets.

	Proactive £	*Reactive* £
Budgeted sales	99,000	93,060
Budgeted costs	40,000	37,600
Budgeted contribution	59,000	55,460
Planning variance (Hot Dog Stall Association levy)	(3,000)	(2,820)
Revised budget contribution	56,000	52,640
Hot Dog consumption variance	(3,360)	–
	52,640	52,640
Operational variance	1,420	1,420
Actual contribution	54,060	54,060

Required

Explain the differences between the two operating statements.

4.6   SOLUTION

The differences may be explained as follows.

Budgeted sales

Proactive's budgeted sales are $10,000 \times 10 \times £0.99 = £99,000$.

Reactive, however, flexes this budget to give $£99,000 \times 9,400/10,000 = £93,060$.

Budgeted costs

Full capacity crowds are not expected, so for Proactive costs are budgeted at $10,000/12,000 \times £48,000 = £40,000$.

Reactive flexes the budget: costs are $9,400/12,000 \times £48,000 = £37,600$.

Planning variance

For Proactive this is 7.5% of the budgeted costs: $£40,000 \times 0.075 = £3,000$.

For Reactive the figure is the revised costs versus the original costs.

	£
Revised ($9,400/12,000 \times £48,000 \times 1.075$)	40,420
Original ($9,400/12,000 \times £48,000$)	37,600
Planning variance	2,820 (A)

Hot dog consumption variance

Proactive now highlights the fact that it did not manage to sell as many hot dogs as it intended. The figure is calculated as follows.

Revised standard contribution per customer per half season = revised budget contribution/ budgeted sales = £56,000/10,000 = £5.60

(Actual sales − expected sales) × standard contribution per customer per half season = (9,400 − 10,000) × £5.60 = £(3,360) (A).

Operational variance

The operational variance is calculated by both companies in the same way:

	£
Actual costs	39,000
Revised budgeted costs (as in (c) above)	40,420
Operational variance	1,420 (F)

The actual contribution can be proved as follows.

	£
Sales (9,400 × 10 × £0.99)	93,060
Actual costs	39,000
Actual contribution	54,060

Conclusion

4.7 The company in George Brown's article adopts the approach of Proactive Ltd and the article goes on to show how the company concerned responds to lower than expected fee income. Neither approach is 'right' or 'wrong': they just reflect a different emphasis.

Chapter roundup

- It is sometimes possible to analyse variances into **mix and yield** variances, but this is only appropriate in certain circumstances.

- An **operational** variance compares actual results with a standard which has been revised in hindsight.

- A **planning** variance compares the original standard with the revised standard.

- There are a number of arguments both **for and against** the use of planning and operational variances. They are useful in association with **feedback** and **feedforward control** mechanisms.

- Operational variances may be split into **sub-variances** as in traditional variance analysis.

- Planning variances may be analysed into sub-variances in **two ways**.

- **Management reports** including planning and operational variances can be drawn up in a variety of formats, depending on what information it is important to convey. Expect the unexpected in the exam.

Quick quiz

1 What are two steps for calculating a materials mix variance? (see para 1.3)

2 What are three steps for calculating a materials yield variance? (1.3)

3 How should sales volume variances be valued? (1.9 - 1.11)

4 When is it relevant to calculate sales mix and quantity variances? (1.12)

5 Explain the meaning of the term 'revision variance'. (2.1)

6 An operational variance compares what with what? (2.1)

7 What is the link between planning and operational variances and feedback and feedforward control? (2.5 - 2.7)

8 What is the ideal layout for an operating statement? (4.1)

Question to try	Level	Marks	Time
14	Exam standard	20	36 mins

BPP PUBLISHING

Part E
Performance measurement and divisional control

Chapter 14

THE PRINCIPLES OF PERFORMANCE MEASUREMENT

Chapter topic list	Syllabus reference
1 Performance measurement	1(b), 1(c), 3(c)
2 Responsibility accounting	1(b), 1(c), 3(c)
3 Accountability	1(b), 1(c), 3(c)
4 Financial performance measures	1(b), 1(c), 3(c)
5 Non-financial performance measures	1(b), 1(c), 3(c)
6 Indices	1(b), 1(c), 3(c)
7 The benefits and problems of performance measures	1(b), 1(c), 3(c)

Introduction

This chapter looks at a wide variety of issues connected with performance measurement ranging from the general aspects of a business that need to be measured to specific techniques that are favoured by the Paper 9 **examiner**.

Performance measurement features regularly in **written** questions and occasionally in numerical ones.

Core areas of the syllabus identified by the examiner and covered in this chapter: **benchmarking**; **accountability and performance measurement**; **benefits and problems of performance measurement**.

1 PERFORMANCE MEASUREMENT

1.1 Performance measurement aims to establish **how well** something or somebody is doing in relation to the **planned activity** and **desired results**. The 'thing' may be a machine, a factory, a subsidiary company or an organisation as a whole. The 'body' may be an individual employee, a manager, or a group of people.

1.2 A typical business requires performance measurement in the following areas.

    (a) In relation to **external parties** (customers, market, suppliers, competitors)
    (b) **Across the organisation** as a whole (divisional performance measurement)
    (c) **Within** each of the main sub-divisions of the business
    (d) At the level of **individual activities**

1.3 Measurement can be in terms of **profitability, activity** and **productivity**.

Point of reference	Comment
Profitability	Profit has two components: cost and income. All parts of an organisation and all activities within it incur costs, and so their success needs to be judged in relation to cost. Only some parts of an organisation receive income, and their success should be judged in terms of both cost and income.
Activity	All parts of an organisation are also engaged in activities (activities cause costs). Activity measures could include the following.
	• Number of orders received from customers, a measure of the effectiveness of marketing
	• Number of deliveries made, a measure of the effectiveness of distribution
	• Number of production runs achieved by a particular factory
	Each of these items could be measured in terms of physical numbers, monetary value, or time spent.
Productivity	This is the quantity of the product or service produced in relation to the resources put in, for example so many units produced per hour, or per employee, or per tonne of material. It defines how *efficiently* resources are being used.

Question 1

An invoicing assistant works in a department with three colleagues. She is paid £8,000 per annum. The department typically handles 10,000 invoices per week. One morning she spends half an hour on the phone to her grandfather, who lives in Australia, at the company's expense. The cost of the call proves to be £32.

Required

From this scenario identify as many different performance measures as possible, explaining what each is intended to measure. Make any further assumptions you wish.

Answer

Invoices per employee per week: 2,500 (activity)
Staff cost per invoice: £0.06 (cost/profitability)
Invoices per hour: 2,500/(7 × 5) = 71.4 (productivity)
Cost of idle time: £32 + £2.14 = £34.14 (cost/profitability)

You may have thought of other measures and probably have slight rounding differences.

Profit and other objectives

1.4 A traditional view has been that a desire to achieve greater profitability often entails a **sacrifice** in some other aspect of performance. One obvious example is quality: if cheaper materials are used to make a product or less highly trained workers deliver a service, money will be saved (increasing profits), but quality will fall.

1.5 In other cases there may not be a clear link between an objective and the profitability objective. A company may aim to improve **working conditions** for its staff, and measure its success in terms of the cost of improved facilities, falls in staff turnover, or absenteeism and so on. Some of the successes are directly contrary to profitability, while others can only with difficulty be linked to extra productivity.

1.6 A third example is where a company aims to fulfil its **social and moral responsibilities,** for example by incurring costs to make a manufacturing process more environmentally friendly.

Control and performance measurement

1.7 Performance measurement is a vital part of **control**: it is the part of the control process where **feedback** is compared with the plan, and it is also a means of **feedforward control** in the sense that it sets targets to be aimed at in the future.

> ### Exam focus point
> An exam question that appeared in **December 1994** referred to the need to exercise control over the process of performance measurement and asked how measurement itself acted as a control mechanism.

Measuring productivity

1.8 Earlier we identified **productivity** as a key area for measurement of a business, so let us see how that might be 'controlled', in other words how we can make sure that the 'right' productivity gets measured.

> ### KEY TERM
>
> **Productivity** expresses a relationship between outputs from a system and the inputs which go into their creation, as output ÷ input

1.9 The lower the input and the higher the output, the higher will be the resulting productivity. However it needs to be understood by those measuring and those being measured that **high productivity is not a virtue** in itself. It might be possible to produce a larger number of items by spreading the inputs available more thinly, but **if the final output does not then serve its intended purpose** high productivity is worthless.

1.10 **Inputs** should be measured accurately and fairly.

(a) In some cases it is very **easy** to measure inputs: the material inputs for a mass-produced product can be **weighed** or **counted** and a standard established. The more finished items that can be got out of standard inputs the more productive the process is.

(b) Sometimes it can be more **difficult**, however, perhaps because **people** do not keep accurate records of the time they put into a task (or falsify records), or because satisfactory outputs depend upon **quality** of input rather than quantity.

(c) Arguably, a fair measure should be **neutral**, that is, not manipulated by the measurer to encourage certain behaviour. An example might be the exclusion from time measurements of an arbitrary allowance for time that management considers to be 'wasted' chatting to colleagues.

1.11 **Outputs** must also be measured fairly and accurately.

(a) In a manufacturing context outputs are likely to consist of finished products, but a fair measurement should also take account of goods subsequently **returned** for repair or replacement.

(b) In a service context (for example, the delivery of products or after-sales care), outputs can be difficult to define: *how* **satisfied** is a satisfied customer, for example?

1.12 The measure needs to exhibit all the qualities of **good information**. For example it needs to be understood by those using it to make decisions, it needs to be available to them on time so that they can act if necessary, it should not cost more to obtain and calculate the measurement than the benefit derived from it, and so on.

1.13 The measurement should be **interpreted in context**. Low productivity in a particular month may be an isolated occurrence or part of a worsening trend. High productivity in one part of the factory may be overburdening workers in the next part of the process, causing them to cut corners and produce less satisfactory finished output.

1.14 As a **means of control**, productivity measures can be used in the following ways.

(a) They can be linked to, and so help to achieve, the organisation's overall **strategy** and **objectives**. (A certain level of productivity may, in fact, be an objective itself.)

(b) Once established they can be used to **predict** future performance.

(c) They can indicate when and **where action is needed** to correct a process that is out of control.

(d) They can be used as a **motivation** device if appropriate incentives are offered for achieving productivity targets (or disincentives for failing to achieve them).

> **Exam focus point**
>
> As noted above the matters covered in Paragraphs 1.7 - 1.14 were the subject of a written question in **December 1994**.

Critical success factors

1.15 The use of critical success factors (CSFs) can help to determine the information requirements of senior management.

> **KEY TERM**
>
> **Critical success factors** are the few key areas of the job where things must go right for the organisation to flourish. They are all critical to the furtherance of the organisation's aims and the organisation cannot afford to fall behind in any of these areas.

1.16 There are usually **fewer than ten** of these factors that any one executive should monitor. They are very **time dependent**, so they should be **re-examined** as often as necessary to keep abreast of the current business climate.

1.17 Critical success factors are derived from the concerns of senior management and cover such areas as industry trends, market positioning and the wider business environment. Here are four sources of CSFs.

(a) The **industry** that the business is in

(b) The **company** itself and its situation within the industry

(c) The **environment,** for example consumer trends and the economy

(d) **Temporal organisational factors** (areas of corporate activity which are currently **unacceptable** and represent a cause of concern, such as high stock levels)

Case example

A famous study of GEC examined a management reporting system that produced reports on the following factors.

(a)	Profitability	(e)	Personnel development
(b)	Market share	(f)	Employee attitudes
(c)	Productivity	(g)	Public responsibility
(d)	Product leadership	(h)	Balance between short-range and long-range goals

---

1.18 One approach to asking users to define the factors which are critical to success in performing their functions or making decisions is as follows.

Step 1. List the organisation's corporate objectives and goals.

Step 2. Determine which factors are critical for accomplishing the objectives.

Step 3. Determine a small number of prime measures for each factor.

1.19 Two separate types of critical success factor can be identified. A **monitoring** CSF is used to keep abreast of existing activities and operations. A **building** CSF helps to measure the progress of new initiatives and is more likely to be relevant at senior executive level.

Exam focus point
A question in **December 1994** asked students to explain the meaning and relevance of the term critical success factors and give examples.

Behavioural implications of performance measurement

1.20 If people **know** that their performance is being measured then this will affect the standard of their performance, particularly if they know that they will be **rewarded** for achieving a certain level of performance.

1.21 Ideally, performance measures will be devised that reward behaviour that maximises the **corporate good**. In practice, however, it is not quite so simple.

(a) There is a danger that managers and staff will concentrate **only** upon what they know is being measured. This is not a problem if every important issue has a measure attached to it, but such a system is difficult to devise and implement.

(b) Individuals have their own **personal goals,** but performance that satisfies their own sense of what is important will not necessarily work towards the corporate good.

1.22 Point (b) is the problem of **goal congruence**.

Attitudes

1.23 There are a number of factors which may affect the **attitude** of staff to their work.

(a) The feeling of **belonging** to a group with similar aims can be a great motivating force.

(b) The feeling of having **fulfilled one's personal potential** by introducing a new method or receiving praise from a customer can motivate staff.

(d) The amount of **resources** available will affect how staff work. If resources provided are inadequate they will feel as if their task is almost impossible.

(e) **Pay, promotion** prospects and bonuses will also be influencing factors.

1.24 Staff attitude can be measured in a number of ways.

(a) By the level of **quality** of their work and their **productivity** relative to other staff.
(b) By responses to **customer questionnaires** about the attitude of staff
(c) By reviews written by **colleagues** and **bosses**.

> **Exam focus point**
> Measurement of the motivation of staff in an educational institution featured in a question set in the **December 1996** exam.

2 RESPONSIBILITY ACCOUNTING

2.1 When performance is measured in terms of accounting results the name given to the procedure is **responsibility accounting**

> **KEY TERMS**
>
> **Responsibility accounting** is a system of accounting that segregates revenues and costs into areas of personal responsibility in order to monitor and assess the performance of each part of an organisation.
>
> A **responsibility centre** is 'A unit or function of an organisation headed by a manager having direct responsibility for its performance'. (CIMA, *Official Terminology*)

2.2 Responsibility accounting aims to provide accounting reports that make every manager aware of all the items which are within his area of authority so that he or she is in a position to explain them and **judge their performance**.

Responsibility centre	Performance measure
Cost centres	Standard costs, variance reports, efficiency measures
Profit centres	Revenues, costs, output levels and, of course, profit
Investment centres	Return on investment (ROI) and subsidiary ratios, residual income (RI), costs, revenues, assets employed and liabilities

Controllable costs and uncontrollable costs

2.3 Managers should only be held accountable for costs over which they have some influence. This may seem quite straightforward in theory, but it is not always so easy in practice to distinguish controllable from uncontrollable costs.

2.4 **Controllable costs** are items of expenditure which can be directly influenced by a given manager within a given time span.

(a) A cost which is not controllable by a **junior manager** or supervisor might be controllable by a **senior manager**. For example, there may be high direct labour costs in a department caused by excessive overtime working. The supervisor may feel obliged to continue with the overtime in order to meet production schedules, but his senior may be able to reduce costs by deciding to hire extra full-time staff, thereby reducing the requirements for overtime.

(b) A cost which is not controllable by a manager in **one department** may be controllable by a manager in **another department**. For example, an increase in material costs may be caused by buying at higher prices than expected (controllable by the purchasing department) or by excessive wastage and spoilage (controllable by the production department).

2.5 Some costs are **non-controllable**, such as increases in expenditure items due to inflation. Other costs are **only controllable in the long term** not in the short term. For example, production costs might be reduced by the introduction of new machinery and technology, but in the short term, management must attempt to do the best they can with the resources and machinery at their disposal.

Question 2

Think of some performance information that could be reported to a divisional manager to assist with decisions on the following.

(a) A new product, just introduced
(b) Employment of personnel
(c) Granting credit to customers

Answer

(a) Volume of sales, relative to potential market, competitors etc.
(b) Overtime hours worked, idle time, numbers relative to other businesses or departments, etc.
(c) Debtors collection period, incidence of bad debts, policies of competitors etc.

There are plenty of other examples.

Managerial performance

2.6 It is difficult to devise performance measures that relate specifically to a manager to judge his or her performance **as a manager**. It is possible to calculate statistics to assess the manager as an **employee** like any other employee (days absent, professional qualifications obtained, personability and so on), but this is not the point.

2.7 As soon as the issue of ability as a manager arises it is necessary to consider him in relation to his **area of responsibility**. If we want to know how good a manager is at marketing the only information there is to go on is the marketing performance of his division, which may or may not be traceable to his own efforts.

2.8 **Subjective measures** may be used, for example ranking performance on a scale of 1 to 5. This approach is obviously highly imprecise but if properly done it should avoid the problems that arise when a good manager is hampered by the poor division. To work well it must be perceived by managers generally to be fair, and this will usually mean that the judgement is made by somebody impartial, but close enough to the work of each manager to appreciate the efforts he has made and the difficulties he faces.

BPP PUBLISHING

2.9   The **judgement of outsiders** can be regarded as a measure of managerial performance. An organisation might, for example, set up a bonus scheme for directors such that they would only receive a reward if the share price outperforms the FT-SE 100 index for more than three years. This is fair in that the share price reflects many aspects of performance, but it is questionable whether they can all be influenced by the directors concerned.

2.10   **Upward appraisal** is used by some businesses. This involves staff giving their opinions on the performance of their managers. To be effective this requires very healthy working relationships, however.

2.11   **Accounting measures** can be used, but must be tailored according to what or whom is being judged. The measure, in essence, is profitability but it is calculated in two different ways.

(a)   As **return on investment** it measures the performance of the **business**.
(b)   As **residual income** it measures the performance of **managers**.

This topic is pursued in depth in Chapter 17.

> **Exam focus point**
> onuses based on various accountancy measures (net profit, RI, ROI and NPV) had to be calculated and discussed in the **December 1999** exam.

Question 3

A production manager is paid a monthly bonus for achieving certain production levels. The bonus is £100 where production is 3,000 units. The bonus is increased by 2% of the additional contribution from units produced in excess of 3,000 units or reduced by 2% of the reduction in contribution from production below 3,000 units.

Devise a formula for the production director's bonus. If actual production is 2,750 and contribution per unit is £5 how much bonus does the production manager get?

Answer

Let the actual bonus = £X, the actual production in any month = Y units, and the contribution per unit = C.

$X = £100 + ((Y - 3{,}000) \times 0.02C)$
$X = £100 + ((2{,}750 - 3{,}000) \times 0.02 \times £5 = £75.$

3   ACCOUNTABILITY

3.1   **Accountability** was covered in a recent article by the examiner ('Accountability and performance measurement', George Brown, *ACCA Students' Newsletter*, August 1998).

Agency theory

3.2   Agency theory considers the **relationship between a principal** (such as the owners of a company, the shareholders) **and an agent** (such as an organisation's managers and employees). The examiner explains (emphasis is BPP's):

> 'The problem is "how can the agent be motivated and monitored?". The motivation may be achieved by the payment of ....a reward. The monitoring may be through the submission of regular accounts...(as a measure of performance). The **key requirements** are that:

- the **agent** must have to **give an account of performance** to the principal; and
- the **principal** must be able to **hold the agent to account**.'

3.3 The examiner goes on to describe the **difficulty of identifying agents and principals in particular circumstances**. In public sector and not-for profit organisations there are likely to be multiple principals (such as the Government and students in the Higher Education sector).

Accounting and accountability

3.4 Accountancy via the use of **management control systems** (budgeting and standard costing) has a key role to play in the development of regimes of accountability. Such control systems provide two forms of accountability.

(a) **Hard accountability** involves consideration of financial and quantitative information and covers three areas.

   (i) Counting (that is, converting activities and outcomes into numbers), such as the number and type of warranty claims.

   (ii) **Ensuring that the numbers are accounted for** (in other words, **reporting on activities and outcomes** and providing a discussion of **how and why they have occurred**). The examiner's example is to report 'we achieved 20% new customers though promising a just-in-time delivery of orders (**how**) and 80% of complaints related to an inability to meet the JIT timetable because of internal failure of the 'pull-through' system due to lack of a synchronised manufacturing system (**why**)'.

   (iii) **Being held accountable for** accounting and also for the events and circumstances leading to the records, such as being held responsible for failing to meet unrealistic production schedules and for failing to take action such as implementing overtime working to try and meet the schedules.

(b) **Soft accountability** involves consideration of the human input to the system and its role in shaping, evaluating and implementing goals. **Self accountability** achieved by employees, for example, will be affected by financial and non-financial rewards offered, training and developments programmes and the way in which employees are grouped in order to achieve specific business outcomes (such as multidisciplinary project teams and quality circles).

3.5 The examiner suggests the **accountability** requires the implementation of the following **steps**.

Step 1. Choose and make public a range of accepted performance measures.

Step 2. Ensure that the benefits of the performance measures have been identified.

Step 3. Identify and understand possible problems in the use of performance measures.

Step 4. Consider ways in which to counter perceived problems in the use of performance measures.

Exam focus point
A discussion on accountability formed part of a Section B question in **December 1998**.

4 FINANCIAL PERFORMANCE MEASURES

4.1 Financial measures (or *monetary* measures) are very familiar to you. Here are some examples, accompanied by comments from a single page of the *Financial Times*.

Measure	Example
Profit	*Profit* is the commonest measure of all. Profit maximisation is usually cited as the main objective of most business organisations: 'ICI increased pre-tax profits to £233m'; 'General Motors... yesterday reported better-than-expected first-quarter net income of $513 (£333m).
Revenue	'the US businesses contributed £113.9m of total group turnover of £409m'.
Costs	'Sterling's fall benefited pre-tax profits by about £50m while savings from the cost-cutting programme instituted in 1991 were running at around £100m a quarter'; 'The group interest charge rose from £48m to £61m'.
Share price	'The group's shares rose 31p to 1,278p despite the market's fall'.
Cash flow	'Cash flow was also continuing to improve, with cash and marketable securities totalling $8.4bn on March 31, up from $8bn at December 31'.

4.2 Note here that monetary amounts stated are only given meaning in **relation to something else**. Here is a list of yard-sticks against which financial results are usually placed so as to become measures, perhaps in the form of **variances.**

- Budgeted **sales, costs** and **profits**
- **Standards** in a standard costing system
- The **trend** over time (last year/this year, say)
- The results of **other parts** of the business
- The results of **other businesses**
- The **economy** in general
- **Future potential**

Modern trends: customer profitability analysis

4.3 In certain circumstances a useful approach to performance evaluation may be the analysis of **profitability by customer** or customer group. Profitability can vary widely between different customers because various overhead costs are, to some extent, variable and '**customer-driven**'. These overheads include things like discounts and distribution costs.

4.4 Customer profitability analysis relates these variabilities in cost to individual customers or customer groups. Managers can use this information to check whether or not individual customers are actually profitable to sell to, and to assess whether profitability can be improved for any customer by switching effort from one type of overhead activity to another, or by reducing spending on some overhead activities.

Modern trends: activity based costing

4.5 The implications of ABC for performance measurement are highly significant. For example if a large part of production overheads used to be known as 'warehousing', but are now recognised as 'materials handling costs' that are incurred in relation to the number of production runs, then a materials handling rate per production run can be established. Many such insights will become possible using ABC and they are useful not only for costing products, but also as a **measurement** that will help in the **management** of costs.

4.6   In the third of the 'Control information and standard process costs' articles (*ACCA Students' Newsletter*, February 1996), **the examiner** suggests using a table of comparative unit costs for assessing performance. Using an ABC approach, actual and budgeted unit costs are calculated for each cost element (labour, material, each type of overhead and so on). As well as allowing actual versus budget comparisons to be made, this 'unit product cost comparison .... for the current period provides an analysis which we can use to study **cost trends** when information is available for a number of periods, and whether a **continuous improvement** pattern is being achieved.'

Modern trends: benchmarking

4.7   **Benchmarking** has been described as 'the formalisation of the basic notion of comparing practices. It is a **systematic analysis of one's own performance against that of another organisation** ... the overall objective of benchmarking is to improve performance by learning from the experience of others' (Smith). Benchmarking, which is becoming increasingly popular, therefore aims to **achieve competitive advantage** by **learning from others' experiences and mistakes**, finding **best practice** and translating this best practice into **use in the organisation**.

Types of benchmarking

4.8   **External benchmarking** involves comparing the performance of an organisation with that of a **direct competitor** - ideally one that is acknowledged to be the 'best in class' (**competitive benchmarking**) or comparing the performance of an internal function with those of the best **external practitioners of those functions**, regardless of the industry within which they operate (**functional benchmarking**). Given that the benchmark is the 'best' in a particular field, it provides a meaningful target towards which the organisation should aim.

        Internal benchmarking, on the other hand, involves comparing the performance of **one part of a business with that of a different part of the same business** with the aim of establishing best practice throughout an organisation. Some external benchmarking is still required, however, in order to establish best practice.

4.9   A 1994 survey of the *The Times* Top 1000 companies (half of which were in manufacturing) revealed that the business functions most subjected to benchmarking in the companies using the technique were **customer services, manufacturing, human resources** and **information services.**

Why benchmark?

4.10   'Perhaps performance measures, when done correctly, help everyone in the company focus on the right things in the right place at the right time. However ... there are many stories of dysfunctional behaviour - the telephone company which pledged to have at least 90% of payphones working, then achieving this figure by simply removing all public payphones from those areas most often vandalised. Or the bus operator which, plagued by delays, decided to pay bonuses to drivers who arrived at the terminus on time. As a result, most buses arrived at the terminus on time - however, drivers no longer tended to stop for passengers along the way!

        Measuring performance by itself has no meaning. Meaning can only be achieved through comparison, either against poor performance, which usually provides no true indication of future or competitive position, or through benchmarking.'   (*Management Accounting*, November 1996)

Limitations

4.11   Both approaches to benchmarking suffer from a number of **limitations**.

(a)   **Limitations of external benchmarking**

- Deciding which activities to benchmark
- Identifying which organisation is the 'best in class' at an activity
- **Persuading that organisation to share information**
- Successful practices in one organisation may not transfer successfully to another

(b)   The principal limitation of **internal benchmarking** centres on the **relevance of the other part of the business**.

- The amount of resources devoted to the units may differ.
- There may be local differences (use of different computer hardware).
- Inputs and outputs may be difficult to define.

4.12   Benchmarking **works,** it is claimed, **for the following reasons**.

(a)   The comparisons are carried out by the **managers who have to live with any changes implemented** as a result of the exercise.

(b)   Benchmarking focuses on improvement in key areas and sets **targets** which are **challenging but 'achievable'**. What is *really* achievable can be discovered by examining what others have achieved: managers are thus able to accept that they are not being asked to perform miracles.

4.13   Benchmarking can also provide **early warning of competitive disadvantage** and should lead to a greater incidence of **teamworking** and **cross-functional learning**.

Exam focus point

In the **June 1998** exam, a benchmarking exercise on the effectiveness of a department against both its current position and industry standards (provided in the question) was required. Benchmarking also appeared in the **December 1998** exam, when six marks were available for discussing ways in which it may be used for performance measurement and improvement focus.

5   NON-FINANCIAL PERFORMANCE MEASURES

Quantitative and qualitative performance measures

5.1   As you know it is possible to distinguish between **quantitative** information, which is capable of being expressed in numbers, and **qualitative** information, which can only be expressed in numerical terms with difficulty.

5.2   An example of a **quantitative** performance measure is 'You have been late for work *twice* this week and it's only Tuesday!'. An example of a **qualitative** performance measure is 'My bed is *very* comfortable'.

5.3   The first measure is likely to find its way into a staff appraisal report. The second would feature in a bed manufacturer's customer satisfaction survey. Both are indicators of whether their subjects are doing as good a job as they are required to do.

5.4   Qualitative measures are by nature **subjective** and **judgmental** but this does not mean that they are not valuable. They are especially valuable when they are derived from several different sources because then they can be expressed in a mixture of quantitative and qualitative terms which is more meaningful overall.

5.5 Consider the following statement.

'Seven out of ten customers think our beds are very comfortable.'

This is a **quantitative** measure of customer satisfaction as well as a **qualitative** measure of the perceived performance of the beds. (But it does not mean that only 70% of the total beds produced are comfortable, nor that each bed is 70% comfortable and 30% uncomfortable: 'very' is the measure of comfort.)

Non-financial indicators (NFIs)

5.6 Financial measures do not convey the full picture of a company's performance, especially in a **modern business environment**.

'In today's worldwide competitive environment companies are competing in terms of product quality, delivery, reliability, after-sales service and customer satisfaction. None of these variables is directly measured by the traditional responsibility accounting system, despite the fact that they represent the major goals of world-class manufacturing companies.'

5.7 Many companies are discovering the usefulness of quantitative and qualitative **non-financial indicators (NFIs)** such as the following.

- Quality
- Lead times
- Rework
- Number of customer complaints and warranty claims
- Delivery to time
- Non-productive hours
- System (machine) down time, and so on

5.8 Unlike traditional variance reports, measures such as these can be provided quickly for managers, per shift, **daily** or even **hourly** as required. They are likely to be easy to calculate, and easier for non-financial managers to understand and therefore to use effectively.

5.9 The beauty of non-financial indicators is that **anything can be compared** if it is **meaningful** to do so. The measures should be **tailored** to the circumstances so that, for example, number of coffee breaks per 20 pages of Study Text might indicate to you how hard you are studying!

5.10 Many suitable measures combine elements from the chart shown below. The chart is not intended to be prescriptive or exhaustive.

Errors/failure	Time	Quantity	People
Defects	Second	Range of products	Employees
Equipment failures	Minute	Parts/components	Employee skills
Warranty claims	Hour	Units produced	Customers
Complaints	Shift	Units sold	Competitors
Returns	Cycle	Services performed	Suppliers
Stockouts	Day	kg/litres/metres	
Lateness/waiting	Month	m^2/m^3	
Misinformation	Year	Documents	
Miscalculation		Deliveries	
Absenteeism		Enquiries	

5.11   Traditional measures derived from these lists like 'kg (of material) per unit produced' or 'units produced per hour' are fairly obvious, but what may at first seem a fairly **unlikely combination** may also be very revealing. 'Absenteeism per customer', for example, may be of no significance at all or it may reveal that a particularly difficult customer is being avoided, and hence that some action is needed.

5.12   There is clearly a need for the information provider to work more closely with the managers who will be using the information to make sure that their needs are properly understood. The measures used are likely to be **developed and refined over time**. It may be that some will serve the purpose of drawing attention to areas in need of improvement but will be of no further relevance once remedial action has been taken. A flexible, responsive approach is essential.

Question 4

Using the above chart make up five non-financial indicators and explain how each might be useful.

Answer

Here are five indicators, showing you how to use the chart, but there are many other possibilities.

(a)   Services performed late v total services performed
(b)   Total units sold v total units sold by competitors (indicating market share)
(c)   Warranty claims per month
(d)   Documents processed per employee
(e)   Equipment failures per 1,000 units produced

Don't forget to explain how the ones that you chose might be useful.

NFIs and financial measures

5.13   Arguably, NFIs are less likely to be **manipulated** than traditional profit-related measures and they should, therefore, offer a means of counteracting short-termism, since short-term profit at any (non-monetary) expense is rarely an advisable goal. The ultimate goal of commercial organisations in the long run is likely to remain the maximisation of **profit**, however, and so the financial aspect cannot be ignored.

5.14   There is a danger that too many such measures could be reported, leading to **information overload** for managers, providing information that is not truly useful, or that sends conflicting signals. A further danger of NFIs is that they might lead managers to pursue detailed **operational goals** and become blind to the **overall strategy** in which those goals are set.

5.15   A **combination** of financial and non-financial indicators is therefore likely to be most successful.

The Paper 9 examiner and NFIs

5.16   In his January and February 1996 *ACCA Students' Newsletter* articles, the examiner considered and calculated a range of non-financial indicators before and after the implementation of a **TQM programme**.

5.17 In the second article he uses the measures to **diagnose the problems** facing the company. Attempt the following exercise to see if you can come up with the right sort of ideas.

Question 5

What do the following indicate about an organisation's operational performance?

(a) Actual late deliveries as a percentage of total orders are greater than the budgeted figure.
(b) Actual process losses as a percentage of input are greater than the budgeted figure.
(c) Actual sales volumes are lower than budgeted sales volumes.

Answer

(a) This could indicate problems with either production planning or distribution.

(b) This could indicate faulty material, poor quality work or machine faults.

(c) This could indicate a fall in demand or too great a proportion of replacements or too many losses in process so that production cannot meet demand.

5.18 In the third article, the indicators calculated before and after the implementation of a TQM programme are used to **facilitate an analysis** of the programme's effects. This part of the article provides a good example of the sort of comments the examiner is looking for when he asks you to interpret data given or calculated in an exam question, so make sure that you do read all of his past articles.

Ratios

5.19 **Ratios** are a useful way of measuring performance for a number of reasons.

(a) It is easier to look at **changes over time** by comparing ratios in one time period with the corresponding ratios for periods in the past.

(b) Ratios are often **easier to understand than absolute measures** of physical quantities or money values. For example, it is easier to understand that 'productivity in March was 94%' than 'there was an adverse labour efficiency variance in March of £3,600'.

(c) Ratios **relate one item to another,** and so help to put performance into context. For example the profit/sales ratio sets profit in the context of how much has been earned per £1 of sales, and so shows how wide or narrow profit margins are.

(d) Ratios can be used as **targets**. In particular, targets can be set for ROI, profit/sales, asset turnover, capacity fill and productivity. Managers will then take decisions which will enable them to achieve their targets.

(e) Ratios provide a way of **summarising** an organisation's results, and **comparing** them with similar organisations. For example, the results of one investment centre/profit centre/company can be compared directly with the results of another.

Percentages

5.20 A **percentage** expresses one number as a proportion of another and gives meaning to absolute numbers. Examples are as follows.

(a) **Market share**. A company may aim to achieve a 25% share of the total market for its product, and measure both its marketing department and the quality of the product against this.

(b) **Capacity levels** are usually measured in this way. 'Factory A is working at 20% below full capacity' is an example which indicates relative inefficiency.

(c) **Wastage** is sometimes expressed in percentage terms. 'Normal loss' may be 10%, a measure of *in*efficiency.

(d) **Staff turnover** is often measured in this way. In the catering industry for example, staff turnover is typically greater than 100%, and so a hotel with a lower percentage could take this as an indicator both of the experience of its staff and of how well it is treating them.

Indices

5.21 **Indices** show how a particular variable has changed **relative to a base value**. The base value is usually the level of the variable at an earlier date. The 'variable' may be just one particular item, such as material X, or several items, such as 'raw materials' generally.

5.22 In its simplest form an index is calculated as (current value/base value) × 100. Thus if materials cost £15 per kg in 19X0 and now (19X3) cost £27 per kg, the 19X0 value would be expressed in index form as 100 (15/15 × 100) and the 19X3 value as 180 (27/15 × 100). If you find it easier to think of this as a percentage, then do so.

5.23 The use of indices for performance measurement is a favourite topic of the **Paper 9 examiner** and it is discussed in more detail in the next section.

6 INDICES

6.1 There is no mystique about indices: the mathematics is easy as you will see if you study the following example and attempt question 6.

6.2 EXAMPLE: WORK STANDARDS AND INDICES

Standards for work done in a service department could be expressed as an index. Suppose that in a sales department there is a standard target for sales representatives to make 25 customer visits per month each. The budget for May 19X9 might be for ten sales representatives to make 250 customer visits in total. Actual results in May might be that nine sales representatives made 234 visits in total. Performance could then be measured as:

Budget	100	(Standard = index 100)
Actual	104	((234/(9 × 25)) × 100)

This shows that 'productivity' per sales representative was actually 4% over budget.

Advantages of indices

6.3 **Advantages of indices**

(a) They are **easily understood**.

(b) Once established, they can be used to evaluate:

- **Actual results** in a period against the **standard**
- **Trends** over time

(c) They can incorporate a **'basket' of different types of job**. In the example of customer visits above, not all customer visits are the same. Travelling time to some customers will be longer than to others, and some customers will take longer to deal with than others. With indexing, **weightings** can be given to different types of visit.

Question 6

An accounts department (of two staff) deals with sales ledger, nominal ledger, purchase ledger and payroll duties. The estimated standard 'units' of time per transaction and the budgeted number of transactions handled by the department per month are as follows.

Transaction	Standard units of time	No of transactions	Standard units of time
Sales ledger	5	1,500	7,500
Nominal ledger	3	300	900
Purchase ledger	4	600	2,400
Payroll	7	200	1,400
			12,200

In August 19X3, the actual volume of transactions handled by the staff was as follows.

	No of transactions
Sales ledger	900
Nominal ledger	220
Purchase ledger	440
Payroll	230

However, one of the two members of staff had one half of the month off work, on holiday.

Required

Use a productivity index to measure actual performances in August 19X3.

Answer

Budget = 12,200/2 = 6,100 standard units per person per month = index ___100___

Actual	Transactions	Weighting	Standard units
Sales ledger	900	× 5	4,500
Nominal ledger	220	× 3	660
Purchase ledger	440	× 4	1,760
Payroll	230	× 7	1,610
			8,530

Combined months worked by two staff = 1½

Output per person per month (8,530/1.50) = 5,686.7 standard units

Actual productivity index = ((5,686.7/6,100) × 100) = ___93.2___

In this example, the productivity of the accounts department in August 19X3 was low, even allowing for the absence on holiday of one of the two staff.

Price and performance level changes

6.4 'Performance' in this context means factors like material usage and labour efficiency. **Examination** questions have been set in the past that require you, for example, to:

(a) Use tables of price and performance indices to prepare budgeted profit and loss accounts for *future* years

(b) Adjust the results of a *past* year using industry average indices for the *current* year, giving an industry norm against which current year actual results can be compared

An example will help to make this clear.

6.5 EXAMPLE: FORECAST PRICE AND PERFORMANCE LEVEL CHANGES

PPI Ltd has prepared forecasts for next year using tables of indices provided by a market intelligence organisation. You are checking the trading account which is shown below.

	This year		Next year	
	£	£	£	£
Sales		10,000		12,650
Less cost of sales				
Direct materials	5,000		5,973	
Direct labour	750		799	
Production overhead	1,550		1,762	
		7,300		8,534
Gross profit		2,700		4,116

Relevant information from the tables of indices is shown below.

Forecast changes in performance level

	Material usage	Labour efficiency	Production overhead utilisation (fixed and variable)
This year	100	100	100
Next year	98	104	102

Forecast changes in price level

	Material price	Labour rate	Overhead expenditure
This year	100	100	100
Next year	106	100	104

Forecast changes in sales and production volume and selling prices

	Sales/production volume	Selling prices
This year	100	100
Next year	115	110

Labour costs contain a fixed element of £500; production overhead contains a fixed element of £750 (both this year's price levels). Within the latter is included a depreciation provision of £150 which will remain constant next year. Material costs, variable labour costs and production overhead vary in proportion to units produced. Utilisation indices monitor changes due to factors other than volume changes.

Required

Show how the figures in the trading account for next year have been calculated.

6.6 SOLUTION

Sales revenue increases because of both the increase in volume and the increase in price, as shown in the third table and so sales = £10,000 × 1.15 ×1.10 = £12,650.

Direct materials costs will decrease due to the 2% usage reduction, but increase due to price increases and increases in production volume and so materials = £5,000 × 0.98 × 1.06 × 1.15 = £5,973.10

Direct labour cost is partly fixed and partly variable.

Labour costs	This year	Labour efficiency	Labour rate	Prod volume	Next year
Variable	250	1.04	1.00	1.15	299
Fixed	500	-	1.00	-	500
	750				799

Production overhead is calculated in a similar way.

	This year	Utilisation	Expenditure	Volume	Next year
Variable	800	1.02	1.04	1.15	976
Depreciation	150	-	-	-	150
Fixed	600	1.02	1.04	-	636
	1,550				1,762

6.7   Questions on this topic are rarely any more difficult than this. The problem is that in a full question you need to be given pages and pages of data and this is so offputting that many students never find out how simple the question really is because they daren't even start it.

The Paper 9 examiner and indices

6.8   An article by George Brown in the ACCA *Students' Newsletter* in October 1989 contained an illustration of the use of price and performance indices where a company is a member of a trade association which gathers information from members and issues industry average indices to each member. The following example is a modified version of the trickiest part of this illustration.

6.9   EXAMPLE: COMPANY COMPARISONS AND INDUSTRY AVERAGE INDICES

NDC Ltd, a manufacturer of components for car telephones joined a newly formed trade association in 2009. The association provides industry average indices to its members using 2009 as the base year (100). NDC's management accountant has just received the indices for 2013 and is starting to calculate figures to compare his company's performance with the average for the industry. Relevant data is as follows.

NDC Ltd

	2009	2013
	£	£
Sales	40,000	140,000
Variable costs	20,000	106,250
Average selling price per component	£0.50	£0.28

Trade Association Indices

Industry average	2009	2013
Sales volume	100	250
Sales price	100	65
Variable costs	100	90

Required

Calculate the industry average contribution per unit in 2013 and using this prepare a statement reconciling the sales that NDC Ltd could have expected to achieve in 2013 (if it were an average member of its trade) with those actually achieved.

6.10   SOLUTION

Step 1.   First calculate the number of units sold by NDC Ltd in each year.

2009: £40,000/£0.50 =   80,000 units
2013: £140,000/£0.28 =   500,000 units

Step 2.   Then determine how many units NDC might have expected to sell if it were typical of its industry.

80,000 × 2.5 =   200,000 units

NDC has sold 300,000 units more than expected.

Step 3.   To calculate the industry average contribution it is necessary to adjust NDC's 2009 figures using the industry average indices for sales price and variable cost.

	2009	Index	2013
Sales	40,000	0.65	26,000
Variable costs	20,000	0.90	18,000
Contribution	20,000		8,000

Contribution per unit = £8,000/80,000 = £0.10

Step 4. Now you can produce your reconciliation statement.

	£	£
Expected contribution 200,000 × 0.10		20,000
Sales factors		
Gain through increased sales volume (300,000 × 0.10)	30,000	
Price loss ((£0.50 × 0.65) - £0.28) × 500,000	(22,500)	
Cost factors		
Expected variable costs (W)	112,500	
Actual costs	106,250	
	6,250	
		13,750
Actual contribution (£140,000 - £106,250)		33,750

Working

2009 variable cost per unit of (£20,000/80,000) £0.25 × 0.9 (industry average index) × NDC Ltd's actual volume (500,000 units)

Conclusion

6.11 It can be seen that NDC won a net market advantage through having lower than average selling prices, and gained further by containing costs to a greater degree than its competitors.

Question 7

G Ltd had the following budgeted and actual revenues and selling prices in the years 2001 to 2003.

	2001 Budget £'000	2001 Actual £'000	2002 Actual £'000	2003 Actual £'000
Sales revenue	10,800	13,680	16,380	19,305
Selling price per unit	£360	£360	£409.50	£438.75

Required

(a) Show the sales revenue, sales volume and sales price indices for the years 2001, 2002 and 2003, taking the 2001 budget as the base (100) and rounding your answers to whole numbers.

(b) What is the mathematical relationship between the three indices?

Answer

(a) First calculate the sales volume for each year.

	2001 Budget	2001 Actual	2002 Actual	2003 Actual
Revenue/price	10,800/360	13,680/360	16,380/409.5	19,305/438.75
Sales volume ('000 units)	30	38	40	44

The indices can now be calculated as follows.

	2001 Actual	2002 Actual	2003 Actual
Revenue index (13,680/10,800; 16,380/10,800 etc)	127	152	179
Volume index (38/30: 40/30, etc)	127	133	147
Price index (360/360; 409.5/360, etc)	100	114	122

(b) Sales revenue index divided by sales price index equals sales volume index (other variants of this would be as good).

7 THE BENEFITS AND PROBLEMS OF PERFORMANCE MEASURES

7.1 George Brown's article on performance measurement ('Accountability and performance measurement' *ACCA Students' Newsletter*, August 1998) includes Berry, Broadbent and Otley's list of **benefits of performance measures**.

1 'Clarifying the objectives of the organisation
2 Developing agreed measures of activity
3 Greater understanding of the processes
4 Facilitating comparison of performance in different organisations
5 Facilitating the setting of targets for the organisation and its managers
6 Promoting accountability of the organisation to its stakeholders'

7.2 Their list of **problems of performance measures** is also included in the article.

Problem	Comment
Tunnel vision	Undue focus on performance measures to the detriment of other areas
Sub-optimisation	Focus on some objectives so that others are not achieved
Myopia	Short-sightedness leading to the neglect of longer-term objectives
Measure fixation	Measures and behaviour in order to achieve specific performance indicators which may not be effective
Misrepresentation	'Creative' reporting to suggest that a result is acceptable
Misinterpretation	Failure to recognise the complexity of the environment in which the organisation operates
Gaming	Deliberate distortion of a measure to secure some strategic advantage
Ossification	An unwillingness to change the performance measure scheme once it has been set up

7.3 Make sure that you read the article as the examiner has included some illustrations set in the context of a UK university. He also suggests ways in which the **problems may be reduced**, and they are summarised here.

(a) **Involvement of staff** at all levels in the development and implementation of the scheme should help to reduce gaming and tunnel vision.

(b) A **flexible use** of performance measures should help to reduce measure fixation and misrepresentation.

(c) Keeping the performance measurement system under **constant review** should help to overcome the problems of ossification and gaming.

(d) Give careful consideration to the **dimensions of performance**. Quantifying all objectives should help to overcome sub-optimisation, while a focus on measuring customer satisfaction should reduce tunnel vision and sub-optimisation.

(e) Consideration should be given to the **audit of the system**. Expert interpretation of the performance measurement scheme should help to provide an idea of the incidence of the problems, while a careful audit of the data used should help to reduce the incidence and impact of measure fixation, misinterpretation and gaming.

(f) **Recognition of the key feature** necessary in any scheme (a long-term view/perspective amongst staff, a sensible number of measures, benchmarks which are independent of past activity) should help to overcome the range of problems listed above.

Chapter roundup

- Key areas for performance measurement are **profitability, activity** and **productivity.** Profitability is often a key objective but other **'success factors'** are also critical. **Benchmarking** is increasingly common.

- Performance measurement in terms of accounting results is one of the aims of **responsibility accounting.** Controllability is a key issue.

- A distinction needs to be made between the performance of **managers** and the performance of **what it is that they manage.**

- Management control systems provide **hard accountability** and **soft accountability.**

- Both quantitative and qualitative performance measures are equally valuable.

- Financial measures generally derive from the accounting system (or other businesses' accounting systems).

- An imaginative approach to performance measurement is becoming a necessity in the modern business environment, and many businesses now recognise the need to supplement traditional financial measures with other, **non-financial indicators.**

- Non-monetary measures also include **ratios, percentages** and **indices.**

- **Indices** can be used in a variety of ways in performance measurement, for example in **forecasting** and for **inter-company comparisons.**

- A recent article by the examiner considers the **benefits and problems of performance measures.**

Quick quiz

1 What is the aim of performance measurement? (see para 1.1)

2 What is productivity? (1.8)

3 What is a critical success factor? (1.15)

4 What is responsibility accounting? (2.1)

5 Give some examples of controllable costs. (2.4)

6 What is soft accountability? (3.4)

7 How can financial performance be measured? (4.1 - 4.2)

8 What are the benefits and drawbacks of non-financial indicators? (5.8, 5.13, 5.14)

9 Why are ratios useful? (5.19)

10 List three advantages of using indices. (6.3)

11 Describe the problem of myopia in relation to performance measurement. (7.2)

Question to try	Level	Marks	Time
15	Exam standard	35	63 mins

Chapter 15

PERFORMANCE MEASUREMENT IN DIFFERENT SECTORS

Chapter topic list	Syllabus reference
1 Performance measures for manufacturing	1(b), 1(c), 3(c)
2 Performance measures for services	1(b), 1(c), 3(c)
3 Performance measurement for non-profit-making organisations	1(b), 1(c), 3(c)

Introduction

In this chapter we discuss the features of performance measurement in the three main sectors of the economy - **manufacturing**, **services** and **non-profit bodies** such as government organisations. There is not much to add about manufacturing that you have not studied already, and the examiner has not shown much interest so far in non-profit bodies, so the chief focus is **services.** Written questions on aspects of service businesses have appeared fairly regularly.

Core areas of the syllabus identified by the examiner and covered in this chapter: **performance measurement in different sectors; performance measurement in the service sector; performance measurement in not-for-profit organisations (value for money and 3Es).**

1 PERFORMANCE MEASURES FOR MANUFACTURING

1.1 Most of this book is about manufacturing businesses because that is the context in which **Paper 9 questions** are most often set. There is no need for us to repeat what you have read already about quality, standard costing and so on. But here are a few points that may help to jog your memory of the key issues and answer questions that ask you what measures are appropriate in what circumstances.

1.2 In a **jobbing** environment each job undertaken is unique and products are made to the specific requirements of individual customers. This has a number of implications for performance measurement.

(a) It will often be difficult to judge in advance the precise requirements for labour, material and overheads because the job will have no standard features. A system of **planning variances** would be highly appropriate in these circumstances.

(b) **Suppliers** may be different for each job, making it harder to set standards for quality, speed of delivery and so on.

(c) **Customer satisfaction** measures are particularly important in this environment (payment might depend contractually upon customer satisfaction). Information on performance in the view of the customer will be easy to obtain, however, because each job has a specific customer.

BPP PUBLISHING

(d) Because each job will be different the organisation will have to be extremely **flexible**. Measures of the manufacturing facility's success in adapting to new requirements will provide a key indicator. Measures of **employee skills** will be equally important.

(e) It is likely that the job will need to be completed within a certain **time** and therefore an ongoing check must be kept of performance in relation to the **deadline**.

1.3 A **contract** or **project** is simply a large job that takes a considerable length of time. The same considerations apply regarding performance measurement as in a jobbing environment, except that:

(a) the consequences of **overspending** may be dire: for instance several contracting companies involved in the London Docklands developments went out of business due to a combination of the recession in the early 1990s and poor cash control;

(b) the longer timescale means that progress must be measured even more carefully, since there is more likelihood of slippage if **deadlines** seem a long way off.

1.4 In **batch** production and **mass production** environments products are more **standardised**, although some costs and activities may be unique to a specific batch. This means that materials requirements and labour and machinery capabilities are more specialised and so **performance standards** can be set for materials quality and usage, labour efficiency, suppliers and so on.

1.5 As you know, the modern trend is towards **cellular** manufacturing, a means of organising the factory floor to facilitate short production runs of a wide diversity of products. This is simply so as to be able to respond promptly to what modern customers require. In the light of this change, as we have seen elsewhere, measures that are gaining importance include the following:

(a) **changeover** times;
(b) number of **common parts** in products;
(c) level of product **diversity**;
(d) number of **different applications** of the same equipment (or worker).

2 PERFORMANCE MEASURES FOR SERVICES

Types of service organisation

2.1 Fitzgerald *et al* (*Performance Measurement in Service Businesses,* (1991)) identify three different types of service organisation, as follows.

(a) **Professional services,** for example an accountancy or law firm. Such services are characterised as being highly adaptable to individual customer needs and dependent upon staff/customer contact. They are people-based and rely on short chains of command and highly autonomous employees.

(b) **Mass services,** for example a railway company. These involve little customisation and limited customer contact. They are predominantly equipment-based and require defined tasks and set procedures to be performed with little exercise of judgement.

(c) **Service shops,** for example, a bank. These fall between the above extremes in terms of customisation, customer contact, people/equipment and levels of staff discretion.

Service businesses

2.2 A service business is one that treats people or provides goods or facilities for them as opposed to an organisation that makes things. To take a homely example, think of a haircut (as opposed, perhaps, to the pair of scissors used to cut the hair).

(a) **Intangibility**. A haircut is intangible in itself, and the performance of the service comprises many other intangible factors, like the music in the salon, the personality of the hairdresser, the quality of the coffee.

(b) **Simultaneity**. The production and consumption of a haircut are simultaneous, and therefore it cannot be inspected for quality in advance, nor can it be returned if it is not what was required.

(c) **Perishability**. Haircuts are perishable, that is, they cannot be stored. You cannot buy them in bulk, and the hairdresser cannot do them in advance and keep them stocked away in case of heavy demand.

(d) **Heterogeneity**. A haircut is heterogeneous and so the exact service received will vary each time: not only will Justin and Nigel cut hair differently, but Justin will not consistently deliver the same standard of haircut.

Question 1

Consider how the factors intangibility, simultaneity, perishability and heterogeneity apply to the various services that you use: public transport, your bank account, meals in restaurants, the postal service, your annual holiday and so on.

Exam focus point

A question in the **June 1996** exam asked for an **explanation** of these four terms and for relevant **examples**, so it is worth doing Question 1!

'Dimensions' of performance measurement

2.3 Performance measurement in service businesses has sometimes been perceived as difficult because of the four factors listed above, but the modern view is that if something is difficult to measure this is because it has not been clearly enough defined. Fitzgerald *et al* and Fitzgerald & Moon provide **building blocks** for **dimensions, standards** and **rewards** for performance measurement systems in service businesses. The **standards** are **ownership, achievability** and **equity**; the **rewards** are **clarity, motivation** and **controllability**. The **dimensions** are as follows.

(a) **Competitive performance,** focusing on factors such as sales growth and market share.

(b) **Financial performance,** concentrating on profitability, capital structure and so on.

(c) **Quality of service** looks at matters like reliability, courtesy and competence.

(d) **Flexibility** is an apt heading for assessing the organisation's ability to deliver at the right speed, to respond to precise customer specifications, and to cope with fluctuations in demand.

(e) **Resource utilisation,** not unsurprisingly, considers how efficiently resources are being utilised. This can be problematic because of the complexity of the inputs to a service and the outputs from it and because some of the inputs are supplied by the customer (he or she brings their own hair, their own taste in coffee and so on). Many measures are possible, however, for example 'number of customers per hairdresser', 'waiting time to haircutting time' and so on. Performance measures can be devised easily if it is known what activities are involved in the service.

(f) **Innovation** is assessed in terms of both the innovation process and the success of individual innovations.

2.4 These dimensions can be divided into two sets, the **results** (measured by financial performance and competitiveness) and the **determinants** (the remainder). Focus on the **examination and improvement of the determinants** should **lead to improvement in the results**.

> ### Exam focus point
> The 'dimensions' featured in questions set in **June 1995, December 1996, June 1997, June 1998** and **December 1998** (see below).

Services and manufacturing

2.5 You may think that the measures identified above sound **little different** from many of those that we have identified for manufacturing businesses. This is true. As all businesses become more and more **customer-oriented**, manufacturers take on more of the characteristics of service providers; as all businesses become more and more **results-oriented**, service businesses realise that most of their activities can be measured, and some can be measured in ways similar to those used in manufacturing.

2.6 There is no need, therefore, to elaborate on **competitive performance**, **financial performance** and **quality of service** issues, all of which have been covered already. The other three dimensions deserve more attention.

Flexibility

2.7 Flexibility has three aspects.

(a) **Speed of delivery**. **Punctuality** is vital in some service industries like passenger transport: indeed punctuality is currently one of the most widely publicised performance measures in the UK, because organisations like railway companies are making a point of it. **Measures** include waiting time in queues, as well as late trains. In other types of service it may be more a question of **timeliness**. Does the auditor turn up to do the annual audit during the appointed week? Is the audit done within the time anticipated by the partner or does it drag on for weeks? These aspects are all easily measurable in terms of '**days late**'. Depending upon the circumstances, 'days late' may also reflect on inability to cope with fluctuations in demand.

(b) **Response to customer specifications**. The ability of a service organisation to respond to **customers' specifications** is one of the criteria by which Fitzgerald *et al* distinguish between the three different types of service. Clearly a professional service such as legal advice and assistance must be tailored exactly to the customer's needs. Performance is partly a matter of customer perception and so **customer attitude surveys** may be appropriate. However it is also a matter of the diversity of skills possessed by the service organisation and so it can be measured in terms of the **mix of staff skills** and the amount of time spent on **training**. In **mass service** business customisation is not possible by the very nature of the service.

(c) **Coping with demand**. This is clearly measurable in quantitative terms in a mass service like a railway company which can ascertain the extent of **overcrowding**. It can also be very closely monitored in service shops: customer **queuing** time can be measured in banks and retailers, for example. Professional services can measure levels of **overtime** worked: excessive amounts indicate that the current demand is too great for the organisation to cope with in the long term without obtaining extra human resources.

Resource utilisation measures

2.8 Resource utilisation is usually measured in terms of **productivity**. The ease with which this may be measured varies according to the service being delivered.

2.9 The main resource of a firm of accountants, for example, is the **time** of various grades of staff. The main output of an accountancy firm is **chargeable hours**.

2.10 In a restaurant it is not nearly so straightforward. Inputs are highly **diverse**: the ingredients for the meal, the chef's time and expertise, the surroundings and the customers' own likes and dislikes. A **customer attitude survey** might show whether or not a customer enjoyed the food, but it could not ascribe the enjoyment or lack of it to the quality of the ingredients, say, rather than the skill of the chef.

2.11 Here are some of the resource utilisation ratios listed by Fitzgerald *et al*.

Business	Input	Output
Andersen Consulting	Man hours available	Chargeable hours
Commonwealth Hotels	Rooms available	Rooms occupied
Railway companies	Train miles available	Passenger miles
Barclays Bank	Number of staff	Number of accounts

Innovation

2.12 In a modern environment in which product quality, product differentiation and continuous improvement are the order of the day, a company that can find innovative ways of satisfying customers' needs has an important **competitive advantage**.

2.13 Fitzgerald *et al* suggest that **individual innovations** should be measured in terms of whether they bring about **improvements in the other five 'dimensions'**.

2.14 The innovating **process** can be measured in terms of how much it **costs** to develop a new service, how **effective** the process is (that is, how innovative is the organisation, if at all?), and how **quickly** it can develop new services. In more concrete terms this might translate into the following.

(a) The amount of **R&D** spending and whether (and how quickly) these costs are recovered from new service sales

(b) The proportion of **new** services to **total** services provided

(c) The time between **identification** of the need for a new service and making it **available**

Question 2

This question is based on one that appeared in **June 1997.** A service business has collected some figures relating to its year just ended.

		Budget	Actual
Customer enquiries:	New customers	6,000	9,000
	Existing customers	4,000	3,000
Business won:	New customers	2,000	4,000
	Existing customers	1,500	1,500
Types of services performed:	Service A	875	780
	Service B	1,575	1,850
	Service C	1,050	2,870
Employees:	Service A	5	4
	Service B	10	10
	Service C	5	8

Required

Calculate figures that illustrate competitiveness and resource utilisation.

Answer

Competitiveness can only be measured from these figures by looking at how successful the organisation is at converting enquiries into firm orders.

Percentage of enquiries converted into firm orders

	Budget	Actual
New customers (W1)	33%	44%
Existing customers (W1)	37.5%	50%

Resource utilisation can be measured by looking at average services performed per employee.

	Budget	Actual	Rise
Service A (W2)	175	195	+11.4%
Service B (W2)	157.5	185	+17.5%
Service C (W2)	175	358.75	+105.0%

Workings

1   For example 2,000/6,000 = 33%
2   For example 875/5 = 175

What comments would you make about these results? How well is the business doing?

The Paper 9 examiner and means to success

2.15   As George Brown points out ('Performance measurement in service businesses', *ACCA Students' Newsletter*, October 1994), 'Competitive performance and financial performance are measures of the **success** of the strategy adopted by the company. The remaining measures – quality, flexibility, resource utilisation, and innovation – are the **means** by which success is achieved.'

3   PERFORMANCE MEASUREMENT FOR NON-PROFIT-MAKING ORGANISATIONS

Non-profit-making organisations

3.1   Commercial organisations generally have market competition and the profit motive to guide the process of managing resources economically, efficiently and effectively. However, non-profit-making organisations (NPMOs) **cannot** by definition be judged by **profitability**

nor do they generally have to be successful against competition, so other methods of assessing performance have to be used.

3.2   A major problem with many NPMOs, particularly government bodies, is that it is extremely difficult to **define their objectives** at all, let alone find *one* which can serve a yardstick function in the way that profit does for commercial bodies.

Question 3

One of the objectives of a local government body could be 'to provide adequate street lighting throughout the area'.

(a)   How could the 'adequacy' of street lighting be measured?

(b)   Assume that other objectives are to improve road safety in the area and to reduce crime. How much does 'adequate' street lighting contribute to each of these aims?

(c)   What is an excessive amount of money to pay for adequately lit streets, improved road safety and reduced crime? How much is too little?

Answer

Mull over these questions and discuss them in class or with colleagues if possible. It is possible to suggest answers, perhaps even in quantitative terms, but the point is that there are no *easy* answers, and no right or wrong answers.

How can performance be measured?

3.3   Performance is usually judged in terms of inputs and outputs and this ties in with the **'value for money'** criteria that are often used to assess NPMOs.

- **Economy** (spending money frugally)
- **Efficiency** (getting out as much as possible for what goes in)
- **Effectiveness** (getting done, by means of (a) and (b), what was supposed to be done)

> **Exam focus point**
> These concepts were examined in **December 1998**.

3.4   More formally, **effectiveness** is the relationship between an organisation's outputs and its objectives, **efficiency** is the relationship between inputs and outputs, and **economy** equates to cost control in the commercial sector.

3.5   These criteria may conflict with each other. In Higher Education, for example, economy may require minimising the cost per graduate, efficiency may require maximising the student:staff ratio but effective teaching may not be possible given these requirements.

3.6   The **problems** with an NPMO are thus twofold.

(a)   NPMOs tend to have **multiple objectives,** so that even if they can all be clearly identified it is impossible to say which is the overriding objective. A Higher Education establishment's principal objective might be to provide education but subsidiary objectives could include being a quality research establishment.

(b) **Outputs** can seldom be measured in a way that is generally agreed to be meaningful. (For example, are good exam results alone an adequate measure of the quality of teaching?)

Inputs

3.7 One possible solution is to judge performance in terms of **inputs**. This is very common in everyday life. If somebody tells you that their suit cost £750 you would generally conclude that it was an extremely well-designed and good quality suit, even if you did not think so when you first saw it. The **drawback**, of course, is that you might also conclude that the person wearing the suit had been cheated, or you may think that no piece of clothing is worth £750, designer label or not. So it is with the inputs and outputs of a NPMO.

Judgement

3.8 A second possibility is to accept that performance measurement must to some extent be **subjective**. Judgements can be made by **experts** in that particular non-profit-making activity or by the persons who **fund** the activity.

Comparisons

3.9 Most NPMOs do not face competition but this does not mean that all NPMOs are unique. Bodies like local governments, health services and so on can judge their performance **against each other** and against the historical results of their predecessors. **Unit cost measurements** like 'cost per patient day' can be established to allow organisations to assess whether they are doing better or worse than their counterparts.

Inputs/outputs

3.10 As a further illustration, suppose that at a cost of £40,000 and 4,000 hours (**inputs**) in an average year, two policemen travel 8,000 miles and are instrumental in 200 arrests (**outputs**). A large number of **possibly meaningful** measures can be derived from these few figures, as the table below shows.

	£40,000	4,000 hours	8,000 miles	200 arrests
Cost £40,000		£40,000/4,000 = £10 per hour	£40,000/8,000 = £5 per mile	£40,000/200 = £200 per arrest
Time 4,000 hrs	4,000/£40,000 = 6 mins patrol per £1 spent		4,000/8,000 = ½ hour to patrol 1 mile	4,000/200 = 20 hours per arrest
Miles 8,000	8,000/£40,000 = 0.2 of a mile per £1	8,000/4,000 = 2 miles patrolled per hour		8,000/200 = 40 miles per arrest
Arrests 200	200/£40,000 = 1 arrest per £200	200/4,000 = 1 arrest every 20 hours	200/8,000 = 1 arrest every 40 miles	

3.11 These measures do not necessarily identify cause and effect or personal responsibility and accountability. Actual performance needs to be **compared** with:

- **Standards,** if there are any
- Similar **external activities**
- Similar **internal activities**

- **Targets**
- **Indices**
- Other time periods - ie **as trends**

NPMOs and profit-making bodies

3.12 If it has struck you that the main issue in the performance measurement of NPMOs is one of **quality,** you may be wondering whether the distinction between profit-making and non-profit-making in this context is worth-making!

3.13 The answer, of course, is that increasingly it is not. The commercial sector's new focus on customers and service quality has much in common with the aims of NPMOs. Conversely NPMOs (in particular government bodies under the former Conservative government) have been forced to face up to elements of **competition** and **market forces**. The distinctions are thus becoming blurred. The problems of performance measurement in NPMOs are to a great extent the problems of performance measurement generally.

Chapter roundup

- In **manufacturing**, the type of environment has an impact on the type of measures that can be or need to be used. The same measure may have a different meaning in a different environment.

- **Service** businesses fall into **three main types**, depending upon how closely the service itself is customised to individual customer requirements. Services should be measured under headings like quality, flexibility and innovation, as well as in more traditional ways such as **competitiveness, financial performance** and **resource utilisation.**

- **Non-profit making organisations** are difficult to measure because they have multiple objectives and output measures are not necessarily meaningful. Comparisons with similar bodies, subjective measures and input/output measures may be used.

Quick quiz

1 What are the implications of jobbing production for performance measurement? (see para 1.2)

2 What are four measures that might apply in a cellular environment? (1.5)

3 What are three types of service business? (2.1)

4 What are the four features that characterise a service? (2.2)

5 What are six dimensions of performance measurement? (2.3)

6 What are three aspects of flexibility? (2.7)

7 Why is innovation important? (2.12)

8 How is success achieved? (2.15)

9 What are the three Es? (3.3)

10 Suggest four ways of measuring the performance of a NPMO. (3.7 - 3.10)

Question to try	Level	Marks	Time
16	Exam standard	25	45 mins

Chapter 16

TRANSFER PRICING

Chapter topic list	Syllabus reference
1 Transfer pricing: basic principles	1(b), 4(a)
2 The use of market price	1(b), 4(a)
3 Cost-based approaches to transfer pricing	1(b), 4(a)
4 Opportunity cost and transfer prices	1(b), 4(a)
5 Negotiated transfer prices	1(b), 4(a)

Introduction

Transfer pricing is an aspect of divisional control concerned with trying to encourage managers to make decisions that are in the best interests of the company as a whole (**goal congruence**). It can involve a variety of techniques that you have studied earlier in this book, including break-even analysis, pricing methods, limiting factor analysis and linear programming, and planning and operational variances.

Questions that have been set so far have been mainly **written** ones, but because the concepts are best illustrated by considering numerical examples, there are quite a lot of numbers to work through in this chapter.

Core areas of the syllabus identified by the examiner and covered in this chapter: **alternative transfer pricing methods; relevance of and problems associated with methods; balance between divisional autonomy and corporate profit maximisation**.

1 TRANSFER PRICING: BASIC PRINCIPLES

1.1 Transfer pricing means charging other divisions of your organisation when you provide them with your division's goods or services. For example, A, a subsidiary of X plc, might make a component that it used in the product of B, another subsidiary of X plc, but can also be sold to the external market, including makers of rival products to B's product.

> **KEY TERM**
>
> A **transfer price** is 'The price at which goods or services are transferred from one process or department to another or from one member of a group to another.'

1.2 A transfer price may be based upon:

- Market price
- The market price, but at a discount
- Marginal cost (or marginal cost with a gross profit margin on top)
- Full cost (or full cost plus)
- A negotiated price, which could be based on any of (a) to (d) above

Three problems with transfer pricing

Divisional autonomy

1.3 Transfer prices are particularly appropriate for **profit centres** because if one profit centre does work for another the size of the transfer price will affect the costs of one profit centre and the revenues of another.

1.4 However, a danger with profit centre accounting is that the business organisation will divide into a number of **self-interested segments**, each acting at times against the wishes and interests of other segments. Decisions might be taken by a profit centre manager in the best interests of his own part of the business, but against the best interests of other profit centres and possibly the organisation as a whole.

1.5 A task of head office is therefore to try to prevent dysfunctional decision making by individual profit centres. To do this, it must reserve some power and authority for itself and so profit centres **cannot** be allowed to make entirely **autonomous decisions**.

1.6 Just how much authority head office decides to keep for itself will vary according to individual circumstances. A **balance** ought to be kept between **divisional autonomy** to provide incentives and motivation, and retaining **centralised authority** to ensure that the organisation's profit centres are all working towards the same target, the benefit of the organisation as a whole (in other words, retaining **goal congruence** among the organisation's separate divisions).

Divisional performance measurement

1.7 Profit centre managers tend to put their own profit **performance** above everything else. Since profit centre performance is measured according to the profit they earn, no profit centre will want to do work for another and incur costs without being paid for it. Consequently, profit centre managers are likely to dispute the size of transfer prices with each other, or disagree about whether one profit centre should do work for another or not. Transfer prices **affect behaviour and decisions** by profit centre managers.

Corporate profit maximisation

1.8 When there are disagreements about how much work should be transferred between divisions, and how many sales the division should make to the external market, there is presumably a **profit-maximising** level of output and sales for the organisation as a whole. However, unless each profit centre also maximises its own profit at this same level of output, there will be inter-divisional disagreements about output levels and the profit-maximising output will not be achieved.

The ideal solution

1.9 Ideally a transfer price should be set at a level that overcomes these problems.

(a) The transfer price should provide an 'artificial' selling price that enables the transferring division to **earn a return** for its efforts, and the receiving division to **incur a cost** for benefits received.

(b) The transfer price should be set at a level that enables profit centre performance to be **measured 'commercially'** (that is, it should be a **fair** commercial price).

(c) The transfer price, if possible, should encourage profit centre managers to agree on the amount of goods and services to be transferred, which will also be at a level that is consistent with the organisation's aims as a whole such as **maximising company profits**.

In practice it is very difficult to achieve all three aims.

Exam focus point

Questions set in Paper 9 exams on transfer pricing have tended to be **written** questions, requiring an understanding of the issues raised above. In the **December 1997** exam, however, candidates were required to calculate divisional ROCE using various transfer pricing bases for the costs of a service division.

Question 1

(a) What do you understand by the term 'divisional autonomy'?

(b) What are the likely behavioural consequences of a head office continually imposing its own decisions on divisions?

Answer

(a) The term refers to the right of a division to govern itself, that is, the freedom to make decisions without consulting a higher authority first and without interference from a higher body.

(b) Decentralisation recognises that those closest to a job are the best equipped to say how it should be done and that people tend to perform to a higher standard if they are given responsibility. Centrally-imposed decisions are likely to make managers feel that they do not really have any authority and therefore that they cannot be held responsible for performance. They will therefore make less effort to perform well.

2 THE USE OF MARKET PRICE

Market price as the transfer price

2.1 If an **external market** price exists for transferred goods, profit centre managers will be aware of the price they could charge or the price they would have to pay for their goods on the external market, and so will **compare** this price with the internal transfer price.

2.2 EXAMPLE: TRANSFERRING GOODS AT MARKET VALUE

A company has two profit centres, A and B. Centre A sells half of its output on the open market and transfers the other half to B. Costs and external revenues in an accounting period are as follows.

	A	B	Total
	£	£	£
External sales	8,000	24,000	32,000
Costs of production	12,000	10,000	22,000
Company profit			10,000

Required

What are the consequences of setting a transfer price at market value?

2.3 SOLUTION

If the transfer price is at market price, A would be happy to sell the output to B for £8,000, which is what A would get by selling it externally instead of transferring it.

	A		B		Total
	£	£	£	£	£
Market sales		8,000		24,000	32,000
Transfer sales		8,000		-	
		16,000		24,000	
Transfer costs		-	8,000		
Own costs	12,000		10,000		22,000
		12,000		18,000	
Profit		4,000		6,000	10,000

The consequences, therefore, are as follows.

(a) A earns the same profit on transfers as on external sales. B must pay a commercial price for transferred goods, and both divisions will have their profit measured fairly.

(b) A will be indifferent about selling externally or transferring goods to B because the profit is the same on both types of transaction. B can therefore ask for and obtain as many units as it wants from A.

A **market-based** transfer price therefore seems to be the **ideal** transfer price.

Adjusted market price

2.4 However, internal transfers are often **cheaper** than external sales, with **savings** in selling and administration costs, bad debt risks and possibly transport/delivery costs. It would therefore seem reasonable for the buying division to expect a **discount** on the external market price.

2.5 The transfer price might be slightly less than market price, so that A and B could **share the cost savings** from internal transfers compared with external sales. It should be possible to reach agreement on this price and on output levels with a minimum of intervention from head office.

> **Exam focus point**
> This point was examined in **December 1999**.

The disadvantages of market value transfer prices

2.6 Market value as a transfer price does have certain disadvantages.

(a) The market price may be a **temporary** one, induced by adverse **economic conditions**, or dumping, or the market price might depend on the volume of output supplied to the external market by the profit centre.

(b) A transfer price at market value might, under some circumstances, act as a disincentive to use up any **spare capacity** in the divisions. A price based on incremental cost, in contrast, might provide an incentive to use up the spare resources in order to provide a marginal contribution to profit.

(c) Many products **do not have an equivalent** market price so that the price of a similar, but not identical, product might have to be chosen. In such circumstances, the option to sell or buy on the open market does not really exist.

(d) The **external market** for the transferred item might be **imperfect**, so that if the transferring division wanted to sell more externally, it would have to **reduce** its price.

3 COST-BASED APPROACHES TO TRANSFER PRICING

3.1 Cost-based approaches to transfer pricing are often used in practice, because in practice the following conditions are common.

(a) There is **no external market** for the product that is being transferred.

(b) Alternatively, although there is an external market it is an **imperfect** one because the market price is affected by such factors as the amount that the company setting the transfer price supplies to it, or because there is only a limited external demand.

In either case there will not be a suitable market price upon which to base the transfer price.

Transfer prices based on full cost

3.2 Under this approach, the **full cost** (including fixed overheads absorbed) incurred by the supplying division in making the 'intermediate' product is charged to the receiving division. If a **full cost plus** approach is used a **profit margin** is also included in this transfer price.

> ### KEY TERM
>
> An **intermediate product** is one that is used as a component of another product, for example car headlights or food additives.

3.3 EXAMPLE: TRANSFERS AT FULL COST (PLUS)

Consider the example introduced in Paragraph 2.2, but with the additional complication of imperfect intermediate and final markets. A company has 2 profit centres, A and B. Centre A can only sell **half** of its maximum output externally because of limited demand. It transfers the other half of its output to B which also faces limited demand. Costs and revenues in an accounting period are as follows.

	A	B	Total
	£	£	£
External sales	8,000	24,000	32,000
Costs of production in the division	12,000	10,000	22,000
Profit			10,000

There are no opening or closing stocks. It does not matter here whether marginal or absorption costing is used and we shall ignore the question of whether the current output levels are profit maximising and congruent with the goals of the company as a whole.

Transfer price at full cost only

3.4 If the transfer price is at full cost, A in our example would have 'sales' to B of £6,000 (costs of £12,000 × 50%). This would be a cost to B, as follows.

	A		B		Company as a whole
	£	£	£	£	£
Open market sales		8,000		24,000	32,000
Transfer sales		6,000		-	
Total sales, inc transfers		14,000		24,000	
Transfer costs			6,000		
Own costs	12,000		10,000		22,000
Total costs, inc transfers		12,000		16,000	
Profit		2,000		8,000	10,000

The transfer sales of A are self-cancelling with the transfer costs of B so that total profits are unaffected by the transfer items. The transfer price simply spreads the total profit of £10,000 between A and B.

3.5 The obvious drawback to the transfer price at cost is that **A makes no profit** on its work, and the manager of division A would much prefer to sell output on the open market to earn a profit, rather than transfer to B, regardless of whether or not transfers to B would be in the best interests of the company as a whole. Division A needs a profit on its transfers in order to be motivated to supply B; therefore transfer pricing at cost is inconsistent with the use of a profit centre accounting system.

Transfer price at full cost plus

3.6 If the transfers are at cost plus a margin of, say, 25%, A's sales to B would be £7,500 (£12,000 × 50% × 1.25).

	A		B		Total
	£	£	£	£	£
Open market sales		8,000		24,000	32,000
Transfer sales		7,500		-	
		15,500		24,000	
Transfer costs			7,500		
Own costs	12,000		10,000		22,000
		12,000		17,500	
Profit		3,500		6,500	10,000

3.7 Compared to a transfer price at cost, **A gains some profit** at the expense of B. However, A makes a bigger profit on external sales in this case because the profit mark-up of 25% is less than the profit mark-up on open market sales. The choice of 25% as a profit mark-up was arbitrary and unrelated to external market conditions.

Divisional autonomy, performance measurement and corporate profit maximisation

3.8 In the above case the transfer price **fails on all three criteria** for judgement.

(a) Arguably, it does not give A fair revenue or charge B a reasonable cost, and so their profit **performance** is distorted. It would certainly be unfair, for example, to compare A's profit with B's profit.

(b) Given this unfairness it is likely that the **autonomy** of each of the divisional managers is under threat. If they cannot agree on what is a fair split of the external profit a decision will have to be imposed from above.

(c) It would seem to give A an incentive to sell more goods externally and transfer less to B. This may or may not be in the best interests of the **company as a whole**.

Question 2

Suppose, in the example, that the cost per unit of A's output is £9 in variable costs and £6 in fixed costs. B's own costs are £25 including a fixed element of £10. What is the minimum price that B should charge for its products to break even?

Answer

A produces £12,000/(£9 + £6) = 800 units and transfers half of them to B for £6,000. The cost for each unit that B buys is therefore £6,000/400 = £15. From B's perspective this is a **variable** cost. B's costs are as follows.

	Cost per unit
	£
Variable cost: transfers from A	15
Own variable costs	15
	30

From B's perspective it must charge more than £30 per unit to earn a contribution. However, from the overall perspective, £6 of the 'variable' cost of transfers is **fixed**. The variable cost is really £9 + £15 = £24, and any price above this will earn a contribution for the organisation as a whole.

Transfer price at variable cost

3.9 A variable cost approach entails charging the variable cost that has been incurred by the supplying division to the receiving division. As above, we shall suppose that A's cost per unit is £15, of which £6 is fixed and £9 variable.

	A		B		Company as a whole	
	£	£	£	£	£	£
Market sales		8,000		24,000		32,000
Transfer sales (£6,000 × 9/15)		3,600		-		
		11,600		24,000		
Transfer costs	-		3,600			
Own variable costs	7,200		6,000		13,200	
Own fixed costs	4,800		4,000		8,800	
Total costs and transfers		12,000		13,600		22,000
(Loss)/Profit		(400)		10,400		10,000

3.10 This result is **deeply unsatisfactory** for the manager of division A who could make an additional £4,400 (£(8,000 – 3,600)) profit if no goods were transferred to division B. For the company overall, however, this action would cause a large fall in profit, because division B could make no sales at all.

3.11 The problem is that with a transfer price at variable cost the **supplying division does not cover its fixed costs**.

Fixed costs and transfer pricing

3.12 There are a number of ways in which this problem could be overcome.

(a) Each division can be given a **share** of the overall contribution earned by the organisation, but it is probably necessary to decide what the shares should be centrally, undermining **divisional autonomy**. Alternatively central management could impose a range within which the transfer price should fall, and allow divisional managers to **negotiate** what they felt was a fair price between themselves.

(b) A second method is to use a **two-part charging system**: transfer prices are set at variable cost and once a year there is a transfer of a fixed fee to the supplying division, representing an allowance for its fixed costs. Care is needed with this approach. It risks sending the message to the supplying division that it need not control its fixed costs because the company will **subsidise any inefficiencies**. On the other hand, if fixed costs are incurred because spare capacity is kept available for the needs of other divisions it is reasonable to expect those other divisions to pay a fee if they 'booked' that capacity in advance but later failed to utilise it. The main problem with this approach once more is that it is likely to conflict with **divisional autonomy**.

(c) A third possibility is a system of **dual pricing**. Be careful not to confuse this term with 'two-part' transfer pricing. Dual pricing means that two separate transfer prices are used.

  (i) For the transfer of goods from the supplying division to the receiving division the transfer price is set at variable cost. This ensures that the receiving division makes optimal **decisions**.

  (ii) For the purposes of **reporting results** the transfer price is based on the *total* costs of the transferring division, thus avoiding the possibility of reporting a loss.

  This method is not widely used in practice.

(d) One final possibility that may be worth mentioning. Given that the problems are caused by the divisional structure, might it not be better to address the **structure**, for example by **merging the two divisions**, or ceasing to treat the transferring division as a profit centre. This may not be practical. Some would argue that the benefits of decentralisation in terms of motivation outweigh any costs that might arise due to slight inefficiencies.

Standard cost versus actual cost

3.13 When a transfer price is based on cost, **standard cost** should be used, not actual cost. A transfer of actual cost would give no incentive to **control costs**, because they could all be passed on. Actual cost-*plus* transfer prices might even encourage the manager of A to overspend, because this would increase the divisional profit, even though the company as a whole (and division B) suffers.

3.14 Suppose, for example, that A's costs should have been £12,000, but actually were £16,000. Transfers (50% of output) would cost £8,000 actual, and the cost plus transfer price is at a margin of 25% (£8,000 × 125% = £10,000).

	A £	A £	B £	B £	Total £
Market sales		8,000		24,000	32,000
Transfer sales		10,000		-	
		18,000		24,000	
Transfer costs		-	10,000		
Own costs	16,000		10,000		26,000
		16,000		20,000	
Profit		2,000		4,000	6,000

A's overspending by £4,000 has reduced the total profits from £10,000 to £6,000.

3.15 In this example, B must bear much of the cost of A's overspending, which is clearly unsatisfactory for responsibility accounting. If, however, the transfer price were at standard cost plus instead of actual cost plus, the transfer sales would have been £7,500, regardless of A's overspending.

	A £	A £	B £	B £	Total £
Market sales		8,000		24,000	32,000
Transfer sales		7,500		-	
		15,500		24,000	
Transfer costs		-	7,500		
Own costs	16,000		10,000		26,000
		16,000		17,500	
Profit/(loss)		(500)		6,500	6,000

The entire cost of the overspending by A of £4,000 is now borne by division A itself as a comparison with the figures in Paragraph 3.14 will show.

Question 3

Why has A's profit fallen by £2,500, not £4,000?

Answer

A was already bearing 50% of its overspending. The fall in profit is £2,000 × 125% = £2,500, which represents the other 50% of its over spending and the loss of the profit margin on transfers to B.

Planning and operational variances and transfer prices

3.16 Using standard costs has a possible drawback in that the standard may become **out of date**, for example due to increases in material prices or other factors beyond the control of the transferor division. This could benefit either party, depending upon whether the standard cost rose or fell.

3.17 To avoid this eventuality transfer prices could be revised on the basis of **planning and operational variances** (see Chapter 13). Changes in the transferor division's costs that are beyond its control will be reported as planning variances and reflected in a revised transfer price. Operational inefficiencies in the transferor division will be reported as operational variances and the consequences will not be passed on.

Market conditions: no external market

3.18 So far we have considered the use of cost-based approaches where the following factors applied.

(a) There was a **limit on the maximum output** of the supplying division.

(b) There was a **limit** to the amount that could be sold in the **intermediate market**.

3.19 We found that a **variable cost** based approach led to the **best decisions** for the organisation overall, but that this was **beset with problems** in maintaining divisional autonomy and measuring divisional performance fairly.

3.20 We shall now consider whether this finding changes in different conditions. We shall remove the limit on output and demand for the final product, but assume that there is *no* intermediate market at all.

3.21 EXAMPLE: UNLIMITED CAPACITY AND NO INTERMEDIATE MARKET

Motivate Ltd has two profit centres, P and Q. P transfers *all* its output to Q. The variable cost of output from P is £5 per unit, and fixed costs are £1,200 per month. Additional processing costs in Q are £4 per unit for variable costs, plus fixed costs of £800. Budgeted production is 400 units per month, and the output of Q sells for £15 per unit. The transfer price is to be based on standard full cost plus. From what *range* of prices should the transfer price be selected, in order to motivate the managers of both profit centres to both increase output and reduce costs?

3.22 SOLUTION

Any transfer price based on **standard** cost plus will motivate managers to cut costs, because favourable variances between standard costs and actual costs will be credited to the division's profits. Managers of each division will also be willing to increase output above the budget of 400 units provided that it is profitable to do so; that is:

(a) in P, provided that the transfer price exceeds the variable cost of £5 per unit;

(b) in Q, provided that the transfer price is less than the difference between the fixed selling price (£15) and the variable costs in Q itself (£4). This amount of £11 (£15 – £4) is sometimes called **net marginal revenue**.

The range of prices is therefore between £5.01 and £10.99.

3.23 Let's do a check. Suppose the transfer price is £9. With absorption based on the **budgeted** output of 400 units what would divisional profits be if output and sales are 400 units or 500 units?

3.24 Overheads per unit are £1,200/400 = £3, so the full cost of sales is £(5 + 3) = £8 in division P. In division Q, full cost is £(4 + 2) = £6, plus transfer costs of £9.

At 400 units:

	P £	Q £	Total £
Sales	-	6,000	6,000
Transfer sales	3,600	-	
Transfer costs	-	(3,600)	
Own full cost of sales	(3,200)	(2,400)	(5,600)
	400	0	400
Under/over absorbed overhead	0	0	0
Profit/(loss)	400	0	400

At 500 units:

	P £	Q £	Total £
Sales	-	7,500	7,500
Transfer sales	4,500	-	-
Transfer costs	-	(4,500)	-
Own full cost of sales	(4,000)	(3,000)	(7,000)
	500	0	500
Over absorbed overhead (100 × £3; 100 × £2)	300	200	500
Profit/(loss)	800	200	1,000

3.25 Increasing output improves the profit performance of both divisions and the company as a whole, and so decisions on output by the two divisions are likely to be **goal congruent**.

Summary

3.26 To summarise the transfer price should be set in the range where:

Variable cost in supplying division $\leq$ Selling price minus variable costs (net marginal revenue) in the receiving division

4 OPPORTUNITY COST AND TRANSFER PRICES

4.1 Ideally, a transfer price should be set that enables the individual **divisions** to maximise their profits at a level of output that maximises profit for the **company as a whole**. The transfer price which achieves this is unlikely to be a market-based transfer price (if there is one) and is also unlikely to be a simple cost plus based price.

> **Exam focus point**
>
> Candidates in the **December 1997** exam had to discuss the acceptability of various bases for transferring the costs of a service division. The general rule was also examined in **December 1999**.

An opportunity cost approach

4.2 If optimum decisions are to be taken transfer prices should reflect **opportunity costs.**

   (a) If profit centre managers are given sufficient autonomy to make their own output and selling decisions, and at the same time their performance is judged by the company according to the profits they earn, they will be keenly aware of all the commercial opportunities.

(b) If transfers are made for the good of the company as a whole, the commercial benefits to the company ought to be **shared** between the participating divisions.

4.3 Transfer prices can therefore be reached by:

(a) recognising the levels of output, external sales and internal transfers that are best for the **company as a whole**; and

(b) arriving at a transfer price that ensures that all divisions maximise their profits at this same level of output. The transfer price should therefore be such that there is **not a more profitable opportunity** for individual divisions. This in turn means that the opportunity costs of transfer should be covered by the transfer price.

> **Exam focus point**
> This general rule of transfer pricing had to be used to set point-maximising transfer prices in three situations in the **December 1998** exam.

Limiting factors and transfer pricing

4.4 When an intermediate resource is in short supply and acts as a limiting factor on production in the transferring division, the **cost of transferring** an item is the variable cost of production plus the contribution obtainable from using the scarce resource in its next most profitable way.

4.5 EXAMPLE: SCARCE RESOURCES

Suppose, for example, that division A is a profit centre that produces three items, X, Y and Z. Each item has an external market.

	X	Y	Z
External market price, per unit	£48	£46	£40
Variable cost of production in division A	£33	£24	£28
Labour hours required per unit in division A	3	4	2

Product Y can be transferred to division B, but the maximum quantity that might be required for transfer is 300 units of Y.

The maximum **external** sales are 800 units of X, 500 units of Y and 300 units of Z.

Instead of receiving transfers of product Y from division A, division B could buy similar units of product Y on the open market at a slightly cheaper price of £45 per unit.

What should the transfer price be for each unit if the total labour hours available in division A are 3,800 hours or 5,600 hours?

4.6 SOLUTION

Hours required to meet maximum demand:

External sales:	Hours
X (3 × 800)	2,400
Y (4 × 500)	2,000
Z (2 × 300)	600
	5,000
Transfers of Y (4 × 300)	1,200
	6,200

Contribution from external sales:

	X	Y	Z
Contribution per unit	£15	£22	£12
Labour hours per unit	3 hrs	4 hrs	2 hrs
Contribution per labour hour	£5.00	£5.50	£6.00
Priority for selling	3rd	2nd	1st
Total hours needed	2,400	2,000	600

(a) If only **3,800 hours** of labour are available, division A would choose, **ignoring transfers to B**, to sell:

	Hours
300 Z (maximum)	600
500 Y (maximum)	2,000
	2,600
400 X (balance)	1,200
	3,800

To transfer 300 units of Y to division B would involve forgoing the sale of 400 units of X because 1,200 hours would be needed to make the transferred units.

Opportunity cost of transferring units of Y, and the appropriate transfer price:

	£ per unit
Variable cost of making Y	24
Opportunity cost (contribution of £5 per hour available from selling X externally): benefit forgone (4 hours × £5)	20
Transfer price for Y	44

The transfer price for Y should, in this case, be less than the external market price.

(b) If **5,600 hours** are available, there is enough time to meet the full demand for external sales (5,000) and still have 600 hours of spare capacity, before consideration of transfers. However, 1,200 hours are needed to produce the full amount of Y for transfer (300 units), and so 600 hours need to be devoted to producing Y for transfer instead of producing X for external sale.

This means that the **opportunity cost** of transfer is this.

(i) The variable cost of 150 units of Y produced in the 600 'spare' hours (£24/unit).

(ii) The variable cost of production of the remaining 150 units of Y (£24 per unit), plus the **contribution forgone** from the external sales of X that could have been produced in the 600 hours now devoted to producing Y for transfer (£5 per labour hour). An average transfer price per unit could be negotiated for the transfer of the full 300 units (see below), which works out at £34 per unit.

	£
150 units × £24	3,600
150 units × £24	3,600
600 hours × £5 per hour	3,000
Total for 300 units	10,200

In both cases, the opportunity cost of receiving transfers for division B is the price it would have to pay to purchase Y externally - £45 per unit. Thus:

Maximum labour hours in A	Opportunity cost to A of transfer	Opportunity cost to B of transfer
	£	£
3,800	44	45
5,600	34 (average)	45

In each case any price between the two opportunity costs would be sufficient to persuade B to order 300 units of Y from division A and for division A to agree to transfer them.

Question 4

Try to explain **in your own words** why transfer prices should reflect opportunity costs.

If you cannot do so, start reading this section again. You probably would not be able to do a Paper 9 transfer pricing question unless you can give this explanation.

4.7   OPTIMAL TRANSFER PRICES: AN EXTENDED EXAMPLE

A group of highly integrated divisions wishes to be advised as to how it should set transfer prices for the following inter-divisional transactions:

(a)   Division L sells all its output of product LX to Division M. To one kilogram of LX, Division M adds other direct materials and processes it to produce two kilograms of product MX which it sells outside the group. The price of MX is influenced by volume offered and the following cost and revenue data are available:

Division L

The variable costs per kg of LX are £4 of direct materials and £2 of direct labour.

The following cost increases are expected at different levels of production per annum:

Direct materials	At 60,000 kg pa increase to £5.00 per kg
	At 90,000 kg pa increase to £5.50 per kg
	At 100,000 kg pa increase to £6.00 per kg
Direct labour	At 80,000 kg pa increases to £2.50 per kg
	At 100,000 kg pa increases to £3.00 per kg

Fixed overhead	Under 70,000 kg	£210,000 pa
	70,000 - 79,999 kg	£260,000 pa
	80,000 - 89,999 kg	£280,000 pa
	90,000 or more kg	£310,000 pa

Division M

To produce one kilogram of product MX, the variable cost incurred for each half-kilogram of LX used is made up of £1.50 of other direct materials and £3.50 processing cost.

The following cost increases are expected at different levels of production of MX per annum:

Other direct materials	At 140,000 kg pa increase to £1.75 per kg
	At 160,000 kg pa increase to £2.00 per kg
Processing	At 180,000 kg pa increases to £4.00 per kg

		£
Fixed overhead	Under 120,000 kg	250,000 pa
	120,000 - 139,999 kg	280,000 pa
	140,000 - 159,999 kg	290,000 pa
	160,000 - 199,999 kg	320,000 pa
	200,000 or more kg	360,000 pa
Selling price	Up to 199,999 kg	£16.00 per kg
	200,000 or more kg	£15.50 per kg

(b) Division N manufactures two products, NA and NB, whose variable production cost and selling prices per unit are:

Product	NA		NB	
	£	£	£	£
Direct materials	8		5	
Direct labour	8		12	
Production cost		16		17
Selling price		32		50

Direct labour is paid at £4.00 per hour. Fixed overhead is £72,000 per annum and total capacity is 960,000 man-hours per annum.

Division N sells product NA either to Division P or outside the group and Division P can buy from either source. Product NB is sold only outside the group. When NA and NB are sold outside the group, variable selling costs of £1.00 and £3.00 per unit respectively are incurred.

Required

(a) Recommend, with supporting calculations and explanations, the most appropriate narrow range of transfer price per kg for product LX between the two divisions; assume that any changes in output are in steps of 10,000 kg of product LX and 20,000 kg of product MX.

(b) Recommend, with supporting calculations and explanations:

  (i) the most appropriate transfer price of product NA between Divisions N and P:

    (1) on the assumption that Division N can just sell all of, but no more than, its capacity;

    (2) on the assumption that Division N could sell more than its existing capacity, though the market price stays the same;

  (ii) in the case of (i) (2) above, what quantities of NA Division P should buy from Division N.

4.8 DISCUSSION AND SOLUTION

Part (a) of the question is long and the calculations might easily be confusing. The **ratio** of 1 kg of LX to 2 kg of MX also complicates the figure-work. It is probably tempting to calculate **unit contribution** rather than **unit net profit**, but in this case it is probably easier to work out unit full costs, because of the stepped changes in fixed costs.

Step 1. The first step in a solution is to work out **what is best for the group as a whole.**

MX costs and profits can be calculated on a unit basis first and then total profitability at each level of output derived.

	Quantity of MX ('000 kg)							
	100	*120*	*140*	*160*	*180*	*200*	*220*	*240*
Division L cost								
(1 kg LX per 2 kg MX)								
	£	£	£	£	£	£	£	£
Direct materials	2.00	2.50	2.50	2.50	2.75	3.00	3.00	3.00
Direct labour	1.00	1.00	1.00	1.25	1.25	1.50	1.50	1.50
Fixed overhead	2.10	1.75	1.86	1.75	1.72	1.55	1.41	1.29
Total	5.10	5.25	5.36	5.50	5.72	6.05	5.91	5.79
Division M costs								
Other materials	1.50	1.50	1.75	2.00	2.00	2.00	2.00	2.00
Processing cost	3.50	3.50	3.50	3.50	4.00	4.00	4.00	4.00
Fixed overhead	2.50	2.33	2.07	2.00	1.78	1.80	1.64	1.50
Total	7.50	7.33	7.32	7.50	7.78	7.80	7.64	7.50
Full unit cost	12.60	12.58	12.68	13.00	13.50	13.85	13.55	13.29
Sales price	16.00	16.00	16.00	16.00	16.00	15.50	15.50	15.50
Unit profit	3.40	3.42	3.32	3.00	2.50	1.65	1.95	2.21
Total profit (£000)	340	410	465	480	450	330	429	530

Below 200,000 kg, profit is maximised at 160,000 kg of MX (£480,000) but this profit figure is exceeded when output rises to 240,000 kg and beyond, by which time profit is rising by £100,000 per extra 20,000 kg of MX. Division M ought to make 240,000 kg or more of MX, up to capacity output.

Step 2. So how do we calculate the **ideal transfer price**? First of all, the transfer price must be **higher than £5.79** per ½ kg of LX, but **not more than £(5.79 + 2.21) = £8** per ½ kg of LX. At the lower price, Division L would make no profit at 240,000 kg of MX and at the higher price, Division M would make no profit.

Step 3. The selection of a transfer price is further complicated by the **changing unit costs** at lower levels of output. The transfer price must give each division an incentive not to want to restrict output to less than 240,000 kg of MX.

(a) Left to its own devices Division M will produce **140,000 kg** because its unit costs are minimised at this level. So Division M will be willing to offer Division L a transfer price that persuades it to produce 140,000 kg and this must at least cover Division L's unit costs at this level of £5.36.

(b) However, overall profit is maximised at the **240,000 kg** level, where unit costs for Division L are £0.43 (£5.79 - £5.36) higher.

$$240,000x > 140,000(x + 0.43)$$
$$100,000x > 60,200$$
$$x > 0.60$$

Our analysis suggests that unless Division L earns a unit profit of at least 60p, the division's manager will need a lot of persuading to increase output above 140,000 kg.

(c) In the case of Division M, a similar analysis can be applied. Unit costs are £0.18 per kg lower at 140,000 kg of output, and so if the unit profit at 240,000 kg is £y, we want a transfer price where:

$$240,000y > 140,000(y + 0.18)$$
$$100,000y > 25,200$$
$$y > 0.25$$

This suggests that unless Division M makes a profit per kg of at least 25p at 240,000 kg of output the division's manager might prefer to halt production and sales at 140,000 kg.

Step 4. The range of transfer prices per kg of MX is therefore narrower than the £5.79 to £8 range we began with. Division L should have a profit of at least £0.60 per kg of MX at 240,000 kg of output and so the minimum transfer price should be (£5.79 + £0.6) **£6.39** per kg of MX. Division M should have a profit of at least £0.25 and so the maximum transfer price should be (£8 – £0.25) **£7.75**.

Conclusion for Division L and Division M. The transfer price per kg of MX should be in the range £6.39 - £7.75, so that the transfer price range per kg of LX (2:1) is £12.78 - £15.50.

Let's now turn our attention to part (b). The situation facing Division N is probably a bit easier to understand.

(a) If Division N can sell all of its capacity but no more, the **opportunity cost** of transferring NA instead of selling it will be the external revenue per unit of NA less the variable selling costs - ie £(32 – 1) = £31 per unit.

(b) In part (2) of the question, N's existing capacity acts as a constraint on total output: labour hours become a scarce resource.

	NA	NB
	£	£
Contribution before variable selling costs	16	33
Variable selling costs	1	3
Net contribution	15	30
Labour hours per unit	2	3
Contribution per labour hour	£7.50	£10

Transferring NA to Division P (rather than making NB) would force Division N to forgo contribution of £10 per labour hour, and the transfer price of NA should reflect this opportunity cost:

	£
Variable cost of making NA	16
Opportunity cost of lost contribution on NB (2 hrs × £10)	20
Transfer price of NA, per kg	36

(c) Since the external market price of NA is only £32, Division P should buy all its supplies externally, and buy nothing from Division N. This would leave Division N free to make NB exclusively, and earn a contribution of £10 per labour hour on all its external sales.

Linear programming and transfer pricing

4.9 Where the decision is subject to a **range of limiting factors** rather than just one, the optimum production programme can be devised using a **linear programming** model. The output from the model would provide a means of calculating the ideal transfer price, because it indicates the **shadow price** of scarce resources. The shadow price is the **opportunity cost** of a scarce resource, the amount of benefit forgone by not having the availability of the extra resources.

5   NEGOTIATED TRANSFER PRICES

5.1   A transfer price based on opportunity cost is often **difficult to identify**, for lack of suitable information about costs and revenues in individual divisions. In this case it is likely that transfer prices will be set by means of **negotiation**. The agreed price may be finalised from a mixture of accounting arithmetic, politics and compromise.

5.2   The process of negotiation will be improved if **adequate information** about each division's costs and revenues is made available to the other division involved in the negotiation. By having a free flow of cost and revenue information, it will be easier for divisional managers to identify opportunities for improving profits, to the benefit of both divisions involved in the transfer.

5.3   A negotiating system that might enable **goal congruent plans** to be agreed between profit centres is as follows.

(a)   Profit centres **submit plans** for output and sales to head office, as a preliminary step in preparing the annual budget.

(b)   Head office **reviews these plans**, together with any other information it may obtain. Amendments to divisional plans might be discussed with the divisional managers.

(c)   Once divisional plans are acceptable to head office and **consistent** with each other, head office might let the divisional managers arrange budgeted transfers and transfer prices.

(d)   Where divisional plans are **inconsistent** with each other, head office might try to establish a plan that would maximise the profits of the company as a whole. Divisional managers would then be asked to negotiate budgeted transfers and transfer prices on this basis.

(e)   If divisional managers fail to agree a transfer price between themselves, a head office **'arbitration' manager** or team would be referred to for an opinion or a decision.

(f)   Divisions **finalise their budgets** within the framework of agreed transfer prices and resource constraints.

(g)   Head office **monitors the profit performance** of each division.

Chapter roundup

- Transfer prices are a way of promoting **divisional autonomy**, ideally without prejudicing the **divisional performance** measurement or discouraging overall **corporate profit maximisation**.

- They may be based on **market price** where there is a market.

- If not, problems arise with **cost-based** transfer prices because one party or the other is liable to perceive them as unfair.

- **Fixed costs** in the supplying division can be accounted for in a number of ways to ensure that it at least breaks even.

- **Standard costs** should be used for transfer prices to avoid encouraging inefficiency in the supplying division.

- If a **profit-maximising output** level has been established the transfer price should be set such that there is **not a more profitable opportunity** for individual divisions. In other words transfer prices should include **opportunity costs** of transfer.

- The problem with this approach is that it entails collecting all the relevant divisional **data** centrally and **imposing** a transfer price, undermining divisional autonomy.

- In practice, **negotiated** transfer prices, **market-based** transfer prices and **full cost-based** transfer prices are the methods normally used.

Quick quiz

1 List five possible bases of a transfer price. (see para 1.2)

2 What three criteria should a transfer price ideally fulfil? (1.3 - 1.8)

3 Why might an *adjusted* market price be used as a transfer price? (2.4 - 2.5)

4 What are the disadvantages of market value transfer prices? (2.6)

5 What is the drawback of setting a transfer price at full cost? (3.5)

6 How can supplying divisions cover their fixed costs by means of transfer prices? (3.12)

7 Why should actual costs not be used to set transfer prices? (3.13)

8 Where there is no external market for an intermediate product in what range should the transfer price be set? (3.26)

9 Why should transfer prices reflect opportunity costs? (4.2 - 4.3)

10 How might a linear programming model be used in transfer pricing? (4.9)

11 Describe a negotiating system for transfer prices. (5.3)

Question to try	Level	Marks	Time
17	Exam standard	35	63 mins

Chapter 17

DIVISIONAL PERFORMANCE EVALUATION

Chapter topic list	Syllabus reference
1 Performance measures in divisionalised organisations	1(b), 3(c)
2 ROI and decision making	1(b), 3(c)
3 Residual income	1(b), 3(c), 4(c)
4 Incompatible signals - solutions to the problem	1(b), 3(c), 4(c)
5 Multiple measures of performance	1(b), 3(c)
6 Divisional autonomy versus corporate goal congruence	1(b), 3(c)

Introduction

In this, the last chapter of the Study Text, we will be looking at the ways in which both the performance of divisions as a whole and the performance of their managers can be measured. The two most important methods of appraisal that we will be considering are **return on investment (ROI)** and **residual income (RI)**. You may think these measures are fairly easy to calculate but they are quite seriously flawed, especially when compared with **DCF techniques**.

When you complete this chapter give yourself a pat on the back. You've completed all 17 chapters. But how much can *you* remember of what was covered in Chapter 1?

Core areas of the syllabus identified by the examiner and covered in this chapter: **financial performance measures including ROI, RI and NPV; balance between divisional autonomy and corporate profit maximisation; balanced scorecard and performance pyramid approaches to performance measurement.**

1   PERFORMANCE MEASURES IN DIVISIONALISED ORGANISATIONS

1.1   Our concern in this chapter is with the performance of **divisions as a whole,** as compared with the performance of other divisions as a whole, and/or in terms of what they contribute to the organisation as a whole.

1.2   Divisions can be assessed and compared in **non-financial** terms but such measures have been discussed elsewhere in this text and the discussion does not need to be repeated here. Our concern is now exclusively with **financial** performance measurement, and more particularly with **profitability.**

Return on investment (ROI)

1.3   Return on investment (ROI), also known as **return on capital employed (ROCE)**, is generally regarded as the key financial performance ratio. The main reasons for its widespread use as a measure of return on investment are that:

(a) it ties in directly with the **accounting process**, and is identifiable from the profit and loss account and balance sheet;

(b) even more importantly, ROI is the **only** measure of performance available (apart from residual income) by which the return on investment for a division or company **as a single entire unit** (or collection of assets) can be measured.

KEY TERM

Return on investment (ROI) shows how much profit has been made in relation to the amount of capital invested and is calculated as profit ÷ capital employed.

1.4 Suppose a company has two investment centres A and B, with the following results.

	A £	B £
Profit	60,000	30,000
Capital employed	400,000	120,000
ROI	15%	25%

1.5 Investment centre A has made double the profits of investment centre B, and in terms of profits alone has therefore been more 'successful'. However, B has achieved its profits with a much lower capital investment, and so has earned a much higher ROI. This suggests that B has been a more successful investment than A.

1.6 ROI can be measured in different ways, such as profit after depreciation as a percentage of **net assets** employed or profit after depreciation as a percentage of **gross assets** employed.

Return on net assets

1.7 This is the most common method but it presents a problem. If an investment centre maintains the same annual profit, and keeps the same assets without a policy of regular fixed asset replacement, its ROI will increase year by year as the assets get older. This can give a **false impression of improving performance** over time.

Exam focus point

Exam questions typically focus on why various measures may give misleading impressions, and on methods of resolving the problem of conflicting signals given by different measures.

1.8 For example, the results of investment centre X, with a policy of straight-line depreciation of assets over a 5-year period, might be as follows.

Year	Fixed assets at cost £'000	Depreciation in the year £'000	Net book value (mid year) £'000	Working capital £'000	Capital employed £'000	Profit £'000	ROI
0	100			10	110		
1	100	20	90	10	100	10	10%
2	100	20	70	10	80	10	12.5%
3	100	20	50	10	60	10	16.7%
4	100	20	30	10	40	10	25%
5	100	20	10	10	20	10	50%

1.9 This table of figures is intended to show that an investment centre can improve its ROI year by year, simply by allowing its fixed assets to depreciate, and there could be a **disincentive** to investment centre managers to **reinvest** in new or replacement assets, because the centre's ROI would probably fall if new assets were bought.

Question 1

A new company has fixed assets of £460,000 which will be depreciated to nil on a straight line basis over 10 years. Working capital will consistently be £75,000, and annual profit will consistently be £30,000. If ROI is measured as return on net assets what is its ROI in year 2 and year 6?

Answer

6.4% in year 2
10.6% in year 6

1.10 A further disadvantage of measuring ROI as profit divided by net assets is that it is **not easy to compare** fairly the performance of **different investment centres**.

1.11 For example, suppose that we have two investment centres:

	Investment centre P		Investment centre Q	
	£	£	£	£
Working capital		20,000		20,000
Fixed assets at cost	230,000		230,000	
Accumulated depreciation	170,000		10,000	
Net book value		60,000		220,000
Capital employed		80,000		240,000
Profit		£24,000		£24,000
ROI		30%		10%

1.12 Investment centres P and Q have the same amount of working capital, the same value of fixed assets at cost, and the same profit. But P's fixed assets have been depreciated by a much bigger amount (presumably P's fixed assets are much older than Q's) and so P's ROI is three times the size of Q's ROI. The conclusion might be that P has performed much better than Q. This comparison, however, would not be 'fair', because the difference in performance might be entirely attributable to the age of their fixed assets.

1.13 The **arguments in favour** using net book values for calculating ROI are these.

(a) It is the '**normally accepted**' method of calculating ROI.

(b) In reality firms are continually **buying new fixed assets** to replace old ones that wear out, and so on the whole, the total net book value of all fixed assets together will remain fairly constant (assuming nil inflation and nil growth).

Return on gross assets

1.14 We could measure ROI as return on gross assets. This would remove the problem of ROI increasing over time as fixed assets get older.

1.15 If a company acquired a fixed asset costing £40,000, which it intends to depreciate by £10,000 pa for 4 years, and if the asset earns a profit of £8,000 pa after depreciation, ROI might be calculated on net book values or gross values, as follows.

Year	Profit £	Net book value (mid-year value) £	ROI based on NBV	Gross value £	ROI based on gross value
1	8,000	35,000	22.9%	40,000	20%
2	8,000	25,000	32.0%	40,000	20%
3	8,000	15,000	53.3%	40,000	20%
4	8,000	5,000	160.0%	40,000	20%

1.16 The ROI based on **net book value** shows an **increasing trend over time**, simply because the asset's value is falling as it is depreciated. The ROI based on **gross book value** suggests that the asset has performed **consistently** in each of the 4 years, which is probably a more valid conclusion.

Question 2

Repeat question 1, measuring ROI as return on gross assets.

Answer

5.6% in year 2
5.6% in year 6

1.17 However, using gross book values to measure ROI has its **disadvantages**. Most important of these is that measuring ROI as return on gross assets ignores the age factor, and does not distinguish between old and new assets.

(a) **Older** fixed assets usually cost **more to repair and maintain**. An investment centre with old assets may therefore have its profitability reduced by repair costs, and its ROI might *fall* over time as its assets get older and repair costs get bigger.

(b) **Inflation** and **technological change** alter the cost of fixed assets. If one investment centre has fixed assets bought ten years ago with a gross cost of £1 million, and another investment centre, in the same area of business operations, has fixed assets bought very recently for £1 million, the quantity and technological character of the fixed assets of the two investment centres are likely to be very different.

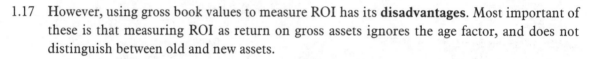

Exam focus point
Using various transfer price bases for a service division, candidates in the **December 1997** exam had to carry out numerous **easy ROCE calculations** and then discuss the acceptability of the charge bases to divisions and the organisation as a whole.

2 ROI AND DECISION MAKING

New investment

2.1 If investment centre performance is judged by ROI, we should expect that the managers of investment centres will probably decide to undertake **new capital investments** *only if* these new investments are likely to increase the ROI of their centre.

2.2 Suppose that an investment centre, A, currently makes a return of 40% on capital employed. The manager of centre A would probably only want to undertake new investments that promise to **yield a return of 40% or more**, otherwise the investment centre's overall ROI would fall. For example, if investment centre A currently has assets of £1,000,000 and expects to earn a profit of £400,000, how would the centre's manager view a new capital investment which would cost £250,000 and yield a profit of £75,000 pa?

	Without the new investment	*With the new investment*
Profit	£400,000	£475,000
Capital employed	£1,000,000	£1,250,000
ROI	40%	38%

The new investment would **reduce** the investment centre's ROI from 40% to 38%, and so the manager would probably decide **not to undertake** the new investment.

2.3 If the group of companies of which investment centre A is a part has a **target ROI** of, say, 25%, the new investment would presumably be seen as **beneficial for the group as a whole**. But even though it promises to yield a return of 75,000/250,000 = 30%, which is above the group's target ROI, it would still make investment centre A's results look worse. The manager of investment centre A in these circumstances, would be motivated to do not what is best for the organisation as a whole, but what is **best for his division**.

The target return for a group of companies

2.4 If a group sets a **target return** for the group as a whole, it might be group policy that investment projects should **only go ahead** if they promise to **earn at least the target return**.

2.5 For example, it might be group policy that:

(a) there should be **no new investment** by any subsidiary in the group unless it is expected to earn at least a 15% return;

(b) similarly, no fixed asset should be **disposed of** if the asset is currently earning a return in excess of 15% of its disposal value;

(c) investments which promise a return of **15% or more** ought to be undertaken (provided that the degree of uncertainty or risk in the project is acceptable).

2.6 A problem with such a policy is that even if investment decisions are based on a target **DCF rate of return**, actual performance can only ever be measured on the basis of an **accounting ROI**, which is by no means the same thing.

2.7 Suppose that an investment in a fixed asset would cost £100,000 and make a profit of £11,000 p.a. after depreciation. The asset would be depreciated by £25,000 pa for four years. It is group policy that investments must show a minimum return of 15%. The DCF net present value of this investment would just about be positive, and so the investment ought to be approved if group policy is adhered to.

Year	Cash flow (profit before dep'n)	Discount factor	Present value
	£	15%	£
0	(100,000)	1.000	(100,000)
1	36,000	0.870	31,320
2	36,000	0.756	27,216
3	36,000	0.658	23,688
4	36,000	0.572	20,592
		NPV	2,816

2.8 If the investment is measured year by year according to the accounting ROI it has earned, its return is less than 15% in year 1, but more than 15% in years 2, 3 and 4.

Year	Profit £	Net book value of equipment (mid-year value) £	ROCE
1	11,000	87,500	12.6%
2	11,000	62,500	17.6%
3	11,000	37,500	29.3%
4	11,000	12,500	88.0%

2.9 In view of the low accounting ROI in year 1, should the investment be undertaken or not?

(a) Strictly speaking, **investment decisions should be based on DCF yield**, and should not be guided by short-term accounting ROI.

(b) Even if accounting ROI is used as a guideline for investment decisions, ROI should be looked at **over the full life** of the investment, not just in the short term. In the short term (in the first year or so of a project's life) the accounting ROI is likely to be low because the net book value of the asset will still be high.

Question 3

Why are DCF techniques not commonly used?

Answer

Because they are perceived as being difficult to calculate and understand and because it is difficult in practice to establish an accurate cost of capital.

DCF v ROI

2.10 In spite of the superiority of DCF yield over accounting ROI as a means of evaluating investments, and in spite of the wisdom of taking a longer term view rather than a short-term view with investments, it is nevertheless an uncomfortable fact that the consideration of short-run accounting **ROI does often influence investment decisions.**

2.11 In our example, it is conceivable that the group's management might disapprove of the project because of its low accounting ROI in year 1. This approach is short-sighted, but it nevertheless can make some sense to a company or group of companies which has to show a satisfactory profit and ROI in its **published accounts** each year, to keep its **shareholders** satisfied with performance.

2.12 A similar mis-guided decision would occur where a divisional manager is worried about the low ROI of his division, and decides to reduce his investment by **scrapping some machinery** which is not currently in use. The reduction in both depreciation charges and assets would immediately improve the ROI. When the machinery is eventually required the manager would then be obliged to buy new equipment. Such a situation may seem bizarre, but it does occur in real life.

2.13 ROI should not be used to guide management decisions but there is a difficult motivational problem. If **management performance** is measured in terms of ROI, any decisions which benefit the company in the long term but which reduce the ROI in the immediate short term would reflect badly on the manager's reported performance. In other words, good investment decisions would make a manager's performance seem worse than if the wrong investment decision were taken instead.

2.14 EXTENDED EXAMPLE: ROI AND DECISION-MAKING

At the end of 20X3, Division S (part of a group) had a gross book value of fixed assets of £300,000, net current assets of £40,000 and net profit before tax of £64,000.

The fixed assets of Division S consist of five separate items each costing £60,000 which are depreciated to zero over 5 years on a straight-line basis. For each of the past years on 31 December it has bought a replacement for the asset that has just been withdrawn and it proposes to continue this policy. Because of technological advances the asset manufacturer has been able to keep his prices constant over time. The group's cost of capital is 15%.

Required

Assuming that, except where otherwise stated, there are no changes in the above data, you are required to deal with the following *separate situations*.

(a) Division S has the opportunity of an investment costing £60,000, and yielding an annual profit of £10,000.

    (i)   Calculate its new ROI if the investment were undertaken.

    (ii)   State whether you would recommend that the investment be undertaken.

(b) Division S has the opportunity of selling, at a price equal to its written-down book value of £24,000, an asset that currently earns £3,900 p.a.

    (i)   Calculate its new ROI if the asset were sold.

    (ii)   State, with brief reasons, whether you would recommend the sale of the asset.

2.15 SOLUTION IN GENERAL

The question does not state whether capital employed should include a valuation of fixed assets at gross historical cost or at net book value. It is assumed that net book value is required. It is also assumed that the fixed asset which has just been bought as a replacement on 31 December 20X3 has not been depreciated at all.

> **Exam focus point**
>
> **Paper 9 questions** usually give you information such as this, but if not, it is worth stating assumptions such as these at the start of your solution. If the problem has not been fully defined, clarify your own assumptions and definitions for the benefit of the marker of your exam script!

The gross book value of the five fixed asset items is 5 × £60,000 = £300,000.

	£
Net book value of asset just bought on 31.12.X3	60,000
NBV of asset bought 1 year earlier	48,000
NBV of asset bought 2 years earlier	36,000
NBV of asset bought 3 years earlier	24,000
NBV of asset bought 4 years earlier	12,000
NBV of all 5 fixed assets at 31.12.X3	180,000
Net current assets	40,000
Total capital employed, Division S	220,000

2.16 SOLUTION TO PART (a)

Part (i)

Part (a) of the solution should begin with a **comparison** of the existing ROI ((64/220) × 100% = 29.1%), which is presumably the typical ROI achieved each year under the current policy of asset replacement, and the ROI with the new investment.

For the ROI with the new investment it is **assumed** that the full asset cost of £60,000 should be included in the capital employed, although the asset will obviously be depreciated over time. It is also assumed that the additional profit of £10,000 is net of depreciation charges. The ROI with the new investment = ((64 + 10)/(220 + 60)) × 100% = 26.4%.

> **Exam focus point**
> A **Paper 9** question might specify a variety of different assumptions, to make the calculation more complex. As always, stay calm and follow the instructions given in the question.

If the investment centre manager based his investment decisions on whether an investment would increase or reduce his ROI, he would not want to make the additional investment. This investment has a **marginal ROI** of (10/60) × 100% = 16.7%, which is **above** the group's **cost of capital** but **below** Division S's **current ROI** of 29.1%. Making the investment would therefore lower the Division's average ROI.

This example illustrates the weakness of ROI as a guide to investment decisions. An investment centre manager might want an investment to show a good ROI from year 1, when the new investment has a high net book value. In the case of Division S, the **average net book value** of the asset over its full life will be 50% of £60,000 = £30,000, and so the **average ROI on the investment over time** will be (£10,000/£30,000) × 100% = 33.3%. Presumably, however, the Division S manager would not want to wait so long to earn a good ROI, and wants to protect his division's performance in the short run as well as the long run.

Part (ii)

The question is clearly calling for a recommendation about the investment, and in the absence of full information, two approaches to a solution could be taken.

(a) The investment's year 1 ROI of 16.7% exceeds the group's cost of capital of 15% and so it is likely to be a worthwhile investment.

(b) If we assumed a project life of 5 years, which is the same as the life of the other fixed assets, and a nil residual value, the minimum annual cash flow required to achieve a return of 15% would be (using DCF tables) £60,000/3.352 = £17,900 pa.

The investment would yield an annual profit of £10,000 after depreciation of £12,000 p.a. and so annual **cash** profits would be £22,000. This exceeds the minimum needed for a 15% yield, and so the investment should go ahead.

2.17 SOLUTION TO PART (b)

Part (b) of the question deals with a **disinvestment** proposal, compared to an acquisition in part (a). The same basic principles apply.

ROI if the asset is sold = ((64 – 3.9)/(220 – 24)) × 100% = 30.7%

This compares favourably with the Division's current average ROI of 29.1%, and so if the manager of Division S made his divestment decisions on the basis of ROI, he would presumably decide to get rid of the asset.

However, the decision would be misguided, because decisions should not be based on the short-term effects on ROI.

The asset which would be sold earns a ROI of $3.9/24 \times 100\% = 16.3\%$ which is higher than the group's cost of capital, but lower than the Division S average.

On the assumption that the asset would earn £3,900 after depreciation for the 2 remaining years of its life, its ROI next year would be $3.9/12 \times 100\% = 32.5\%$

More importantly, the **cash flows** involved in the decision would be as follows.

Cash profits = £3,900 + £12,000 (depreciation) = £15,900 p.a.

Year	Cash flow	Discount factor	Present value
	£	15%	£
0	(24,000)*	1.000	(24,000)
1 - 2	15,900	1.626	25,853
		NPV	1,853

* Sale price forgone if asset is not sold.

The correct decision is **not to sell the asset**, because the present value of cash flows is positive.

3 RESIDUAL INCOME

3.1 An alternative way of measuring the performance of an investment centre, instead of using ROI, is residual income (RI).

KEY TERM

Residual income is a measure of a division's profits after deducting a notional or imputed interest cost.

- The divisional profit is after deducting depreciation on capital equipment.

- The imputed cost of capital might be the organisation's cost of borrowing or its weighted average cost of capital.

Question 4

A division with capital employed of £400,000 currently earns a ROI of 22%. It can make an additional investment of £50,000 for a 5 year life with nil residual value. The average net profit from this investment would be £12,000 after depreciation. The division's cost of capital is 14%. Calculate the residual income before and after the investment.

Answer

	Before investment	After investment
	£	£
Divisional profit	88,000	100,000
Imputed interest		
(400,000 × 0.14)	56,000	
(450,000 × 0.14)		63,000
Residual income	32,000	37,000

The advantages and weaknesses of RI compared with ROI

3.2 The **advantages** of using RI are as follows.

   (a) Residual income will **increase** when investments earning above the cost of capital are undertaken and when investments earning below the cost of capital are eliminated.

   (b) Residual income is **more flexible** since a different cost of capital can be applied to investments with different **risk** characteristics.

3.3 The **weaknesses** of RI are that it does not facilitate **comparisons** between investment centres and it does not relate the **size** of a centre's **income** to the **size** of the **investment**.

RI versus ROI: marginally profitable investments

3.4 Residual income will increase if a new investment is undertaken which earns a profit in excess of the imputed interest charge on the value of the asset acquired. Residual income will go up even if the investment only just exceeds the imputed interest charge, and this means that '**marginally profitable' investments are likely to be undertaken** by the investment centre manager.

3.5 In contrast, when a manager is judged by ROI, a marginally profitable investment would be less likely to be undertaken because it would reduce the average ROI earned by the centre as a whole.

3.6 EXAMPLE: RESIDUAL INCOME AND DECISION MAKING

In the previous example in Paragraph 2.16, whereas ROI would have worsened with the new investment opportunity (part (a)) and improved with the disinvestment (part (b)) **RI would have done the opposite** - improved with the new investment and worsened with the disinvestment. The figures would be as follows.

(a) *Part (a)*

	Without new investment *£*	*Division S* *Investment* *£*	*With new investment* *£*
Profit before notional interest	64,000	10,000	74,000
Notional interest (15% of 340,000)	51,000	9,000*	60,000
	13,000	1,000	14,000

* 15% of £60,000

If the manager of Division S were guided by residual income into making decisions, he would **approve the new investment**. This happens to coincide with the recommendation that a DCF analysis would produce, and so the manager would make the right decision, albeit on a less satisfactory basis.

(b) *Part (b)*

	Without disinvestment *£*	*Disinvestment* *£*	*With disinvestment* *£*
Profit before notional interest	64,000	3,900	60,100
Notional interest	51,000	3,600 *	47,400
Residual income	13,000	300	12,700

*15% of £24,000

If the investment centre manager is guided by residual income, he would decide to **keep the asset** instead of selling it off. Again, this would coincide with the recommendation based on DCF analysis, and so the investment centre manager would make the right decision but for the wrong reason.

3.7 Residual income does not **always** point to the right decision, because notional interest on accounting capital employed is **not the same as DCF yield** on cash investment. However, residual income is more likely than ROI to improve when managers make correct investment/divestment decisions, and so is probably a 'safer' basis than ROI on which to measure performance.

3.8 EXAMPLE: ROI VERSUS RESIDUAL INCOME

Suppose that Department H has the following profit, assets employed and an imputed interest charge of 12% on operating assets.

	£	£
Operating profit	30,000	
Operating assets		100,000
Imputed interest (12%)	12,000	
Return on investment	———	30%
Residual income	18,000	

Suppose now that an additional investment of £10,000 is proposed, which will increase operating income in Department H by £1,400. The effect of the investment would be:

	£	£
Total operating income	31,400	
Total operating assets		110,000
Imputed interest (12%)	13,200	
Return on investment	———	28.5%
Residual income	18,200	

If the Department H manager is made responsible for the department's performance, he would **resist** the new investment if he were to be judged on **ROI**, but would **welcome** the investment if he were judged according to **RI**, since there would be a marginal increase of £200 in residual income from the investment, but a fall of 1.5% in ROI.

The marginal investment offers a return of 14% (£1,400 on an investment of £10,000) which is above the 'cut-off rate' of 12%. Since the original return on investment was 30%, the marginal investment will reduce the overall divisional performance. Indeed, any marginal investment offering an accounting rate of return of less than 30% in the year would reduce the overall performance.

Conclusion

3.9 Residual income should not be used as a means of making asset purchasing decisions; nevertheless, it may be a useful alternative to ROI where there is a **conflict between investment decisions** indicated by a positive NPV in discounted cash flow, and the resulting reduction in divisional ROI which 'reflects badly' on management performance.

Exam focus point

Straight forward RI and ROI calculations were necessary in the **December 1999** exam to provide the basis for bonus calculations.

331

4   INCOMPATIBLE SIGNALS - SOLUTIONS TO THE PROBLEM

4.1   As we have seen, ROI and RI do not always point to the right decision and so, whenever possible, a DCF approach to decision making should be adopted. Two possible **refinements** to the normal approach to calculating ROI and RI exist, however, and these can be adopted if it is not possible to calculate an NPV or an IRR.

The Paper 9 examiner and incompatible signals

4.2   An article by the **Paper 9 examiner** in the August 1995 edition of the *ACCA Students' Newsletter* (George Brown, 'Performance Measurement and Investment Decisions - Potential Conflict?'), looked at this very topic.

> **Exam focus point**
>
> A question in the **December 1995** exam was based on the contents of the article.

4.3   Our example which follows covers the same points as those made by George Brown.

4.4   Suppose that Division M is considering an investment of £200,000 which will provide a net cash inflow (before depreciation) of £78,000 each year for the four years of its life. It is group policy that investments must show a minimum return of 15%.

4.5   As the working below shows, using net book value at the start of each year and **depreciating on a straight line basis** to a nil residual value, in year 1 the RI would be negative and the ROI below the target rate of return of 15%. If management were to take a short-term view of the situation, the **investment would be rejected** if either of the measures were to be used, despite the fact that the investment's NPV is positive and that in years 2 to 4 the RI is positive and the ROI greater than the target rate of return.

	Years			
	1	*2*	*3*	*4*
	£	£	£	£
NBV of investment at start of year	200,000	150,000	100,000	50,000
Cash flow (before depreciation)	78,000	78,000	78,000	78,000
Less depreciation	(50,000)	(50,000)	(50,000)	(50,000)
Net profit	28,000	28,000	28,000	28,000
Less inputed interest (at 15%)	(30,000)	(22,500)	(15,000)	(7,500)
RI	(2,000)	5,500	13,000	20,500
ROI	14.00%	18.67%	28.00R	56.00%

Net present value = (£200,000) + (£78,000 × 2.855) = £22,690.

Annuity depreciation method

4.6   However, if instead of using straight line depreciation we use what is known as **annuity depreciation** we get a different story.

4.7   To calculate annuity depreciation we need to determine an **annual equivalent cash flow** which represents the annual net cash inflow required so that, in present value terms, the investment would break even. This annual equivalent cash flow is calculated for our example as (initial investment/cumulative discount factor at 15% for 4 years) = £200,000/2.855 = £70,052.54.

4.8 As the annual equivalent cash flow is the annual cash inflow which ensures that the investment **breaks even**, it is the total of the 'costs' that the investment will cause, those 'costs' being interest and depreciation.

FORMULAE TO LEARN

Annual equivalent cash flow = depreciation + interest

Annuity depreciation = annual equivalent cash flow – imputed interest on capital employed

---

Year 1 annuity depreciation = £70,052.54 – (0.15 × 200,000) = £40,052.54

Year 2 annuity depreciation = £70,052.54 – (0.15 × (200,000 – 40.052.54)) = £46,060.42

and so on, the imputed interest depending on the NBV of the investment at the start of the year, which in turn depends on the annuity depreciation charged in the previous year.

	Years			
	1	*2*	*3*	*4*
	£	£	£	£
NBV of investment at start of year	200,000.00	159,947.46	113,887.04	60,917.56
Cash flow (before depreciation)	78,000.00	78,000.00	78,000.00	78,000.00
Less depreciation	(40,052.54)	(46,060.42)	(52,969.48)	(60,914.91)
Net profit	37,947.46	31,939.58	25,030.52	17,085.09
Less inputed interest (at 15%)	(30,000.00)	23,992.12	17,083.06	9,137.63
RI	7,947.46	7,947.46	7,947.46	7,947.46
ROI	18.97%	19.97%	21.98%	28.05%

Note that the use of annuity depreciation produces an increasing charge for depreciation but that the total depreciation charged still totals to £200,000 (with a small difference for rounding).

4.9 In the first year of the investment's life using annuity depreciation, the **ROI is in excess of the target rate of return** and the **RI is positive**. This means that the investment would be considered acceptable, even if management are taking a short-term view. The use of annuity depreciation therefore helps to make the ROI/RI and NPV measures **compatible**.

4.10 Moreover, this approach has **smoothed the ROI figures** reported each year compared with those reported when using straight-line depreciation and has produced a **constant RI** for each of the four years.

4.11 Note that if the RI were to be **discounted** in the same way as cash flows in the NPV approach, the overall discounted RI= £7,947.46 × 2.855 = £22,690 = the investment's NPV.

Variable annual cash flows

4.12 In the example above, the annual net cash inflows were constant. If they vary from year to year annuity depreciation does not overcome the problem of the incompatibility of the indications given by ROI/RI and NPV for decision making.

Discounted future earnings method

4.13 **This** problem can be overcome if the valuation of the investment and hence the calculation of depreciation are based on the **discounted future earnings method.**

> *Step 1.* Begin by calculating the present value of the cash inflows in the usual way over the four years' of the project's life. This is the discounted future earnings of the investment in the first year of its life.

> *Step 2.* The year 1 cash flow then falls out of consideration and the PV of the cash inflows of years 2 to 4 are calculated and totalled, treating them as if they were years 1 to 3. This is the discounted future earnings of the investment in the second year of its life.

> *Step 3.* The discounted future earnings for years 3 and 4 are calculated in a similar way.

4.14

	Years			
	1	*2*	*3*	*4*
	£	£	£	£
Discounted future earnings	201,528.01	161,757.21	121,020.79	52,173.91
Cash flow (before depreciation)	70,000.00	65,000.00	87,000.00	60,000.00
Depreciation (W)	(39,770.80)	(40,736.42)	(68,846.88)	(52,173.91)
Net profit	30,229.20	24,263.58	18,153.12	7,826.09
Imputed charge	(30,229.20)	(24,263.58)	(18,153.12)	(7,826.09)
RI	0.00	0.00	0.00	0.00
ROI	15%	15%	15%	15%

Working

Depreciation is the difference between one year's discounted future earnings and the next year's, so £(201,528.01 – 161,757.21) = £39,770.80, and so on.

4.15 Note that for each year, the **ROI** comes out as a **constant figure** (the target rate of return) and the **RI** is now **zero.** Using this approach, ROI/RI and NPV would therefore give **consistent signals** to management.

> **Exam focus point**
>
> The examiner has confirmed that you will not be required to perform discounted future earnings calculations.

4.16 The examiner concluded in his article that although the above methods are 'ways in which the accept/reject signals for ROI, RI and NPV could be made compatible', the problems of **uncertainty** and the dominance of **conventional accounting procedures** mean that the methods are **unlikely to be used in practice.**

5 MULTIPLE MEASURES OF PERFORMANCE

5.1 Although segments of a business may be measured by a single performance indicator such as ROI, profit, or cost variances, it might be more suitable to use multiple measures of performance where each measure reflects a **different aspect of achievement.** Where multiple measures are used, several may be **non-financial.**

The balanced scorecard

5.2   The most popular approach in current management thinking is the use of a '**balanced scorecard**' consisting of a variety of indicators both financial and non-financial.

5.3   The balanced scorecard focuses on four different perspectives, as follows.

Perspective	Question
Customer	What do existing and new **customers** value from us? This perspective gives rise to targets that matter to customers: cost, quality, delivery.
Internal business	What **processes** must we excel at to achieve our financial and customer objectives? This perspective aims to improve internal processes and decision making.
Innovation and learning	Can we continue to **improve** and create future value? This perspective considers the business's capacity to maintain its competitive position through the acquisition of new skills and the development of new products. Suitable measures include the percentage of sales derived from new products compared with established ones, and time to market.
Financial	How do we create **value** for our shareholders? Traditional measures such as growth, profitability and shareholder value are set through talking to the shareholder(s) direct.

5.4   **Performance targets** are set once the key areas for improvement have been identified, and the balanced scorecard is the main monthly report.

5.5   The scorecard is '**balanced**' as managers are required to think in terms of **all four** perspectives, to prevent improvements being made in one area at the expense of another.

5.6   Important features of this approach are as follows.

(a)   It looks at both **internal and external** matters concerning the organisation.
(b)   It is related to the key elements of a company's **strategy**.
(c)   **Financial and non-financial** measures are linked together.

5.7   'The scorecard adds to the traditional financial focus by seeking to monitor the internal business perspective in non-financial terms, to monitor change and improvement in products and methods and to provide an external focus aiming at ensuring customer satisfaction and continued increased business from them.' (George Brown, 'Product costing/pricing strategy', **ACCA Students Newsletter,** August 1999).

The performance pyramid

5.8   Lynch and Cross viewed business as a **performance pyramid.** As shown in the diagram below, the four-level pyramid links strategy and operations. It includes a range of objectives for both external effectiveness (such as related to customer satisfaction) and internal efficiency (such as related to productivity) which are achieved through measures at various levels.

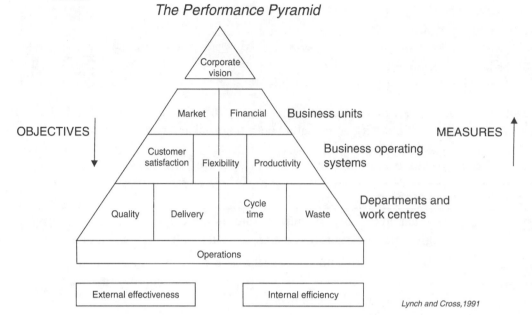

The Performance Pyramid

Lynch and Cross, 1991

(a) **Corporate vision** oversees the business. Corporate vision or mission is forward looking and involves defining markets and the basis on which an organisation will compete (pricing policy, production innovation, quality and so on.

(b) Each **business unit** should be distinct in terms of competitors, business concepts and mission, manage its strategies independently, and use short-term and long-term **financial** and **marketing measures**.

(c) Each **business operating system** is geared to achieve specific objectives and will cross departmental/functional boundaries. Performance focus will be on **customer satisfaction, flexibility** and **productivity**.

(d) The objective in **departments and work centres** is to increase quality and delivery and decrease cycle time and waste. **NFIs** will be used.

The four levels are linked by attempts to achieve objectives. For example, a reduction in waste (an improvement in internal efficiency), should lead to increased productivity and hence improved financial performance. An improvement in external effectiveness (in terms of quality and delivery) should increase customer satisfaction and hence affect marketing.

> **Exam focus point**
> A discursive and quantitative analysis of a proposal based specifically on viewing an organisation as a performance pyramid, was required in the **December 1999** exam.

6 DIVISIONAL AUTONOMY VERSUS CORPORATE GOAL CONGRUENCE

6.1 The conflict between divisional autonomy on the one hand and corporate goal congruence on the other has been a recurrent theme in this part of the text, both in the chapter on transfer pricing and in the present chapter. It will therefore be appropriate to end this final chapter with a summary of the **benefits and drawbacks of divisionalisation**.

6.2 Advantages of divisionalisation (or 'decentralisation')

(a) **Better quality decisions**. The divisional manager is more familiar with local conditions and can make a more informed judgement.

(b) **Motivation** of divisional managers. They are given the authority to act to improve their measures of performance (profit, ROI, added value and so on).

(c) The head office '**bureaucracy**' should be **reduced** in size, because many administrative decisions will be decentralised.

(d) Where transfer pricing schemes are in operation, there is a greater **awareness of market conditions** and market prices, since these often provide the basis for determining what the transfer prices should be.

6.3 The major **disadvantage** of divisionalisation is '**dysfunctional decision making**'. This is where a decision is made by a divisional manager which profits his own division, but creates greater off-setting losses (or benefits forgone) to the company as a whole.

Question 5

In what sense do these points reflect the **title** of Paper 9?

Chapter roundup

- **Return on investment** is the main measure of divisional performance, but it is flawed in a number of ways. There is no generally agreed method of calculating ROI.

- ROI can lead to **dysfunctional decisions**. An alternative measure is **residual income**, which can sometimes give results that avoid the problem of dysfunctionality. RI is preferable for judging *managerial* performance.

- Better are **multiple measures**, each reflecting a different aspect of achievement.

Quick quiz

1 Why is ROI considered important? (see para 1.3)

2 What are the arguments in favour of using net book values for calculating ROI? (1.13)

3 Why might the ROI be used as a guideline for investment in spite of the superiority of the DCF approach? (2.11)

4 How is residual income calculated? (3.1)

5 What are the advantages and weaknesses of RI compared with ROI? (3.2, 3.3)

6 What is an annual equivalent cash flow? (4.8)

7 How are discounted future earnings calculated? (4.13)

8 What are the four different perspectives of the balanced scorecard? (5.3)

9 What are the advantages of divisionalisation? (6.2)

Question to try	Level	Marks	Time
18	Exam standard	25	45 mins

BPP
PUBLISHING

Articles by the Paper 9 examiner

ARTICLES BY THE PAPER 9 EXAMINER

Here is a list of all the articles published by George Brown, the Paper 9 examiner, in recent years up to the date of publication of this Study Text (**June 2000**). The contents of all of these are reflected in this Study Text. The three most recent articles are reproduced in this Appendix.

Students' Newsletter	Article
November 1992	A feedback and feedforward control model
March 1994	Management accounting and strategic management
October 1994	Performance measurement in service businesses
December 1994	Is this a spreadsheet I see before me?
April 1995	Planning and operational variances in a service business
August 1995	Performance measurement and investment decisions - potential conflict?
December 1995	Control information and standard process costs - part 1
January 1996	Control information and standard process costs - part 2
February 1996	Control information and standard process costs - part 3
August 1998	Accountability and performance measurement
March 1999	Standard costing - a status check
August 1999	**Product costing/pricing strategy**
April 2000	**Quantitative applications in Paper 9, part 1**
May 2000	**Quantitative applications in Paper 9, par 2**

BPP PUBLISHING

Product costing/ pricing strategy

Relevant to paper 9

by George Brown, the Examiner for paper 9

Product costing and pricing strategies will interact in helping to achieve competitive advantage. Main areas of focus will be on the retention/increase of market share and the maintaining/ improving of profit levels. The retention/increase of market share will involve consideration of price as one of a number of influences. Porter (1980) offers a model (**Figure 1**) which suggests the importance of pressure from five competitive forces:

- rivalry between existing competitors;

- the threat of new entrants;

- the threat of substitutes;

- the bargaining power of buyers and;

- the bargaining power of suppliers.

Each force will require in-depth analysis of a checklist of factors. Examples of each of the factors may be viewed as follows:

- intensity of rivalry between existing competitors may be linked to determinants such as the number of competitors, marketing power, brand identity, product differences and cost structure. The rivalry will extend to the seeking of new markets and new products;

- the threat of new entrants will be affected by determinants such as the barriers to entry and the expected reaction from existing firms. New entrants will incur high capital costs of entry plus experience costs of developing expertise and the costs of brand identity development;

- the threat of substitutes may be determined by the level of innovation of existing producers, the ability of existing competitors to finance responses to the threat (switching costs) and the propensity of buyers to substitute, possibly because of price considerations;

- the bargaining power of buyers may be linked to buyer concentration. Where there are many buyers (e.g. of chocolate bars) they have little direct ability to negotiate the price of the product. Where there are few buyers (e.g. of aircraft fleets) they are likely to have a much greater level of bargaining power in relation to price;

- the bargaining power of suppliers may be viewed in a similar context to that of buyers. Supplier power and impact on costs will be greater where there are few of them. This principle may be viewed in the context of individual inputs for materials, labour and services.

The maintaining or improving of profit levels may also be viewed by considering the competitive strategy of the firm. Porter cited strategies with respect to competitive position, which may be used to provide competitive advantage:

- **Cost leadership** is characterised by a cost-conscious approach to operations, the pursuit of technical advantage and acknowl-

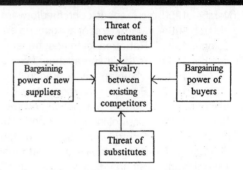

Figure 1: The Five Forces Model (Porter 1980)

edged lowest costs in the industry. Note that this low cost should not be equated with a 'cheap' product philosophy. Also, low cost does not necessarily mean low price. It does mean the ability to lower price in time of severe price competition and provides a cushion to defend profit levels against competitors;

- **Product differentiation** is characterised by the use of multiple products, each branded and promoted. Competitors are forced to compete simultaneously on many fronts and must overcome brand loyalty through price cutting. Product differentiation should add attributes that are valued by the customer and that the customer is therefore, willing to pay for. This should aim to maximise the profit gap between price and cost;

- **Niche marketing** targets markets in which the company can focus on cost and quality in response to customer needs in a specific market. This should lead to higher profits in the short term;

Other models

Efforts to achieve retention and/or increase of market share and the maintenance or improvement of profit levels may also be viewed in the context of other 'models' proposed in the 1990s.

Lynch and Cross (1991), viewed business as a performance pyramid (see Figure 2). The levels in the pyramid link strategy and operations. Corporate vision is seen as looking forward through defining markets and the basis on which the company will compete. The bases of competing may include pricing policy, product innovation and quality, features such as quality of sales force, after-sales service, financial aid to customers and point of sale amenities. The pyramid views a range of objectives for both external effectiveness and internal efficiency. These objectives are to be achieved through measures at various levels as shown in the pyramid. These measures are seen to interact with each other both horizontally at each level and vertically across the levels in the pyramid.

August 1999

ACCA Students' Newsletter

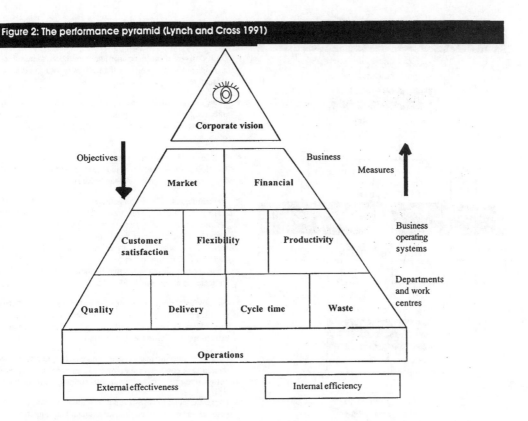

Figure 2: The performance pyramid (Lynch and Cross 1991)

Kaplan and Norton (1992) devised the 'balanced scorecard' as a way in which to improve the range and linkage of performance measures. **Figure 3** illustrates four perspectives: financial, customer, internal business and innovation and learning. These perspectives seek to answer the questions as stated in **Figure 3**. The scorecard adds to the traditional financial focus by seeking to monitor the internal business perspective in non-financial terms, to monitor change and improvement in products and methods and to provide an external focus aiming at ensuring customer satisfaction and continued or increased business from them.

Fitzgerald et al (1993) and Fitzgerald and Moon (1996), focus on performance in service businesses. **Figure 4** shows their building blocks for dimensions, standard and rewards. The model focuses on results measured by financial performance and competitiveness. Improved competitiveness should lead to retention or increase in market share and improved financial performance. The determinants by which the results should be achieved are quality, flexibility, resource utilisation and innovation.

Product Life Cycles
Product life cycle is a relevant factor in the determining of product market strategies and the price/cost relationships which are factors in the pricing and profitability of a product. Smith (1997), illustrates the product life cycle as in **Figure 5**. The **introductory phase** of product uptake and volume will be affected by the level of advantage on price or quality over rival products. Also, investment in the improvement of product promotion, distribution and after-sales warranties will help to overcome customer resistance and any perception of relative lack of reliability and

longevity of the product. This view fits with aspects of the discussion of the Lynch and Cross performance pyramid and Kaplan and Norton's balanced scorecard in focusing on customer satisfaction and confidence. The **growth phase** will be characterised by reduced uncertainty about the product, repeat buyers and brand loyalty and a perception of price and/or quality advantages by consumers. The **maturity phase** requires focus on retention of existing customers and attracting new ones. Also, a recognition of the need for competitive pricing over advertising. The **decline phase** and the rate of such decline may depend on the degree of changes in fashion or technological change. The rate of decline may also be linked to the comparative price/quality advantages of emerging products.

Producers may attempt to rejuvenate products through product and user innovation, corresponding to positions A and B in Smith's life cycle illustration **(Figure 5)**. Position A may focus on major product improvements and a repositioning of the product from a customer viewpoint. Position B may seek additional distribution outlets, perhaps through exports or through identifying new markets for the existing product.

Boston Consulting Group (BCG) Portfolio Matrix
The BCG portfolio matrix provides a useful framework for the analysis of a whole into the sum of its component parts. One area of use of such analysis is in the relative positioning of products through their life cycles. **Figure 6** shows an illustration of the components of the matrix. The vertical axis shows market growth rate as a measure of market attributes. The horizontal axis shows relative market share as a measure of competitive strength. Products and their phase in their

46   TECHNICAL

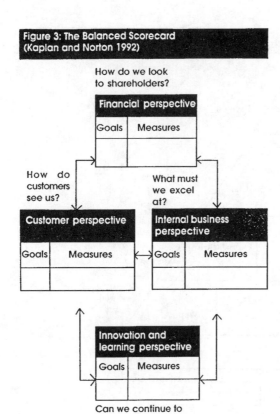

Figure 3: The Balanced Scorecard (Kaplan and Norton 1992)

How do we look to shareholders?

Financial perspective

Goals	Measures

How do customers see us?

What must we excel at?

Customer perspective

Goals	Measures

Internal business perspective

Goals	Measures

Innovation and learning perspective

Goals	Measures

Can we continue to improve and create value?

Figure 4: The Building blocks for performance measurement systems (Fitzgerald and Moon 1996)

Dimensions
Profit
Competitiveness
Quality
Resource utilisation
Flexibility
Innovation

Standards
Ownership
Achievability
Equity

Rewards
Clarity
Motivation
Controllability

life cycles may be linked to the Cash Cows, Stars, Dogs and Question marks (?) of the matrix. The products may be viewed as:

- **Cash Cows** are in a mature market and enjoy the economies of scale and high profits with low growth rate. Few investment resources are required;

- **Stars** are market leaders and enjoy higher growth, but still require injection of investment and promotional expenditure to maintain their position and reputation. They will eventually turn into cash cows;

- **Dogs** are products which are now uncompetitive in static markets. No further investment or promotional expenditure is justified. They are unlikely to do more than break even;

- **Question marks (?)** are competitive products which have yet to make a significant market impact. They have the potential to become stars, but a question mark hangs over their ability to achieve sufficient market penetration to justify further investment. Price, cost and other factors such as quality and brand loyalty are all factors in the overall strategy. It is important that a balance is achieved in the management of the matrix. Basic strategies listed by Smith (1997) are:

- **build** by increasing market share, even at the expense of short term profits. For example turning question marks (?) into stars. This may require a penetration pricing policy and investment in establishing quality and brand loyalty;

- **hold** by preserving market share and ensuring that cash cows remain cash cows. This may require additional investment in customer retention through competitive pricing and marketing;

- **harvest** through the use of funds to promote products with the potential to become future stars or to support existing stars;

- **divest** through the elimination of under-performing dogs and question marks (?) whose use of resources is inefficient.

Approaches to pricing

The implementation of strategies which will achieve retention/increase of market share and which will maintain/improve profit levels may take place in conjunction with the application of one of a number of costing and pricing techniques. Accounting systems may use one or more of the following in their attempts to provide relevant information:

- traditional cost plus profit mark-up approach to product costing and price setting;

- an activity based approach to cost management and pricing;

- the use of target costing and pricing;

- price/demand relationships and pricing;

- relevant costs and pricing decisions.

Traditional cost plus profit mark-up approach

This approach uses a functional/process analysis. An example of the total cost built up may be illustrated as shown in **Figure 7**. The information required for the cost build up may differ considerably depending on the type of product. Consider the different analysis required in each of the following situations:

Figure 5: The Product Life Cycle (Smith 1997)

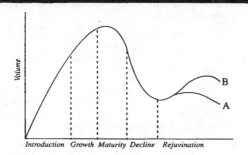

Introduction   Growth   Maturity   Decline   Rejuvination

1   a batch of light fittings made to customer specification.

2   a chemical produced in a multi-stage process cycle.

3   the construction of a bridge.

The mix of direct and indirect costs and the bases for the absorption of overhead costs will vary considerably for each situation. **(Paper 9 — June 1998, Q5 solution provides background discussion to these three situations).**

In the case of the batch of light fittings and the bridge construction, the company will be in a position of having to determine a selling price at which it wishes to offer to complete the work. This may require submitting a price in competition with other companies seeking the work. The profit mark-up percentage added will be subject to taxation and must then provide for dividends to shareholders, reinvestment in the business to replace existing assets or to finance new ventures and to protect the business against erosion of its capital base in periods of inflation.

In the case of the chemical product, the profit element may be the difference between market price and total cost. The product may be sold in a competitive market where a market price prevails which may be affected by a number of variables including level of customer demand and degree of competition. In this situation, the profit element may not provide the return which a cost plus profit mark-up approach would suggest.

A number of arguments can readily be raised against the use of a traditional cost plus profit mark-up approach to pricing. These include:

● lack of accuracy of the various cost allocations and apportionments;

● problems in determining the profit mark-up percentage;

● lack of flexibility in pricing since it assumes a single activity level when determining the absorption rate for fixed costs;

● does not take into account price: demand relationship considerations;

● does not allow for special pricing situations which consider factors such as the existence of spare capacity, the relevance of product specific or customer specific costs and the use of opportunity cost in 'one-off' situations.

Consider some alternatives which are available in deciding on an acceptable price starting with the model in **Figure 7:**

1   A smaller profit may be deemed acceptable if considerable competition exists. For example the price could be set at £8,500 which gives a profit of £1,220 (approximately 17% mark up on total cost).

2   If competition is very tough, the price could be set equal to total cost i.e., £7,280. This will at least be contributing to the fixed costs of the company which have to be paid whatever level of sales is achieved.

3   The company may have spare capacity which will be idle if no orders are obtained. In this situation only the variable costs are avoidable if the order is not obtained. The minimum price acceptable in such circumstances is therefore, the total variable (marginal) cost. It is unlikely that such a price would be accepted, but it could be used as a starting point in deciding on the acceptability of a price below total cost where spare capacity exists. Assume that additional information relating to the situation in **Figure 7** shows that:

● prime cost is a variable cost;

Figure 6: The BCG Portfolio Matrix (Smith 1997)

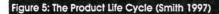

Figure 7: Traditional total cost plus profit mark-up pricing model

	£	£
Direct material cost		820
Direct wages cost:		
Preparation	380	
Assembly	180	
Finishing	225	785
Direct expenses		332
Prime cost		1,937
Production overhead cost		
Preparation	2,470	
Assembly	660	
Finishing	750	3,880
Production cost		5,817
Administration and selling cost		1,163
Distribution cost		300
Total cost		7,280
Profit (25% on sales = 33.33% on total cost)		2,427
Selling price		9,707

- production overhead cost is 40% variable and 60% fixed;

- administration/selling cost is total fixed;

- distribution cost is a variable cost (e.g. outside carrier is used).

The total variable (marginal) cost of the order is now:

	£
Prime cost	1,937
Production overhead cost (40% of £3,880)	1,552
Distribution cost	300
Total variable cost	3,789

If a selling price of £4,250 could be negotiated, should it be accepted? Where spare capacity exists this would give a net cash inflow of £461. In the absence of any more profitable orders it would be worthwhile having this order.

4   There may be some product (order) specific fixed costs which are avoidable if the **order did not** go ahead. For example there may be special supervision costs or sales and marketing costs which relate specifically to the order. In the **Figure 7** example, assume that £800 of administration and selling cost is specifically incurred by the order. In this situation, the marginal cost of the order must include this amount in addition to the £3,789 calculated above. The price of £4,250 is no longer acceptable on financial grounds, since it will result in a net cash outflow of £339 (£4,250 - £3,789 - £800).

Activity based approach to costing and pricing

The traditional cost analysis model illustrates the functional analysis of indirect/overhead costs, with allocation and apportionment to departments/cost centres. The absorption of a share of overhead costs by product units tends to be implemented using a single volume related absorption basis such as direct labour hours or machine hours. An activity based approach will operate in conjunction with an activity based budgeting system which requires a move from a mainly functional focus to a focus on activities. A number of questions may be asked to help in the development of an activity model:

- what activities are being carried out and do they need to be carried out? Activities may be classified as primary or support activities.

The cutting of steel sheet will be a primary activity. The maintenance of cutting machinery will be a necessary support activity. Activities may also be classified as value-added or non-value added. The cutting of steel sheet is value-added, unnecessary aspects of a support activity such as maintenance are non-value-added, unnecessary movement of steel sheet is a non-value-added activity;

- how effectively are activities being carried out and to what quality and standard? This would require a study of the steel sheet cutting activity in terms of type of machinery used, the skills level of machine operators and the efficiency of the machinery;

- what is the principal cost driver which determines the level of resource required for an activity? In the cutting example this may be the number of cuts required. Could the number of cuts be reduced from (say) six cuts per sheet to four cuts per sheet?

- what is the relationship between an activity cost driver and its root cause? In the cutting example the number of cuts may be linked to the steel sheet purchasing policy. If the root cause of requiring six cuts per sheet is the size of **sheet** purchased, should this be overcome by reducing the size of sheet purchased?

Figure 8 shows the unit costs for each of three products where overhead costs are absorbed using

(a) a traditional rate per labour hour and

(b) an activity-based approach.

The products pass through a single production process in which three activities and cost drivers have been identified. The activities are material receipt and inspection, machine processing and material handling with cost drivers of number of batches of material, number of drilling operations and square metres of material handled respectively. Competitive prices per unit for the products X, Y and Z are £360, £400 and £700 respectively. The company normally requires a profit mark-up of 25% on cost for a product to be considered viable.

The information in **Figure 8** shows that where a traditional absorption approach is used, product X (27.7%) easily meets the profit mark-up requirement. Product Z (21.7%) is barely above the requirement. Product Y (10.1%) is clearly below the requirement. This information may lead management to pursue a strategy of:

- a planned expansion of sales of product X;

- consideration of the elimination of product Y;

Figure 8: Traditional volume related vs ABC cost analysis

	Product X Traditional £	Product X ABC £	Product Y Traditional £	Product Y ABC £	Product Z Traditional £	Product Z ABC £
Direct material cost	100.00	100.00	60.00	60.00	120.00	120.00
Direct wages cost	32.00	32.00	53.33	53.33	80.00	80.00
Overhead cost:						
Material receipt and inspection	48.00	50.32	80.00	33.55	120.00	201.29
Power	60.00	129.30	100.00	64.65	150.00	43.10
Material handling	42.00	56.28	70.00	84.42	105.00	42.21
Total cost	282.00	367.90	363.33	295.95	575.00	486.60
Profit/loss	78.00	-7.90	36.67	104.05	125.00	213.40
Selling price	360.00	360.00	400.00	400.00	700.00	700.00
Net profit/loss: total cost (%)	27.7%	-2.1%	10.1%	35.2%	21.7%	43.9%

- attempt to increase the price of product Z.

The ABC information in **Figure 8** indicates that product X is being sold at a net loss (2.1%), product Y is earning a healthy profit (35.2%) and product Z is earning a much higher profit than thought (43.9%). The original strategy based on the traditional cost figures would, therefore, be inappropriate.

The benefits of the activity-based cost system may not be as straightforward as the above example would imply. Problems which may be difficult to overcome include:

- the selection of the relevant activities and cost drivers;

- the collection of data to enable accurate cost driver rates to be calculated;

- the problem of cost driver denominator level — similar to that in a traditional volume related system;

- achieving the required level of management commitment to the change.

An additional problem is the application of cost driver rates to products. This may require a hierarchical approach (Drury 1996). Activity sub-sets may be chosen which determine that costs may be identified as being incurred at different levels. These may be **unit based** such as direct labour or power costs; **batch based** such as work-in-progress movement or machine set up costs; **product sustaining** such as material scheduling or design and testing costs; **product line sustaining** such as line development or line maintenance. Other costs may be **factory sustaining** and not readily charged to products other than on an arbitrary basis. **(Paper 9 — December 1998, Q3 solution provides a quantitative illustration of this approach).**

Target costing and pricing

Target costing has been used for some years in many of Japan's assembly oriented industries. **Figure 9** provides an illustration of the target setting process. Sakurai (1989), indicated the move towards products being increasingly tailored to meet customer requirements with a shortened life cycle expectation. The stages in the implementation of the target costing process may be summarised as follows:

- a product specification is determined for which an anticipated sales volume is estimated;

- a target selling price is set at which the company will be able to achieve a desired market share;

- the required profit is estimated based on return on sales (%) or return on investment;

- the target cost is calculated as target selling price minus target profit

- an estimated cost for the product is compiled based on the anticipated design specification and current cost levels

- estimated cost minus target cost represents any 'cost gap' which exists;

- efforts are made to close the cost gap. This is more likely to be successful if efforts are made to 'design out' costs prior to production, rather than to 'control out' costs during the production phase. This process will involve the application of a number of techniques. Value engineering may be carried out in order to evaluate the necessary features of the product such as the quantity and quality of materials and components and the conversion processes required to achieve the desired quality of finished product. This will involve discussions by members of various disciplines, including design, production and purchasing. An activity-based approach will be useful in determining value-added activities and non-value-added activities. It will also allow focus on cost drivers and their root causes

- final negotiations may take place with the customer before a decision is made whether the project will go ahead. Sakurai (1989), in his article indicated that an increase in selling price may be negotiated with the customer where the company can demonstrate that it has made all reasonable efforts to close the cost gap.

(Paper 9 — June 1996, QI provides a scenario which illustrates and requires comment on, aspects of the target costing process).

Price/demand relationships and pricing

Demand for products may be viewed as a function of a number of variables. Such variables may be internally or externally influenced. The level of promotion of a product, its brand image, its quality status and customer care, may all be addressed by the firm. The degree of competition, changing tastes of customers, technological progress and level of purchasing power are all external influences.

Prices may be viewed as being set by overall market supply and demand forces. The Economist's model assumes that the firm will attempt to set the selling price at a level where profits are maximised. An algebraic

Figure 9: The target setting process

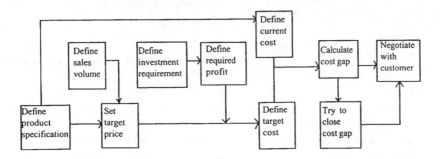

representation of the model may be constructed as follows:

- for monopolistic/imperfect competition, the model assumes that the lower the price, the larger will be the volume of sales. This relationship is known as the demand curve which may be expressed as $P_x = P_o - aX$, where P_x = price at X units, P_o = price at zero units, a = rate of change of demand with price and X = number of units;

- the total revenue (TR) line may be constructed by multiplying the demand curve by the quantity (X) units. We have $TR_x = P_o X - aX^2$;

- the total cost line may be viewed as constructed from the basic accounting model of a fixed element and a variable element which varies in proportion to volume. This may be expressed as $TC_x = b + cX$, where b = fixed cost, c = variable cost per unit and X = number of units;

- The Economist's model submits that the volume of production and sale should be increased to the point where the additional (or marginal) revenue (MR) is equal to the additional (or marginal) cost (MC). The selling price at which this sales volume occurs can then be determined. This process may be implemented by visual inspection of a tabulation of the data, the use of a graphical approach or the application of simple differential calculus.

A simple example may be used to illustrate the above procedures.

Saffro Systems plc has estimated that the demand/price relationship for one of its products is linear and the following data are available for the coming period:

Selling price per unit:	£90	£60
Demand (in units)	400	1,000

The price at which the product will be marketed will be somewhere between the above parameters and will be a multiple of £5.

A preliminary estimate is that variable cost per unit will be £40 with fixed costs of £5,000 for the period. All fixed costs are an apportionment of company unavoidable fixed cost.

Saffro Systems plc wishes to determine the profit maximising selling price and sales volume.

Solution: The demand curve is $P_x = P_o - aX$

The price: demand relationship (a) = (£90 – £60)/(1,000 – 400) = 0.05 Note that this represents a downward sloping demand curve as volume increases. Starting with any point on the curve, the price at zero demand (P_o) may be calculated.

A price of £90 (P_x) applies where demand is 400 units (X)

Hence 90 = P_o – 0.05 x 400. Solving gives P_o = 110

Alternatively this may be obtained from a graph by plotting the price: demand curve (P_x) as in **Figure 10**.

Total revenue may now be calculated by applying the equation formulated above where P_o = £110 and a = 0.05.

$TR_x = P_o X - aX^2$

Giving $TR_x = 110X - 0.05X^2$

For example where demand (X) is 500 units:

Total revenue (TR) = 110 x 500 – 0.05 x 500^2 = £42,500

Total cost (TC_x) = b + cX where b = £5000 and c = £40

For example where demand is 500 units:

Total cost (TC) = 5,000 + 40 x 500 = £25,000

A table may be constructed as follows:

Table 1						
Demand	Price	Total Revenue	Marginal Revenue	Total Cost	Marginal Cost	Total Profit
(units)	£	£	£	£	£	£
400	90	36,000		21,000		15,000
500	85	42,500	6,500	25,000	4,000	17,500
600	80	48,000	5,500	29,000	4,000	19,000
700	75	52,500	4,500	33,000	4,000	19,500
800	70	56,000	3,500	37,000	4,000	19,000
900	65	58,500	2,500	41,000	4,000	17,500
1,000	60	60,000	1,500	45,000	4,000	15,000

The table shows that total profit is maximised at £19,500 where the price is set at £75 giving a demand of 700 units.

Figure 10 shows a graphical representation of the situation. The total revenue (TR_x) and total cost (TC_x) curves are shown with the optimum position where the difference between the two is maximised. Note that the total revenue curve (TR_x) shows a decreasing slope as demand increases, which is reflected in the downward sloping marginal revenue curve (MR_x). The total cost curve (TC_x) is a straight line in the Saffro Systems plc example, indicating the assumption of a basic fixed cost and a constant variable cost element per unit. This means that the marginal cost line (MC_x) is a horizontal straight line in this case. Most textbook illustrations of the model would assume an increasing slope of total cost and an upward sloping marginal cost line. Examples of the increasing nature of costs might be the need for premium rates of pay for overtime working or increased material costs in order to obtain additional quantities at higher output levels.

The graphs show that the marginal revenue and marginal cost curves intersect where demand is 700 units, where price is £75 per unit and where profit (difference between TR_x and TC_x curves) is £19,500.

The application of differential calculus provides a concise representation and solution of the problem.

$TR = 110X - 0.05X^2$

$MR = \dfrac{dTR}{dX} = 110 - 0.1X$

$TC = 5,000 + 40X$

$MC = \dfrac{dTC}{dX} = 40$

MR = MC for optimum solution

$110 - 0.1X = 40$

$X = 700$ units

Substituting in the price: demand equation to get the selling price at this demand level:

$P = 110 - 0.05X = 110 - 0.05 \times 700 = £75$

The Economist's model may be criticised as being difficult to apply in practice.

The following points may be raised:

- it is likely to be very difficult to quantify price: demand relationships. At best an approximation can be ventured;

Figure 10

Saffro Systems plc — Graphical representation of model for establishing the optimum price and demand

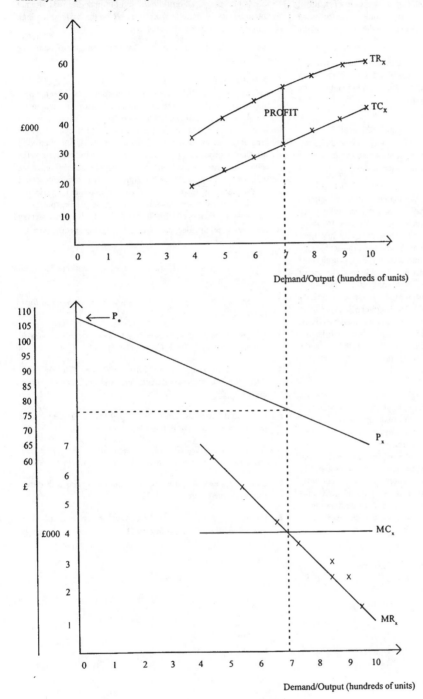

- the total cost and marginal cost functions prepared by the accounting system are likely to be only an approximation of the true cost function;

- many factors other than price affect quantity demanded. These include the amount and quality of sales effort, product design and quality and customer care;

- the model assumes the pursuit and application of a profit maximising strategy. However a variety of competitive forces are likely to influence the strategy implemented during the life cycle of any product.

(Paper 9 — December 1997, Q1 required the use of price/demand relationships in estimating the price at which to launch a product in order to gain market share which it is then hoped to hold in the face of future increased competition.)

Relevant costs and pricing decisions

Pricing decisions may require consideration of the specific circumstances in which the decision is being made and the relevant costs for that decision. Examples of such circumstances are:

- **the use of spare capacity.** This was discussed earlier where it was illustrated that a marginal cost approach might be applied where any contribution to company fixed costs earned by comparing the best price available with marginal cost is worth having in the short term where no better alternative use of the resources is available. Another illustration of this might be the acceptance of a one-off contract after taking into account the opportunity cost of inputs. For example a contract may be able to make use of materials which have an inventory value of £100,000 but which are old stock which if not used on the proposed contract could only be sold at a scrap value of £10,000. The contract price appears to be £50,000 less than total cost on a conventional total cost basis. However, given that the opportunity cost of the materials is only £10,000 and not the £100,000 included in the current figures, the contract price may be viewed as £40,000 in excess of total relevant costs on an incremental opportunity cost basis;

- **the identification of customer specific costs** may be relevant in deciding on a profit maximising sales strategy. Consider a situation where product A is sold to two customers X and Y by Alpha plc. The existing system charges costs to the product without considering customer specific aspects of cost. Product profit per unit is estimated as £23.25 per unit based on production/sales of 9,000 units sold in equal numbers to customers X and Y, giving a total profit of £209,250. Customers X and Y currently require 8,000 units and 5,000 units respectively. Only 9,000 units worth of production capacity is available. An investigation of costs by Alpha plc reveals that some costs are customer specific and a revised profit analysis per unit is as follows:

	Customer X	Customer Y
Common costs	50	50
Rebates to customers	5	12.50
Service back-up costs	8	4
Distribution cost	6	18
Total cost	69	84.50
Net profit	31	15.50
Selling price	100	100

Alpha plc would now sell 8,000 units to customer X and 1,000 units to customer Y in order to maximise profit. Total profit would now be 8,000 × £31 + 1,000 × £15.50 = £263,500. It may be however, that Alpha plc will decide to adopt a different strategy. Customer Y may be a valued client who also buys other products and with whom business is expected to grow. It may be known that customer B has trading problems and future sales may fall off rapidly. Alpha plc may decide to accept a lower overall profit in the short term and/or may attempt to obtain a price increase from customer Y on the basis of the high distribution cost incurred on sales to it.

(Paper 9 — December 1997, Q3 — illustrates the use of customer specific costs)

Conclusion

The above discussion has indicated that price may be affected by a number of factors. Price may be used when seeking to retain or increase market share (e.g., to deter new entrants to the market). It may be used in different ways at different stages in a product life cycle (e.g. the milking of cash cows). It may be affected by the basis on which costs are attached to products (e.g., the impact of an ABC analysis to the perceived unit cost/price relationships). It may be determined at the outset in a short life product (with a focus on how to reduce costs to a target level necessary to give the required level of return). The Economist's price/demand model may be conceptually appealing (but ignore a number of other factors which influence demand). Relevant cost may be important in pricing decisions (such as customer specific costs).

References

1 Drury, *Management and Cost Accounting*, International Thomson Business Press, (1996).

2 Fitzgerald, *et al, Performance Measurement in Service Businesses,* CIMA, (1993).

3 Fitzgerald and Moon, *Performance Measurement in Service Industries: Making it Work,* CIMA, (1996).

4 Kaplan and Norton, *Harvard Business Review,* "The Balanced Scorecard — Measures that Drive Performance," January/February, (1992).

5 Lynch and Cross, *Measure Up! — Yardsticks for Continuous Improvement,* Blackwell, (USA), (1991).

6 Sakurai, *Journal of Cost Management for the Manufacturing Industries,* "Target Costing and how to use it," iii No 2, (1989)

7 Smith, *Strategic Management Accounting — text and cases,* Butterworth/Heinemann, (1997).

8 Porter, *Competitive Strategy: techniques for analysing industries and competitors,* Free Press, (1980).

66   TECHNICAL   by George Brown

Quantitative applications in paper 9 — Part 1

Relevant to paper 9

George Brown is the Examiner for paper 9

Quantitative applications in paper 9 have been and will be examined in the context of management accounting situations. Questions may require:

- The manipulation of data;
- The interpretation of information which has already been processed;
- The application or explanation of a number of techniques.

The above requirements are not mutually exclusive. For example, the manipulation of data may be in the context of techniques such as CVP analysis or throughput accounting. The interpretation of information may be where we are first asked to implement some processing/manipulation before discussing its meaning and relevance. The application or explanation of a technique may require manipulation and/or the interpretation of output information.

In this article we will assume some prior knowledge of the applications which are illustrated and discussed. The main focus will be on interpretation and explanation, although some manipulation of data will be included. Questions from past examination diets of paper 9 provided a useful source of illustrations and will be referred to where relevant.

Manipulation of data

There are a number of ways in which you may be asked to manipulate data. A list of possible situations are as follows:

- use and present data/information, for example as part of a report;
- form a model of a situation e.g., a decision tree;
- use formulae/models provided e.g., learning curve;
- apply algebraic principles in order to obtain a required solution.

Interpretation of information already processed

In paper 9 questions, you may be provided with information in a table or appendix which you are required to use and/or comment on. Examples of such situations are:

- information provided as a data table from a spreadsheet model. You may be asked to explain the relevance of the information in the data table. You may also be expected to use the information as part of a broader interpretation of a situation;
- information provided as an Activity Based Budget matrix. You may be required to demonstrate your understanding of the content and structure of the matrix. You may also be required to use information from the matrix.

April 2000

Application of techniques with a quantitative focus

You will be expected to understand the structure and application of a number of techniques. You may also be required to comment on the relevance of the information produced from their application. Relevant areas of focus include:

- maximax/maximin/minimax regret analysis;
- formulation and interpretation of a linear programming model;
- CVP analysis and throughput accounting.

Illustrative examples

Example 1: Use and present data/information

Paper 9, June 1995 Q2(b) asks for comment on the business performance in BS Ltd using data provided in **Figure 1.1**. The business provides consultancy services offering administrative, data processing and marketing advice. Consultants work partly in the clients' premises and partly in BS Ltd premises. Consultants also spend some time negotiating with potential clients, attempting to secure contracts from them. Other relevant information is as follows:

- contract negotiation and remedial work hours are not charged directly to each client;
- BS Ltd policy is to retain 60 consultants on an ongoing basis;
- clients are invoiced at £75 per chargeable consultant hour;
- consultant salaries are budgeted at £30,000 per consultant per annum. Actual salaries include a bonus for hours in excess of budget paid for at the budgeted average rate per hour;
- sundry operating costs were budgeted at £3,500,000. Actual was £4,100,000;
- BS Ltd capital employed (start year) was £6,500,000.

The answer requires illustration of quantitative measures and comment in respect of each of financial performance, competitive performance, quality of service, flexibility, resource utilisation and innovation.

ACCA Students' Newsletter

BPP
PUBLISHING

When answering this sort of question you must back up any comment which you make with relevant quantitative analysis, indicating where relevant how you arrived at any ratios or percentages which you provide.

An abbreviated illustration of a possible answer, which focuses on the incorporation of relevant quantitative aspects might be as follows:

Financial performance

The summary profit and loss account **(Figure 1.2)** has been prepared after implementing the following calculations:

Note 1: Revenue from clients:

- Budget: (12,000 + 88,800)hours x £75 = £7,560,000
- Actual: (6,600 + 85,800)hours x £75 = £6,930,000

Note 2: Consultant salaries:

- Budget: 60 x £30,000 = £1,800,000
- Actual: budgeted average hours per consultant = 120,000/60 = 2,000 hours

    budgeted average rate per hour = £30,000/2,000 = £15

    actual total salaries = 132,000 hours x £15 = £1,980,000

The information shows that BS Ltd has a poor financial performance during the year to 30 April 1995 compared to that budgeted. Client income is down and operating costs have increased. It would be useful, however, to have a more detailed analysis which attempts, where possible, to link the fall in profit to quality, flexibility, resource utilisation and innovation factors. In addition, it would be useful to have a longer term trend of financial results in order to see whether the current year figures are representative of a continuing decline or are due to specific short-term conditions.

Competitiveness

Competitiveness may be measured in terms of the relative success/ failure in obtaining business from clients. **Figure 1.1** data shows that the budgeted uptake from client enquiries is 40% (180/450) for new systems and 75% (300/400) for existing systems advice. The actual percentages are 35% and 80% respectively. For new systems business the percentage has fallen, but the number of new systems worked on has increased from budget (210 from 180). For existing systems advice, although the percentage uptake is higher than budget, the total number of clients is down (288 from 300) on budget.

Quality

Key quality factors must be identified and monitored in quantitative and/or qualitative ways. To some extent the increased level of remedial advice, an extra 5,520 hours compared to budget, may indicate a quality problem. The question does indicate, however, that this is an innovation on the part of BS Ltd with a view to future demand improvement. The information in **Figure 1.1** indicates that client complaints were four times the budgeted level (20 compared with 5). Also, the number of clients requiring remedial advice was 75 compared to a budget level of 48. BS Ltd should investigate the reasons for the increases in order to identify and eliminate quality problems.

Flexibility

This may relate to the company being able to cope with flexibility of volume, delivery speed or job specification. We are told that BS Ltd retains 60 consultants in order that it has increased flexibility in meeting demand. The mix of consultants available will be another indicator of flexibility. **Figure 1.1** shows a change in mix from that budgeted which may indicate a high level of awareness of market changes and the need to provide for such changes. Delivery speed should be aided by the policy of retaining consultants and the mix of staff available. The ability to cope with a range of job specifications may be linked to the mix of consultants available. BS Ltd has moved to a work ratio of new

Figure 1.1: BS Ltd Sundry Statistics for year ended 30 April 1995

	Budget	Actual
Number of consultants:		
Administration	30	23
Data processing	12	20
Marketing	18	17
Consultants hours analysis:		
Contract negotiation hours	4,800	9,240
Remedial advice hours	2,400	7,920
Other non-chargeable hours	12,000	22,440
General development work hours (charge)	12,000	6,600
Customer premises contract hours (charge)	88,800	85,800
Gross hours	120,000	132,000
Chargeable hours analysis:		
New systems	70%	60%
Existing systems advice	30%	40%
Number of client enquiries received:		
New systems	450	600
Existing systems advice	400	360
Number of client contracts worked on:		
New systems	180	210
Existing systems advice	300	288
Number of client complaints	5	20
Contracts requiring remedial advice	48	75

Figure 1.2: BS Ltd Summary profit and loss account for the year ended 30 April 1995

	Budget £000	Actual £000
Revenue from client contracts	7,560	6,930
Costs:		
Consultant salaries	1,800	1,980
Sundry operating costs (given)	3,500	4,100
	5,300	6,080
Net profit	2,260	850
Capital employed (given)	6,500	6,500
Financial ratios: (budget workings shown)		
Net profit: Turnover (£2,260,000/£7,560,000)	29.9%	12.3%
Turnover:Capital employed (£7,560,000/£6,500,000)	1.16 times	1.07 times
Net profit: Capital employed (£2,260,000/£6,500,000)	34.8%	13.1%

68   TECHNICAL

systems: existing systems advice of 40%:60% compared to a budget ratio of 30%:70% which may indicate an ability to be flexible in response to market demands.

Resource utilisation

This may be measured in terms of output to input consultant hours. In the budget the hours charged to clients represents 84% of gross hours (100,800/120,000). The actual percentage for the year to 30 April 1995 was 70% of gross hours (92,400/132,000). There is a trade-off between resource utilisation, flexibility and innovation. The strategy implemented must be viewed not only in terms of the results for the current year, but also in terms of the likely impact on future levels of client demand. The increased level of remedial advice (6% of gross hours compared to 2% in the budget) may be viewed as a longer-term investment.

Innovation

This should be viewed in terms of its impact on financial performance, competitiveness, quality, flexibility and resource utilisation in both the short and long term. BS Ltd has an innovative feature in allowing 'free' remedial advice after the completion of a contract. In the short term this is adversely affecting financial performance. Actual remedial advice hours of 7,920 hours are 5,280 hours in excess of the standard allowance of 2,640 hours (i.e., 2% of 132,000 gross hours). The excess hours may also indicate that the **process** of remedial advice needs to be reviewed.

Example 2: Form a model of a situation

Paper 9, December 1994 Q2(d) focuses on an extension to a question which is investigating standard cost variance analysis trends in a company. The company now wishes to investigate a high level of machine idle time variance. A decision is required whether to investigate the variance based on an analysis of the likely financial implications. The following figures should be used in the investigation:

● The average excess idle time variance will be eliminated at the end of March 19x5 as an existing total quality management programme takes effect. Until that time it is estimated that the excess idle time variance will continue to occur each month at a level equal to 75% of the November 19x4 variance of £12,000. The December 19x4 idle time variance will remain unaffected irrespective of the action taken, and should not be included in your calculations.

● The additional investigation will have an initial cost of £1,500 to determine whether the variance is controllable in the January to March 19x5 period.

● The cost of taking control action will be £7,000 per month, which would eliminate the variance from January 19x5 onwards if the variance responds to the planned control action. The variance may not respond to the control action and remain unchanged.

● The probability that the variance is controllable in the January to March 19x5 period is 0.4.

● The probability that the variance will respond to the proposed control action is 0.8.

You are required to advise management of the expected net cost or benefit of the investigation proposal and comment on the reliability of the results obtained. Your answer should include a decision tree illustration of the situation.

April 2000

Figure 2.1 Decision tree analysis of variance investigation

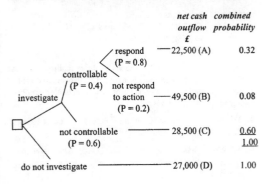

The first step is for you to visualise the structure of the problem. One approach is to create a decision tree which may be shown as in **Figure 2.1.**

The relevant time period is the three months January to March 19x5. After this period we are told to assume that the idle time variance will be eliminated as an existing total quality programme takes effect.

The net cash outflows for the decision tree are calculated as follows:

	A £	B £	C £	D £
Initial investigation cost	1,500	1,500	1,500	nil
Control action cost (£7,000 x 3)	21,000	21,000	nil	nil
Idle time variance cost:				
If non-controllable (£12,000 x 75% x 3)	nil	nil	27,000	27,000
If controllable and responds	nil	nil	nil	nil
If controllable but does not respond	nil	27,000	nil	nil
Total	22,500	49,500	28,500	27,000

Check that you are able to determine the source of each value in Figure 2.1 by referring to the data provided earlier.

Starting from the left hand side, the decision tree shows the decision point between investigate the variance or do not investigate the variance.

● One choice is that we do not investigate the problem. In this case the net cash outflow (D) is £27,000 with a probability of 1.00. This is the payoff or expected value.

● The alternative choice is that we investigate the problem. In this case the payoff or expected value of cash outflow is £22,500 x 0.32 + £49,500 x 0.08 + £28,500 x 0.6 = £28,260.

This indicates that the decision tree shows that the net cost over the January to March period of investigating the excess idle time variance is £28,260 – £27,000 = £1,260. It is better, therefore, not to investigate.

A less expansive solution could have been presented by focusing on the net benefits and costs of investigation over the three month period January to March 19x5. The benefits are the saving of 75% of the variance for three months. The costs are the cost of the initial investigation and the cost of control action for three months. The benefits occur only if the variance responds to the control action (0.4 x 0.8 = 0.32 probability). The initial cost has a probability of 1.00. The control action is only implemented if, on investigation, the variance is found to be controllable (0.4 probability). This may be shown as:

net benefits − net costs
$$= £9,000 \times 3 \times 0.32 - (£1,500 + (3 \times £7,000 \times 0.4))$$
$$= £8,640 - £1,500 - £8,400$$
$$= -£1,260$$

The reliability of the solution depends on the reliability of the data used. Additional questions may be asked. The answers to these may help management in deciding whether or not to investigate the problem. Examples of such questions are:

- How accurate is the estimate of the excess idle time cost during the January to March period?

- What is the basis for the probabilities used? Are they based on historic observations which may not apply in the present TQM situation?

- How accurate are the estimates of the costs of control action and the variance saving which will result therefrom?

Example 3: Use formulae/models provided

You may be provided with a formula or model as part of an examination question. It will be necessary for you to be able to substitute appropriate values for each variable in the formula/model in order that you can calculate the desired solution.

Paper 9, June 1999 Q2 contains a demand projection model given as:

$$D_q = K(4D_{q-1} + 3D_{q-2} + 2D_{q-3})/9$$

Where D_q = number of batches for quarter q
   K = a constant which reflects the impact of a number of key variables on demand.

Paper 9, June 1996 Question 1 required the use of the learning curve formula $y = ax^b$ where:

   y = average cost per batch;

   a = cost of initial batch;

   x = total number of batches;

   b = learning factor.

The learning factor may be provided in the question e.g., $b = -0.3219$ for an 80% learning rate. Alternatively you may simply be told that the learning rate is 80% and be expected to calculate the learning factor. This may be done by calculating the value for the learning factor which may be determined as $b = \log(\text{percentage learning})/\log 2$. We have $b = \log(0.8)/\log 2 = -0.3219$.

In the June 1999 paper 9 question values are provided for variables D_{q-1} etc. and for the constant K. This enables you to calculate the value of D_q. It is also necessary to suggest internal and external variables which might affect the value of the constant K. Examples might include advertising effort and product design changes (internal) or change in customer taste and degree of competition (external). Note that although set in the context of the forecasting model, the ability to name such variables is part of your fundamental knowledge of management accounting.

In the June 1996 paper 9 question you are provided with data which includes:

- Monthly production = 100 batches (i.e., 600 batches for six months).

- Learning rate = 80%.

- Labour cost of the initial batch = 500 hours at £5 per hour = £2,500.

- Variable overhead = 40% of labour rate.

Applying the learning curve formula $y = ax^b$ we can calculate the average cost per batch for the first six months as: $y = 2,500 \times 600^{-0.3219}$

Using a scientific calculator we can readily calculate that $y = £318.90$. You should note that the *Students' Newsletter* regularly carries a note indicating that all candidates for paper 9 should bring to the examination hall and be able to use a scientific calculator with function keys.

Example 4: Apply algebraic principles in order to obtain a required solution

This type of application is relevant where you are asked to calculate the value of a specific variable at which a given outcome will occur and all other variables in the model remain unchanged.

In the paper 9, June 1996 Q1 which was previously used in Example 3, an extension of the scenario is as follows:

- The learning rate and other data given in **Example 3** still applies.

- The net cash inflow from the scenario for the first 6 months is £91,124. You are required to calculate this figure in the examination.

- *You are required to determine the labour hours for the initial batch which would result in the scenario providing the required cash inflow of £100,000 which would provide the target return on investment. All other variables remain as before.*

- You are also told that the labour + variable overhead cost at which the required return will be achieved is £259,000.

This scenario requires you to go through the following sequence of problem solving:

- Required increase in net cash inflow = £100,000 − £91,124 = £8,876.

- We also know that the increase in net cash inflow will be achieved when labour and overhead total is £259,000 for the first six months.

- Since variable overhead is 40% of labour cost we can show a combined labour cost + variable overhead cost factor = 1.00 + 0.4 = 1.40. If labour + overhead = £259,000, we have labour cost = £259,000/1.4 = £185,000.

- To achieve the target return we require: (number of batches x average labour cost per batch) = £185,000 where number of batches = 600; average cost per batch = y.

- We have 600y = £185,000. Solving we have y = £185,000/600 = £308.33.

- But learning curve formula is $y = ax^b$. Substituting we have 308.33 = a x $600^{-0.3219}$; Using a scientific calculator we can readily solve to show that a = £2,417.

- Since the labour rate per hour = £5, initial batch labour hours = £2,417/£5 = 483.4 hours.

Follow through the logic of this process and carry out the calculations on your calculator as additional practice.

Example 5: Information provided as a data table from a spreadsheet model

In paper 9, June 1999 Q3 the early parts of the question requires the calculation of product unit costs for three products. A later part of the question asks the following:

● Cinque division has a proposed strategy to redesign container Uno. There is some controversy as to the effect of the redesign on the number of cuts required per unit, which is seen as a key cost driver in the production process and also on the quantity of direct material which will be required per product unit. Probabilities have been estimated for the level at which the key variables will occur. Number of cuts and quantity of material are independent of each other. The estimates are as follows:

Direct material per unit (sq.m)	Probability	Number of cuts per unit	Probability
1.6	0.3	40	0.3
1.2	0.4	35	0.2
0.8	0.3	25	0.5

You are required to prepare a summary which shows the range of possible activity-based unit cost outcomes for Uno showing the combined probability of each outcome. The two-way data table (**Figure 5.1**) monitors the effect of the proposed redesign on the activity-based product unit cost for product Uno . This may affect the direct material per unit (range 1.6 to 0.8 sq.m) and the number of cuts per unit (range 25 to 50).

In addition, you are required to comment on the likely impact of management's attitude to risk on their decision whether or not to implement the redesign strategy for Uno on financial grounds. Calculation of, and comment on, the expected value of product specific cost for Uno is required in the answer.

Figure 5.1 — Two-way data table

		Number of cuts				
	82.41	25	30	35	40	50
	1.6	94.31	95.38	96.30	97.10	98.42
	1.4	87.00	88.08	89.00	89.80	91.12
Material required	1.2	79.62	80.69	81.61	82.41	83.73
(sq.m)	1	72.14	73.21	74.13	74.93	76.25
	0.8	64.56	65.63	66.55	67.35	68.67

The relevant summary of the range of unit cost outcomes and their probabilities is readily prepared after reference to the above table of probabilities and the two-way datatable (**Figure 5.1**) for the range of values of direct material per product unit and number of cuts per product unit.

The summary of the range of unit cost outcomes is as shown in **Figure 5.2.**

Note that the unit cost values in **Figure 5.2** may be read directly from the data table (**Figure 5.1**). No calculations are required. For example where material required is 1.2sq.m and the number of cuts per unit is 35 we simply read the value of £81.61 from the data table.

April 2000

Many candidates did not realise that the relevant unit costs for Uno were contained in the data table. They attempted to calculate the nine unit costs despite that fact that there was insufficient data in the question to allow this procedure!!

Figure 5.2 — Range of Unit Cost outcomes

Direct Material Sq. m	probability	Number of cuts	probability	Combined probability	Unit cost
1.6	0.3	40	0.3	0.09	97.10
		35	0.2	0.06	96.30
		25	0.5	0.15	94.31
1.2	0.4	40	0.3	0.12	82.41
		35	0.2	0.08	81.61
		25	0.5	0.20	79.62
0.8	0.3	40	0.3	0.09	67.35
		35	0.2	0.06	66.55
		25	0.5	0.15	64.56
				1.00	

In order to calculate the expected value unit cost we multiply the combined probability by the unit cost in each row of the above summary and sum the answers. The answer is £80.74. *Check that you are able to carry out this procedure.*

The quantitative information in **Figure 5.2** may be used when discussing the likely impact of the management's attitude to risk on their decision about the implementation of the redesign. Management may be risk neutral, risk seeking or risk averse. They may view the likely change from the existing ABC cost of £82.41 as the basis for their views. *(Note that the existing ABC cost of £82.41 was calculated in an earlier part of the question. Candidates could have checked their calculations by referring to the data table.)*

● A risk neutral manager may take the view that since the EV unit cost of £80.74 is less than the existing ABC cost, the redesign strategy is worth pursuing;

● There is a 21% likelihood (0.06 + 0.15) of a unit cost less than £67.35 which is approximately a 20% reduction from the current value of £82.41. A risk seeking manager might see this as an attractive possibility;

● There is a 30% likelihood (0.09 +0.06 + 0.15) of a unit cost greater than the existing level of £82.41. This might be enough to lead a risk averse manager to reject the redesign strategy.

This article will be concluded in next month's issue. Part 2 will contain examples to illustrate and comment on:

● information provided an an activity-based matrix;

● maximax/maximin/minimax regret analysis;

● formulation and interpretation of a linear programming model;

● CVP analysis and throughput accounting.

ACCA Students' Newsletter

Technical May 2000

Quantitative applications in paper 9 — Part 2

By George Brown, the Examiner for paper 9

Relevant to paper 9

In part 1 of this article in the April 2000 *Students' Newsletter* we indicated a range of management accounting situations in which quantitative applications have been, and will be, examined in paper 9. Illustrative examples were included as follows:

- use and interpretation of data/information, for example as part of a report;

- form a model of a situation, e.g., a decision tree;

- use formulae/models provided e.g., learning curve;

- apply algebraic principles in order to obtain required solution;

- information provided as a data table from a spreadsheet model to be explained and used.

The remaining topics will be illustrated in **Examples 6 to 9** which follow. These topics are:

- interpretation of information provided as an activity-based budget matrix;

- maximax/maximin/minimax regret analysis;

- formulation and interpretation of a linear programming model;

- CVP analysis and throughput accounting.

Example 6: Information provided as an activity-based budget matrix

Where activity-based budgeting is in use, the budget information may be shown in a matrix format. **Figure 6.1** shows the activity cost matrix for a sales order department as illustrated in paper 9, June 1998 Q2. A brief analysis of the structure of the matrix is as follows:

- The left hand column shows the total budgeted cost by expense type for the sales order department.

- The remaining six columns show the costs for each activity which is part of the sales order department. Customer negotiation, processing of orders (home and export) and implementing dispatches are value added activities. Sales literature and general administration are non-value added activities which support the primary, value added activities.

- Cost drivers have been identified for the value added activities. For example customer negotiation costs are seen as being driven by the number of negotiations taking place.

The question in paper 9 provides additional information which indicates the cost and volume changes which it is estimated will occur on purchase of additional computer software with internet links in order to improve the effectiveness of the sales order department. Candidates were required to use the following additional information in order to prepare an amended activity cost matrix:

1 Reduction in overall salaries by 10% per annum, applied to the existing salary apportionments.

2 Reduction of 60% in the stores/supplies cost in the sales literature activity only.

3 £20,000 of the computer software cost will be allocated to the sales literature activity. The balance will be shared by the other activities in proportion to their existing share of IT costs.

4 Sundry costs for customer negotiation, processing of orders and implementing despatches will vary in proportion to the number of units of each activity. Sundry costs for sales literature and general administration will be unchanged.

5 Amended volume of activity will be: total customers 2,600; customer negotiations 6,000; home orders 5,500; export orders 2,000; despatches to customers 18,750.

Figure 6.1 Activity Cost Matrix — Sales order department

	Total Cost	Customer Negotiations	Processing of orders		Implement Despatches	Sales Literature	General Admin
			Home	Export			
Cost element	£000	£000	£000	£000	£000	£000	£000
Salaries	500	80	160	100	90	20	50
Stores/supplies	90		16	6	8	60	
IT	70	10	30	20	10		
Sundry costs	80	8	10	6	20	10	26
Total	740	98	216	132	128	90	76
Volume of activity:	2,000 Customers	3,000 Negotiations	5,000 orders	1,200 orders	11,500 despatches		

Figure 6.2 Activity Cost Matrix — Sales Order Department (after IT changes)

Cost element	Total Cost	Customer Negotiations	Processing of orders Home	Export	Implement Despatches	Sales Literature	General Admin
	£000	£000	£000	£000	£000	£000	£000
Salaries	450	72	144	90	81	18	45
Stores/supplies	54		16	6	8	24	
IT	300	40	120	80	40	20	
Sundry costs	106	16	11	10	33	10	26
Total	910	128	291	186	162	72	71
Volume of activity:	2,600 Customers	6,000 Negotiations	5,500 orders	2,000 orders	18,750 despatches		

The impact of the above changes on the activity cost matrix have been implemented in the amended matrix shown in Figure 6.2. As a useful learning aid, use the additional information and the original matrix (per Figure 6.1) in order to check that you can arrive at the values in the amended matrix.

Recent industry average statistics for sales order department activities in businesses of similar size, customer mix and product mix are available (these were provided in the June 1998 question). You are required to carry out a benchmarking exercise which compares these industry averages with original and post-IT changes figures from Cognet plc. To do this requires you to abstract information from **Figures 6.1** and **6.2** and carry out calculations as relevant. In addition, you are required to comment on differences between the figures. An appropriate analysis is shown in **Figure 6.3**.

Figure 6.3

	Industry average	Cognet plc Original	Post-IT
Cost per customer per year (£)	300	370	350
Cost per home order (£)	50	43.20	52.91
Cost per export order (£)	60	110	93
Cost per despatch (£)	8	11.13	8.64
Sales literature per customer (£)	35	45	27.69
Average orders per customer (units)	4.1	3.1	2.89
Average despatches per order (units)	3.3	1.85	2.5
Activity measures (numbers of):			
Customers		2,000	2,600
Negotiations		3,000	6,000
Home orders		5,000	5,500
Export orders		1,200	2,000
Despatches		11,500	18,750

Check that you are able to arrive at the analysis in Figure 6.3 using the information from the original and amended activity cost matrices.

A summary of relevant comments relating to the analysis in **Figure 6.3** might be:

- From an internal benchmarking viewpoint, the sales order department (SOD) of Cognet plc will achieve a fall of 5.4% in its average cost per customer. This is however, still 16.7% above the industry average figure.

- Cognet plc will increase its number of customers by 30%. Home orders will increase by 10% and export orders by 67%. We are not provided with industry average figures for such measures. It would also be useful to have information which would enable us to calculate the estimated increase in contribution earned by Cognet plc and whether this would exceed the estimated extra SOD cost of £170,000 for the year.

- The proportion of export orders to total orders for Cognet plc will move from 19.4% to 26.7%. This may be seen as an appropriate move in developing the market base for Cognet plc. Similar information for the industry would be useful.

- The costs per order comparison raises a number of points. Cognet plc cost per home order will rise above the industry average following the IT initiative. The cost per export order will still be 55% higher than the industry average, but will be 15.5% lower than the pre-IT level. We do know that the industry has an average orders per customer ratio of 4.1 compared to the post-IT level of 2.89 for Cognet plc.

- The question indicates that the despatch of part orders has benefits for both Cognet plc and its customers in areas such as stock holding costs and work flow management respectively. The statistics show that the post-IT position for Cognet plc of 2.5 despatches per order is an 'improvement' on the 1.85 despatches per order which applied previously. The new figure is still below the industry average of 3.3 despatches per order.

- The cost per despatch will fall considerably following the IT initiative from £11.13 to £8.64 which is very close to industry average of £8. Since many of the costs are indicated to be mainly fixed in nature, this improvement at Cognet plc may be a function of the increased volume of despatches.

- The sales literature cost per customer will fall from £45 to £27.69 at Cognet plc. The level after the IT initiative will be below the industry average of £35. This may be viewed as an indication of the effectiveness of the new system insofar as it is linked to a 30% increase in customer numbers.

Note that the ability to select relevant quantitative values, ratios and percentages and comment on their possible significance to management for future decision-making and strategic planning changes is a relevant examination focus for paper 9. You should check that you follow the logic and sources of the above comments.

Example 7: maximax/maximin/minimax regret analysis

Stow Health Centre specialises in the provision of sports/ exercise and medical/dietary advice to clients (paper 9, June 1998 Q1). The demand (in client days) is related to the client fee charged. In addition, it is estimated that the variable cost per client day may occur at one of three levels, namely £95, £85 or £70.

Figure 7.1 summarises the total estimated contribution per year for each level of client fee and for each level of variable cost. This gives a total of nine possible budgeted outcomes.

Figure 7.1

Stow Health Centre: budgeted outcome analysis

Client days	Fee per client day £	Variable cost per client day £	Contribution per client day £	Total contrib. per year £
15,750	180	95	85	1,338,750
15,750	180	85	95	1,496,250
15,750	180	70	110	1,732,500
13,125	200	95	105	1,378,125
13,125	200	85	115	1,509,375
13,125	200	70	130	1,706,250
10,500	220	95	125	1,312,500
10,500	220	85	135	1,417,500
10,500	220	70	150	1,575,000

The columns in **Figure 7.1** for client days and fee per client day were compiled in the paper 9 question from data provided. Contribution per client day is fee per client day minus variable cost (e.g., 180 – 95 = 85). The contribution per year is client days x contribution per day (e.g., 15,750 x £85 = £1,338,750).

The **maximax rule** looks for the largest possible contribution from all outcomes. In this case the decision maker will choose a client fee of £180 per day where there is a possibility of a contribution of £1,732,500. This may be seen as the adoption of a risk seeking posture by the decision maker.

The **maximin rule** looks for the strategy which will maximise the minimum possible contribution. In this case the decision-maker will choose a client fee of £200 per day where the lowest contribution is £1,378,125. This is better than the worst possible outcome from client fees per day of £180 or £220 which will provide contribution of £1,338,750 and £1,312,500 respectively. This may be viewed as a risk averse posture by the decision-maker.

The **minimax regret rule** requires the choice of the strategy which will minimise the regret from making the wrong decision. Regret in this context is the opportunity lost through making the wrong decision. Using the calculations from our table of outcomes (**Figure 7.1**), we may create a regret matrix as shown in **Figure 7.2**.

Figure 7.2 — Regret matrix

State of variable cost	Client fee per day strategy £180	£200	£220
High (£95)	39,375	0	65,625
Most likely (£85)	13,125	0	91,875
Low (£70)	0	26,250	157,500
Maximum regret	**39,375**	**26,250**	**157,500**

As examples of the workings for **Figure 7.2** we may show that at the low level of variable cost (£70), the best strategy would be a client fee of £180. The opportunity loss from using a fee of £200 or £220 per day would be £26,250 (1,732,500 – 1,706,250) or £157,500 (1,732,500 – 1,575,000) respectively. This process is repeated for the high (£95) and medium (£85) levels of variable cost. (**Check that you can follow the calculations in the high and most likely rows of Figure 7.2**).

The maximum regret is then calculated for each client fee rate. This is done by selecting the highest figure from each column. This gives maximum regret figures of £39,375, £26,250 and £157,500 for client fee rates of £180, £200 and £220 respectively. The minimum regret strategy (client fee £200 per day) is that which minimises the maximum regret (i.e., £26,250 in the maximum regret row).

Example 8: Formulation and interpretation of a Linear Programming model

Questions may be asked in paper 9 which require the formulation and interpretation of a linear programming model. Solving the model through the application of the simplex technique through successive iterations is not examinable. Examination questions may require the formulation of the model detailing its parameters and constraints together with a requirement to interpret the optimal solution of the model. This solution will be shown as a print out from a computer model of the situation. Any future examination questions will use a computer print-out from the use of the Microsoft Excel Spreadsheet 'Solver' add-on facility. Paper 9, June 1997 Q2 may be used to illustrate the formulation and interpretation process.

The paper 9, June 1997 question indicates that the Alphab Group has five divisions A, B, C, D and E. Group management wish to increase overall group production capacity per year by up to 30,000 hours. Part of the strategy will be to require that the minimum increase at any one division must be equal to 5% of its current capacity. The maximum funds available for the expansion programme are £3,000,000.

Additional information relating to each division is as follows:

Division	Existing capacity (hours)	Investment cost per hour £	Average contribution per hour £
A	20,000	90	12.50
B	40,000	75	9.50
C	24,000	100	11
D	50,000	120	8
E	12,000	200	14

Figure 8.1: Divisional Investment evaluation Optimal solution — detailed report

(Including sensitivity analysis of objective function coefficients and RHS values)

Name	Final value
Contribution	359263.6364

	Hours
Name	Final value
Div A	22090.90909
Div B	2000
Div C	1200
Div D	2500
Div E	2209.090909

Name	Final value	Objective coefficient	Allowable increase	Allowable decrease
Div A	22090.91	12.50	1.50	1.8
Div B	2000.00	9.50	2.80	1E+30
Div C	1200.00	11.00	1.64	1E+30
Div D	2500.00	8.00	4.91	1E+30
Div E	2209.09	14.00	13.78	1.5

Name	Final value	Shadow price	Constraint R.H. Side	Allowable increase	Allowable decrease
Hours	30000.00	11.27	30000	1966.67	11600
Funds	3000000.00	0.01	3000000	2320000.00	177000
Div A	22090.91	0.00	1000	21090.91	1.0E+30
Div B	2000.00	-2.80	2000	18560.00	2000
Div C	1200.00	-1.64	1200	17700.00	1200
Div D	2500.00	-4.91	2500	5900.00	2500
Div E	2209.09	0.00	600	1609.09	1.0E+30

A linear programme of the plan has been prepared in order to determine the strategy which will maximise additional contribution per annum and to provide additional decision-making information. **Figure 8.1** shows a print-out of the optimal solution to an LP model of the situation.

A mathematical model of the situation is required in order that the relevant data can be input to the LP programme and the optimal solution calculated. The relevant model would be as follows:

Maximise $C = 12.5A + 9.5B + 11C + 8D + 14E$ (contribution)
where $A + B + C + D + E \leq 30,000$ (capacity)
and $90A + 75B + 100C + 120D + 200E \leq 3,000,000$ (funds)
Subject to $A \geq 1,000$ (hours)
$\quad\quad\quad B \geq 2,000$ (hours)
$\quad\quad\quad C \geq 1,200$ (hours)
$\quad\quad\quad D \geq 2,500$ (hours)
$\quad\quad\quad E \geq 600$ (hours)
$\quad A,B,C,D,E \geq 0$

Note that all relevant input data is provided in the question as outlined above. We are told that the minimum extra capacity requirements for each division are 5% of current capacity. For example for division A = 20,000 x 5% = 1,000 hours, as indicated in the above quantification of the situation.

It is likely that an examination question will be structured into a series of smaller requirements each of which relates to a specific aspect of

the interpretation of the optimal solution print-out. The interpretation of the **Figure 8.1** information may be summarised as follows:

- The objective function shows that the maximum contribution from the additional 30,000 hours within the overall budget of £3,000,000 of additional funds is £359,263.6.

- The maximum contribution is achieved where the investment provides additional hours in each division as follows:

Division	Hours
A	22,090.9
B	2,000
C	1,200
D	2,500
E	2,209.1
Total	30,000

Note that only divisions A and E have been allocated more hours than the minimum required.

- The shadow prices indicate the opportunity cost of the constraints. For divisions B,C and D the shadow prices measure the cost per hour of choosing to provide the minimum quantity according to group strategy. For example for division D the cost is a loss of contribution of £4.91 per hour. There are no net opportunity costs for divisions A and E.

- For the hours and investment constraints the shadow prices indicate the extra contribution which would be available for each extra hour of machine time (£11.27) or additional £ of investment (£0.01, actually 1.36pence if shown to 4 decimal places of a £).

- The contribution coefficient analysis shows the sensitivity of the plan to changes in the contribution per hour. For example, decreases in contribution would have no effect on the planned allocation in respect of divisions B, C and D (as evidenced by the infinity value (1E+30) allowable decrease). For division A the allowable increase is £1.50 and the allowable decrease is £1.80. This means that contribution would have to rise above £14 per hour (£12.50 + £1.50) or fall below £10.70 per hour (£12.50 – £1.80) for a change in the planned allocation of hours between divisions to occur. For division E corresponding contributions per hour of £27.78 (£14 + £13.78) and £12.50 (£14 – £1.50) respectively would apply.

- If the group relaxes the 30,000 hours capacity constraint, additional contribution could be earned. This could be achieved by transferring investment from Division E to Division A. We could transfer 1609.1 hours from division E (2,209.1 – 600). This would leave the minimum requirement of 600 hours in Division E. The investment released from Division E (at £200 per hour) is £200 x 1609.1 = £321,820. This investment would provide 3,575.77 hours in division A (£321,820/£90) where investment is required at £90 per hour. Note that the net additional hours = 3,575.77 – 1,609.1 = 1,966.67 hours. This is the allowable increase (in excess of 30,000) shown in the sensitivity of RHS values table in **Figure 8.1**. Note that the additional contribution which would be earned from this strategy is (extra hours x shadow price per hour) = 1,966.67 x £11.27 = £22,164.

- The allowable decrease in funds per **Figure 8.1** is £177,000 i.e., from £3,000,000 to £2,823,000. This will result in a fall in contribution which may be calculated as (fall in investment (£) x shadow price per £) = £177,000 x 1.36p = £2,407. (Note that the shadow price shown in **Figure 8.1** is £0.01, actually 1.36p if shown to 4 decimal places). This strategy would occur by reducing the hours in division E from 2,209.1 to the allowable minimum of

600 hours. This will release 1,609.1 hours to division A. This will reduce the investment in division E by 1,609.1 hours x £200 = £321,820. The additional investment required in division A will be 1,609.1 x £90 = £144,820. The net reduction in investment = £321,820 – £144,820 = £177,000 (as indicated above).

This type of analysis requires a clear understanding of the business situation and of the LP model which is used to represent it. In order to satisfy yourself that you understand the procedure, you should check carefully the quantitative manipulations, sources of the quantitative data and explanations provided in the above analysis.

Linear programming has a number of features which limit its usefulness for planning purposes. Examples are as follows:

● It is assumed that all the variables are infinitely divisible which undermines the credibility of the solution. For example in the Alphab situation, 2,209.091 hours are allocated to division E.

● All relevant relationships are assumed to be linear in nature. For example, the model does not allow for economies of scale or diminishing marginal returns.

● The model does not allow for uncertainty, hence all relationships must be stated with certainty and without the incorporation of probability distributions.

● The model is only as accurate as its formulation. For example, all possible uses of scarce resources must have been identified and incorporated into the model.

Example 9: CVP analysis and throughput accounting

The basic principles of contribution analysis suggest that contribution per unit of product is a more relevant measure than net profit per product unit when comparing one product against another. Contribution is seen as a measure of the net cash flow from each product unit of sale. Net profit per unit is calculated after the deduction of an arbitrary apportionment of fixed costs using some appropriate absorption basis. Where there is a limitation on the availability of some input resource, contribution per unit of that limiting factor may be used to rank the products in order that the best financial results will be obtained from the use of the limited resource.

Consider a situation where a company makes and sells two products Basic and Deluxe, each of which passes through the same automated production processes. The following estimated information is available for period 1:

● Product unit data:

	Basic	Deluxe
Direct material cost (£)	5	100
Variable production overhead cost (£)	70	10

● Production/sales of products Basic and Deluxe are currently being planned as 240,000 units and 90,000 units respectively. The selling prices per unit for Basic and Deluxe are £175 and £200 respectively.

● Maximum demand for Basic and Deluxe is 288,000 units and 108,000 units respectively.

● Total fixed production overhead cost is £20,000,000. This is deducted from contribution in order to calculate net profit.

One of the production operations has a maximum capacity of 15,375 hours which has been identified as a bottleneck which limits the overall production/sales of products Basic and

Deluxe. The bottleneck hours required per product unit for products Basic and Deluxe are 0.05 and 0.0375 respectively. We are required to investigate the situation in the context of CVP analysis and throughput accounting.

We can check the bottleneck resource by determining the hours of the resource required for the planned production/sales of Basic and Deluxe. Total hours required = (240,000 x 0.05) + (90,000 x 0.0375) = 15,375 hours. If the company wishes to maximise its profit in period 1, it should consider the product mix that would achieve this.

A CVP analysis of the situation per product unit will show the following:

	Basic	Deluxe
	£	£
Direct material cost	5	100
Variable overhead cost	70	10
Total variable cost	75	110
Selling price	175	200
Contribution per unit	100	90
Bottleneck hours per product unit	0.05	0.0375
Contribution per bottleneck hour	£2,000	£2,400

Note that the total net profit for period 1 from the current plan would be:

		£
Contribution for product Basic = 240,000 x £100		24,000,000
Contribution from product deluxe = 90,000 x £90		8,100,000
Total contribution		32,100,000
Less: fixed overhead cost		20,000,000
Net profit		12,100,000

In this situation the company should change its product mix from the current plan in order to maximise the proportion of the bottleneck resource that is used on product Deluxe which has a contribution per bottleneck hour of £2,400 whereas that of product Basic is only £2,000 per bottleneck hour.

The company should produce and sell product Deluxe up to its maximum demand and then product Basic with the remaining capacity.
Maximum demand of product Deluxe = 108,000 units
Bottleneck hours required for Deluxe

= 108,000 x 0.0375 = 4,050 hours

Bottleneck hour available for Basic = 15,375 – 4,050 = 11,325 hours
Output of product Basic which is possible
= 11,325/0.05 = 226,500 units

The maximum net profit may be calculated as:	£
Contribution product Basic 226,500 x £100	22,650,000
Contribution product Deluxe 108,000 x £90	9,720,000
Total contribution	32,370,000
Less: Fixed overhead cost:	20,000,000
Net profit	12,370,000

Goldratt's theory of constraints (1986) noted that production bottlenecks often limit production output and that producing excessively on non-bottleneck facilities would lead, not to sales but to excess work-in-progress. His theory of constraints focuses on:

● throughput: the rate at which the system generates money. This is viewed as (sales – material costs);

- inventory: is all the money invested in achieving the goods for sale. This is defined as all assets (including stock);

- operational expense: is all the money spent in converting inventory into throughput.

The model may be viewed as:

$$\text{ROI} = \frac{\text{Throughput} - \text{Operational expense}}{\text{Inventory}}$$

Improvement in ROI may be achieved through a combination of increased throughput, reduced operational expense and reduced inventory. This may be viewed as a combination of throughput control, TQM and JIT. TQM should lead to improved product quality and customer satisfaction leading to improved throughput. Its emphasis will be on the effective application of operational expense rather than cost reduction. JIT should lead to a smoother flow of production and should lead to reduced inventory and increased throughput.

Galloway and Waldron (1988) suggested that a revised view was required for manufacturing, to replace traditional concepts such as direct/indirect costs, economic batch sizes and the idea of adding value to stock. It was put forward that principles of throughput accounting may be viewed as:

- the distinction between indirect and direct costs is no longer useful. It is more useful and simpler to consider all cost, excluding material cost, as fixed;

- it is the rate at which the factory earns money that determines profitability, not the contribution from each product;

- inventory is the product of unsynchronised manufacturing and stands between the business and profit;

- profit is a function of material cost, total remaining factory cost and throughput.

Measures relevant to a throughput accounting are seen as:

- return per bottleneck hour = (sales price – material cost)/bottleneck hours per unit;

- cost per bottleneck hour = total overhead cost/total hours of bottleneck resource;

- throughput Accounting (TA) ratio may then be calculated as: **TA Ratio = Return per bottleneck hour/Cost per bottleneck hour.**

We can consider the throughput accounting principles in the context of our example of the company that is producing and selling products Basic and Deluxe.

Consider that the variable overhead should be classified as fixed in the short term and that it will occur at the total value as determined by the original plan of the company for period 1 i.e., 240,000 units of Basic x £70 + 90,000 units of Deluxe x £10 = £17,700,000.

Applying throughput accounting principles we have:

- Return per bottleneck hour
   = (selling price – material cost)/ bottleneck hours per unit
   Product Basic = (175 – 5)/0.05 = £3,400
   Product Deluxe = (200 – 100)/0.0375 = £2,666.67

The company should sell product Basic up to its maximum demand and then product Deluxe using the remaining capacity.

Maximum demand of product Basic = 288,000 units
Bottleneck hours required for product Basic = 288,000 x 0.05 = 14,400 hours
Bottleneck hour available for product Deluxe
= 15,375 – 14,400 = 975 hours

Output of product Deluxe which is possible
= 975/0.0375 = 26,000 units

The maximum net profit may be calculated as:

	£
Throughput return product Basic 288,000 x (£175 – 5)	48,960,000
Throughput return product Deluxe 26,000 x (£200 – 100)	2,600,000
Total throughput return	51,560,000
Less: Overhead cost:	
Shown as variable in original plan now classified as fixed	(17,700,000)
Originally classified as fixed	(20,000,000)
Net profit	13,860,000

Where throughput accounting principles are applied, a product is worth producing and selling so long as its throughput return per bottleneck hour is greater than the average production cost per throughput hour. This may be measured by the throughput accounting ratio. Where the ratio is greater than 1.00, return exceeds cost and the focus should be on improving the size of the ratio.

As discussed above, the throughput accounting ratio = throughput return per bottleneck hour/overall average overhead cost per bottleneck hour.

Using component Deluxe to illustrate, we may calculate the component elements as follows:

Throughput return per bottleneck hour for product Deluxe (as calculated above)

$$= (200 - 100)/0.0375 = £2,666.67$$

The average overhead cost per bottleneck hour
$$= (£17,700,000 + £20,000,000)/15,375$$
$$= £2,452.03$$

This means that we have a throughput accounting ratio for product Deluxe = £2,666.67/£2,452.03 = 1.0875

This is an acceptable return since it is greater than 1.00. However, efforts may be made to improve the position for each product and in total by focusing on areas such as:

- improved throughput (£) per unit by increasing selling price or reducing material cost per unit. Product Deluxe has a high material element (£100 per unit);

- improving the throughput (£) per unit by reducing the time required on the bottleneck resource. Reducing the time for product deluxe from 0.0375 to (say) 0.03 hours per unit through methods changes would improve its ratio;

- improving the overall position by reducing the cost of spare capacity in other areas. This could possibly be achieved by operational re-design aimed at reducing or eliminating the impact of the bottleneck.

Summary

A number of management accounting situations that require some quantitative input have been illustrated in this article. Candidates for paper 9 are required to apply and interpret a wide range of management accounting decision situations which require some quantitative input. Candidates should attempt to improve their ability to manipulate and interpret quantitative information. This may be helped through study of the principles involved and through practice of questions involving quantitative aspects. The presentation of answers is an important feature where the question scenarios include a quantitative element. Improvement of presentation skills is probably best achieved through attempting examination type questions under examination conditions and then checking with the suggested solutions. ∎

Exam question bank

1 CRITERIA FOR INFORMATION (15 marks)

27 mins

Management accounting information should comply with a number of criteria including verifiability, objectivity, timeliness, comparability, reliability, understandability and relevance if it is to be used in planning, control and decision-making.

(a) Explain briefly the meaning of *each* of the criteria named above and give a specific example to illustrate each. (12 marks)

(b) Give a brief explanation of how the criteria detailed in (a) might be in conflict with each other giving examples to illustrate where such conflict might arise. (3 marks)

2 FLAT'S STRATEGY (15 marks)

27 mins

A management consultant has just submitted a report on a publishing company called FLAT Ltd which is struggling to survive in a competitive market. The overall conclusion was that: 'the market leaders maintain their position through their ability to supply high quality books quickly in response to demand ... FLAT Ltd have not been able to match this in either respect.'

Further extracts from the report (with emphasis added by BPP) are shown below.

'... quarterly summarised profit and loss accounts appear to be the only available indicator of *performance* ...'

'The plan for the current year was to reach a market share in excess of 50%. It should have been evident from the outset that this was quite *unachievable* ...'

'... operational staff seem *not to have been made aware* of the company's strategic aims, instead pursuing *their own goals* ...'

Required

(a) Taking account of the competitive environment described in the consultant's conclusion, describe the likely impact on *costs* of the problems highlighted above.

(8 marks)

(b) Explain what is meant by planning at operational level and at strategic level and list the notable traits of the planning process at each level. (7 marks)

3 NELUMBO PLC (35 marks)

63 mins

Nelumbo plc produce truck silencers. The silencers are produced in batches. The production process involves cutting, bending and welding stainless steel sheets and tubing using a special shaping machine. The silencers are then finished by hand.

Three models of silencer are produced: the PN8; the ES6; the LV4. Current selling price are as follows: PN8 £55; ES6 £45; LV4 £35.

Set out below is the budget data for the year ending 30 September 19X5.

	Model		
	PN8	ES6	LV4
Per unit:			
Direct materials weight (kg)	25.00	20.00	15.00
Direct materials cost (£)	12.00	10.00	9.00
Direct labour time (hours)	0.60	0.40	0.60
Direct labour cost (£)	5.40	3.60	5.40
Shaping machine time (hours)	0.30	0.20	0.05
Budgeted output in year (units)	2,200	1,800	600
Standard batch size	10	12	20

Budgeted overheads for the year:	£
Inspection costs	36,000
Shaping machine costs	63,000
Material handling costs	21,000

At present the company attributes overheads to products using absorption costing principles. Overhead is absorbed by product units using rates per direct labour hour. Nelumbo is considering introducing activity based costing (ABC). The following cost drivers have been identified.

365

Inspection costs   Number of production batches
Shaping machine costs   Shaping machine hours
Material handling costs   Weight of material handled

Required

(a)   Calculate the *unit* cost for each model of silencer using the following.

       (i)   The existing absorption costing approach   (9 marks)
       (ii)   The proposed ABC approach   (12 marks)

(b)   Comment on your findings in (a) above.   (5 marks)

(c)   Advocates of ABC claim that use of the concept should not be restricted to calculating product costs. Explain other ways in which Nelumbo could use the activity based concept and the benefits that the company could hope to gain.   (9 marks)

4   RABBIT (20 marks)   *36 mins*

Standard cost information concerning one unit of Hare, the product made by Rabbit Ltd, is as follows.

Sales price	£90
Direct material A	15 kg at £2 per kg
Machine cost	£22 per available hour
Machine operating hours	1.3 hours

Other information concerning Rabbit's operations is as follows.

(a)   Machine processing faults lead to a loss of 6% of material A input to the process.

(b)   Goods receiving procedures and storage of material A costs 18 pence per kg. Inefficiencies in goods receiving procedures and in stores control result in 4% of material A being scrapped.

(c)   The costs of inspection, supplier vetting and other checking procedures amount to £21,000 per month.

(d)   9% of units are rejected during the inspection process at the end of the production cycle. Rejected units are sold as grade B units at 80% of the sales price for a perfect unit.

(e)   4% of units delivered to customers are returned as faulty and are replaced free of charge, incurring a delivery cost of £6 per unit. 60% of the returned units can be rectified in 0.5 hours of machine operating time per unit. These units are sold as grade C units at 40% of the sales price for a perfect unit. The remaining 40% of returned units are sold as scrap for £3 per unit.

(f)   Production volume is increased to allow for inspection rejects and customer returns.

(g)   Product liability insurance and the cost of dealing with other complaints and claims from customers amounts to 2% of the sales revenue from perfect units.

(h)   Machine idle time is currently 18% of available machine hours.

(i)   Selling, distribution and administration overhead amounts to £28,000 per month.

(j)   Customer demand for Hares amounts to 7,000 units per month.

(k)   Finished goods stocks are not held and material stocks are maintained at a constant level.

Rabbit Ltd has been making some attempt to reduce inefficiencies and losses in their operating procedures. The cost of this prevention programme is currently £14,000 per month.

The company is now considering the implementation of total quality management (TQM) procedures. This will increase the cost of the prevention programme by a further £49,000 per month. It is expected that these TQM procedures will lead to the following reductions in inefficiencies and losses.

Operating problem/cost incurred	*Expected reduction*
Material A losses in production	Reduced to 3.5% of material input to process
Material A losses in receiving and stores	Reduced to 2% of material received
Inspection, supplier vetting and checking costs	Reduced by 18% of current amount
Units rejected during inspection process	Reduced to 2.5% of units inspected
Units returned as faulty by customers	Reduced to 1.5% of units delivered
Product liability insurance and customer claims	Reduced to 1.5% of sales revenue from perfect units
Machine idle time	Reduced to 11% of available machine hours
Selling, distribution and administration overhead	Reduced by 5% of current amount
Machine operating hours	Reduced to 1.0 hours per unit

Required

Assuming that Rabbit wishes to satisfy customer demand for 7,000 units per month, calculate the following amounts for each month for the current situation and for the proposed situation once the TQM procedures have been installed.

(a)	Production units required before inspection process	(5 marks)
(b)	Purchases of material A in kg	(4 marks)
(c)	Available machine hours required	(4 marks)
(d)	Monthly profit or loss	(7 marks)

Perform all calculations to the nearest whole number.

5   AB LTD (30 marks)   *54 mins*

AB Ltd produces a consumable compound X, used in the preliminary stage of a technical process that it installs in customers' factories worldwide. An overseas competitor, CD, offering an alternative process which uses the same preliminary stage, has developed a new compound, Y, for that stage which is both cheaper in its ingredients and more effective than X.

At present, CD is offering Y only in his own national market, but it is expected that it will not be long before he extends its sales overseas. Both X and Y are also sold separately to users of the technical process as a replacement for the original compound that eventually loses its strength. This replacement demand amounts to 60% of total demand for X and would do so for Y. CD is selling Y at the same price as X (£64.08 per kg).

AB Ltd discovers that it would take 20 weeks to set up a production facility to manufacture Y at an incremental capital cost of £3,500 and the comparative manufacturing costs of X and Y would be:

	X	Y
	£ per kg	£ per kg
Direct materials	17.33	4.01
Direct labour	7.36	2.85
	24.69	6.86

AB Ltd normally absorbs departmental overhead at 200% of direct labour: 30% of this departmental overhead is variable directly with direct labour cost. Selling and administration overhead is absorbed at one-half of departmental overhead.

The current sales of X average 74 kgs per week and this level (whether of X or of Y if it were produced) is not expected to change over the next year. Because the direct materials for X are highly specialised, AB Ltd has always had to keep large stocks in order to obtain supplies. At present, these amount to £44,800 at cost. Its stock of finished X is £51,900 at full cost. Unfortunately, neither X nor its raw materials have any resale value whatsoever: in fact, it would cost £0.30 per kg to dispose of them.

Over the next three months AB Ltd is not normally busy and, in order to avoid laying off staff, has an arrangement with the trade union whereby it pays its factory operators at 65% of their normal rate of pay for the period whilst they do non-production work. AB Ltd assesses that it could process all its relevant direct materials into X in that period, if necessary.

There are two main options open to AB Ltd:

(a)   to continue to sell X until all its stocks of X (both of direct materials and of finished stock) are exhausted, and then start sales of Y immediately afterwards;

(b)   to start sales of Y as soon as possible and then to dispose of any remaining stocks of X and/or its raw materials.

Required

(a)   Recommend with supporting calculations, which of the two main courses of action suggested is the more advantageous from a purely cost and financial point of view.   (16 marks)

(b)   Identify three major non-financial factors that AB Ltd would need to consider in making its eventual decision as to what to do.   (6 marks)

(c)   Suggest one other course of action that AB Ltd might follow, explaining what you consider to be its merits and demerits when compared with your answer at (a) above.   (8 marks)

6   MANCASTLE CITY (35 marks)   *63 mins*

Mancastle City Football Club intends to sell its present stadium in five years time. In the interim the directors face a decision about the stadium's pitch. A number of experts in the property market have been consulted and most agree that an all-weather pitch will enable the stadium to be sold for £90,000 more (at the end of year 5) than would otherwise be the case. The payment will be received in six years time.

The directors therefore have three options.

(a)   They can retain the present natural grass pitch.

(b)   They can replace the grass pitch with Astroturf (a sort of plastic grass).

(c)   They can replace the grass pitch with a new synthetic material called 'I Can't Believe It's Not Grass', but nicknamed ICING.

The decision also needs to take account of the club's cost of capital (8%) and incorporate inflation, which industry commentators have predicted will show the following pattern.

19X0	(ie year 0)	100
19X1		103
19X2		103
19X3		105
19X4		105
19X5		107

(a)   Upkeep of the present *natural grass pitch* entails the following expenditure.

(i)	Fertiliser, grass seed, chemicals, etc	£53,000
(ii)	Groundspersons' salaries (proportion)	£42,000

The groundspersons also look after the seating area, leisure areas, and offices of the stadium. The above proportion is an allocation of total salary costs on the basis of time spent.

The club built up a store of chemicals some time ago in anticipation of price rises: if bought today the club would have to pay 15% more for its chemicals. These have no alternative uses or sales value, but there are enough chemicals to last for another three years, so actual costs in this category will be £10,000 per annum less than that stated above for this period.

(b)   As for the *all-weather* options, Astroturf costs £29 per square metre while Icing is sold in units of 5 square metres and costs £800 per unit. The pitch (and its surrounding verge) will measure 110m by 90m. If either option is chosen, payment will be made *now* (ie the end of 19X0).

If either type of all-weather pitch is introduced it will become possible to use the main stadium for practice purposes some of the time. This in turn will enable the use of the current practice pitch to be reduced. Last year Mancastle City paid a fixed flat fee of £25,000 for the use of a practice ground and a further £78,000 in 'session' fees, chargeable at a rate per training session (3 hours). Astroturf will enable the number of sessions at the practice ground to be cut by 55%. If the slightly more delicate Icing is used the number of sessions will be reduced by 45%.

Upkeep of an all-weather pitch (of either type) entails the following annual expenditure.

(i)	Replacement of damaged 'turfs' (year 1 price)	£23,000
(ii)	Groundspersons' salaries (proportion) (year 1 price level)	£25,000

It is estimated that the cost of replacement turfs will be 10% greater in year 2 and a further 5% greater in each of years 3 to 5. (This is in addition to general inflation.)

No change in overall groundsperson's salaries is anticipated.

Required

(a)   Identify the costs, revenues or cashflows that are *not* relevant to the decision, and explain why not.   (4 marks)

(b)   Perform calculations so as to advise the club's board of directors whether it is worthwhile to replace the natural grass pitch and if so with which of the two alternative all-weather pitches.   (17 marks)

(c)   One expert's forecast of the likely improvement in the disposal value of the stadium in five years time would leave the club indifferent between keeping the present pitch and replacing it with an Astroturf pitch. How much of an improvement did this expert forecast?   (4 marks)

(d) The directors have expressed dissatisfaction with the information they have been given to help them reach their decision.

    (i)   A lot of estimates have been used.

    (ii)   There may be other matters that have not been taken into account.

Required

Explain how the first problem could be overcome and give examples of other information that may affect the calculations. (10 marks)

---

7 THISTLEKILM PLC (20 marks)   *36 mins*

Thistlekilm plc is a food processing group with a number of subsidiaries producing similar but differently branded products. Zilch Ltd, for example, produce FA, which is a sugar-free version of the product of Nowt Ltd, which is called SFA.

Both products contain base ingredients Nix and Nill which are obtained from O division and Z division respectively of the parent company. SFA requires 1 kg of Nix and 4 kgs of Nill per batch. FA requires 2 kgs of Nix and 3 kgs of Nill per batch.

Divisions O and Z produce only these ingredients and do so for the exclusive use of companies within the group. However, they are unable to produce enough Nix and Nill to allow Nowt Ltd and Zilch Ltd to exploit the demand for SFA and FA to the full. Production of SFA is also subject to the availability of the sweetener, Sucradam, which is obtained from sources external to the group.

All of the necessary details have been fed into a computer whose linear programming facility has come up with the following print-out.

Thistlekilm plc

LP optimal solution - detailed report

			Value
1:	*Variable*		
2:	1	SFA	960.00
3:	2	FA	480.00
4:	3	Slack A	0.00
5:	4	Slack B	0.00
6:	5	Slack C	240.00
7:			

	Constraint	*Type*	*RHS*	*Slack*	*Shadow price*
8:					
9:	Nix	≤	2,400.00	0.00	–120.00
10:	Nill	≤	2,400.00	0.00	–20.00
11:	Sucradam	≤	1,200,00	240.00	0.00
12:					
13:	*Objective function value*		336,000.00		
14:					

	Sensitivity analysis of objective function coefficients		
15:			
16:	*Variable*	*Current coefficient*	*Allowable minimum*	*Allowable maximum*
17:	SFA	200.00	100.00	225.00
18:	FA	300.00	266.67	600.00
19:				

	Sensitivity analysis of RHS values			
20:				
21:	*Constraint*	*Type*	*Current value*	*Allowable minimum*	*Allowable maximum*
22:	Nix	≤	2,400.00	1,000.00	3,600.00
23:	Nill	≤	2,400.00	1,500.00	4,800.00
24:	Sucradam	≤	1,200.00	960.00	∞

Required

Explain what the values in the print-out mean and how they are relevant to management.

BPP PUBLISHING

8   **ALLEGRO FINISHES LTD   (15 marks)**   *27 mins*

(a)   Allegro Finishes Ltd is about to launch an improved version of its major product - a pocket chess computer - onto the market. Sales of the original model (at £65 per unit) have been at the rate of 50,000 per annum but it is now planned to withdraw this model and the company is now deciding on its production plans and pricing policy.

The standard variable cost of the new model will be £50 which is the same as that of the old, but the company intends to increase the selling price 'to recover the research and development expenditure that has been incurred'. The research and development costs of the improved model are estimated at £750,000 and the intention is that these should be written off over 3 years. Additionally there are annual fixed overheads of approximately £800,000 allocated to this product line.

The sales director has estimated the *maximum* annual demand figures that would obtain at three alternative selling prices. These are as follows:

Selling price £	Estimated maximum annual demand physical units
70	75,000
80	60,000
90	40,000

The sales director has estimated for each selling price, an optimistic, a pessimistic and a most likely demand figure and associated probabilities for each of these. For the £90 price the estimates are:

	Annual demand	Probability of demand
Pessimistic	20,000	0.2
Most likely	35,000	0.7
Optimistic	40,000	0.1
		1.0

On the cost side, it is clear that the standard unit variable cost of £50 is an 'ideal' which has rarely been achieved in practice. An analysis of the past 20 months shows that the following pattern of variable cost variances (per unit of output) has arisen:

(i)   an adverse variance of around £10 arose on 4 occasions
(ii)   an adverse variance of around £5 arose on 14 occasions
(iii)   a variance of around 0 arose on 2 occasions.

There is no reason to think that the pattern for the improved model will differ significantly from this or that these variances are dependent upon the actual demand level.

Required

From the above, calculate the expected annual profit for a selling price of £90.   (5 marks)

(b)   A tabular summary of the result of an analysis of the data for the other two selling prices (£70 and £80) is as follows:

	£70	£80
Probability of a loss of £500,000 or more	0.02	0.00
Probability of a loss of £300,000 or more	0.07	0.05
Probability of a loss of £100,000 or more	0.61	0.08
Probability of break-even or worse	0.61	0.10
Probability of break-even or better	0.39	0.90
Probability of a profit of £100,000 or more	0.33	0.52
Probability of a profit of £300,000 or more	0.03	0.04
Probability of a profit of £500,000 or more	0.00	0.01
Expected value of profit (loss)	(£55,750)	£68,500

You are required to compare your calculations in part (a) with the above figures and to write a short memo to the sales director outlining your advice and commenting on the use of subjective discrete probability distributions in problems of this type.   (10 marks)

9   ABC LTD (25 marks)   *45 mins*

(a)   ABC Ltd Manufactures a wide range of components for use in various industries.   It has developed a new component called the unit.   It is the practice of ABC Ltd to set a 'list' selling price for its components and charge this price to all customers.   It sells its components directly to customers all over the UK and abroad.

ABC Ltd has surplus capacity available to enable it to produce up to 350,000 units per year without any need to acquire new facilities or cut back on the production of other products.

Market research indicates that the demand for units per year will move as follows in response to changes in selling price.

(i)   At a selling price of £9.00 per unit, no units will be sold.

(ii)   For every 3p the selling price is reduced below that figure sales will increase by 1,000 units until total sales reach 100,000 units.

(iii)   From that point, the selling price must be reduced by 4p for each additional 1,000 units increase in sales.

Research into production costs indicates that the marginal costs for unit production in any given year are as follows.

(i)   *Labour*: initially £2.00 per unit but falling by 2.5p per unit for each extra 1,000 units produced, thus the first 1,000 units produced incurs a labour cost of £2,000, the second 1,000 incurs a labour cost of £1,975, the third 1,000 incurs a labour cost of £1,950 and so on until output reaches 80,000; output can be increased beyond 80,000 units per year without incurring any additional labour costs.

(ii)   *Materials*: 50p per unit constant at all levels of output.

(iii)   *Overhead*: initially £1.00 per unit and remaining constant until output reaches 100,000 units per year; the overhead cost per unit of producing at above that level rises by 0.25p for each extra 1,000 units produced, thus the 101st thousand units produced incurs an overhead cost of £1,002.50, the 102nd thousand units produced incurs an overhead cost of £1,005 and so on.

Required

Calculate (accurate to the nearest penny) the selling price per unit that will maximise ABC Ltd's profit from unit production.   (15 marks)

(b)   'There are various problems arising from setting a single price for your product and charging all the customers the same. For one thing, you forgo revenue from customers who would be prepared to pay a higher price. For another thing you turn away customers who would be prepared only to pay a lower price but one which exceeds variable production costs.'

Required

Discuss this statement with reference to ABC Ltd and its sale of units.   (10 marks)

10   ZBB LTD (20 marks)   *36 mins*

ZBB Ltd has two service departments - material handling and maintenance, which are in competition for budget funds which must not exceed £925,000 in the coming year. A zero base budgeting approach will be used whereby each department is to be treated as a decision package and will submit a number of levels of operation showing the minimum level at which its service could be offered and two additional levels which would improve the quality of the service from the minimum level.

The following data have been prepared for each department showing the three possible operating levels for each.

Material handling department

Level 1. A squad of 30 labourers would work 40 hours per week for 48 weeks of the year. Each labourer would be paid a basic rate of £4 per hour for a 35 hour week. Overtime hours would attract a premium of 50% on the basic rate per hour. In addition, the company anticipates payments of 20% of gross wages in respect of employee benefits. Directly attributable variable overheads would be incurred at the rate of 12p per man hour. The squad would move 600,000 kilos per week to a warehouse at the end of the production process.

Level 2. In addition to the level 1 operation, the company would lease 10 fork lift trucks at a cost of £2,000 per truck per annum. This would provide a better service by enabling the same volume of output as for level 1 to be moved to a customer collection point which would be 400 metres closer to the main factory gate. Each truck would be manned by a driver working a 48 week year. Each driver would receive a fixed weekly wage of £155.

Directly attributable overheads of £150 per truck per week would be incurred.

Level 3. A computer could be leased to plan the work of the squad of labourers in order to reduce their total work hours. The main benefit would be improvement in safety through reduction in the time that work in progress would lie unattended. The computer leasing costs would be £20,000 for the first quarter (3 months), reducing by 10% per quarter cumulatively thereafter.

The computer data would result in a 10% reduction in labourer hours, half of this reduction being a saving in overtime hours.

Maintenance department

Level 1. Two engineers would each be paid a salary of £18,000 per annum and would arrange for repairs to be carried out by outside contractors at an annual cost of £250,000.

Level 2. The company would employ a squad of 10 fitters who would carry out breakdown repairs and routine maintenance as required by the engineers. The fitters would each be paid a salary of £11,000 per annum.

Maintenance materials would cost £48,000 per annum and would be used at a constant rate throughout the year. The purchases could be made in batches of £4,000, £8,000, £12,000 or £16,000. Ordering costs would be £100 per order irrespective of order size and stock holding costs would be 15% per annum. *The minimum cost order size would be implemented.*

Overheads directly related to the maintenance operation would be a fixed amount of £50,000 per annum.

In addition to the maintenance squad it is estimate that £160,000 of outside contractor work would still have to be paid for.

Level 3. The company could increase its maintenance squad to 16 fitters which would enable the service to be extended to include a series of major overhauls of machinery. The additional fitters would be paid at the same salary as the existing squad members.

Maintenance materials would now cost £96,000 per annum and could be used at a constant rate throughout the year. Purchases could be made in batches of £8,000, £12,000 or £16,000. Ordering costs would be £100 per order (irrespective of order size) and stock holding costs would now be 13.33% per annum. In addition, suppliers would now offer discounts of 2% of purchase price for orders of £16,000. The minimum cost order size would be implemented.

Overheads directly related to the maintenance operation would increase by £20,000 from the level 2 figure.

It is estimated that £90,000 of outside contractor work would still have to be paid for.

Required

(a) Determine the incremental cost for each of levels 1, 2 and 3 in each department. (16 marks)

(b) In order to choose which of the incremental levels of operation should be allocated the limited budgeted funds available, management have estimated a 'desirability factor' which should be applied to each increment. The ranking of the increments is then based on the 'incremental cost x desirability factor' score, whereby a high score is deemed more desirable than a low score. The desirability factors are estimated as:

	Material handling	Maintenance
Level 1	1.00	1.00
Level 2 (incremental)	0.60	0.80
Level 3 (incremental)	0.50	0.20

Use the above ranking process to calculate which of the levels of operation should be implemented in order that the budget of £925,000 is not exceeded. (4 marks)

11   **BLYTHELY LTD   (15 marks)**   *27 mins*

Blythely Ltd make a single product and operate a standard costing system in respect of labour and materials, but not overheads (which are all fixed). The standards per unit of output in the first half of 19X5 were as follows.

Material   4 kg at £60 per kg
Direct labour   50 hours at £2.50 per hour

When reviewing the results for the first half of 19X5 the company's new operations manager came to the conclusion that the standards for materials had been inappropriately set. He challenges you, as the management accountant, to take action.

Required

(a)   Set out the alternative bases which might have been used in setting the original standards and compare these alternatives in terms of the significance of variances arising from the use of each of them respectively.   (10 marks)

(b)   Answer a criticism by the operations manager that, given time and usage standards, in hours and kg respectively, he could control the business satisfactorily without the use of any cost standards.
                                                                                        (5 marks)

It is not necessary to make calculations in answering this question.

12   **A1 TRADITIONAL TRADES (20 marks)**   *36 mins*

A1 Traditional Trades Ltd is a firm that employs a number of local tradespersons and offers a variety of building services to domestic customers and small businesses. As at the beginning of the year under discussion the company employed a total of 25 tradespersons at an average annual salary of £18,000. Staff turnover in this type of industry tends to be high, although qualified and experienced staff are easy to recruit.

Essentially the work is divisible into 24-hour emergency services and longer-term work. However an activity analysis has also identified that tradespersons spend a significant amount of time on activities whose costs cannot be passed on to customers.

(a)   Travelling between jobs, paperwork etc

(b)   Estimates, which have to be provided free to match local competitors

(c)   Return visits to finish off jobs or rectify faults. Finishing-off visits are often necessary (for example after plumbing has 'settled in' or plaster has dried), especially with emergency work. It is now company policy not to charge for such visits, as part of a marketing initiative.

The company is presently analysing its performance for the year just finished. The following information has been collected.

Tradespersons' timesheets analysis

	Budget Hours	Actual Hours
Long-term work	25,000	11,531
Emergency work	10,000	25,480
Travelling, administration	8,000	9,875
Return visits	5,000	9,920
Estimates	2,000	3,194
Total hours	50,000	60,000

Additional hours worked are paid at the same average rate as budgeted hours.

Where time can be billed to customers the charge-out rate is £40 per hour.

Direct costs of materials are always recovered in full from customers. Budgeted overheads were £525,000. Actual overheads were £794,000.

Required

(a)   Analyse the timesheet information so as to provide a meaningful comparison, in terms of both *hours and money*, between each category of time spent. Variances should be valued at the standard charge-out rate.   (17 marks)

(b) Prepare a summary statement showing budgeted and actual profit or loss for the year (variances are not required), and comment on the company's financial performance. Capital employed is £800,000. (3 marks)

13 LEARNING CURVE EFFECT (25 marks)   *45 mins*

(a) Z plc experiences difficulty in its budgeting process because it finds it necessary to quantify the learning effect as new products are introduced. Substantial product changes occur and result in the need for retraining.

An order for 30 units of a new product has been received by Z plc. So far, 14 have been completed; the first unit required 40 direct labour hours and a total of 240 direct labour hours has been recorded for the 14 units. The production manager expects an 80% learning effect for this type of work.

The company uses standard absorption costing. The direct costs attributed to the centre in which the unit is manufactured and its direct material costs are as follows:

Direct material	£30.00 per unit
Direct labour	£6.00 per hour
Variable overhead	£0.50 per direct labour hour
Fixed overhead	£6,000 per four-week operating period

There are ten direct employees working a five-day week, eight hours per day. Personal and other downtime allowances account for 25% of the total available time.

The company usually quotes a four-week delivery period for orders.

Required

(i) Determine whether the assumption of an 80% learning effect is a reasonable one in this case, by using the standard formula $y = ax^b$

where y = the cumulative average direct labour time per unit (productivity)
       a = the average labour time per unit for the first batch
       x = the cumulative number of batches produced
       b = the index of learning. (5 marks)

(ii) Calculate the number of direct labour hours likely to be required for an expected second order of 20 units. (5 marks)

(iii) Use the cost data given to produce an estimated product cost for the initial order, examining the problems which may be created for budgeting by the presence of the learning effect. (10 marks)

(b) It is argued that in many areas of modern technology, the 'learning curve' is of diminishing significance. An 'experience curve' effect would still be present and possibly strengthened in importance. However, the experience curve has little to do with short-term standard setting and product costing.

You are required to discuss the validity of the above statement, in particular the assertion that the experience curve has little relevance to costing. (5 marks)

14 WIMBRUSH LTD (20 marks)   *36 mins*

The management of Wimbrush Ltd feel that standard costing and variance analysis have little to offer in the reporting of some of the activities of their firm.

'Although we produce a range of fairly standardised products' states the accountant of Wimbrush Ltd, 'prices of many of our raw materials are apt to change suddenly and comparison of actual prices with pre-determined, and often unrealistic, standard price is of little use. For some of our products, we can utilise one of several equally suitable raw materials and we always plan to utilise the raw material which will, in our opinion, lead to the cheapest total production costs. However, we are frequently caught out by price changes and the material actually used often proves, after the event, to have been more expensive than the alternative which was originally rejected.

For example, consider the experience over the last accounting period of two of our products, Widgets and Splodgets. To produce a Widget we can use either 5 kg of X or 5 kg of Y. We planned to use X as it appeared it would be the cheaper of the two and our plans were based on a cost of X of £3 per kg.

Due to market movements the actual prices changed and if we had purchased efficiently the costs would have been:

Material X   £4.50 per kg

Material Y   £4.00 per kg

Production of Widgets was 2,000 units and usage of X amounted to 10,800 kg at a total cost of £51,840.

A Splodget uses only one raw material, Z, but again the price of this can change rapidly. It was thought that Z would cost £30 per tonne but in fact we only paid £25 per tonne and if we had purchased correctly the cost would have been less as it was freely available at only £23 per tonne. It usually takes 1.5 tonnes of Z to produce 1 Splodget but our production of 500 Splodgets used only 700 tonnes of Z.

So you can see that with our particular circumstances the traditional approach to variance analysis is of little use and we don't use it for materials, although we do use it for reporting on labour and variable overhead costs'.

Required

(a)   Analyse the material variances for both Widgets and Splodgets, utilising:

  (i)   traditional variance analysis; and
  (ii)   an approach which distinguishes between planning and operational variances.

                                                                                                   (11 marks)

(b)   Write brief notes which:

  (i)   explain the approach to variance analysis which distinguishes between planning and operational variances; and

  (ii)   indicate the extent to which this approach is useful for firms in general and for Wimbrush Ltd in particular; and

  (iii)   highlight the main difficulty in the application of this approach.   (9 marks)

15   NARUD PLC (35 marks)   *63 mins*

Use the accompanying tables to answer the following question.

Narud plc is nearing the end of year 7 and has prepared summary profit and loss account data for year 6 (actual) and year 7 (projected actual) as shown in Table 1. Table 1 also shows the bank overdraft at the end of year 6 and the projected bank overdraft at the end of year 7. Sales and production mix may be taken as constant from year 6 to year 9, with all production being sold in the year of production.

Budgeted direct material cost is variable with output volume but budgeted direct labour cost contains a fixed element of £50,000 in year 6 with the remainder varying with production volume and used in the calculation of the labour efficiency index in Table 2.

Production overhead contains a fixed element of £150,000 (at year 6 price levels). Included within this fixed element is a depreciation provision of £30,000 which will remain unaltered irrespective of price level changes.

Variable production overhead varies in proportion to units produced.

Budgeted administration/selling overhead is wholly fixed, whilst distribution expense should vary with sales volume.

The financial charges figure for each year is calculated as the average borrowing for the year times the borrowing rate (taken as 20%), ie financial charges per year = $((2x - y) \times 0.20)/2$.

where   x = previous year end overdraft and
             y = net profit for current year before financial charges and depreciation.

Narud plc are concerned about the level of borrowing and high financial charges. A number of changes are planned in order to attempt to eliminate the overdraft by the end of year 9, eg:

(a)   change the type of material used from year 8 onwards as a means of reducing scrap and hence improving efficiency;

(b)   it is anticipated that the material change per (i) above, together with extra training of operatives in each of years 8 and 9 will improve labour efficiency;

(c)   selling prices will be cut in years 8 and 9 in order to stimulate demand.

Tables 2 and 3 show cost indices for performance and price respectively which show the projected changes from a year 6 base of 100. The performance indices show the cost effect of performance changes, eg material usage in year 8 indicates a 5% cost reduction for the base year level because of the reduced scrap level of material per product unit referred to in (i) above.

Table 4 shows the sales volume and price movements from a 6 year base of 100.

Required

(a) Give detailed working calculations which show how the year 7 projected figures (per Table 1) have been arrived at for (i) labour cost (ii) production overhead and (iii) financial charges, using the year 6 data per Table 1 as the starting point and using indices from Tables 2, 3 and 4 as necessary. (10 marks)

(b) Prepare forecast profit and loss accounts for years 8 and 9 and calculate the forecast bank balance or overdraft at the end of years 8 and 9, assuming that the overdraft is affected only by net profit adjusted for the non-cash effect of the depreciation charge. (15 marks)

(c) Enumerate *three* items not incorporated in the profit and loss account which may affect cash flow. (5 marks)

(d) Explain how the calculations in (b) above demonstrate the use of a feed-forward control model. (5 marks)

Table 1
Narud plc Summary profit and loss account

	Year 6 £	Year 7 £
Sales revenue	2,000,000	2,310,000
Less cost of sales:		
Direct material cost	1,000,000	1,201,200
Direct labour cost	150,000	163,300
Production overhead	310,000	350,124
Admin/selling overhead	100,000	115,500
Distribution overhead	140,000	158,466
Financial charges	130,000	124,859
	1,830,000	2,113,449
Net profit	170,000	196,551
Bank overdraft	800,000	573,449

Table 2
Indices reflecting the cost effect of changes in performance level from year 6

Year	Material usage	Labour efficiency	Production overhead utilisation (fixed and variable)	Admin/selling overhead utilisation	Distribution overhead utilisation
6	100	100	100	100	100
7	104	103	103	110	98
8	95	99	99	105	95
9	85	97	97	100	95

Note: utilisation indices monitor the cost effect of a change in the quantity of a cost item used (a) other than changes due to a change in the number of units produced and (b) even where the cost is defined as fixed by the company.

Table 3
Indices reflecting the cost effect of price level changes from year 6

Year	Material price	Labour rate	All overheads expenditure
6	100	100	100
7	105	100	105
8	120	110	112
9	125	115	118

Table 4
Indices for sales/production volume changes and sales price changes from year 6

Year	Sales volume	Sales price
6	100	100
7	110	105
8	120	103
9	130	101

16 NOT FOR PROFIT ORGANISATIONS (25 marks) 45 mins

(a) The absence of the profit measure in Not for Profit (NFP) organisations causes problems for the measurement of their efficiency and effectiveness.

You are required to explain:

(i) why the absence of the profit measure should be a cause of the problems referred to;
(9 marks)

(ii) how these problems extend to activities within business entities which have a profit motive. Support your answer with examples. (4 marks)

(b) A public health clinic is the subject of a scheme to measure its efficiency and effectiveness. Amongst a number of factors, the 'quality of care provided' has been included as an aspect of the clinic's service to be measured. Three features of 'quality of care provided' have been listed:

(i) Clinic's adherence to appointment times
(ii) Patients' ability to contact the clinic and make appointment without difficulty
(iii) The provision of a comprehensive patient health monitoring programme

You are required:

(i) to suggest a set of quantitative measures which can be used to identify the effective level of achievement of each of the features listed; (9 marks)

(ii) to indicate how these measures could be combined into a single 'quality of care' measure.

(3 marks)

17 TRANSFER PRICING (35 marks) 63 mins

(a) Consider the advantages and disadvantages of the following.

(i) Market price based transfer prices.
(ii) Cost based transfer prices.

Outline the main variants that exist under each heading. (13 marks)

(b) Black and Brown are two divisions in a group of companies and both require intermediate products Alpha and Beta which are available from divisions A and B respectively. Black and Brown divisions convert the intermediate products into products Blackalls and Brownalls respectively. The market demand for Blackalls and Brownalls considerably exceeds the production possible because of the limited availability of intermediate products Alpha and Beta. No external market exists for Alpha and Beta and no other intermediate product market is available to Black and Brown divisions.

Other data are as follows.

Black division
Blackalls: Selling price per unit £45
Processing cost per unit £12
Intermediate products required per unit:
Alpha: 3 units
Beta: 2 units

Brown division

Brownalls:	Selling price per unit £54
	Processing cost per unit £14
	Intermediate products required per unit:
	Alpha: 2 units
	Beta: 4 units

A division

| *Alpha:* | Variable cost per unit £6 |
| | Maximum production capacity 1,200 units |

B division

| *Beta:* | Variable cost per unit £4 |
| | Maximum production capacity 1,600 units |

The solution to a linear programming model of the situation shows that the imputed scarcity value (shadow price) of Alpha and Beta is £0.50 and £2.75 per unit respectively and indicates that the intermediate products be transferred such that 200 units of Blackalls and 300 units of Brownalls are produced and sold.

Required

(i)   Calculate the contribution earned by the group if the sales pattern indicated by the linear programming model is implemented.   (3 marks)

(ii)   Where the transfer prices are set on the basis of variable cost plus shadow price, show detailed calculations for the following.

   (1)   The contribution per unit of intermediate product earned by divisions A and B.
   (2)   The contribution per unit of final product earned by Black and Brown divisions.
                                                                                      (4 marks)

(iii) Comment on the results derived in (b) and on the possible attitude of management of the various divisions to the proposed transfer pricing and product deployment policy.
                                                                                      (6 marks)

(iv)   In the following year the capacities of divisions A and B have each doubled and the following changes have taken place.

   Alpha: There is still no external market for this product, but A division has a large demand for other products which could use the capacity and earn a contribution of 5% over costs. Variable cost per unit for the other products would be the same as for Alpha and such products would use the capacity at the same rate as Alpha.

   Beta: An intermediate market for this product now exists and Beta can be bought and sold in unlimited amounts at £7.50 per unit. External sales of Beta would incur additional transport costs of 50p per unit which are not incurred in inter-divisional transfers.

   The market demand for Blackalls and Brownalls will still exceed the production availability of Alpha and Beta.

   (1)   Calculate the transfer prices at which Alpha and Beta should now be offered to Black and Brown divisions in order that the transfer policy implemented will lead to the maximisation of group profit.

   (2)   Determine the production and sales pattern for Alpha, Beta, Blackalls and Brownalls which will now maximise group contribution and calculate the group contribution thus achieved. It may be assumed that divisions will make decisions consistent with the financial data available.   (9 marks)

18   **RED OCHRE LTD (25 marks)**   *45 mins*

Red Ochre Ltd is divided into ten operating divisions, each of which is autonomous. The cost of capital for the group is 12% per annum and it is currently earning 15% on its capital employed.

In the ROCE calculation, return is equated with net profit and capital employed is the figure at the beginning of the financial year. All fixed assets are depreciated on a straight-line basis. Investments in new projects include incremental working capital. Projects sold or withdrawn from operation are treated as consisting of fixed assets only.

If no new capital expenditure transactions take place the position of four of the divisions would be:

Division	Capital employed as at 1 January 19X0	Net profit	Budgeted for 19X0 Sales
	£000	£000	£000
P	320	80	800
Q	450	150	1,400
R	280	84	700
S	200	26	200

The following transactions are proposed:

Division P   Investment of £100,000 to yield sales of £150,000 per annum and net profit of £20,000 per annum.

Division Q   Sale for £75,000 of a project that is budgeted to yield a net profit of £15,000 in 19X0. The original equipment cost £600,000 seven years ago with an expected life of eight years.

Division R   (a) sale of product line at book value. The original equipment cost £60,000 two years ago with an expected life of three years. This line is budgeted to yield a net profit of £20,000 in 19X0; combined with

   (b) replacement of (a) above by investing £100,000 in a new product to yield £30,000 per annum.

Division S   Investment of £80,000 in a project to yield sales of £36,000 per annum and a net profit of £11,200 per annum.

(*Note.* In connection with each of the above transactions, you are to assume that the sale and/or investment would be completed by 1 January 19X0 so as to be included in the relevant ROCE calculations for the year 19X0. Ignore taxation and inflation considerations and assume that actual results are as budgeted.)

Required

(a)   On the assumption that each transaction goes ahead:

   (i)   calculate the new ROCE for each division for the year ending 31 December 19X0;

   (ii)   identify those divisional managers whose bonuses will be higher if they receive annual bonuses directly related to the level of their respective ROCE;

   (iii)   state, in respect of each division, whether the group's interests will be favourably or adversely affected by the proposed transactions. Explain briefly why in each case.

(10 marks)

(b)   Identify, with brief reasons, which proposals the group would approve if its new capital expenditure were limited to £200,000 for the four divisions.   (3 marks)

(c)   (i)   Compare the old results of division P and division S, both of which are in the same type of business, and briefly advise the divisional manager of S how he might improve his performance based on the data concerning division P.

   (ii)   Comment briefly on how the new project for division S fits in with the advice given in (c)(i) above.   (3 marks)

(d)   Calculate the lowest price at which the equipment should be sold by division Q if the transaction proposed is to break even financially for the group.   (3 marks)

(e)   (i)   Explain briefly the concept of 'residual income' in the context of performance evaluation.

   (ii)   Calculate the residual income for each division for 19X0 on the assumption that each transaction goes ahead, and compare this with the original residual income figures budgeted for 19X0.   (6 marks)

Exam answer bank

1   CRITERIA FOR INFORMATION

> *Tutorial note.* To answer it well you need to draw on concepts that you studied at earlier levels as well as material in this Chapter 1. Your explanations should be brief and they **must include examples**, otherwise you would not pass on this question.

(a)   *Criteria for judging management information*

(i)   *Relevance.* Recipients of management accounting information should not be required to search through irrelevant information in order to locate what is relevant to them. Information is likely to be ignored if it is largely irrelevant. The preparation of budgetary statements using the exceptions principle is an example of a technique to ensure that management attention is drawn only to those items which are important and relevant.

(ii)   *Comprehensibility.* Management accounting information should be presented in a way that is understandable to its recipient. For instance, information prepared by the management accountant for the finance director can reasonably contain some technical financial terms. However, a report prepared for the factory foreman may not be understandable if it contains the same amount of jargon.

(iii)   *Reliability.* Managers should be able to rely on management accounting information as being consistent in quality and accuracy. The reliability of information can be improved through the use of standardised procedures. The inclusion of standard assumptions and instructions in a budget manual is an example of an attempt to improve the reliability of budgetary planning information.

(iv)   *Comparability.* Management accounting information must be prepared in such a way that useful comparisons can be made effectively. If two mutually exclusive contracts are under consideration then the data and information used to analyse the contracts must be comparable. If different assumptions and valuation bases have been used then the comparison will not be valid. An effective way of valuing resources which can be used in a variety of ways is to use opportunity cost as a common valuation basis.

(v)   *Timeliness.* Management accounting information must be made available in sufficient time for management action to be taken. For example, budgetary control reports should be prepared as soon as possible after the end of the period, otherwise variances can continue uncontrolled. Information which arrives too late for any action to be taken is of little use to management.

(iii)   *Objectivity.* Management accounting information should be prepared without being coloured by the preparer's own opinions and beliefs: any forecasts should be as objective as possible. It is easier to exercise objectivity in some circumstances than in others. For instance, it may be comparatively straightforward to estimate the material usage per unit for a future period, using work study techniques. However the determination of the total material to be used in all production will depend on the forecast production volume, an estimate which is likely to be less objective.

(iv)   *Verifiability.* Management accounting information should be verifiable. This means that it must be possible to establish how the information was prepared and the data sources and assumptions used. For instance, if the management accountant prepares a job cost estimate as the basis of a quotation then it must be possible to ascertain how each figure in the estimate was determined. The means that all data sources should be well documented.

(b)   *Area of conflict*

The main conflict arises between timeliness and the other criteria.

(i)   It can take some time to present the information in a fully understandable format. Budgetary control reports can be rushed out quickly if abbreviations and rough formats can be used. It takes more time to prepare clear statements and accounts without the use of abbreviations.

(ii)   Reliability of data can be improved if more time is taken in its preparation. For instance, the management accountant may be able to arrive at a rough estimate of job costs for a quotation fairly quickly, but there could be some doubt as to the reliability of such information.

(iii) Similarly, information which is prepared quickly may not be as well documented, leading to difficulties in verifying it later.

2 FLAT'S STRATEGY

> *Tutorial note.* Paper 9 questions offer you a traditional management accounting 'peg' to hang on to even when dealing with strategic and management issues. This question is: it seems to be about competitive advantage at first sight, but what it actually asks you to do is to comment on *cost* implications. You may feel that this restricts your ability to comment sensibly on the scenario. We would agree – it is *very* difficult not to repeat your examples – but you *must* learn to answer the question that is set, not the one you would like to be set.
>
> Part (b) here can be answered from book knowledge.

(a) (i) A lack of suitable *performance indicators* will mean that the business has little idea of which areas are performing well and which need attention. If quality of product and speed of delivery are the main sources of competitive advantage a business needs to know how good it is at these things.

For example, if a company measures only conventional accounting results it will know how much stock it has and how much it has spent on 'carriage out'. It will not know the opportunity cost of cancelled sales through not having stock available when needed, or not being able to deliver it on time.

Equally the quality of products needs to be measured in terms not only of sales achieved, but also in terms of customer complaints and feedback: again the cost is the opportunity cost of lost sales.

(ii) *Unachievable targets* will force staff to try too hard with too few resources. Mistakes and failure are almost inevitable. This means poor quality products: costs include lost sales, arranging for returns, and time wasted dealing with complaints and rectification work.

Overambitious targets may also mean that more stocks are produced than the business could realistically expect to sell (meaning the costs of write-offs, opportunity costs of wasted production resources, and unnecessary stock holding costs).

(iii) *Lack of awareness* of strategic aims is the fault of senior management who have failed to communicate with operational staff. *Lack of goal congruence* is not necessarily the fault of senior management: operational staff may wilfully choose to go their own way and act in their own best interests. The consequences in either case are the same.

The implications depend on how individuals respond to lack of direction: some operational managers, for example, may choose to focus on quality of product while others determine to produce as many products as possible as quickly as they can; still others will simply keep their heads down and do as little as possible. This will lead to lack of co-ordination: there will be bottlenecks in some operational areas, needing expensive extra resources in the short term, and wasteful idle time in other areas.

(b) (i) Operational planning works out what specific tasks need to be carried out in order to achieve the strategic plan. For example a strategy may be to increase sales by 5% per annum for at least five years, and an operational plan to achieve this would be sales reps' weekly sales targets. (*Note.* We use the words 'strategic' and 'operational' in the senses implied in the well known work of Robert Anthony.)

Notable characteristics of operational planning are the speed of response to changing conditions, and the use and understanding of non-financial information such as data about customer orders or raw material input.

(ii) Strategic planning is the process of setting or changing the long-term objectives or strategic targets of an organisation. These would include such matters as the selection of products and markets, the required levels of company profitability, the purchase and disposal of subsidiary companies or major fixed assets, and so on.

Notable characteristics of strategic planning are as follows.

(1) It will generally be formulated in writing, and only after much after discussion by committee (the Board)

(2) It will be (or should be) circulated to all interested parties within the organisation, and perhaps even to the press.

(3) It will trigger the production not of direct action but of a series of lesser plans for sales, production, marketing and so on.

3   NELUMBO PLC

(a)   (i)

		PN8		ES6		LV4
		£		£		£
Direct material		12.00		10.00		9.00
Direct labour		5.40		3.60		5.40
Overheads (W)	(0.6×£50)	30.00	(0.4×£50)	20.00	(0.6 × £50)	30.00
		47.40		33.60		44.40

Working

Direct labour hours	PN8	0.6 × 2,200 =		1,320 hrs
	ES6	0.4 × 1,800 =		720 hrs
	LV4	0.6 × 600 =		360 hrs
				2,400 hrs

Total overheads = £(36,000 + 63,000 + 21,000) = £120,000

OAR per hour = £120,000/2,400 = £50 per direct labour hour

(ii)

		PN8		ES6		LV4
		£		£		£
Direct material		12.00		10.00		9.00
Direct labour		5.40		3.60		5.40
Overheads (W):						
Inspection costs	9.00		7.50		4.50	
Shaping machine costs	18.00		12.00		3.00	
Material handling costs	5.25		4.20		3.15	
		32.25		23.70		10.65
		49.65		37.30		25.05

Working

	PN8	ES6	LV4	Total
Number of production batches	220	150	30	400
Share of inspection costs (in total)	£19,800 (220/400 × £36,000)	£13,500	£2,700	£36,000
Share per unit	£9	£7.50	£4.50	
Number of shaping machine hours	660 (0.3 × 2,200)	360	30	1,050
Share of shaping machine costs (in total)	£39,600 (660/1,050 × £63,000)	£21,600	£1,800	£63,000
Share per unit	£18	£12	£3	
Total weight of material handled (kg)	55,000 (25 × 2,200)	36,000	9,000	100,000
Share of material handling costs (in total)	£11,550 (55/100 × £21,000)	£7,560	£1,890	£21,000
Share per unit	£5.25	£4.20	£3.15	

(b)   Using the existing absorption costing approach, overheads are absorbed into products on the basis of direct labour hours. This means that the same amount of overhead is absorbed into the PN8 and the LV4. The overheads do not seem to be caused by the number of direct labour hours worked, however. The cost drivers identified do seem to be the more probable cause of an increase in overheads. The number of production batches, shaping machine hours and weight of material handled associated with the LV4 were budgeted to be less than those associated with the PN8 and ES6 and hence, since those appear to 'drive' the overhead costs, it would seem only fair for the LV4 to bear a smaller overhead cost than the PN8 and ES6. The ABC approach provides product costs which reflect this and which would appear to be more accurate and fair since the overhead absorbed per unit of LV4 is only half that absorbed per unit of the ES6 and one third of that absorbed per unit of PN8.

(c)   Nelumbo could use the activity based cost concept for budgeting. Activity based budgeting (ABB) (sometimes termed activity cost management) involves defining the *activities* that underlie the financial figures in the budget and using the level of activity to decide how much resource should be allocated, how well it is being managed and to explain variances from budget. This avoids the weakness inherent in a traditional budgeting system of making managers responsible for activities which are driven by factors beyond their control. For example, the cost of setting up new

BPP
PUBLISHING

personnel records and of induction training is driven by the number of new employees required by managers *other than* the personnel manager.

Further benefits of ABB have also been claimed.

(i)   Provides stronger links between an organisation's strategic objectives and the objectives of the individual activities within an organisation for which departmental managers are responsible

(ii)   Identifies cost improvement opportunities

(iii)   Offers a focused, participative approach to guide and sustain continuous improvement

(iv)   Encourages new thinking (can the activity be carried out more effectively, does the activity represent value for money?)

(v)   Facilitates a more focused view of cost control, since trends can be monitored and comparisons with other organisations can be made (bench marking)

(vi)   Identifies value and non-value added activities

4   RABBIT

(a)   *Production units required before inspection process*

		Current situation Units		With TQM procedures Units
Perfect units required		7,000		7,000
Returns from customers	(4%)	280	(1.5%)	105
		7,280		7,105
Inspection process rejections	(9/91)	720	(2.5/97.5)	182
Units required before inspection		8,000		7,287

(b)   *Purchases of material A*

		kg		kg
Material in inspected units	(8,000 × 15kg)	120,000	(7,287 × 15kg)	109,305
Losses due to processing faults	(6/94)	7,660	(3.5/96.5)	3,964
Process input required		127,660		113,269
Losses in stores and receiving	(4/96)	5,319	(2/98)	2,312
Purchases of material A required		132,979		115,581

(c)   *Available machine hours*

		Hours		Hours
Hours for perfect units	(8,000 × 1.3)	10,400	(7,287 × 1.0)	7,287
Rectifying hours	(280 × 60% × 0.5)	84	(105 × 60% × 0.5)	32
Operating hours required		10,484		7,319
Idle time	(18/82)	2,301	(11/89)	905
Available machine hours required		12,785		8,224

(d)   *Monthly profit or loss*

		Current situation £		With TQM procedures £
Sales				
Sales income: Perfect units	(7,000 × £90)	630,000		630,000
Grade B units	(720 × £72)	51,840	(182 × £72)	13,104
Grade C units	(168 × £36)	6,048	(63 × £36)	2,268
Scrap	(7,000 × 4% × 40% × £3)	336	(7,000 × 1.5% × 40% × £3)	126
Total sales income		688,224		645,498

Costs

Material A	(132,979 × £2)	265,958	(115,581 × £2)	231,162
Goods receiving etc	(132,979 × £0.18)	23,936	115,581 × £0.18)	20,805
Machine costs	(12,785 × £22)	281,270	(8,224 × £22)	180,928
Delivery costs for replacements	(280 × £6)	1,680	(105 × £6)	630
Inspection, supplier vetting etc		21,000	(× 82%)	17,220
Product liability insurance etc	(2% × 630,000)	12,600	(1.5% × 630,000)	9,450
Selling, distn and admin		28,000	(× 95%)	26,600
Prevention programme		14,000		63,000
		648,444		549,795
Monthly profit		39,780		95,703

5   AB LTD

Tutorial note. This question has four ingredients of a good and testing problem on decision making.

(a)   It tests your ability to grasp the nature of a decision problem, and think about the assumptions you may have to make.

(b)   It tests your knowledge of relevant costs.

(c)   It includes a consideration of non-financial factors.

(d)   Part (c) of the question introduces the very practical issue of searching for alternative opportunities. Have all the possible courses of action been identified and considered?

(a)   It is assumed that stock in hand of finished X, valued at £51,900 at full cost, is valued at the full cost of production and not at the full cost of sale. This would be in keeping with SSAP 9, although the wording of the question is ambiguous on this point.

The full cost of production per kg of X is:

	£
Direct materials	17.33
Direct labour	7.36
Production overhead (200% of labour)	14.72
	39.41

The quantity of stock-in-hand is therefore £51,900/£39.41 = 1,317 kg

At a weekly sales volume of 74 kg, this represents 1,317/74 = about 18 weeks of sales

It will take 20 weeks to set up the production facility for Y, and so stock in hand of finished X can be sold before any Y can be produced. This finished stock is therefore irrelevant to the decision under review; it will be sold whatever decision is taken.

The problem therefore centres on the stock in hand of direct materials. Assuming that there is no loss or wastage in manufacture and so 1 kg of direct material is needed to produce 1 kg of X then stock in hand is £44,800/£17.33 = 2,585 kg.

This would be converted into 2,585 kg of X, which would represent sales volume for 2,585/74 = 35 weeks.

If AB Ltd sells its existing stocks of finished X (in 18 weeks) there are two options.

(i)   To produce enough X from raw materials for 2 more weeks, until production of Y can start, and then dispose of all other quantities of direct material - ie 33 weeks' supply.

(ii)   To produce enough X from raw materials to use up the existing stock of raw materials, and so delay the introduction of Y by 33 weeks.

The relevant costs of these two options must be considered.

(i)   *Direct materials.* The relevant cost of existing stocks of raw materials is £(0.30). In other words the 'cost' is a benefit. By using the direct materials to make more X, the company would save £0.30 per kg used.

(ii)   *Direct labour.* It is assumed that if labour is switched to production work from non-production work in the next three months, they must be paid at the full rate of pay, and not at 65% of normal rate. The *incremental* cost of labour would be 35% of the normal rate (35% of £7.36 = £2.58 per kg produced).

Relevant cost of production of X

	£
Direct materials	(0.30)
Direct labour	2.58
Variable overhead (30% of full overhead cost of £14.72)	4.42
Cost per kg of X	6.70

Relevant cost per kg of Y

	£
Direct materials	4.01
Direct labour	2.85
Variable overhead (30% of 200% of £2.85)	1.71
	8.57

(*Note*. Y cannot be made for 20 weeks, and so the company cannot make use of spare labour capacity to produce any units of Y.)

It is cheaper to use up the direct material stocks and make X (£6.70 per kg) than to introduce Y as soon as possible, because there would be a saving of (£8.57 - £6.70) = £1.87 per kg made.

AB Ltd must sell X for at least 20 weeks until Y could be produced anyway, but the introduction of Y could be delayed by a further 33 weeks until all stocks of direct material for X are used up. The saving in total would be about £1.87 per kg x 74 kg per week x 33 weeks = £4,567.

(*Note*. The £3,500 capital cost of Y will be incurred whatever course of action is taken, although with the recommended alternative the spending could be deferred by 33 weeks. Selling and administration overhead has been assumed to be a fixed cost and so is irrelevant to the decision.)

(b) There are several non-financial factors that must be considered in reaching the decision. Three major items to consider are the workforce, customers' interests and competition in the market from CD.

(i) *The workforce*. If the recommended course of action is undertaken, the workforce will produce enough units of X in the next 13 weeks to satisfy sales demand over the next year, (with 18 weeks' supply of existing finished goods stocks and a further 35 weeks' supply obtainable from direct materials stocks). When production of Y begins, the direct labour content of production will fall to £2.85 per kg - less than 40% of the current effort per kg produced - but sales demand will not rise. The changeover will therefore mean a big drop in labour requirements in production. Redundancies seem inevitable, and might be costly. By switching to producing Y as soon as possible, the redundancies might be less immediate, and could be justified more easily to employees and their union representatives than a decision to produce enough X in the next 3 months to eliminate further production needs for about 9 months.

(ii) *Customers' interests*. Product Y is a superior and 'more effective' compound than X. It would be in customers' interests to provide them with this improved product as soon as possible, instead of delaying its introduction until existing stocks of direct materials for X have been used up.

(iii) *Competition*. CD is expected to start selling Y overseas, and quite possibly in direct competition with AB Ltd. CD has the advantage of having developed Y itself, and appears to use it in the preliminary stage of an alternative technical process. The competitive threat to AB Ltd is two-fold:

(1) CD might take away some of the replacement demand for Y from AB Ltd so that AB Ltd's sales of X or Y would fall.

(2) CD might compete with AB Ltd to install its total technical process into customers' factories, and so the competition would be wider than the market for compound Y.

(c) An alternative course of action would be:

(i) to produce enough units of X in the next 13 weeks to use up existing stocks of direct materials; but

(ii) to start sales of Y as soon as possible, and to offer customers the choice between X and Y. Since X is an inferior compound, it would have to be sold at a lower price than Y.

The merits of this course of action are that:

(i) the work force would be usefully employed for the next 13 weeks and then production of Y would begin at once. Although redundancies would still seem inevitable, the company would be creating as much work as it could for its employees;

(ii) AB's customers would be made aware of the superiority of Y over X in terms of price, and of AB's commitment to the new compound. AB's marketing approach would be both 'honest' and would also give customers an attractive choice of buying the superior Y or, for a time, an inferior X but at a lower price. This might well enhance AB's marketing success.

The demerits of this course of action are that:

(i) it is unlikely to be a profit-maximising option, because selling X at a discount price would reduce profitability;

(ii) customers who get a discount on X might demand similar discounts on Y;

(iii) some customers might query the technical differences between X and Y, and question why AB Ltd has been selling X at such a high price in the past - this might lead to some customer relations difficulties;

(iv) AB Ltd must decide when to reduce the price of X, given that Y cannot be made for 20 weeks. The timing of the price reduction might create some difficulties with customers who buy X just before the price is reduced.

(*Tutorial note.* This alternative course of action seems the most obvious one to suggest, but you might think otherwise, and a sensible alternative would be equally acceptable as a solution.)

6   MANCASTLE CITY

> *Tutorial note.* At heart this is a fairly standard incremental cash flows question, made far more complex by the need to work out when cash flows occur for discounting purposes and to take inflation into account. Part (d) (ii) has a wide variety of possible answers: you may have other valid suggestions besides those we suggest. Not that you are asked about other matters that might affect the *calculations*, not about other matters in general.

(a) The salaries of the groundspersons are not relevant because they will be paid whatever decision is made.

The cost of the stocks of chemicals is a sunk cost and not relevant to the decision.

(b) The net cash flows are calculated by subtracting the Grass cash flows from the Icing cash flows and the Astroturf cash flows respectively, and then discounting by the relevant factor.

Year	Df	Grass (W3)	Icing (W3)	Net Icing	DCF	Astroturf (W3)	Net Astroturf	DCF
0	1.000	-	316,800	316,800	316,800	287,100	287,100	287,100
1	0.926	124,630	67,187	(57,443)	(53,192)	59,153	(65,477)	(60,632)
2	0.857	124,630	69,487	(55,143)	(47,258)	61,453	(63,177)	(54,143)
3	0.794	127,050	72,126	(54,924)	(43,610)	63,936	(63,114)	(50,113)
4	0.735	139,125	73,480	(65,645)	(48,249)	65,290	(73,835)	(54,269)
5	0.681	141,775	76,328	(65,447)	(44,569)	67,982	(73,793)	(50,253)
6	0.630		(90,000)	(90,000)	(56,700)	(90,000)	(90,000)	(56,700)
					23,222			(39,009)

Positive incremental cash flows are shown in brackets. The analysis indicates that Astroturf is the best option to choose: it has a positive discounted cash flow as compared with Grass of £39,009.

Workings

1   *Turf costs*

There is 110m × 90m to cover. This will require (110 × 90) 9,900 units of Astroturf or 9,900 ÷ 5m^2 = 396 units of Icing.

Astroturf:	9,900 × £29	£287,100
Icing:	396 × £800	£316,800

2   *Indexed cash flows*

Emboldened figures refer to W3.

Year	0	1	2	3	4	5
Index	100	103	103	105	105	107

Training session fees (W4)

Grass	78,000	**80,340**	80,340	81,900	81,900	83,460
Astroturf (As grass × (100 − 55)%)	35,100	36,153	**36,153**	36,855	36,855	37,557
Icing (As grass × (100 − 45)%)	42,900	44,187	44,187	**45,045**	45,045	45,903

Fertiliser, chemicals etc (W5)

Stock	-	-	-	-	12,075	12,305
Purchased	43,000	44,290	44,290	45,150	45,150	46,010
Total	43,000	**44,290**	44,290	45,150	57,225	58,315

Turf replacement (Astroturf and Icing) (W6)   23,000 **25,300** **27,081** 28,435 30,425

3   *Summary of cash flows*

Emboldened figures here correspond with emboldened figures in W2 to indicate the derivation of totals.

Year	1	2	3	4	5
Grass	**124,630**	124,630	127,050	139,125	141,775
Astroturf	59,153	**61,453**	63,936	65,290	67,982
Icing	67,187	69,487	**72,126**	73,480	76,328

4   *Training session fees*

For grass the fee of £78,000 is increased by the index figure for each year. For example for year 1 the figure is £78,000 × 1.03 = £80,340.

The figures for Astroturf and Icing are the grass fees reduced by the appropriate percentage.

5   *Fertiliser, chemicals*

Purchases are reduced by £10,000 to £43,000 in year 0. In later years this figure is multiplied by the appropriate index number. For year 5: £43,000 × 1.07 = £46,010.

Stocks last for three years. In year 4 these have to be purchased. The price is adjusted to year 0 value (£10,000 × 1.15 = £11,500) and then indexed up to year 4 and year 5 values (£11,500 × 1.05 = 12,075; £11,500 × 1.07 = £12,305).

6   *Replacement turfs*

Turfs are quoted at year 1 prices. They need to be adjusted to year 0 prices before the general (103, 105 etc) and specific (10%, 5%) inflation indexes can be applied.

Year 2: (£23,000/1.03) × 1.1 × 1.03   = £25,300
Year 3: (£23,000/1.03) × 1.1 × 1.05 × 1.05   − £27,081

and so on.

(c)   For this to hold true the NPV of the Astroturf option would need to be nil. In other words the NPV of the increase in disposal income would need to be £39,009 less. Adjusted to year 0 values the improvement forecast was £(56,700 − 39,009)/0.630 = £28,081.

(d) (i)   The problem of uncertainty can never be fully overcome, but allowances can be made for it in a variety of ways.

        (1)   The data could be set up on a spreadsheet with an input section for all the variables as stated in the question and an output section consisting of formulae and cell references to represent the relationships between the variables. It would then be possible to change any of the input variables that are uncertain and see the effect that this has on the output. This is known as 'what-if' analysis.

        (2)   One-way and two-way data tables could be set up on the spreadsheet to show ranges of NPVs that would result from different values of one or two of the key variables.

(3) Probabilities could be assigned to ranges of values for the uncertain variables and NPVs in the best and worst scenarios calculated.

(4) The club could seek the reassurance of further guidance from experts in the economy or the relevant industries.

(ii) Some of the other matters to be considered are as follows.

(1) The impact of the use of an all-weather pitch may affect the team's performance and that of their opponents. If the team performs well this will increase usage of the stadium and so the costs of wear and tear (both of the pitch and of other facilities).

(2) There may be opposition to the scheme on environmental grounds, which may cause adverse PR for the club and affect attendance levels and so income.

(3) It may be possible to charge spectators to watch the team training at the stadium.

(4) The club will lose the skills of grass pitch maintenance, which may be needed (and will therefore will cost money to acquire again) when they move to a new stadium.

7 THISTLEKILM PLC

- **Lines 2 to 6** show that the optimal production plan is to produce 960 units of SFA and 480 units of FA. All of the available supply of Nix and Nill will be used up if this plan is pursued (Slack A and Slack B are 0.00 kg), but 240 kgs of Sucradam will still be available.

- **Lines 8 to 11** indicate:

  o the types of constraint involved. Each constraint limits the usage of resources to an amount less than or equal to the value shown in the column headed RHS;

  o the maximum amounts of each resource that are available (shown in column headed RHS);

  o all the available resources of Nix and Nill are used up by the optimal solution (slack variables have a value of 0.00 kg). The slack variable of 240 kg for Sucradam means that not all of the available supply is needed in the optimal solution;

  o the shadow prices of Nix and Nill, that is, the marginal contribution that can be earned from each unit of scarce resource that becomes available. The shadow price of Nix is £120, and of Nill £20.

- **Line 13** gives the value of the objective function in the optimal solution (£336,000). This tells management the maximum contribution that can be earned given the scarcity of resources.

- **Lines 16 to 18** show the current contribution per unit of SFA and FA (£200 and £300 respectively), and the minimum and maximum contribution per unit of each product at which the present optimal production mix will remain unchanged.

- **Lines 21 to 24** show the minimum and maximum quantity of each resource that may be available without the shadow price being affected. For example, an infinite amount of Sucradam could come onto the market without affecting its shadow price, which is £0.00 because more than enough is already available. However if less than 960 kg were to be supplied it would acquire a shadow price because the shortage would mean that the optimal solution could not be achieved.

8 ALLEGRO FINISHES LTD

(a) The variable cost per unit is estimated as follows:

	£		Probability	
(i)	60		0.2	(4 out of 20)
(ii)	55		0.7	(14 out of 20)
(iii)	50		0.1	(2 out of 20)

A table of possible outcomes can be constructed, for a selling price of £90.

Demand	Prob.	Variable £	Unit £	Total £'000	Prob.	Joint prob.	EV £
20,000	0.2	60	30	600	0.2	0.04	24.00
		55	35	700	0.7	0.14	98.00
		50	40	800	0.1	0.02	16.00
35,000	0.7	60	30	1050	0.2	0.14	147.00
		55	35	1225	0.7	0.49	600.25
		50	40	1400	0.1	0.07	98.00
40,000	0.1	60	30	1200	0.2	0.02	24.00
		55	35	1400	0.7	0.07	98.00
		50	40	1600	0.1	0.01	16.00

EV of contribution	1,121.25
Fixed costs: (amortised R & D)	250.00
other	800.00
EV of profit	71.25

The EV of profit is £71,250, at a price of £90, but the fixed costs ought to be irrelevant for the decision about selecting the preferred selling price. (They are included here because the question calls for their inclusion.)

(b)   A cumulative probability table can be constructed, to compare the 3 prices.

	Price £70	Price £80	Price £90	
Probability of				
a loss of £500,000 or more*	0.02	0.00	0.00	
a loss of £300,000 or more	0.07	0.05	0.18	(0.04 + 0.14)
a loss of £100,000 or more	0.61	0.08	0.20	(0.18 + 0.02)
breakeven or worse**	0.61	0.10	0.34	
breakeven or better	0.39	0.90	0.80	
a profit of £100,000	0.33	0.52	0.66	(0.8 - 0.14)
a profit of £300,000 or more	0.03	0.04	0.15	(0.66 - 0.49 - 0.02)
a profit of £500,00 or more	0.00	0.01	0.01	
EV of profit/loss	(£55,750)	£68,500	£71,250	

*   ie a contribution of £550,000 or less, given
** ie a contribution of £1,050,000, or worse

Memo

To: Sales director
From: Management accountant

Subject: Sales price of pocket chess computer

(i)   A cumulative probability table of profits with each sales price indicates that although the EV of profit is slightly higher at a price of £90 than at a price of £80, there is a greater risk in a decision to select a price of £90.

   (1)   There is a greater probability of making a loss at a price of £90 compared with a price of £80. For example, the probability of making a loss of £100,000 or more is 0.20 at a price of £90 but only 0.08 at a price of £80.

   (2)   There is, on the other hand, a greater probability of making higher profits at the £90 price. For example, the probability of profits of £300,000 or more is only 0.04 at a price of £80 but is 0.15 at a price of £90.

(ii)   A risk-averse decision maker might therefore opt for £80 as the selling price, although a risk seeker might prefer the higher price of £90.

(iii)   The cumulative probability table reinforces the impression given by the expected values, that £70 would not be a suitable price to select. In all respects it is less attractive than a price of £80.

(iv)   The estimates are based, of course, on point estimate probabilities (discrete probabilities) which are either subjective, in the case of sales demand, or based on limited data, in the case of unit variable costs. Even so, it is better to consider risk with these estimates than to ignore risk altogether, and provided that the selling price decision is taken with an understanding of how the outcome might vary from expectation, and the likelihood that it will do so, the use of these probability distributions is likely to help you to reach your decision about the selling price.

(v)   Notional fixed costs are irrelevant to any decision, including selling price decisions. Allocated fixed overheads and the amortisation of development costs are both notional costs, and do not reflect incremental cash flows. The general effect of changing the accounting treatment of these costs is non-existent, and the analysis of the problem is unchanged.

9   **ABC LTD**

Tutorial note. There was quite a lot of information in part (a). The way to tackle this sort of question is to read through the information twice and then to formulate it mathematically, taking care to define your variables as you go. You should then find that you have condensed all the information into a few simple equations.

(a)   Profit will be maximised when marginal costs (MC) equals marginal revenue (MR). MR and MC are the first derivatives with respect to quantity of total revenue (TR) and total costs (TC) respectively.

Let x = the number of thousands of units sold.

Let p = the unit price in pounds.

TR, MR, TC and MC will all be in thousands of pounds, and MR and MC will be per thousand extra units produced.

For values of x up to 100 (values of p down to £6.00), we have

$$p = 9 - 0.03x$$
$$TR = px = 9x - 0.03x^2$$
$$MR = dTR/dx = 9 - 0.06x$$

For values of x above 100 (values of p below £6.00), we have

$$p = 6 - 0.04 (x - 100) = 10 - 0.04x$$
$$TR = px = 10x - 0.04x^2$$
$$MR = dTR/dx = 10 - 0.08x$$

For values of x up to 80,

$$MC = 2 - 0.025x + 0.5 + 1 = 3.5 - 0.025x$$

For values of x between 80 and 100,

$$MC = 0.5 + 1 = 1.5$$

For values of x above 100,

$$MC = 0.5 + 1 + 0.0025(x - 100) = 1.25 + 0.0025x$$

If the profit-maximising output is below 80,000 units, it is at

$$9 - 0.06x = 3.5 - 0.025x$$
$$5.5 = 0.035x$$
$$x = 157.14$$

This is above 80,000 units, so the profit-maximising output is not below 80,000 units.

If the profit-maximising output is between 80,000 and 100,000 units, it is at

$$9 - 0.06x = 1.5$$
$$7.5 = 0.06x$$
$$x = 125$$

This is above 100,000 units, so the profit-maximising output is not between 80,000 and 100,000 units.

The profit-maximising output is therefore at

$$10 - 0.08x = 1.25 + 0.0025x$$
$$8.75 = 0.0825x$$
$$x = 106.061$$

The profit-maximising price is, to the nearest penny,

p = 6 - 0.04 (106.061 - 100) = £5.76

Alternative solution

The marginal cost line and marginal revenue line can be plotted on a graph as shown below. The profit-maximising output is when the marginal cost and marginal revenue lines cross, that is when (MC) 1.25 + 0.0025x = (MR) 10 - 0.08x. The profit-maximising price is, as before, £5.76.

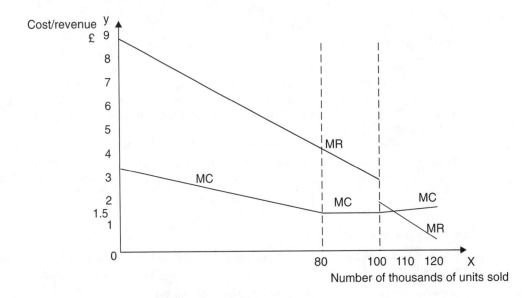

(b) It is normal for a company which advertises a single product to customers generally to set one price, perhaps giving discounts for large orders or for a commitment to place a series of orders. Such discount terms are, however, themselves available to all customers who meet the conditions.

ABC Ltd has chosen to adopt the policy of a single published price, and this may well be the most sensible approach for its type of product and for the market. The company does not appear to be in the position of a contractor negotiating with customers individually, where the pricing policy might be based on cost plus a standard minimum mark-up plus a further mark-up related to the customer's willingness to pay.

Price discrimination does have the advantages suggested by the statement in the question, but as already suggested ABC Ltd may not be in a position to use it. The following points should be considered if price discrimination is to be attempted.

(i) The seller must be able to assess customers' willingness to pay a high price, and this is difficult if there are many customers.

(II) There must be a way of preventing customers from buying goods at a low price and then selling the goods to high-price customers at an intermediate price.

(iii) More generally, groups of customers paying different prices for the same product must be isolated from each other by such factors as distance or national boundaries (where import duties or controls may apply). Because ABC Ltd sells in the UK and abroad, this may well be possible.

(iv) As an alternative to the separation of groups of customers paying different prices for the same product, it may be possible to create different versions of what is basically the same product. The product could be packaged in different ways, or one version could incorporate minor refinements or a high price could be charged for quick delivery.

(v) Products with a short life cycle are a special case. A high price can be charged at first, with sales being made to customers willing to pay a high price. The price can then be lowered to attract other customers.

10   ZBB LTD

(a)   *Material handling department*

Level 1	£
Labourers' wages:	
Basic rate: 30 x 40 hours x £4 x 48 weeks	230,400
Overtime premium: 30 x 5 hours x £2 x 48 weeks	14,400
	244,800
Employee benefits 20% x £244,800	48,960
Variable overheads 30 x 40 x £0.12 x 48 weeks	6,912
Incremental cost	300,672

Level 2	£
Incremental costs:	
Leasing costs 10 x £2,000	20,000
Drivers' wages 10 x £155 x 48 weeks	74,400
Overheads 10 x £150 x 48 weeks	72,000
Incremental costs	166,400

Level 3	£	£
Incremental costs:		
Computer leasing costs:		
Quarter 1		20,000
2 (20,000 x 90%)		18,000
3 (18,000 x 90%)		16,200
4 (16,200 x 90%)		14,580
		68,780

Less savings in labour costs:

Hours saved	= 10% x 30 x 40 hrs x 48 = 5,760 hrs		
∴ Overtime hours saved	= 2,880		
∴ Savings in labourers' basic wages	= 5,760 x £4 =	23,040	
Savings in overtime premium	= 2,880 x £2	5,760	
Savings in variable overheads	= 5,760 x £0.12	691	
			29,491
Incremental cost			39,289

Maintenance department

Level 1	£
Engineer's salaries 2 x £18,000	36,000
Outside contractors' cost	250,000
Incremental cost	286,000

Level 2	£
Incremental costs:	
Fitters' salaries 10 x £11,000	110,000
Maintenance materials	48,000
Stock ordering and holding costs (W1)	1,200
Overheads	50,000
	209,200
Less: saving in outside contractors' cost £(250,000 - 160,000)	90,000
Incremental costs	119,200

		£	£
Level 3			
Incremental costs:			
Additional fitters' salaries 6 x £11,000			66,000
Additional maintenance materials £(96,000 - 48,000)		48,000	
Less supplier discount (W3)		1,920	
			46,080
Increase in stock ordering and holding costs (W2)			445
Increase in overheads			20,000
			132,525
Less saving in outside contractors' cost £(160,000 - 90,000)			70,000
Incremental cost			62,525

Workings

1 Economic order quantity $= \sqrt{2 \times £100 \times £48,000/0.15} = $ £8,000

	£
∴ Stock ordering costs = (£48,000/£8,000) orders per annum × £100 =	£600
Stock holding costs = (£8,000/2) average stock × 15% =	£600
	£1,200

2 Economic order quantity $= \sqrt{2 \times £100 \times £96,000/0.1333} = $ £12,000

A discount is available for orders of £16,000, therefore the total annual cost of purchasing in batches of £12,000 must be compared with the cost for batches of £16,000.

Total cost of ordering £12,000 per batch:		£
Ordering cost	= (£96,000/£12,000) order per annum x £100	800
Stock holding cost	= (£12,000/2) average stock x 13.33 %	800
Annual materials cost		96,000
Total cost		97,600

Total cost of ordering £16,000 per batch:		£
Ordering cost	= (£96,000/£16,000) orders per annum x £100	600
Stockholding cost	= (£16,000/2) x 98% average stock value x 13.33	1,045
Annual materials cost (£96,000 x 98%)		94,080
Total cost		95,725

This is less than the cost of ordering £12,000 per batch, therefore orders should be placed for £16,000 per batch.

Increase in stockholding and ordering costs	£
Level 3 costs (600 + 1045)	1,645
Level 2 costs (W1)	1,200
Increase	445

3 Supplier discount of 2% will be obtained because the purchase value per batch will be £16,000 (W2). Supplier discount = £96,000 x 2% = £1,920.

(b)

	Material handling			Maintenance		
Level	Incremental cost £	Desirability factor	Score	Incremental cost £	Desirability factor	Score
1	300,672	1.00	300,672	286,000	1.00	286,000
2	166,400	0.60	99,840	119,200	0.80	95,360
3	39,289	0.50	19,645	62,525	0.20	12,505

The available budget should be allocated to the incremental levels of expenditure according to the calculated scores, until all funds have been allocated, or until there are insufficient funds available for the next required increment of cost.

	Level	Cost	Cumulative cost
		£	£
Material handling	1	300,672	300,672
Maintenance	1	286,000	586,672
Material handling	2	166,400	753,072
Maintenance	2	119,200	872,272
Material handling	3	39,289	911,561

Material handling should be operated at level 3, but maintenance should be operated at level 2 because the budget of £925,000 will be exceeded if level 3 is implemented.

11 BLYTHELY LTD

(a) A standard cost for direct labour or direct material is made up from a standard level of efficiency or usage and a standard price or rate.

A problem arises in setting a standard for efficiency because there are basically four types of performance standard.

Ideal standards of efficiency are based on perfect operating conditions, ie no wastage, no inefficiencies, no idle time, no breakdowns etc. Variances from ideal standards are useful for pinpointing areas where a close examination may result in large savings, but they are likely to have an unfavourable motivational impact. Employees will often feel that the goals are unattainable and will not work so hard, because the reported variance will always be adverse.

Current standards of efficiency are based on current working conditions and recorded levels of achievement. Variances may therefore be favourable or adverse in any given control period, but in the long run, they should 'cancel out'. The disadvantage of current standards is that if the work force is not working as efficiently as it might, the variance reports will provide no incentive to improve performance.

Target (or attainable) standards of efficiency can be set, which are below 'ideal' standards but which reflect some improvements on current standards.

Well set target standards provide a useful psychological incentive by giving employees a realistic, but challenging target of efficiency. There are often insuperable problems, however, in motivating employees to accept higher attainable standards, above current levels of achievement, and if the workforce does not accept the targets, there will be adverse variances every period which management will be unable to control.

Basic standards of efficiency are standards which are kept unaltered over a long period of time, and may be out of date. These are used to show changes in efficiency or performance over a long period of time. Basic standards are perhaps the least useful and least common type of standard in use, because with changes in working conditions (greater automation etc) variances should always be favourable, even when the workforce is operating at relatively low levels of efficiency.

Material price levels may also be ideal, current, target or basic prices, and the significance of variances would be the same as for efficiency standards. Labour rates will probably be current wage rates.

Because of inflation, there is a problem in deciding how to set standard price levels. One basis is to use current prices at the time the standard is set. When this occurs, adverse price variances will be reported as soon as prices go up. An alternative basis is to use expected mid-year price levels. When this occurs, favourable price variances should be expected for the first half year and adverse price variances for the second half year, because the rate of inflation will eventually overtake the standard prices. In both cases, the significance of price variances will be difficult to assess.

(b) The advantage of putting money prices to efficiency and usage variances is that they indicate the effect on profit of that inefficiency, provided that the standard prices for materials or labour are realistic. For example, a manager might be more concerned with an adverse usage variance of 2,000 units of material than with an adverse efficiency variance of 500 hours. However, if the material only costs 30p per unit, and labour costs £6 the effect on costs and profits of each variance would be £600(A) and £3,000(A) respectively. The labour variance would be more significant.

Variances in production should also be viewed in the context of the organisation as a whole. Management must be able to compare an adverse usage of 4,000 kg of material A in department A, an adverse usage of 3,000 kg of material B in department B, a shortfall in achieving the sales

BPP
PUBLISHING

quota in sales department C and excess mileage travelled by lorries in distribution department D. The obvious basis for comparison is achieved by converting all variances into a monetary value.

On the other hand many control measures can be reported, at least in the first instance, in a non-financial form as stated by the operations manager. Such information is quicker to produce for control purposes and may be more easily understood by the personnel responsible for day to day operational control.

12   A1 TRADITIONAL TRADES

> *Tutorial note.* Part (a) is difficult because the information is not presented in the usual way, although you only need to do standard variance analysis on the data, once you have sorted out what it means.

(a)   In total 10,000 extra hours were worked. Chargeable hours can be analysed as follows.

	Budget Hours	*Actual* Hours	*Variance (W1)* Hours	*Variance (W2)* £
Emergencies	10,000	25,480	15,480	619,200
Long-term work	25,000	11,531	(13,469)	(538,760)
Total	35,000	37,011	2,011	80,440

The time spent on extra chargeable activities gives rise to an increase in total revenue of £80,440. This figure can be further analysed by flexing the budget as follows.

	Budget Hours	*Flexed (W3)* Hours	*Variance (W4)* Hours	*Variance (W2)* £
Emergencies	10,000	12,000	2,000	80,000
Long-term work	25,000	30,000	5,000	200,000
Chargeable hours	35,000	42,000	7,000	280,000

This table indicates that of the 60,000 hours worked 42,000 should have been chargeable (35,000/50,000 × 60,000), so turnover *should* have risen by (42,000 – 35,000) × £40 = £280,000. We need to look at non-chargeable hours to find out why not.

	Budget Hours	*Flexed (W3)* Hours	*Actual* Hours	*Variance (W5)* Hours	*Variance (W2)* £
Return visits	5,000	6,000	9,920	(3,920)	(156,800)
Estimates	2,000	2,400	3,194	(794)	(31,760)
Travelling, administration	8,000	9,600	9,875	(275)	(11,000)
Non-chargeable	15,000	18,000		(4,989)	(199,560)
Total	50,000	60,000		2,011	80,440

In fact an extra 4,989 hours were not chargeable (see above; check: 42,000 – 4,989 = 37,011, the actual chargeable hours) and valued at £40 per hour these reduce the potential increase by £199,560.

	£
Gain in capacity	280,000
Capacity used on non-chargeable activities	(199,560)
Net gain	80,440

Workings

1   This is actual minus budgeted hours

2   This is the variance in hours valued at £40 per hour

3   10,000/50,000 × 60,000 = 12,000
     25,000/50,000 × 60,000 = 30,000
     5,000/50,000 × 60,000 = 6,000 and so on.

4   This is flexed minus budgeted hours.

5   This is actual minus flexed hours.

(b)

	Budget	Actual
Revenue (at £40 per hour)	1,400,000	1,480,440

Costs		
Salaries (W6)	450,000	540,000
Overheads (as given)	525,000	794,000
	975,000	1,334,000
Net profit	425,000	146,440

The standard financial ratios are as follows.

Return on investment (net profit/capital employed, £800,000)	0.531	0.183
Profit margin (profit/sales)	0.304	0.099
Asset turnover (sales/capital employed)	1.75	1.85

Financial performance during the year looks poor in comparison with budget. Although turnover is up by around £80,000 this is more than cancelled out by the extra amount paid in salaries. Overheads have increased substantially (by over 50%).

Further information would be useful to enable us to judge whether the increase in overheads is a one-off occurrence or is part of a longer-term trend.

Attention needs to be given to the company's inability to charge for the extra hours it is paying staff for. Inspection of the variance data in (a) indicates that the main problem by far is time spent on return visits.

Working

6   Budgeted salaries are £18,000 × 25 = £450,000.

Actual salaries include payment for the additional hours:

£450,000/50,000 × 60,000 = £540,000.

13   LEARNING CURVE EFFECT

(a)   (i)   Learning curve formula is $y = ax^b$

where $b = -\left[\log \text{of} (1 \div \text{learning rate})/\log \text{of } 2\right]$

When the learning rate is 80%, $b = -(\log(1 \div 80\%)/\log 2) = -(\log 1.25/\log 2) = -0.0969/0.3010 = -0.322$.

The first unit took 40 hours and so the average time for the first 14 units should be

$$y = ax^b = 40 (14^{-0.322}) = 40 (1 \div 14^{0.322}) = 17.1$$

If the average time per unit for the first 14 units is 17.1 hours, the total time for the units will be (14 × 17.1) = 239.4 hours.

Actual time was 240 hours.

Actual time is therefore consistent with an 80% learning curve effect, and is therefore reasonable to assume in this case.

(ii)   The number of hours needed for the second order, after the first order of 30 units has been completed, will be the time required to produce units 31-50, assuming an 80% learning curve. This is the difference between the total time required to make the first 50 units, and the total time required to make the first 30 units.

1st 30 units

$y = ax^b = 40 (30^{-0.322})$
$= 40 (1 \div 30^{0.322}) = 13.38$ hours

1st 50 units

$y = 40 (50^{-0.322})$
$= 40 (1 \div 50^{0.322}) = 11.35$ hours

	Direct labour
Total time for first 50 units (50 x 11.35)	567.5
Total time for first 30 units (30 x 13.38)	401.4
Total time for 2nd order (units 31-50)	166.1

399

Tutorial note. Due to rounding, your own solution might be *slightly* different from this.

(iii) *Estimated cost for the initial order of 30 units.*

	£
Direct material (30 x £30)	900.0
Direct labour (401.4 hours x £6) (see note (a))	2,408.4
Variable overhead (401.4 hours x £0.5)	200.7
Fixed overhead (see note (b)) (401.4 hours x £5)	2,007.0
	5,516.1

Cost per unit	£183.87, say, £184.

Notes

(a) The hourly rate which is given for labour is assumed to be the cost per productive hour: labour rate paid per hour = £4.50, cost of productive time = £6 per hour.

(b) Fixed overhead is assumed to be absorbed on a direct labour hour basis.

Budgeted fixed overhead per 4-week period		£6,000
Direct labour hours per 4-week period		
Gross (10 x 8 x 5 x 4)	1,600 hours	
less downtime allowance (25%)	400 hours	
		1,200 hours
Absorption rate per direct labour hour		£5

Problems

1   A major problem with the learning effect is that unit costs of production fall considerably as extra units are produced, especially during the early period of a product's manufacture.

With a cost per hour of £11.50 for direct labour and overhead in this case, the actual average unit cost for the first 14 units was approximately (£30 material + (17.1 x £11.5)) = £227, which is much higher than the expected average cost of £184 per unit for the first 30 units.

The budgeting problems are the assumptions that the learning curve effect will continue and that there will be an 80% learning curve effect. If either of these assumptions is incorrect, budgeted unit costs could be inaccurate.

In particular, there is a danger of underestimating costs (and if prices are based on a cost-plus formula, there will be a danger of losses on the contract).

2   A further problem with assumptions about the learning curve effect is budgeting for the use of manufacturing capacity. If estimates of learning rate are incorrect, actual capacity will be either higher or lower than budgeted, with the consequences that there will be either surplus idle capacity in the budget period or an inability to meet sales orders on schedule.

3   The company uses standard costing, but when there is a learning curve effect, standard costs can only be an expected average cost, based on budgeted output volume in the period and budgeted learning rate. There is consequently a strong possibility that actual costs will differ from standard costs due to variance in output volume and/or learning rate, thus *possibly* reducing the control value of variance analysis.

(b) It is *correct* to state that in many areas of modern technology, the learning curve effect is of diminishing significance. This is because of the increase in automated production using robotics and so on, and the declining role of direct labour in manufacturing. In modern systems, the pace and quality of production are dictated by machines rather than labour, and the scope for learning to take place is therefore significantly reduced, even for the labour force that is still employed.

The learning curve effect has a short-term and immediate effect on labour times and thus on product costs and short-term standard setting. Consequently, the diminishing effect of the learning curve has direct consequences for product costing and short-term standard setting.

The experience curve, in contrast, describes the process of acquiring skills and ability through experience of working in a particular environment. In modern manufacturing systems, for example, managers and other employees will gain experience in modern technology and engineering systems and in time they should have developed an ability to apply their expertise to make improvements in the systems they operate. Experience takes time to acquire, and so the benefits will not be apparent in the short term.

Consequently, it is *correct* to state that the experience curve has little relevance to short term standard setting and product costing. It may have some relevance, however, to strategic planning and longer-term cost estimates within a system of strategic management accounting.

14   WIMBRUSH LTD

(a) (i)   Traditional variance analysis:

2,000 Widgets	should use (x 5 kg)	10,000	kg of X
	and did use	10,800	kg
Material X usage variance		800	kg (A)
x standard cost per kg		x £3	
		£2,400	(A)

		£	
10,800 kg of X	should cost (x £3)	32,400	
	but did cost	51,840	
Material X price variance		19,440	(A)

500 Splodgets	should use (x 1.5 tonnes)	750	tonnes of Z
	and did use	700	tonnes
Material Z usage variance		50	tonnes (F)
x standard cost per tonne		x £30	
		£1,500	(F)

		£	
700 tonnes of Z	should cost (x £30)	21,000	
	but did cost (x £25)	17,500	
Material Z price variance		3,500	(F)

Summary

	Material X/Y variances £	Material Z variances £	# Total £
Price variance	19,440 (A)	3,500	15,940 (A)
Usage variance	2,400 (A)	1,500 (F)	900 (A)
	21,840 (A)	5,000	16,840 (A)

(ii) Planning and operational variances:

(1) *Widgets*: the revised standard, given the choice of material X instead of Y was 5 kg at £4.50 per kg.

		£	
10,800 kg of X	should have cost (x 4.5)	48,600	
	but did cost	51,840	
Material X price variance (operational variance)		3,240	(A)

Usage variance for X = 800 kg (A) x £4.5 = (operational variance)	£3,600	(A)

The planning variance is:

	£	
Original standard (using X) 2,000 units x 5 kg x £3 =	30,000	
Revised standard (using X) 2,000 units x 5 kg x £4.50 =	45,000	
Planning variance £1.50 (A) per kg, or	15,000	(A)

(*Note*. The variance is adverse because the original standard was too optimistic, overstating the profits by understating the realistic cost.)

Since a perfect substitute, Material Y, is available, part of this planning variance is possibly avoidable.

	£	£
Original standard (using X) 2,000 units x 5 kg x £3	30,000	
Possible standard (using Y) 2,000 units x 5 kg x £4	40,000	
Unavoidable planning variance (£1 (A) per kg)		10,000 (A)
Rev std (using X) 2,000 units x 5 kg x £4.50	45,000	
Possibly avoidable planning variance (£0.5 (A) per kg)		5,000 (A)
Total planning variance		15,000

(2) *Splodgets*: the revised realistic standard is 1.5 tonnes of Z at £23 = £34.5

	£
700 tonnes of Z should cost (x £23)	16,100
did cost (x £25)	17,500
Material Z price variance (operational variance)	1,400 (A)

Material Z usage variance = 50 tonnes (F) x £23 (op var) =	£1,150 (F)

Planning variance

	£
Original standard 500 units x 1.5 tonnes x £30 per tonne =	22,500
Revised standard 500 units x 1.5 tonnes x £23 per tonne =	17,250
Total planning variance (£7 per tonne) (F) or	5,250 (F)

Material

	£		£		£	
Price variance	3,240	(A)	1,400	(A)	4,640	(A)
Usage variance	3,600	(A)	1,150	(F)	2,450	(A)
Op variances	6,840	(A)	250	(A)	7,090	(A)

Material

Plan variances:	£		£		£	
Unavoidable	10,000	(A)	5,250	(F)	4,750	(A)
Possibly avoidable	5,000	(A)	-		5,000	(A)
Total	15,000	(A)	5,250	(F)	9,750	(A)
Total variances	£21,840	(A)	£5,000	(F)	£16,840	(A)

(b) (i) The distinction between planning and operational variances is a development of the opportunity cost approach to variance analysis. Demski argued that more helpful and meaningful information will be provided for management control decisions if variances are reported using a standard which in hindsight should have been used when the actual standard used (or the budget) is unrealistic for the conditions which actually prevailed. Thus, when it is realised in retrospect that the original standard is inaccurate, a more realistic standard should be used to calculate operational variances. The final reconciliation between budgeted and actual profit would then be made as a planning variance, which measures the extent to which the budget targets are at fault because the standard used was incorrect.

(ii) The opportunity cost approach may be useful to companies because it indicates more clearly the actual loss sustained by faults which gave rise to the particular variances. There is an attempt to equate variances with the amount of profit or loss sustained, which traditional variances often fail to do.

(1) Traditional absorption costing variances for sales volume and production volume do not show the true effect of the variations from budget on company profitability.

(2) When a standard is incorrect, traditional variances will mislead managers about the true costs incurred. In the case of Wimbrush Ltd the error in the original standard price of materials X and Z mean that traditional variances would have reported a misleading variance to the purchasing department for price, and a mis-valuation of the usage variance would report the cost of the adverse usage of material X and the favourable usage of Z incorrectly.

Planning and operational variances attempt to indicate constructively what the real cost of variances should be; which of these variances might have been controllable by better management performance and which were unavoidable; and the effect on financial targets of a failure to construct realistic standards.

(iii) The main difficulty with the approach is deciding in retrospect what the realistic standard should have been. Unless some objective, readily available yardstick is available, the selection of a revised standard might be subjective and designed to provide a cover-up of responsibility rather than to reveal constructive control information.

15   NARUD PLC

(a)   (i)

Labour costs	Year 6	Labour efficiency	Labour rate	Sales volume	Year 7
	£				£
Variable (W)	100,000	1.03	1.00	1.10	113,300
Fixed	50,000	-	1.00	-	50,000
Projected labour cost					163,300

Working

	£
Year 6 direct labour cost	150,000
Less fixed element	50,000
Variable element	100,000

(ii)

Overheads	Year 6	Utilisation index	Expenditure index	Sales volume	Year 7
	£				£
Variable	160,000	1.03	1.05	1.10	190,344
Depreciation	-	-	-	-	30,000
Fixed	120,000	1.03	1.05	-	129,780
					350,124

Working

	£
Year 6	310,000
Depreciation	(30,000)
Fixed element	(120,000)
Variable element	160,000

(iii)   *Finance charges*

Year 7 - net profit before finance charges and depreciation
= £196,551 + £124,859 + £30,000 = £351,410.

Finance charges for year 7 = £((2 × 800,000) − 351,410)/2 × 20% = £124,859

(b)   *Year 8 forecast profit and loss account and bank overdraft*

	Year 7 £	Performance indices	Price indices	Sales indices	Year 8 £
Sales revenue	2,000,000	-	-	× 1.20 × 1.03	2,472,000
Direct material	1,000,000	× 0.95	× 1.20	× 1.20	1,368,000
Direct labour					
variable	100,000	× 0.99	× 1.10	× 1.20	130,680
fixed	50,000	-	× 1.10	-	55,000
Production o/hd					
variable	160,000	× 0.99	× 1.12	× 1.20	212,890
depreciation	30,000	-	-	-	30,000
other fixed	120,000	× 0.99	× 1.12	-	133,056
Admin/selling o/hd	100,000	× 1.05	× 1.12	-	117,600
Distribution o/h	140,000	× 0.95	× 1.12	× 1.20	178,752
Finance chgs (W1)	130,000				87,088
Total costs					2,313,066
Net profit					158,934
Overdraft (W2)					384,515

Year 9 forecast profit and loss account and bank overdraft

	Year 7 £	Performance indices	Price indices	Sales indices	Year 8 £
Sales revenue	2,000,000	-	-	× 1.30 × 1.01	2,626,000
Direct material	1,000,000	× 0.85	× 1.25	× 1.30	1,381,250
Direct labour					
variable	100,000	× 0.97	× 1.15	× 1.30	145,015
fixed	50,000	-	× 1.15	-	57,500
Production o/hd					
variable	160,000	× 0.97	× 1.18	× 1.30	238,077
depreciation	30,000	-	-	-	30,000
other fixed	120,000	× 0.97	× 1.18	-	137,352
Admin/selling o/hd	100,000	× 1.00	× 1.18	-	118,000
Distribution o/hd	140,000	× 0.95	× 1.18	× 1.30	204,022
Finance chrgs (W3)					42,425
Total costs					2,353,641
Net profit					272,359
Overdraft (W4)					82,156

Workings

1   Year 8 net profit before finance charges and depreciation = £276,022

    Year 8 finance charges = £((2 × 573,449) − 276,022)/2 × 20% = £87,088

2

		£	£
Year 7	overdraft		573,449
Year 8	net profit	158,934	
	add back non-cash item - depreciation	30,000	
			188,934
Year 8	overdraft		384,515

3   Year 9 net profit before finance charges and depreciation = £344,784

    Year 9 finance charges = £((2 × 384,515) − 344,784)/2 × 20% = £42,425

4

		£	£
Year 8	overdraft		384,515
Year 9	net profit	272,359	
	add back non-cash item - depreciation	30,000	
			302,359
			82,156

(c)   Items not incorporated in the profit and loss account which may affect cash flow include:

   (i)   changes in debtors/prepayments;
   (ii)   changes in creditors/accruals;
   (iii)   capital expenditure;
   (iv)   sale of fixed assets;
   (v)   other large capital movements such as share and debenture issues.

   (*Tutorial note*. In the examination you should list only three items.)

(d)   A management accounting model is used to simulate future events, incorporating all variables which could affect the final outcome under consideration.

   Feedforward control involves the comparison of forecasts of future outcomes with company goals and objectives, taking corrective action as appropriate to correct any deviations.

   The calculations in (b) demonstrate the use of a feedforward control model to determine whether planned actions will achieve desired objectives.

   Management may feel that a positive cash balance in the bank is an inefficient use of working capital, and may take this opportunity to reformulate their investment plans on the assumption that investing in the business generates a greater return than any interest income receivable, or any reduction in finance charges payable.

16   NOT FOR PROFIT ORGANISATIONS

> *Tutorial note*. Like many examination questions, part (a) can be answered by taking a logical, structured approach that is offered to you by the wording of the question itself. You can take (1) efficiency and (2) effectiveness in turn (this solution opts to deal with effectiveness first) and explain for each why the absence of a profit measure causes problems. This suggest that you need to explain why the *presence* of a profit measure helps with the assessment of efficiency and effectiveness.

(a)   (i)   *Effectiveness* refers to the use of resources so as to achieve desired ends or objectives or outputs.

   In a profit-making organisation, objectives can be expressed financially in terms of a target profit or return. The organisation, or profit centres within the organisation, can be judged to have operated effectively if they have achieved a target profit within a given period.

   In NFP organisations, effectiveness cannot be measured in this way. The organisation's objectives cannot be expressed in financial terms at all, and non-financial objectives need to be established. The effectiveness of performance in NFPs could be measured in terms of whether targeted non-financial objectives have been achieved, but there are several problems involved in trying to do this.

   (1)   The organisation might have several different objectives which are difficult to reconcile with each other. Achieving one objective might only be possible at the expense of failing to achieve another. For example, schools have the objective of providing education. They teach a certain curriculum, but by opting to educate students in some subjects, there is no time available to provide education in other subjects.

   (2)   A NFP organisation will invariably be restricted in what it can achieve by the availability of funds. The health service, for example, has the objective of providing health care, but since funds are restricted there is a limit to the amount of care that can be provided, and there will be competition for funds between different parts of the service.

   (3)   The objectives of NFP organisations are also difficult to establish because the *quality* of the service provided will be a significant feature of their service. For example, a

local authority has, amongst its various different objectives, the objective of providing a rubbish collection service. The effectiveness of this service can only be judged by establishing what standard or quality of service is required.

(4) With differing objectives, none of them directly comparable, and none that can be expressed in profit terms, *human judgement* is likely to be involved in deciding whether an organisation has been effective or not. This is most clearly seen in government organisations where political views cloud opinion about the government's performance.

Efficiency refers to the rate at which resources are consumed to achieve desired ends. Efficiency measurements compare the output produced by the organisation with the resources employed or used up to achieve the output. They are used to control the consumption of resources, so that the maximum output is achieved by a given amount of input resources, or a certain volume of output is produced within the minimum resources being used up.

In profit-making organisations, the efficiency of the organisation as a whole can be measured in terms of return on capital employed. Individual profit centres or operating units within the organisation can also have efficiently measured by relating the quantity of output produced, which has a *market value* and therefore a quantifiable financial value, to the resources (and their costs) required to make the output.

In NFP organisations, output does not usually have a market value, and it is therefore more difficult to measure efficiency. This difficulty is compounded by the fact that since NFP organisations often have several different objectives, it is difficult to compare the efficiency of one operation with the efficiency of another. For example, with the police force, it might be difficult to compare the efficiency of a serious crimes squad with the efficiency of the traffic police, because each has its own 'outputs' that are not easily comparable in terms of 'value achieved'.

In spite of the difficulties of measuring effectiveness and efficiency, control over the performance of NFP organisations can only be satisfactorily achieved by assessments of 'value for money' ie of economy, efficiency and effectiveness.

(ii) The same problems extend to support activities within profit-motivated organisations, where these activities are not directly involved in the creation of output and sales. Examples include research and development, the personnel function, the accountancy function and so on.

(1) Some of the outputs of these functions cannot be measured in *market values*.
(2) The objectives of the functions are not easily expressed in quantifiable terms.

Examples

(1) Within the personnel department, outputs from activities such as training and some aspects of recruitment can be given market price values by estimating what the same services would cost if provided by an external organisation. Other activities, however, do not have any such market valuation. Welfare is an example. Its objective is to provide support for employees in their personal affairs, but since this objective cannot easily be expressed as quantifiable targets, and does not have a market price valuation, the effectiveness and efficiency of work done by welfare staff cannot be measured easily.

(2) Within the accountancy department, outputs from management accountants are management information. This does not have an easily-measured market value, and information's value depends more on quality than quantity. The contribution of management accounting to profitability is difficult to judge, and so the efficiency and effectiveness of the function are difficult to measure.

(b) (i) To measure effectiveness, we need to establish objectives or targets for performance. Since these cannot be expressed financially, non-financial targets must be used. The effective level of achievement could be measured by comparing actual performance against target.

Adherence to appointment times

Measures might be:

(1) percentage of appointments kept on time

(2)   percentage of appointments no more than 10 minutes late

(3)   percentage of appointments kept within 30 minutes of schedule

(4)   percentage of cancelled appointments

(5)   average delay in appointments.

A problem with these measures is that there is an implied assumption that all patients will be at the clinic by their appointed time. In practice, this will not always be the case.

Patients' ability to contact the clinic and make appointments

Measures might be:

(1)   percentage of patients who can make an appointment at their first preferred time, or at the first date offered to them;

(2)   average time from making an appointment to the appointment date;

(3)   number of complaints about failure to contact the clinic, as a percentage of total patients seen;

(4)   if the telephone answering system provides for queuing of calls, the average waiting-for-answer times for callers and the percentage of abandoned calls.

Comprehensive monitoring programme

Measures might be based on the definition of each element or step within a monitoring programme for a patient, It would then be possible to measure:

(1)   percentage of patients receiving every stage of the programme (and percentage receiving every stage but one, every stage but two, and so on);

(2)   if each stage has a scheduled date for completion, the average delay for patients in the completion of each stage;

(ii)   A single quality of care measure would call for subjective judgements about

(1)   the key objective/objectives for each of the three features of service;

(2)   the relative weighting that should be given to each.

The objectives would have to be measured on comparable terms, and since money values are inappropriate, an index based on percentage or a points-scoring system of measurement might be used. A target index or points score for achievement could then be set, and actual results compared against the target.

17   TRANSFER PRICING

(a)   (i)   The main variants of market price based transfer prices are as follows.

(1)   Full market price

(2)   Market price discounted by any costs saved by making internal transfers.

The advantages of market price based transfer prices are as follows.

(1)   The use of market price simulates the competitive characteristics of the free market and ensures that both transferor and transferee behave as if at arm's length. It is argued that this will lead to optimal decision making.

(2)   The market price (as discounted if necessary) should be seen to be fair by both the transferor and the transferee.

(3)   The profit sharing achieved under such a system can be considered to be objective since it is based on external factors and is not distorted by subjective or internal considerations.

The disadvantages of market price based transfer prices are as follows.

(1)   The market price may be a temporary one, induced by adverse economic conditions, or dumping.

(2)   A transfer price at market value might, under some circumstances, act as a disincentive to use up any spare capacity in the buying divisions. A price based on incremental cost, in contrast, might provide an incentive to use up the spare resources in order to provide a marginal contribution to profit.

(3)   Many products in a part-finished state do not have a market price.

(ii) The main variants of cost based transfer prices are as follows.

(1) Full cost plus
(2) Marginal cost plus

Furthermore, each variant could be operated on the following basis.

(1) Standard cost
(2) Actual cost

In the absence of a market price the optimum transfer price is likely to be one based on standard cost plus. Its advantages are as follows.

(1) The transfer price can be fixed and agreed in advance without being subject to external fluctuations.

(2) Such a transfer price should motivate divisional managers to increase output and reduce expenditure levels.

(3) The transfer price can be set in such a way as to ensure a fair division of profit between divisions.

The disadvantages of a cost based transfer pricing system are as follows.

(1) Reaching agreement between the transferor and the transferee as to an appropriate mark-up can be difficult.

(2) Such a system is dependent on cost behaviour and can only be used for ranges of production over which costs vary linearly with output.

(3) The use of a cost based transfer price may encourage dysfunctional behaviour if one division feels that the price is wrong.

(b) (i)

Total annual contribution	£
Blackalls 200 units x £7 =	1,400
Brownalls 300 units x £12 =	3,600
	5,000

	Blackalls		*Brownalls*	
	£/unit	£/unit	£/unit	£/unit
Selling price		45		54
Processing cost	12		14	
Intermediate products:				
Alpha (3 x 6)	18		(2 x 6) 12	
Beta (2 x 4)	8		(4 x 4) 16	
		38		42
Contribution per unit		7		12
Units produced and sold		200		300
Contribution		1,400		3,600

Total contribution earned by   £5,000

(ii)

	Variable cost	*+ Shadow price*	*= Transfer price*
∴ Alpha transfer price =	£6	+ £0.50	= £6.50
Beta transfer price =	£4	+ £2.75	= £6.75

(1)

	Division A	*Division B*
	£/unit	£/unit
Transfer price	6.50	6.75
Variable cost	6.00	4.00
Contribution per unit (= shadow price)	0.50	2.75

(2)

	Black division		Brown division	
	£/unit	£/unit	£/unit	£/unit
Selling price		45		54
Processing cost	12.00		14	
Intermediate products:				
Alpha (3 x 6.50)	19.50		(2 × 6.50) 13	
Beta (2 x 6.75)	13.50		(4 × 6.75) 27	
		45		54
Contribution per unit		nil		nil

(iii) When shadow prices are used to set transfer prices, all of the contribution is deemed to be earned in the divisions which produce the scarce resource. The result is that no contribution is attributed to Black and Brown divisions.

The management of Black and Brown divisions are likely to be demotivated by the proposed transfer pricing policy, as the pricing system implies that their divisions earn no contribution. Such a situation is obviously absurd. There is no external market for Alphas and Betas, and it is the sales of Blackalls and Brownalls produced by Black and Brown which generate revenue.

The management of divisions A and B are more likely to have a positive attitude towards the transfer pricing policy because they can earn a contribution. However the manager of division A may feel that the 8.3% mark-up of 50p on a cost of £6.50 is too low when compared with that for B which earns £2.75 mark-up (68%) on a cost of £4.

The product development policy will result in a larger volume of work for Black division than for Brown division in respect of these products. This may cause behavioural problems if the manager of the Brown division perceives the allocation of resources to be unfair, particularly if staff become demotivated through lack of work or if redundancies become necessary.

(iv) (1) The same basic formula should be used to calculate the transfer prices, but the shadow price from the linear programming model will be replaced with an *opportunity cost*, calculated from the data in the question.

The opportunity cost for Alpha is the contribution which could be earned if the capacity was used for other products = £6 x 5% = £0.30.

The opportunity cost for Beta is the contribution which could be earned from external sales:

	£/unit
Selling price	7.50
Less: transport costs	(0.50)
variable costs	(4.00)
Contribution	3.00

Using the formula: *variable cost*   +   *opportunity cost*   =   *transfer price*

Alpha, transfer price =	£6	+	£0.30	=	£6.30
Beta, transfer price =	£4	+	£3.00	=	£7.00

(2) Summary

2,400 Alphas will be made for the use of the Black division. 3,200 Betas will be made, of which 1,600 are transferred to the Black division and 1,600 are sold.

The company will discontinue production of Brownalls, but will make 800 Blackalls each year.

Group contribution
Beta 1,600 x £3	4,800
Blackalls 800 x £7	5,600
	10,400

Workings

1

	Blackalls		Brownalls	
	£/unit	£/unit	£/unit	£/unit
Selling price		45.00		54.00
Processing cost	12.00		14.00	
Intermediate products:				
Alpha (3 x 6.30)	18.90		(2 × 6.30) 12.60	
Beta (2 x 7.00)	14.00		(4 x 7.00) 28.00	
		44.90		54.60
Contribution		0.10		(0.60)

If divisions will make decisions which are consistent with the financial data available, then the manager of Brown division will be willing to cease production of Brownalls.

Black division will therefore be able to take all available output of Alpha and Beta to make Blackalls.

2　　Maximum production capacity has been doubled to 2,400 Alphas and 3,200 Betas. Blackalls require more Alphas than Betas.

Maximum achievable production = 2,400/3 = 800 Blackalls.

800 Blackalls require 1,600 Betas. The remaining Betas will be sold externally.

(*Tutorial note.* The contributions earned on internal transfers of Betas and Alphas should be excluded, as they are *internal* to the group.)

18　RED OCHRE LTD

(a)　(i)

		Budget			*With the transaction*	
Division P	ROCE	(80/320) × 100%	= 25%		(100/420) × 100%	= 23.8%
Division Q	ROCE	(150/450) × 100%	= 33.3%		(135/375) × 100%	= 36%

(*Note.* The asset has a book value of £75,000 and there would be no profit or loss on the sale.)

Division R	ROCE	(84/280) × 100%	= 30%		(94/360) × 100%	= 26.1%

Workings

Profits per budget	84	Assets per budget		280
Less profit from asset sold	20	Less asset sold		20
	64			260
Plus profit from asset bought	30	Add asset bought		100
Revised profit	94	Revised assets		360

Division S ROCE (26/200) × 100% = 13%　　　　　(37.2/280) × 100% = 13.3%

(ii)　The managers of divisions Q and S would receive higher bonuses for a higher ROCE.

(iii)　Each transaction should be evaluated by DCF techniques, at a discount rate of 12%. The incremental cash flows over the life of the project would be required, but since we have neither the cash flows (net profit is after deduction of depreciation) nor the life of each project, a DCF analysis is not possible in this case.

The only approach we can take, which is very unsatisfactory, is to consider the 19X0 ROCE for each individual project, excluding division Q's (which is dealt with later).

	Division		
	P	R	S
Incremental profit	20	10	112
Incremental assets	100	(100 – 20)	80
ROCE on marginal project	20%	12.5%	14%
Cut-off rate	12%	12%	12%

A tenuous argument is that since the incremental ROCE on P, R and S division projects exceeds the company's cut-off rate, there may be some justification for implementing them. The decline in the budgeted total ROCE for divisions P and R is due to the fact that the original budgeted ROCE is higher than the incremental ROCE of the marginal project, whereas for the division S project, the incremental ROCE of 14%, by exceeding the original budget of 13%, would raise the expected ROCE to 13.3%.

Division Q is difficult to measure, since the decision to sell would earn £75,000 in year 0, but lose maybe (£15,000 profit + £75,000 depreciation) = £90,000 in cash flow in year 1. We could argue, however, that since the division would be deprived of a marginal ROCE of (£15,000/£75,000) = 20%, which is in excess of the group's cut-off rate of 12%, the sale would not be justified. The original budgeted ROCE of division Q was 33% and the increase without the asset to 36.1% is due to the fact that the 'marginal investment' earns only 20%, so that by removing it, the divisional average is increased.

The major conclusion, however, is that ROCE is a poor and inadequate guide for decision makers.

(b) It is assumed that projects must be accepted in their entirety and that no alternative investments are available, so that options are to accept:

	Cost £	Profit in first year £
P and R	200,000	30,000
R and S	180,000	21,200
P and S	180,000	31,200 * optimal choice

(c) (i) Division P   Budgeted profit/sales   10%
                      Budgeted asset turnover 2.5 times
        Division S   Budgeted profit/sales   13%
                      Budgeted asset turnover 1 times

The division manager of S has a favourable profit/sales ratio compared with P, but a poor asset turnover ratio (assuming the assets in each division are valued at similar price levels and are of the same age profile). It appears that the manager of division S should look to generate more sales; an increase in asset turnover to 2.5 times would boost the ROCE of division S to (2.5 x 13) 32.5%. On the other hand, division S could attempt to reduce its capital, whilst maintaining the same sales volume.

(ii) The new project has a profit margin of 31% which is high and an asset turnover of 0.45 times, which is very low. Although the incremental ROCE is 14%, just in excess of the 12% cut-off rate, it is not consistent with the advice in (c)(i).

(d) Red Ochre Ltd evaluates decisions by their effect on the ROCE calculation. Red Ochre Ltd's cost of capital is 12%, which is therefore the minimum annual rate of return required of any asset. Consequently, the capital value of any asset sold must bear some relation to the rate of return required of it: by selling the asset, it should be possible to replace the profit forgone.

If we assume that 12% pa x asset value = £15,000, then asset value = £15,000/12% = £125,000

It is far better to use discounted cash flows in decisions of this kind.

(e) (i) Residual income is the net income of a profit centre (or division), less the 'imputed' interest on the capital invested in the profit centre. Divisional managers are encouraged to maximise their reported residual income, and as long as the division undertakes incremental projects which earn an accounting rate of return in excess of the cut-off rate (in our example, 12%) acceptance of the project would increase residual income and would therefore be favoured by the divisional managers.

(A positive residual income, however, does not necessarily indicate that an investment is financially viable, although it is tempting for divisional managers to assume that this is so.)

The advantage of residual income over ROCE is that when a divisional manager is considering a marginal investment which would earn an accounting rate of return in excess of the cut-off rate of return, but below the ROCE of the rest of the assets in the division, acceptance of the project would increase residual income but reduce the overall divisional ROCE. Residual income as a measure of performance is therefore more likely to encourage managers to buy new assets.

BPP PUBLISHING

(ii) 19X0 residual income

	P £000	Q £000	R £000	S £000
Original budget				
Profit	80.0	150	84.0	26
Less imputed interest at 12%	38.4	54	33.6	24
Residual income	41.6	96	50.4	2
	£000	£000	£000	£000
With the projects:				
Profit	100.0	135	94.0	37.2
Less imputed interest				
(see (a) for capital employed)	50.4	45	43.2	33.6
Residual income	49.6	90	50.8	3.6

The projects in divisions P, R and S would improve residual income, but the disinvestment project in division Q would lower residual income.

Mathematical tables, List of key terms and Index

PRESENT VALUE TABLE

Present value of 1 ie $(1+r)^{-n}$

where r = discount rate
       n = number of periods until payment

Periods					Discount rates (r)					
(n)	1%	2%	3%	4%	5%	6%	7%	8%	9%	10%
1	0.990	0.980	0.971	0.962	0.952	0.943	0.935	0.926	0.917	0.909
2	0.980	0.961	0.943	0.925	0.907	0.890	0.873	0.857	0.842	0.826
3	0.971	0.942	0.915	0.889	0.864	0.840	0.816	0.794	0.772	0.751
4	0.961	0.924	0.888	0.855	0.823	0.792	0.763	0.735	0.708	0.683
5	0.951	0.906	0.863	0.822	0.784	0.747	0.713	0.681	0.650	0.621
6	0.942	0.888	0.837	0.790	0.746	0.705	0.666	0.630	0.596	0.564
7	0.933	0.871	0.813	0.760	0.711	0.665	0.623	0.583	0.547	0.513
8	0.923	0.853	0.789	0.731	0.677	0.627	0.582	0.540	0.502	0.467
9	0.914	0.837	0.766	0.703	0.645	0.592	0.544	0.500	0.460	0.424
10	0.905	0.820	0.744	0.676	0.614	0.558	0.508	0.463	0.422	0.386
11	0.896	0.804	0.722	0.650	0.585	0.527	0.475	0.429	0.388	0.350
12	0.887	0.788	0.701	0.625	0.557	0.497	0.444	0.397	0.356	0.319
13	0.879	0.773	0.681	0.601	0.530	0.469	0.415	0.368	0.326	0.290
14	0.870	0.758	0.661	0.577	0.505	0.442	0.388	0.340	0.299	0.263
15	0.861	0.743	0.642	0.555	0.481	0.417	0.362	0.315	0.275	0.239

	11%	12%	13%	14%	15%	16%	17%	18%	19%	20%
1	0.901	0.893	0.885	0.877	0.870	0.862	0.855	0.847	0.840	0.833
2	0.812	0.797	0.783	0.769	0.756	0.743	0.731	0.718	0.706	0.694
3	0.731	0.712	0.693	0.675	0.658	0.641	0.624	0.609	0.593	0.579
4	0.659	0.636	0.613	0.592	0.572	0.552	0.534	0.516	0.499	0.482
5	0.593	0.567	0.543	0.519	0.497	0.476	0.456	0.437	0.419	0.402
6	0.535	0.507	0.480	0.456	0.432	0.410	0.390	0.370	0.352	0.335
7	0.482	0.452	0.425	0.400	0.376	0.354	0.333	0.314	0.296	0.279
8	0.434	0.404	0.376	0.351	0.327	0.305	0.285	0.266	0.249	0.233
9	0.391	0.361	0.333	0.308	0.284	0.263	0.243	0.225	0.209	0.194
10	0.352	0.322	0.295	0.270	0.247	0.227	0.208	0.191	0.176	0.162
11	0.317	0.287	0.261	0.237	0.215	0.195	0.178	0.162	0.148	0.135
12	0.286	0.257	0.231	0.208	0.187	0.168	0.152	0.137	0.124	0.112
13	0.258	0.229	0.204	0.182	0.163	0.145	0.130	0.116	0.104	0.093
14	0.232	0.205	0.181	0.160	0.141	0.125	0.111	0.099	0.088	0.078
15	0.209	0.183	0.160	0.140	0.123	0.108	0.095	0.084	0.074	0.065

ANNUITY TABLE

Present value of an annuity of 1 ie $\dfrac{1-(1+r)^{-n}}{r}$

where   r = interest rate

n = number of periods

Periods					Discount rates (r)					
(n)	1%	2%	3%	4%	5%	6%	7%	8%	9%	10%
1	0.990	0.980	0.971	0.962	0.952	0.943	0.935	0.926	0.917	0.909
2	1.970	1.942	1.913	1.886	1.859	1.833	1.808	1.783	1.759	1.736
3	2.941	2.884	2.829	2.775	2.723	2.673	2.624	2.577	2.531	2.487
4	3.902	3.808	3.717	3.630	3.546	3.465	3.387	3.312	3.240	3.170
5	4.853	4.713	4.580	4.452	4.329	4.212	4.100	3.993	3.890	3.791
6	5.795	5.601	5.417	5.242	5.076	4.917	4.767	4.623	4.486	4.355
7	6.728	6.472	6.230	6.002	5.786	5.582	5.389	5.206	5.033	4.868
8	7.652	7.325	7.020	6.733	6.463	6.210	5.971	5.747	5.535	5.335
9	8.566	8.162	7.786	7.435	7.108	6.802	6.515	6.247	5.995	5.759
10	9.471	8.983	8.530	8.111	7.722	7.360	7.024	6.710	6.418	6.145
11	10.37	9.787	9.253	8.760	8.306	7.887	7.499	7.139	6.805	6.495
12	11.26	10.58	9.954	9.385	8.863	8.384	7.943	7.536	7.161	6.814
13	12.13	11.35	10.63	9.986	9.394	8.853	8.358	7.904	7.487	7.103
14	13.00	12.11	11.30	10.56	9.899	9.295	8.745	8.244	7.786	7.367
15	13.87	12.85	11.94	11.12	10.38	9.712	9.108	8.559	8.061	7.606
	11%	12%	13%	14%	15%	16%	17%	18%	19%	20%
1	0.901	0.893	0.885	0.877	0.870	0.862	0.855	0.847	0.840	0.833
2	1.713	1.690	1.668	1.647	1.626	1.605	1.585	1.566	1.547	1.528
3	2.444	2.402	2.361	2.322	2.283	2.246	2.210	2.174	2.140	2.106
4	3.102	3.037	2.974	2.914	2.855	2.798	2.743	2.690	2.639	2.589
5	3.696	3.605	3.517	3.433	3.352	3.274	3.199	3.127	3.058	2.991
6	4.231	4.111	3.998	3.889	3.784	3.685	3.589	3.498	3.410	3.326
7	4.712	4.564	4.423	4.288	4.160	4.039	3.922	3.812	3.706	3.605
8	5.146	4.968	4.799	4.639	4.487	4.344	4.207	4.078	3.954	3.837
9	5.537	5.328	5.132	4.946	4.772	4.607	4.451	4.303	4.163	4.031
10	5.889	5.650	5.426	5.216	5.019	4.833	4.659	4.494	4.339	4.192
11	6.207	5.938	5.687	5.453	5.234	5.029	4.836	4.656	4.486	4.327
12	6.492	6.194	5.918	5.660	5.421	5.197	4.988	4.793	4.611	4.439
13	6.750	6.424	6.122	5.842	5.583	5.342	5.118	4.910	4.715	4.533
14	6.982	6.628	6.302	6.002	5.724	5.468	5.229	5.008	4.802	4.611
15	7.191	6.811	6.462	6.142	5.847	5.575	5.324	5.092	4.876	4.675

These are the terms which we have identified throughout the text as being KEY TERMS. You should make sure that you can define what these terms mean; go back to the pages highlighted here if you need to check

BPP PUBLISHING

BPP
PUBLISHING

BPP
PUBLISHING

See overleaf for information on other
BPP products and how to order

ACCA Order

To BPP Publishing Ltd, Aldine Place, London W12 8AA

Tel: 020 8740 2211. Fax: 020 8740 1184

Mr/Mrs/Ms (Full name) _____

Daytime delivery address _____

Postcode _____

Daytime Tel _____   Date of exam (month/year) _____

	6/99 Texts	1/99 Kits	1/99 Psscrds	2/99 Tapes	2/99 Videos	1999 CDs
FOUNDATION						
1 The Accounting Framework	£18.95 ☐	£9.95 ☐	£5.95 ☐	£12.95 ☐	£25.00 ☐	
2 The Legal Framework	£18.95 ☐	£9.95 ☐	£5.95 ☐	£12.95 ☐	£25.00 ☐	
3 Management Information	£18.95 ☐	£9.95 ☐	£5.95 ☐	£12.95 ☐	£25.00 ☐	
4 The Organisational Framework	£18.95 ☐	£9.95 ☐	£5.95 ☐	£12.95 ☐	£25.00 ☐	
CERTIFICATE						
5 Information Analysis	£18.95 ☐	£9.95 ☐	£5.95 ☐	£12.95 ☐	£25.00 ☐	
6 The Audit Framework	£18.95 ☐	£9.95 ☐	£5.95 ☐	£12.95 ☐	£25.00 ☐	
7 The Tax Framework (Finance Act 99) (8/99 Text, 1/00 P/C, 1/00 Kit)	£18.95 ☐	£9.95 ☐	£5.95 ☐	£12.95 ☐	£25.00 ☐	£39.95 ☐ (6/99-FA98)
8 Managerial Finance	£18.95 ☐	£9.95 ☐	£5.95 ☐	£12.95 ☐	£25.00 ☐	£39.95 ☐
PROFESSIONAL						
9 Information for Control and Decision Making	£19.95 ☐	£10.95 ☐	£5.95 ☐	£12.95 ☐	£25.00 ☐	£39.95 ☐
10 Accounting and Audit Practice (Accounting)	£15.95 ☐	£10.95 ☐ }	£5.95 ☐	£12.95 ☐	£25.00 ☐	£39.95 ☐
10 Accounting and Audit Practice (Auditing)	£13.95 ☐					
11 Tax Planning (Finance Act 99) (8/99 Text, 1/00 P/C, 1/00 Kit)	£19.95 ☐	£10.95 ☐	£5.95 ☐	£12.95 ☐	£25.00 ☐	
12 Management and Strategy	£19.95 ☐	£10.95 ☐	£5.95 ☐	£12.95 ☐	£25.00 ☐	
13 Financial Reporting Environment	£19.95 ☐	£10.95 ☐	£5.95 ☐	£12.95 ☐	£25.00 ☐	
14 Financial Strategy	£19.95 ☐	£10.95 ☐	£5.95 ☐	£12.95 ☐	£25.00 ☐	
INTERNATIONAL STREAM						
1 The Accounting Framework	£18.95 ☐	£9.95 ☐				
6 The Audit Framework	£18.95 ☐	£9.95 ☐				
10 Accounting and Audit Practice (Accounting)	£15.95 ☐	£10.95 ☐ }	£5.95 ☐			
10 Accounting and Audit Practice (Audit)	£13.95 ☐					
13 Financial Reporting Environment	£19.95 ☐	£10.95 ☐ (9/99)				

POSTAGE & PACKING

Study Texts

	First	Each extra	
UK	£3.00	£2.00	£
Europe*	£5.00	£4.00	£
Rest of world	£20.00	£10.00	£

Kits/Passcards/Success Tapes

	First	Each extra	
UK	£2.00	£1.00	£
Europe*	£2.50	£1.00	£
Rest of world	£15.00	£8.00	£

Master CDs/Breakthrough Videos

	First	Each extra	
UK	£2.00	£2.00	£
Europe*	£2.00	£2.00	£
Rest of world	£20.00	£10.00	£

Grand Total (Cheques to *BPP Publishing*) I enclose

a cheque for (incl. Postage)   £ ☐

Or charge to Access/Visa/Switch

Card Number ☐☐☐☐ ☐☐☐☐ ☐☐☐☐ ☐☐☐☐

Expiry date _____   Start Date _____

Issue Number (Switch Only) _____

Signature _____

£ _____

We aim to deliver to all UK addresses inside 5 working days. Orders to all EU addresses should be delivered within 6 working days. All other orders to overseas addresses should be delivered within 8 working days.

* Europe includes the Republic of Ireland and the Channel Islands.

REVIEW FORM & FREE PRIZE DRAW

All original review forms from the entire BPP range, completed with genuine comments, will be entered into one of two draws on 31 January 2000 and 31 July 2000. The names on the first four forms picked out on each occasion will be sent a cheque for £50.

Name: _____   Address: _____

_____

_____

How have you used this Text?
(Tick one box only)

☐ Home study (book only)

☐ On a course: college _____

☐ With 'correspondence' package

☐ Other _____

Why did you decide to purchase this Text?
(Tick one box only)

☐ Have used BPP Texts in the past

☐ Recommendation by friend/colleague

☐ Recommendation by a lecturer at college

☐ Saw advertising

☐ Other _____

During the past six months do you recall seeing/receiving any of the following?
(Tick as many boxes as are relevant)

☐ Our advertisement in *Students' Newsletter*

☐ Our advertisement in *Pass*

☐ Our brochure with a letter through the post

Which (if any) aspects of our advertising do you find useful?
(Tick as many boxes as are relevant)

☐ Prices and publication dates of new editions

☐ Information on Text content

☐ Facility to order books off-the-page

☐ None of the above

Your ratings, comments and suggestions would be appreciated on the following areas

	Very useful	Useful	Not useful
Introductory section (Key study steps, personal study plan etc)	☐	☐	☐
Chapter introductions	☐	☐	☐
Key terms	☐	☐	☐
Explanations	☐	☐	☐
Case examples and examples	☐	☐	☐
Questions and answers	☐	☐	☐
Chapter roundups	☐	☐	☐
Quick quizzes	☐	☐	☐
Exam focus points	☐	☐	☐
Exam question bank	☐	☐	☐
Exam answer bank	☐	☐	☐
List of key terms and index	☐	☐	☐
Icons	☐	☐	☐

	Excellent	Good	Adequate	Poor
Overall opinion of this Text	☐	☐	☐	☐

Do you intend to continue using BPP Study Texts/Kits?   ☐ Yes   ☐ No

Please note any further comments and suggestions/errors on the reverse of this page.

Please return to: Katy Hibbert, BPP Publishing Ltd, FREEPOST, London, W12 8BR

REVIEW FORM & FREE PRIZE DRAW (continued)

Please note any further comments and suggestions/errors below

FREE PRIZE DRAW RULES

1 Closing date for 31 January 2000 draw is 31 December 1999. Closing date for 31 July 2000 draw is 30 June 2000.

2 Restricted to entries with UK and Eire addresses only. BPP employees, their families and business associates are excluded.

3 No purchase necessary. Entry forms are available upon request from BPP Publishing. No more than one entry per title, per person. Draw restricted to persons aged 16 and over.

4 Winners will be notified by post and receive their cheques not later than 6 weeks after the relevant draw date. Lists of winners will be published in BPP's *focus* newsletter following the relevant draw.

5 The decision of the promoter in all matters is final and binding. No correspondence will be entered into.